INTRODUCTION TO WINDOWS PROGRAMMING

INTRODUCTION TO WINDOWS PROGRAMMING

by

Guy Quedens

and

Pamela S. Beason

Scott, Foresman and Company

Glenview, Illinois London

Cover photo: Image Bank

Trademarks for *Windows Programming* Book by Quedens/Beason

Microsoft® and MS-DOS® are registered trademarks of Microsoft Corporation.

IBM® is a registered trademark of International Business Machines Corporation.

INTEL® is a registered trademark of Intel Corporation.

Library of Congress Cataloging-in-Publication Data

Quedens, Edmund Guy.
Introduction to windows programming.

Includes index.
1. IBM Personal Computer—Programming. 2. Microsoft Windows. (Computer programs) I. Beason, Pamela S.
II. Title.
QA76.8. I2594Q84 1988 005.4'3 88-18538
ISBN 0-673-38058-0

123456-KPF-93 92 91 90 89 88

ISBN 0-673-38058-0

Notice of Liability

The information in this book is distributed on an "As Is" basis, without warranty. Neither the author nor Scott, Foresman and Company shall have any liability to customer or any other person or entity with respect to any liability, loss, or damage caused or alleged to be caused directly or indirectly by the programs contained herein. This includes, but is not limited ot, interruption of service, loss of data, loss of business or anticipatory profits, or consequential damages from the use of the programs.

Scott, Foresman professional books are available for bulk sales at quantity discounts. For information, please contact Marketing Manager, Professional Books Group, Scott, Foresman and Company, 1900 East Lake Avenue, Glenview, IL 60025.

CONTENTS

To my parents, without whom I would never be who I am.—G.Q.

To Mike—P.B.

INTRODUCTION

- The Benefits of Developing Applications for Windows
- Who Should Read This Book
- System Requirements for Developing Windows Applications

1.1 THE BENEFITS OF DEVELOPING APPLICATIONS FOR WINDOWS

Why do you, as a software developer, want to invest in producing a Windows application? What does Microsoft have to offer that will make your life a little easier? Let's look at some of the benefits of using Windows.

First, it's easier for you to develop a Windows application because Microsoft has already taken care of much of the work for you.

For one thing, you don't need to worry about continually updating your application because of changes in the operating system. Windows is part of Microsoft's long-term MS-DOS strategy, so Windows automatically evolves with MS-DOS while preserving your development investment. New features such as bigger memory models, real multitasking, and protected mode are automatically supported: there's no need for an application developer (or the developer's customers) to be concerned about compatibility problems with new versions of DOS. Windows keeps up with new developments in microcomputers: for example, there's a Windows package developed for 8086- and 8088-based machines, there's Windows/286 for 80286 based computers, and there's Windows/386, developed to take advantage of the power of the Intel® 80386 microprocessor. Windows also runs on the Personal System/2 Series computer. So Windows is a path to the future, which protects your application from becoming obsolete.

Another advantage is that a Windows application is device-independent. That means your application will run on any computer and with any device that is compatible with Windows. Your application won't need to directly address a piece of hardware; instead, you'll talk to Windows in "logical" terms. This saves you a lot of development time. No more writing printer drivers and screen drivers. No more confusion about a variety of input devices—for example, you don't need to worry about the user who has a joystick instead of a mouse. Microsoft takes care of these issues for you by ensuring that all devices running with Windows are responsible for sending and receiving information in a predefined Windows format.

Because of this device independence, Windows is prepared to automatically support new I/O devices. Graphics coprocessors, laser printers, touch screens, light pens, and many other devices can be easily incorporated. If a device is intelligent, Windows can delegate work to the device; if not, Windows can ensure that the device performs a task by breaking the task down into small predefined operations and making the device complete those operations as quickly as possible.

Windows takes on the responsibility of translating your desires into reality.

Windows manages the system display, leaving you free to concentrate on your application, which runs in its own window. A Windows application can be highly flexible, however, because you have full control over your application's screen area. Windows gives you the ability to create, rearrange, and re-size multiple windows easily. Windows also provides a selection of stock graphic objects you can use in your application, or you can create your own graphics using Windows tools.

Windows has a complete memory management system. This includes load-on-demand code, discardable memory, moveable memory segments, and shared code and data.

Windows applications can talk to each other through data exchange channels, including the user-controlled Windows clipboard and automatic Dynamic Data Exchange (DDE). You can exchange text, bitmaps, or graphic operations.

If you're developing applications for overseas markets, you can easily create international versions using discrete Windows resources that are kept separate from the source code. Windows also includes geographically local keyboards, an extended character set (ANSI), and Japanese Kanji.

Most important of all, Microsoft has made it easier for you to sell your application because there's an established market for Windows applications. You're working with a standardized user interface that makes your new application easy to learn and easy to use. Microsoft has already worked out both the mouse and keyboard methods for editing text, scrolling, choosing commands and options, and sizing and rearranging windows. The Windows environment makes users feel confident and comfortable because all Windows applications look and feel the same.

The popularity of Windows is growing daily. If you design your application to take full advantage of all the features Windows has to offer, you'll have a head start on the general applications market.

I.2 WHO SHOULD READ THIS BOOK

This book is for programmers developing applications for Windows, Windows/286, and Windows/386. Most of the book is dedicated to examining sample programs that demonstrate the process of developing a simple Windows application.

To keep this book down to a readable size, we had to make some assumptions about your knowledge as a reader. First of all, we assume that Windows developers are not programming novices.

Windows programs can be written in C, Pascal, or assembly language. Because C is the preferred language for Windows applications, this book uses C program listings. We assume that you have a working knowledge of C, including an understanding of the various memory models, calling conventions, and data structures.

If you have used DOS development tools (LINK, MAPSYM, MAKE, SYMDEB, etc.), you're already familiar with most of the utilities you'll be using to develop Windows programs. Although Chapter 2 of this book provides a general description of the Windows application development process and the development utilities you'll use, we won't teach you how to use those utilities here. The *Windows Programming Tools* manual included with the Windows Software Development Kit provides instructions on using the utilities you'll need.

Although it is not required for understanding this book, Windows developers would find it helpful to be fairly well versed in the 8086/286/386 assembly language, including register models and segment:offset addressing; and to have an understanding of the basic MS-DOS structure, including function calls and device drivers.

1.3 SYSTEM REQUIREMENTS FOR DEVELOPING WINDOWS APPLICATIONS

Hardware

The minimum Windows development workstation should consist of:

- an AT computer with 640K;
- an EGA display monitor;
- a *fast* fixed disk (25 ms or faster);
- for debugging—an additional computer, keyboard, and monitor, or at least an additional monochrome monitor;
- a mouse;
- a graphics printer or laser printer if your application needs print services.

The following are also desirable, but not required:

- a multi-megabyte RAM card for use as a RAM drive and/or disk cache;
- other displays to test the appearance of your application.

Software

To develop Windows applications, you need the following software:

- MS-DOS or PC-DOS version 3.0 (Windows) or 3.01 (Windows/386) or later;
- a Windows-compatible language compiler;
- Microsoft Windows, Windows/286, or Windows/386;
- Microsoft Windows Software Development Kit;
- a text editor.

1

BASIC WINDOWS CONCEPTS

- Windows is a Graphical Interface
- Windows is a Cooperative Environment
- Windows is Device-Independent
- Windows Application Design Considerations

Before you start designing your application, you should be familiar with the concepts that make Windows applications different from other programs. This chapter discusses the ideas that are basic to Windows and examines how these concepts affect the design of your application.

1.1 WINDOWS IS A GRAPHICAL INTERFACE

Windows is a graphical interface that uses visual clues to tell users which programs are running and what those programs are doing at any time. Windows displays each application in its own main *window*, a rectangular portion of the screen that the application controls. Each window can contain several visual devices, such as *menus* and *scroll bars*, that allow users to interact with the application. When an application needs to get the user's attention before proceeding, it displays special "popup" windows called *dialog boxes* or *message boxes*. You can see examples of all these devices in Figure 1.1.

Figure 1.1

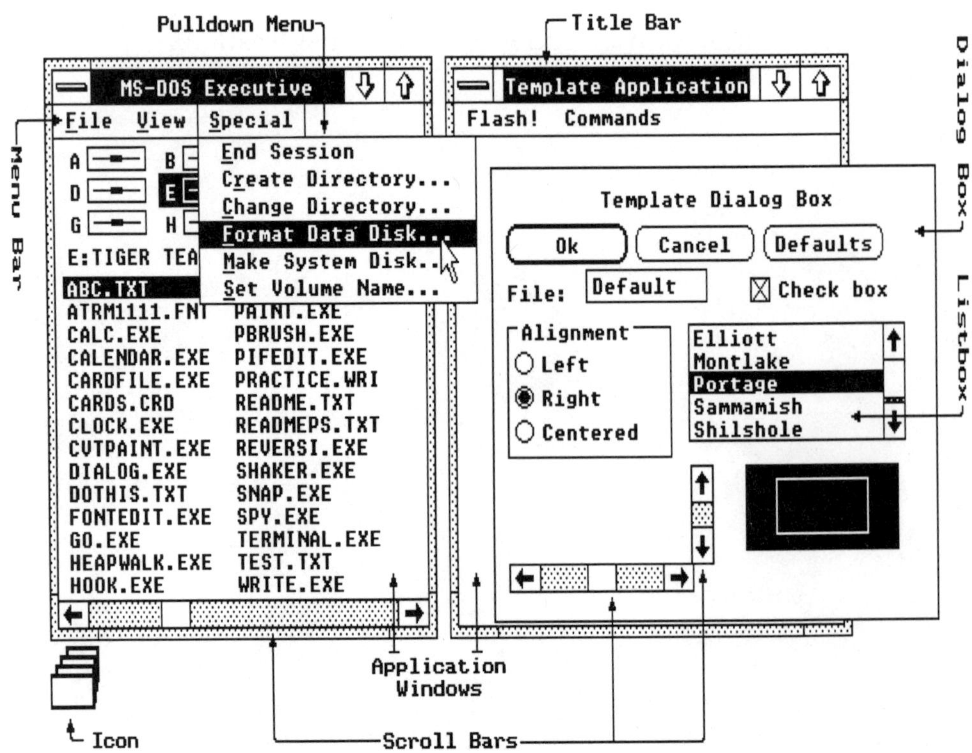

Windows allows both keyboard and mouse users to rearrange and resize windows on the display at will. When users are not interacting with applications but want to keep them readily available, they can shrink application windows down into *icons*, tiny pictorial representations of open programs. These icons can be quickly transformed into active windows again when they are needed.

Windows controls the display through its Graphics Device Interface (GDI), which is a library of routines you call to draw and remove graphics objects from your application's window. Because several applications can have access to the system display at one time, Windows must have a mechanism for controlling each program's graphic output. Otherwise, an application could destroy another application's window. To control graphic output, Windows uses special data structures called *display contexts*, or *DCs*, which contain information defining a window's attributes. All output to the display is routed through GDI, which uses the DCs to control continuity.

The Windows Software Development Kit comes with a variety of fonts and with many stock graphic objects, including menus, scroll bars, cursors, and icons. You can save time and program code and maintain interface consistency by including these existing objects in your application. You're not restricted to using the graphics objects provided with the Development Kit, however. The Kit also includes tools that allow you to create your own graphic objects. The Icon Editor lets you use pens and brushes to draw and color shapes on the system display or on a printer or plotter. You can even create your own pens and brushes, and you can also use Microsoft Paint with the Icon Editor to create sophisticated graphics. The Dialog Editor lets you make your dialog boxes look just the way you want. And the Font Editor allows you to modify existing fonts or create your own.

In the Windows environment, data and graphics objects—such as icons, cursors, fonts, menus, dialog boxes, and strings—are treated as *resources* and are kept in files separate from the program source code. Keeping resources in separate files makes it much easier for you to make changes to them, reduces the size of your program's data segment, and allows multiple instances of your application to share resources.

1.2 WINDOWS IS A COOPERATIVE ENVIRONMENT

One of the key features of Windows is that it allows different applications and multiple instances of the same application to run simultaneously. However, although multiple processes can run concurrently, only one can process a task (use the processor) at any one time. So there's a big difference between *running* and *processing* in the Windows environment. And just as only one application can process a task at any time, only one application can be *active* (receive input from the user) at any time.

Windows depends on *messages* to control the sharing of processing time in the multitasking environment. Windows automatically provides input messages from the keyboard and the mouse to every window on the display. When Windows delivers a message to your application, it also delivers the processor so that your application can take appropriate action. In fact, the only way your application can get the processor is to receive a message. And messages are the only way your application can respond to events generated by the user, by Windows, or by the application itself. So receiving, interpreting, and reacting to messages is the primary duty of any Windows application.

1.3 WINDOWS IS DEVICE-INDEPENDENT

Windows achieves hardware independence by defining the allowable input and output. Any input devices running with Windows must either use the predefined input or provide software to translate their input into Windows' approved code. This ensures that messages to your application will contain only device-independent virtual keycodes, no matter what kind of keyboard the user is typing on.

Windows provides device-independent graphics operations. Your program can use the same calls and the same data to draw on both high- and low-resolution devices. Device drivers provided by equipment manufacturers do the conversion work for specific devices.

This device independence frees you from having to address hardware in specific terms. It also means that you must use Windows routines to control your application's communication with devices.

1.4 WINDOWS APPLICATION DESIGN CONSIDERATIONS

To make the most of the Windows environment, a programmer should keep several key points in mind when designing a Windows application. Your application should:

1 Be highly interactive;
2 Use graphics whenever possible;
3 Share data with other applications;
4 Share system resources;
5 Maintain a consistent user interface.

A Windows application should be as interactive as possible, providing immediate response, feedback, and reinforcement to the user. It should also be interruptible and present alternatives when appropriate.

A Windows application is, because of the nature of Windows, graphical. So use graphics whenever possible—a picture is worth a thousand words! When applicable, use icons to represent options that mouse users can point to and "click on" to select.

As much as possible, your application should allow the user to copy data to and from the Windows clipboard to communicate at will with other Windows applications. The ability to transfer information between applications is, after all, one of the key features of the Windows environment.

As explained previously, Windows is a cooperative system. Make sure your application doesn't demand rights to the complete system; share the resources. Remember that the processor itself is a system resource: all applications need time on it. Windows is a "non-preemptive" system which means that the applications must yield control, so break up long loops to give other applications a chance to process their tasks.

Memory is usually in high demand, so don't hog it! Use Windows routines to manage the memory resources. Use memory incrementally; that is, use it as you need it and release it when you are done. Also, lock memory only as necessary, and unlock it when done. This allows Windows to satisfy all memory requests by moving blocks around and combining free segments.

Above all, your application should maintain consistency with the Windows interface. Most users are resistant to new ways of doing things. A good Windows application should allow users to easily control the program with both keyboard and mouse. Most keyboard and mouse functionality is already built into the Windows functions you'll use, but there are additional steps you can take to make your application easier to use.

For example, to make access easier for keyboard users, the application should include *accelerators*—key combinations that can be used to quickly select a command or dialog box option. The Windows interface uses two types of accelerators. One type is mnemonic: unique letters in option names are underlined to signal users that those letters can be used in combination with the Alt key to select that option. For example, if the option "Close" is displayed in a dialog box, users may select that option either by moving the cursor to the option or by pressing [ALT + C]. The other type of accelerator is a function key or key combination that appears beside a command or menu name. For example, if "Save F1" is displayed on a menu, users may select "Save" by moving the cursor to it or by pressing F1, the accelerator key associated with that command.

Using accelerators is just one of many ways to make your application consistent with the Windows user interface. There are also Windows standards for providing visual clues, such as indicating the default choices in dialog boxes, and Windows standards for consistent terminology and behavior. Microsoft has gone to a lot of trouble to write down all the guidelines for you in the *Windows Application Style Guide*, so follow those guidelines when you create your application. Use all the tools and power that Windows provides to make your program as powerful and as easy to use as it can be. Your customers will appreciate you for it.

. . . .

In this chapter, you've explored some of the basic concepts of Windows. In Chapter 2, you'll learn how to set up your file system, and you'll see an overview of the application development process.

2

PREPARING TO DEVELOP WINDOWS APPLICATIONS

- Setting Up Your System
- Improving Processing Speed
- An Overview of the Development Process
- A Survey of Windows Utilities and Tools

As you may have already noticed, the Windows development environment is *big!* You need a compiler, a linker, several libraries, Windows, a text editor, a debugger, and other assorted programs. If you're not well organized from the beginning, your system could quickly degenerate into a confusing maze of tools and source files from which your dream application may never emerge. This chapter shows you how to structure your file system for maximum efficiency, presents an overview of the development process, and gives you a brief tour of the tools you will be using from the Windows Software Development Kit.

2.1 SETTING UP YOUR SYSTEM

Included with the Windows Software Development Kit are a number of utilities, libraries, include files, and Windows development applications. Because the Windows development environment is so large, it's essential that your system be orderly from the outset. We cannot stress enough the importance of using many small subdirectories: this allows you to more easily control your source code, and also makes DOS respond more quickly. We recommend that you set up your system as described in the following steps:

1. Within the root directory, create the following subdirectories:

Name	*Description*
BIN	DOS-related programs
INCLUDE	Header files
LIB	Linker libraries
UTIL	Development utilities
WINDOWS	Windows runtime files
WINDEV	Development source files

2. In the BIN subdirectory, place all your DOS programs such as FORMAT, DISKCOPY, etc. Generally, these are version-bound programs, so you should keep them separate from other executable programs.

3. In the INCLUDE subdirectory, place all the .H header files (also known as "include files") supplied with your language compiler, and the following files from the Windows Development Kit:

Filename	*Description*
STYLE.H	Windows style definitions
WINDOWS.H	Windows include file for C applications
CMACROS.INC	Include file of assembler macros

4 In the LIB subdirectory, place the following library files used by the development linker, LINK4.

Filename	*Description*
LIBW.LIB[1]	Standard Windows library
WINLIBC.LIB[1]	Start-up library for Windows libraries

5 In the UTIL subdirectory, place all binary development executable files, such as your favorite program editor, language compiler, any other development utilities you want to use, and the following programs from the Development Kit:

Filename	*Description*
EXEHDR.EXE	Displays Windows application file header
IMPLIB.EXE	Creates dynamic-linkable library files
LIB.EXE	Creates and maintains library (.LIB) files
LINK4.EXE	Windows linker
MAKE.EXE	Automatic file maintenance utility
MAPSYM.EXE	Symbol file generator
RC.EXE	Windows resource compiler
RCPP.EXE	Resource script file preprocessor
SYMDEB.EXE	Symbolic debugger for Windows applications

6 The WINDOWS subdirectory will contain all programs placed here by the Windows SETUP program. Also, you should place the following binary executable Windows applications in this subdirectory:

[1] LIBW.LIB and WINLIBC.LIB are prefixed with a C, L, M, or S, according to the memory model size: compact, large, medium, or small, respectively. For example, a compact memory model would use CLIBW.LIB and CWINLIBC.LIB.

Filename	*Description*
DIALOG.EXE	Dialog box editor
FONTEDIT.EXE	Font editor
HEAPWALK.EXE	Enumerates allocation of the global heap
ICONEDIT.EXE	Creates icons, cursors, and bitmaps
SHAKER.EXE	Randomly allocates global memory
WINSTUB.EXE	Old-style application "stub" program

7 Place your application source files in subdirectories of the WINDEV directory. For example, you might create a \WINDEV \CLOCK subdirectory and place the following CLOCK application files in it:

Filename	*Description*
CLOCK.	"Make" script file
CLOCK.C	C language source file
CLOCK.H	Header file
CLOCK.RC	Resource script file
CLOCK.DEF	Link definition file
CLOCK.OBJ	Object file created by language compiler
CLOCK.RES	Binary source file created by resource compiler
CLOCK.MAP	Map file created by LINK4
CLOCK.SYM	Symbol file created by MAPSYM
CLOCK.EXE	Windows executable application file

Some of the filename extensions shown above may be unfamiliar to you. You'll find out about special types of Windows files in the following chapters.

8 Put the following statements in your CONFIG.SYS file:

```
FILES = 32
BUFFERS = 96
SHELL = C:\COMMAND.COM /p/e:256
```

The SHELL statement expands the environment to allow additional environment variables.

9 Put the following statements in your AUTOEXEC.BAT file:

```
SET INCLUDE = C:\INCLUDE
SET LIB = C:\LIB
SET TMP = C:\
SET PATH = C:\BIN;C:\UTIL;C:\WINDOWS
```

2.2 IMPROVING PROCESSING SPEED

A typical program "make" process, which involves compiling a source module, compiling a resource file, linking, and applying the resources, can take anywhere from two to five minutes or more. Here are a couple of ways you can improve your compiler's performance:

- Windows includes a RAM drive program, RAMDRIVE, and a disk-cache program, SMARTDRIVE. Using both of these programs will speed up your development process.
- You can reformat your hard disk using the Advanced Diagnostics from IBM and set your disk to an interleave factor of 1:2. This will yield a 30% increase in access over the IBM recommendation of 1:3. **Important: reformatting the hard disk destroys all data on the disk, so be sure to back up all data before you reformat the disk!**

2.3 AN OVERVIEW OF THE DEVELOPMENT PROCESS

This section describes the general process you'll go through to create a Windows application, as shown in Figure 2.1.

1 Input the .H header file and all source (.C) files for your application.

The header file is the connection between the C program and the resource script file. The names specified in the header file allow the source code (.C files) to find resources.

2 Create and/or identify all the resources your application will use. You can use existing Windows graphics objects or you can use Icon Editor to create icons, cursors, and bitmaps; Font Editor to create fonts; and Dialog Editor to create and modify dialog boxes.

Figure 2.1

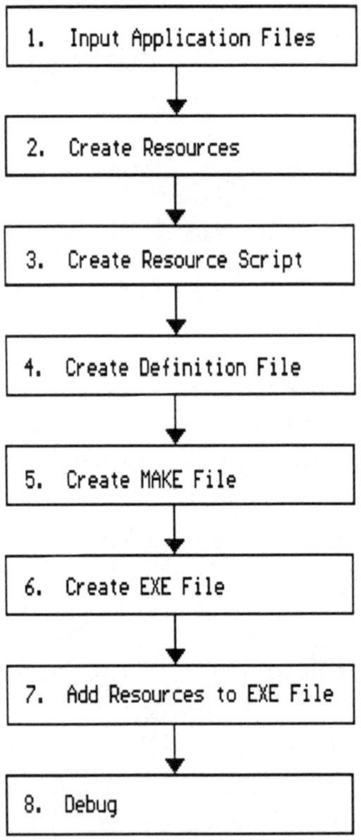

3 Define all resources used in your application in a resource script (.RC) file.

A *resource script file* consists of "resource statements" that define names and attributes of resources to be added to your program's executable file.

4 Create the module definition (.DEF) file.

A *module definition file* is an ASCII text file that defines the system requirements and contents of a Windows application or library. A definition file typically includes the name of the application, the size of the heap, and most importantly, the list of routines to be executed from outside your application, which is known as the *export list*. The export list must include the names of all window procedures and all dialog box procedures.

5 Create a make file.

A *make file* contains a list of the commands and files needed to build a Windows application.

6 Use MAKE (which will in turn use MAPSYM, the C compiler, and LINK4) to compile and link all C language files in an executable (.EXE) file.

7 Use RC to compile the resource script file into a binary resource (.RES) file, and add the .RES file to the .EXE file.

8 Use SYMDEB to debug your application as necessary.

Figure 2.2 illustrates the files used to generate a Windows application. DOS programmers should already be familiar with most of these files and with this process. Most Windows applications have four source code files, plus a file containing instructions to the MAKE program. In Figure 2.2, the source files are EXAMPLE.RC, EXAMPLE.H, EXAMPLE.C, and EXAMPLE.DEF.

EXAMPLE.RC and EXAMPLE.H are the input to the resource compiler preprocessor. As noted earlier, the resource compiler assimilates the resources and places them into a binary file, labelled EXAMPLE.RES in the figure.

Figure 2.2

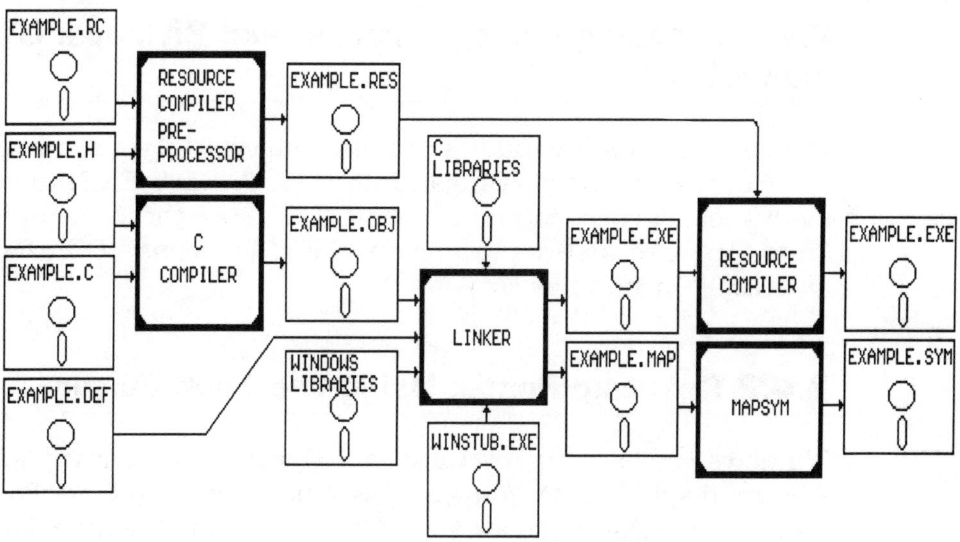

The C compiler accepts EXAMPLE.H and EXAMPLE.C and produces EXAMPLE.OBJ, the object file.

The link phase involves a number of source files: EXAMPLE.OBJ, the C libraries, the Windows Development Kit libraries, a stub file (WINSTUB.EXE), and a module definition file (EXAMPLE.DEF). Output from LINK4 consists of two files: EXAMPLE.EXE and EXAMPLE.MAP. The .MAP file is a listing of all symbols used in the program. The .EXE file is a Windows application that is not quite ready to run.

Next, the resource compiler, RC, takes the .RES file (binary resources) and binds it to the .EXE file. This completes the Windows application module, EXAMPLE.EXE.

To debug the module, MAPSYM is used to convert the .MAP file into a .SYM symbol file, which can be read by the symbolic debugging program, SYMDEB.

2.4 A SURVEY OF WINDOWS UTILITIES AND TOOLS

In the following sections you'll see a brief description of the development utilities and the Development Kit tools you'll be using to create and perfect your Windows application. All these tools are described in depth in the *Microsoft Windows Programming Tools* manual, part of the Software Development Kit.

2.4.1 Creating Icons, Cursors, and Bitmaps: Using the Icon Editor

You can use stock Windows graphics objects in your application, or you can use the Windows Icon Editor (ICONEDIT.EXE) to create and modify icons, cursors, and bitmaps. You'll save these resources in separate files with distinct extensions: .ICO for icons, .CUR for cursors, and .BMP for bitmaps.

2.4.2 Creating Fonts: Using the Font Editor

Windows comes with several default fonts that your application can use to display text. You can also use the Windows Font Editor (FONTEDIT.EXE) to create your own fonts or modify the existing fonts. Like all resources, fonts should be kept in separate files with distinct extensions; in this case, .FON.

2.4.3 Creating Dialog Boxes: Using the Dialog Editor

The Windows Dialog Editor (DIALOG.EXE) lets you create a dialog box on the display screen, then save a definition of that dialog box in a resource file. Using the Dialog Editor, you can create a dialog box outline, add controls, and define how those controls will be used.

2.4.4 Defining Resources: Using RC

As previously mentioned, resources are kept separate from source code in Windows applications. To use resources in your application, you create the resources you need, define those resources in a resource script file, then compile resources and add them to the executable file.

2.4.4.1 Creating Resource Script Files

To formally define an application's resources, you create a *resource script* file, which contains statements describing the resources' symbolic names, types, and other details about the resources, as well as directives defining actions to perform on the script file before it is compiled.

If you can define a resource with text, as in the case of menus, character strings, and dialog boxes, you can define the resource within the resource script file. If a resource cannot be defined with text, as is the case with icons, bitmaps, fonts, and cursors, you must define the resource in its own file and specify that file in the resource script file.

Using resource script files makes it easier to create country- or language-specific versions of an application, because you'll keep all the program's text strings in the resource script file. The source code will merely operate on those objects.

The following example is a resource script file for a program called **SAMPLE.**

```
#include sample.h
SAMPLEICON                          ICON    sample.ico
STRINGTABLE
BEGIN
        IDSTITLE,                   'Sample Program'
        IDSFOO,                     'More text'
END
```

SAMPLE's resources include an icon, called **SAMPLEICON,** which is defined in the file SAMPLE.ICO, and two strings known as **IDSTITLE** and **IDSFOO. SAMPLEICON, IDSTITLE**, and **IDSFOO** are equated to simple integers and are defined in SAMPLE.H. Whenever SAMPLE wants a resource, it need only be referenced by name.

2.4.4.2 Compiling Resource Files

Before your application can use the resources you've created and defined in the resource script file, you must compile them with the RC compiler into a binary resource (.RES) file.

When you've defined the script file as described in the previous section, you'll use the following syntax to compile it into a binary resource module:

```
rc [-r] filename [executable-file]
```

The **-r** switch causes RC to invoke RCPP, the Resource Compiler Pre-Processor, which compiles the resource script and saves the binary result in a file with the extension .RES.

You'll use RC once again (without the **-r** switch) after LINK4 has completed its task. This final RC operation will bind the binary resource file to its executable file—that is, the resources will be appended to the .EXE file created by LINK4.

2.4.5 Maintaining Your Program: Using MAKE

MAKE, the program maintenance utility, automatically updates a program after any of its source files have changed. To use MAKE, you create a MAKE description file, which includes the commands you want to carry out, and supplies the names of the files needed to carry out those commands. You can use MAKE to control the processes of compiling and building your application.

2.4.6 Compiling Source Files: Using C Compiler

Microsoft has slightly modified its C Compiler to support Windows. The C Compiler supports six memory models, and has four additional keywords that enable Windows calling conventions.

Windows supports both the Pascal and C programming languages. How can it support both? The answer lies in the subroutine calling convention. As long as Pascal and C call a subroutine with the same calling convention, Windows doesn't know (or care) which language is used. Since the C and Pascal calling procedures differ somewhat, Microsoft has added a command line switch to the C Compiler: the **PLM**-switch. This switch tells the compiler to use Pascal calling conventions for all procedures.

The six memory models and their respective code and data sizes are as follows:

Model	*Code*	*Data*	*Description*
Small	<= 64K	<= 64K	Code and data segments each less than or equal to 64K
Medium	N*64K	<= 64K	Only one data segment less than or equal to 64K but multiple code segments, each less than or equal to 64K
Large	N*64K	N*64K	Multiple code and data segments; data items do not span segment boundary
Compact	<= 64K	N*64K	Data items span segment boundary
Huge	N*64K	N*64K	Data items span segment boundary
Mixed	N*64K	N*64K	Mixed 16- and 32-bit addresses (uses near and far keywords)

The new keywords are:

Keyword	*Meaning*
PASCAL	Push parameters left to right, callee pops parms
CDECL	Push parameters right to left, caller pops parms
FAR	Use 32-bit addressing
NEAR	Use 16-bit addressing

The C Compiler accepts the .H and .C files, and compiles them into object (.OBJ) files, which will be used by LINK4.

2.4.7 Creating an Executable File: Using LINK4

Windows applications must be linked with LINK4, the Windows Linker. LINK4 creates two files: a .EXE executable file, and a .MAP map file, which can be processed with MAPSYM into a symbol file to be debugged with SYMDEB.

LINK4 differs from previous versions of LINK in the following ways:

First, LINK4 has a new feature called "dynamic linking," which enables applications to dynamically export and import procedures at run time. This means that the application need not keep a copy of the code it needs in its own module. Instead, it can call a subroutine at runtime as it would, for example, an operating system call.

Second, LINK4 has a fifth command line argument that prompts for a .DEF definition file, the text file that defines the contents and system requirements of a Windows application or library.

Third, the "4" in LINK4 refers to the fact that LINK4 creates a DOS version 4.0 executable file. Basically, the new .EXE format looks like this:

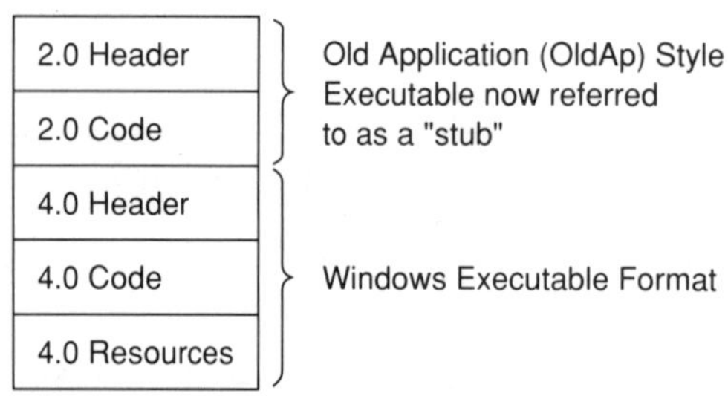

The "stub" file, which is appended to the front of the module, is simply an old-style DOS application that gains control if the user attempts to execute the Windows program from the DOS command prompt. You can write your own stub program to take the actions you want, or you can use the default stub program supplied by Microsoft (WINSTUB.EXE), which simply displays the message:

This program requires Microsoft Windows.

2.4.8 The Debugging Tools: MAPSYM and SYMDEB

The MAPSYM program takes the symbol (.MAP) files created by LINK4 and transforms them into symbol (.SYM) files that can be used with SYMDEB.

SYMDEB, Microsoft's symbolic debugging utility, is much like the DOS program DEBUG, both in appearance and function. This section will deal primarily with those features that affect the Windows development environment.

SYMDEB is of little use to programmers with only one computer and one display. To use SYMDEB effectively, you need one of two possible debugging configurations, illustrated in Figures 2.3 and 2.4.

Figure 2.3

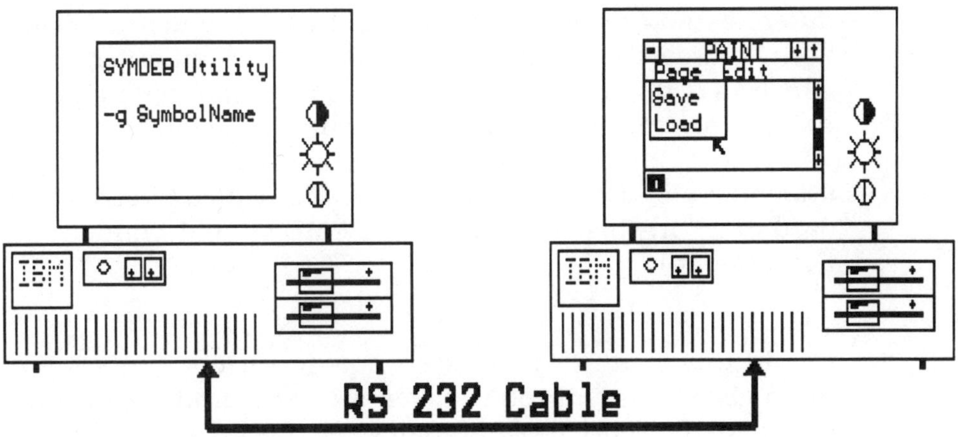

Figure 2.4

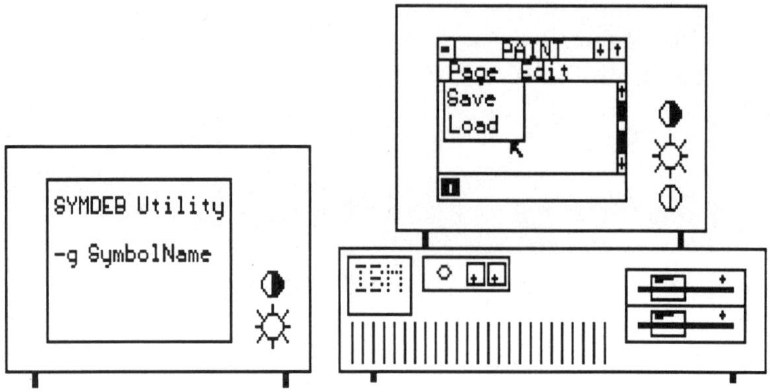

Figure 2.3 shows the preferred configuration, in which two computers communicate via an RS-232 cable, which SYMDEB uses for both "standard in" and "standard out." One computer runs SYMDEB, which in turn runs Windows. The other computer simply echoes anything it receives and transmits anything typed at the keyboard.

Figure 2.4 illustrates the second possible configuration: the attachment of a monochrome monitor to which SYMDEB sends "standard out." In this configuration, SYMDEB and Windows must share the keyboard.

. . . .

In this chapter you've seen how to set up your system for maximum efficiency, and you've taken a brief tour of the development process and the tools you'll be using as you create your application. In Chapter 3, you'll learn about the basic structures of windows, of Windows applications, and of the messages that manage the environment.

3

BASIC STRUCTURES: WINDOWS, WINDOWS APPLICATIONS, AND MESSAGES

- Components of Windows
- Types of Windows
- The Basic Structure of a Windows Application
- Windows Data Types and Structures
- The Structure of Messages

Before we can discuss the design of a Windows application, you should understand what types of windows are available, what each window can contain, and the terminology Windows uses to describe the different types of windows and different parts of windows. You also need to understand what a message contains and how Windows uses messages. This chapter discusses the types of windows you can use, then proceeds into an examination of the basic structures of Windows applications and of the messages they'll use.

3.1 COMPONENTS OF WINDOWS

Windows are made up of several common components, as shown in Figure 3.1.

Figure 3.1

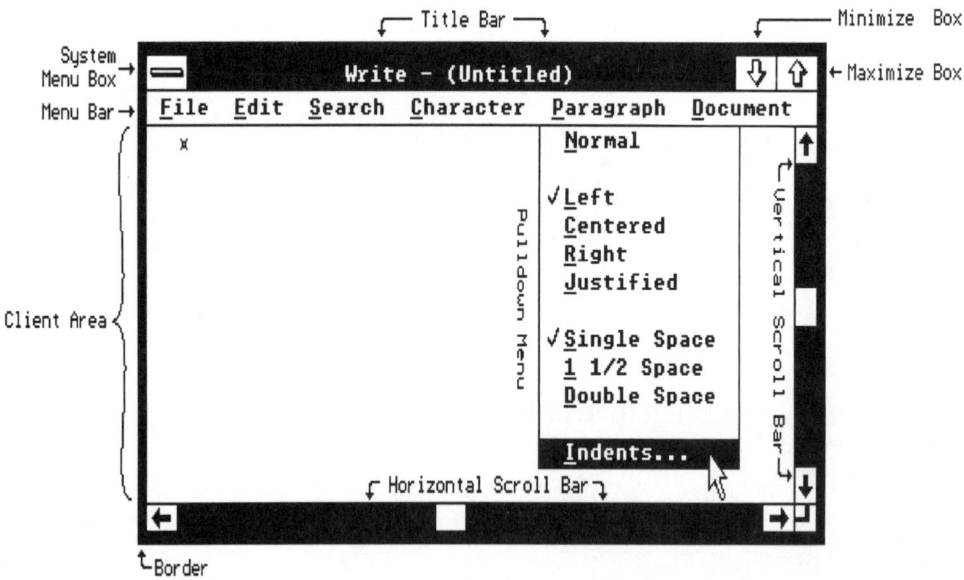

System menu A predefined Windows menu, identified by a spacebar icon at the left end of the title bar. A mouse button click or the [ALT+SPACEBAR] combination from the keyboard displays the system menu. This menu is also called the *control menu*.

Title bar Provides space for the application's name and allows the user with a mouse to move the window.

Menu bar Appears beneath the window's title bar and contains the names of all menus used in the application.

Pulldown Menu A list of menu items that "pulls down" from the menu bar. Windows menus are called *pull-down* menus.

Maximize box A small box with an up-arrow icon in the window's upper right corner. Allows the user with a mouse to enlarge a window to its maximum size.

Minimize box A small box with a down-arrow icon in the window's upper right corner. Allows the user with a mouse to shrink a window to an icon.

Client area The "work area" of the window over which the application has complete control.

Scroll bars Bars at the right and bottom of a window. A window can have a *vertical scroll bar*, located at the right of the client area, and/or a *horizontal scroll bar*, located at the bottom of the client area. Scroll bars allow the mouse user to scroll the contents of the client area by dragging the scroll box.

Scroll box A small square that appears in the scroll bar. The position of the scroll box within the scroll bar indicates the relative position of the displayed information within the file. Sometimes called an *elevator*.

3.2 TYPES OF WINDOWS

Windows has several types of windows that you can create using the Windows functions:

Overlapped window An overlapped window is always a top-level window: it never has an owner or belongs to any other window. It has a client area, border, and title bar; and can also have a system menu, minimize and maximize boxes, scroll bars, and its own menus. Every overlapped window has a corresponding icon that Windows displays in the icon area when the window is closed.

Popup window A popup window can overlap any other window and can be displayed anywhere. This type of window is most often used to display important information about a current command or to request information from the user (in a message box or a dialog box). It has a client area, but does not have a border or title bar or any other feature unless you explicitly request it. If requested, a popup window can also have a system menu or other menus, minimize and maximize boxes, and scroll bars. You can also request a dialog frame instead of a border to distinguish it from an overlapped window.

Child window A child window is confined to the client area of an owner (also called a parent) window. A child window is most often used to split the client area of an owner window into areas with different functions. A child window has a client area, but not any other features unless you explicitly request them. Many applications use several borderless child windows that are "transparent" to the user, who perceives the display as one main window.

Figure 3.2 shows several types of windows. This screen has two overlapped windows titled "Reversi" and "MS-DOS Executive." Both the Reversi window and the MS-DOS Executive have child windows that

Figure 3.2

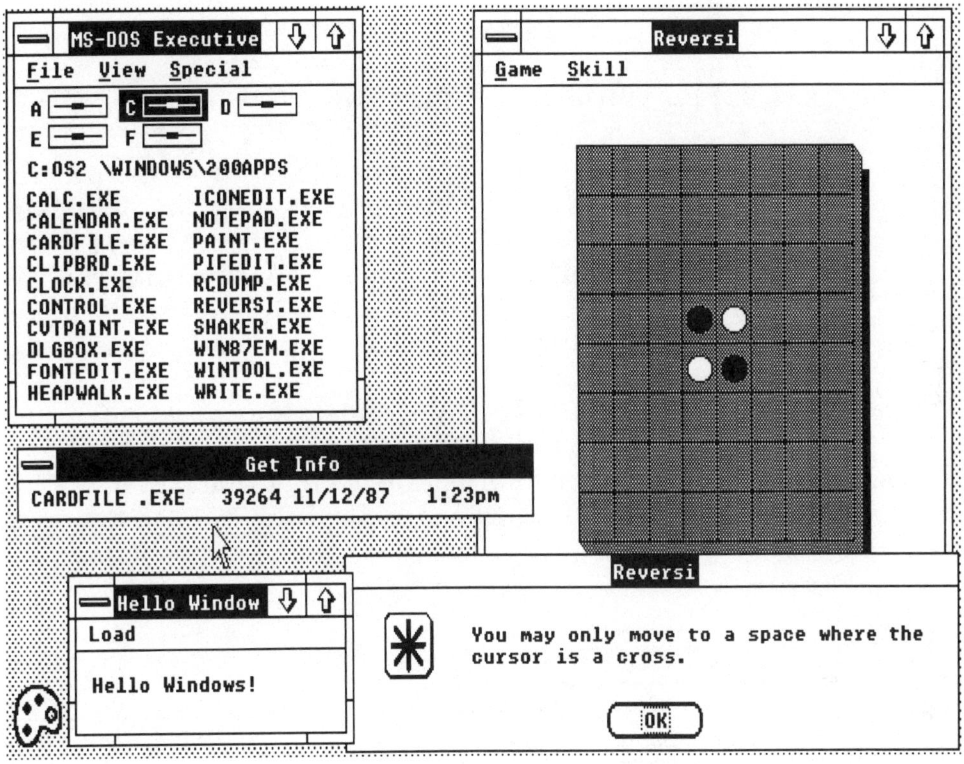

are also popup windows: Reversi has a message box, and the MS-DOS Executive has a dialog box. Another popup window named "Hello" can be seen in the lower right corner of the Reversi window. In the lower left corner of the display we see an artist's palette icon, which represents a closed Paint program window.

You specify how you want your window to look by specifying *window styles* when you create the window. All window styles are defined in STYLE.H, the header file included in the Development Kit. You'll see how to create windows and assign styles in Chapter 4.

3.3 THE BASIC STRUCTURE OF A WINDOWS APPLICATION

Every C language Windows program must define these four elements:

- *main function*, always called **WinMain,**
- *window class*,

- *window function*, and
- *main window.*

3.3.1 The WinMain Function

The **WinMain** function is the starting point of the program, and is similar to MAIN() in a conventional C program. **WinMain** must be declared with the **PASCAL** keyword. As illustrated in Figure 3.3, **WinMain** must accomplish several tasks after gaining control. First, it must go through its initialization process. **WinMain's** first objective is to load resources, such as icons, cursors, fonts, menus, dialog boxes, and strings.

Next, **WinMain** defines and registers a *window class* for the window that it intends to use. A window class is simply a data structure that specifies general information about a window. To define a window class, you'll fill in a WNDCLASS data structure with information about

Figure 3.3

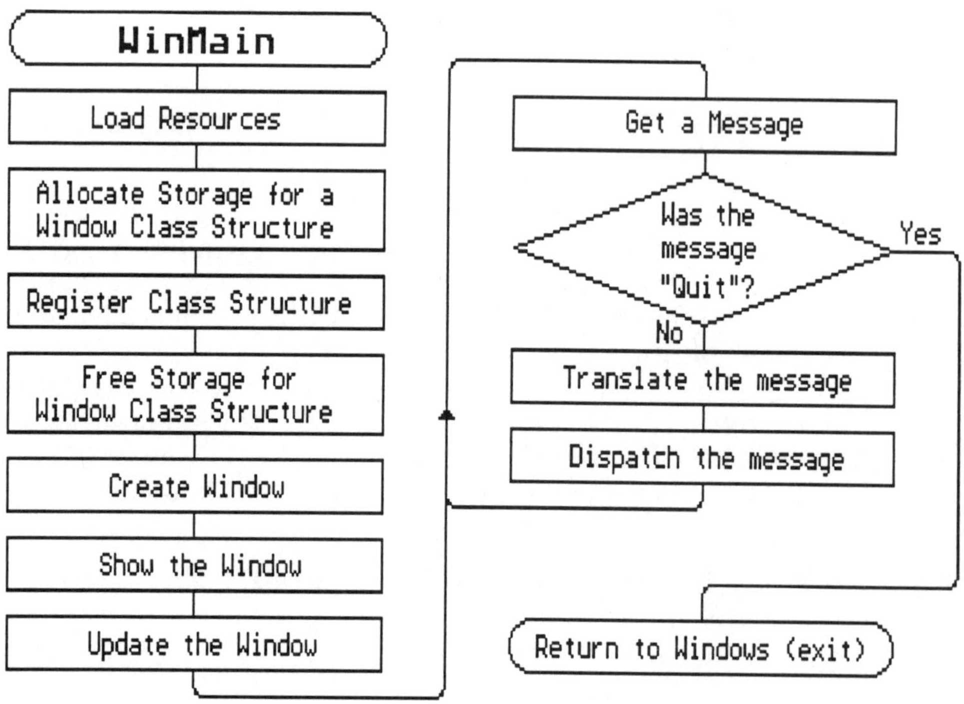

the window's attributes, then pass that information as a parameter to the **RegisterClass** function. The window's attributes include the names of the cursors, icons, and menus, the color of the window's client area background, style selections, and the name of the window function. Subsequent instances of the application can use the class structure defined by the previous instance by referring to the class name. The program doesn't have to go through the registration process again; Windows remembers the class information from the previous instance.

Following class registration, **WinMain** creates the window by placing a call to Windows. After successfully creating a window, **WinMain** displays the window (creating a window doesn't automatically display one). Finally, **WinMain** updates the window, a process that fills in the client area. This process is commonly called *painting*. At this point, initialization is finished and the application has displayed a window that is complete and ready to receive input from the user.

Now **WinMain** begins its primary duty: pulling, translating, and dispatching messages. Any input—such as pressing a key or clicking a mouse button—is recognized by Windows as an *event*. When an event occurs, Windows determines where the focus is (which application and window the event belongs to). Windows then transforms the event into a message and places the message in that application's *input queue*. The application pulls the messages one by one from its input queue. If the message is "Quit," the application terminates; otherwise, the message must be translated and dispatched to the appropriate window function. When **WinMain** dispatches a message, Windows determines which window function is to receive the message. If the queue is empty (no messages are waiting to be processed), Windows allows other processes to execute. This is how Windows achieves multitasking.

WinMain translates messages by changing virtual keystrokes into character messages. For example, if a menu item is selected from the keyboard, **WinMain** translates the keystrokes into menu messages. Then the message is dispatched to the window function (**MainWndProc**) of the application's main window, which processes it.

After **MainWndProc** processes the message, it returns control to Windows, which returns control to **WinMain**. As Figure 3.3 indicates, the program jumps back to **WinMain**'s top and repeats the loop until the "Quit" message is received.

As you can see, no real "work" is performed in **WinMain:** it just initializes the window and passes messages to the window function.

3.3.2 The Window Function

Every window must have a *window function* to respond to messages from Windows. A window function, also called a window procedure or window processor, can be named anything the programmer desires. In this book, we're calling our window function **MainWndProc**.

A window function's structure is basically that of an interrupt handler. It expects to receive certain types of messages and processes them according to their contents. For example, if the user presses the left mouse button, **WinMain** dispatches the resulting message to **MainWndProc**. Then it's up to **MainWndProc** to take the appropriate action.

Figure 3.4 illustrates **MainWndProc's** cascading structure. It's a switch—when **MainWndProc** gets one message, it takes one action; when it gets another, it takes another action, and so on. Any messages that are not specifically handled by the application are passed on to the Windows default procedure, **DefWindowProc**.

Figure 3.4

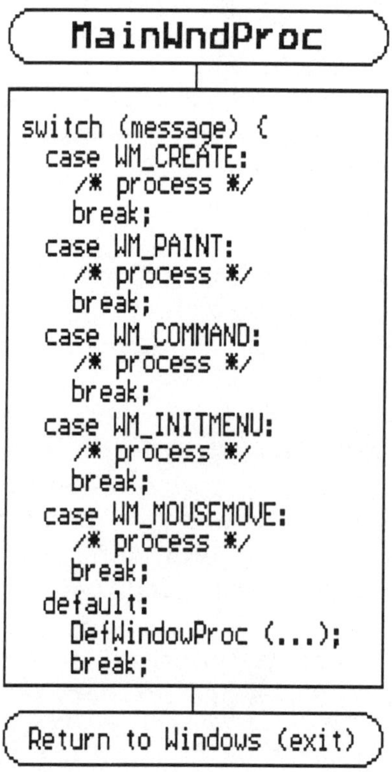

3.4 WINDOWS DATA TYPES AND STRUCTURES

In general, Windows uses many more data types than typical C programs. The Windows data types are defined in the WINDOWS.H include file, which should be included in each of your source files.

Here are some common Windows data types that are used in the sample programs in this book:

Type	*Meaning*
HANDLE	A 16-bit, unsigned integer used as a handle
HWND	A 16-bit, unsigned integer used as a handle to a window
WORD	A 16-bit, unsigned integer
LONG	A 32-bit, signed integer
LPSTR	A 32-bit pointer to a **char** type
FARPROC	A 32-bit pointer to a function

Here are some commonly used Windows data structures you'll see in the sample programs:

Structure	*Defines . . .*
WNDCLASS	A window class
MSG	The fields of an input message
PAINTSTRUCT	A paint structure used to draw within a window
RECT	A rectangle

3.5 THE STRUCTURE OF MESSAGES

Every message is addressed to a specific window, and each message contains these four fields:

- the handle of the window (a 16-bit word),
- the message type (a 16-bit word),
- a WORD parameter (a 16-bit word), and
- a LONG parameter (a 32-bit doubleword).

The *handle* is an identifier—in this case, the identifier of the window the message is addressed to. The message type is a name identifying the type of message. For example, window messages, the most common type of messages, always begin with the letters **WM**. The WORD and LONG parameters contain specific information about an event. For example, these two fields might contain information about a mouse button click, a keystroke, or a selected menu item.

. . . .

Now you have a basic understanding of the structure of windows, the structure of a Windows application, and the structure of messages. In the next chapter, we'll leave the generalities behind and look at our first Windows program.

4

CREATING A MAIN WINDOW

- Introduction to PGM1
- The C Header File: PGM1.H
- The Resource Script File: PGM1.RC
- The C Language Source File: PGM1.C
- Creating and Using Your Own Icons
- The Definition File: PGM1.DEF
- The Make File: PGM1.

The first step in coding a Windows application is creating a main window in which your application will run. This chapter examines a sample program that creates a main window. By the end of the chapter, you'll also understand how Windows applications process messages, and how you can create multiple instances of an application.

4.1 INTRODUCTION TO PGM1

PGM1, the sample program we will examine in this chapter, requires five source files:

Filename	*Description*
PGM1.H	C language program header
PGM1.RC	Resource script file
PGM1.C	Code for PGM1
PGM1.DEF	Definition file (required by LINK4)
PGM1.	Input instructions to the MAKE utility

As stated earlier, we strongly recommend that you place your source files for each program in a separate subdirectory. For example, the files for PGM1 could be kept in C:\WINDEV\PGM1.

Figure 4.1 illustrates the result of running PGM1: a basic window is displayed on the screen. While this particular achievement may not amaze your colleagues, it's the first step in creating your Windows application. This window has a system menu (indicated by the space-bar icon in the upper left corner), a window title, minimize and maximize boxes, and a line of text in the client area. And you can do a lot with this window—you can move it, size it, maximize it. You can reduce it to an icon. You can move the mouse cursor all over it. And you can destroy it. So although PGM1 may at first glance seem simple, it really does a lot.

The following sections show you the code in each of PGM1's files, followed by a detailed description of what the code in each file does.

Figure 4.1

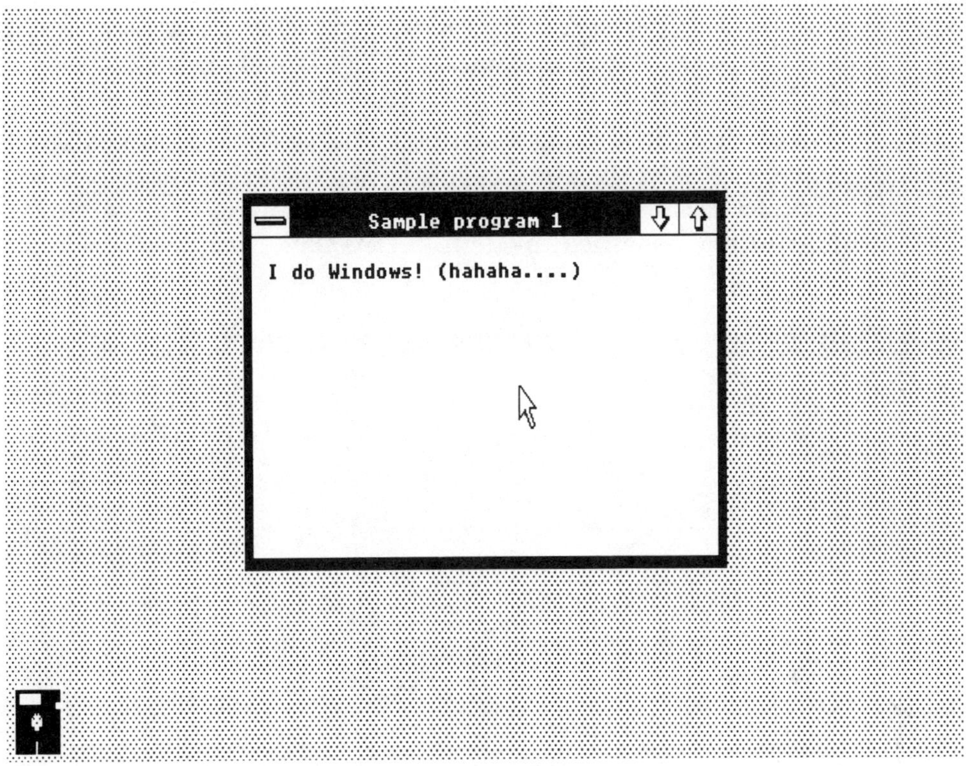

4.2 THE C HEADER FILE: PGM1.H

```
/**********************************************************************/
/* Filename:     PGM1.H                                               */
/*                                                                    */
/* Description:  PGM1.C  header file                                  */
/*--------------------------------------------------------------------*/

#define IDSTITLE        1000     /* String table constants       */
#define IDSSTRING1      1010

/*--------------------------------------------------------------------*/
/* End of file:  PGM1.H                                               */
/**********************************************************************/
```

PGM1.H, a C language header file, defines symbols common to both PGM1.C and PGM1.RC. Thus, PGM.H becomes the link between the two files.

The .H (pronounced "dot H") file contains two equates:

```
#define IDSTITLE                                    1000
#define IDSSTRING1                                  1010
```

These two lines assign symbolic names to resources (in this case, strings) needed by the program. When PGM1 wants to use these two strings, it will load the strings by referencing the symbolic names, or *identifiers*, assigned to them in this file.

4.3 THE RESOURCE SCRIPT FILE: PGM1.RC

```
/***********************************************************************/
/* Filename:     PGM1.RC                                               */
/*                                                                     */
/* Description:  PGM1.EXE resources                                    */
/*---------------------------------------------------------------------*/

#include "pgm1.h"

STRINGTABLE
BEGIN
    IDSTITLE,    "Sample program 1"
    IDSSTRING1, "I do Windows! (hahaha....)"
END

/*---------------------------------------------------------------------*/
/* End of file:  PGM1.RC                                               */
/***********************************************************************/
```

PGM1.RC is the resource script file for PGM1, and contains the strings used in PGM1's title bar and client area.

The statement:

```
#include "pgm1.h"
```

includes the .H file just as in a conventional C program.

The statement STRINGTABLE signifies the beginning of a string resource. The general form of STRINGTABLE is:

```
STRINGTABLE [load-option] [mem-option]
BEGIN
string-definitions
END
```

where **string-definitions** are one or more null-terminated ASCII strings preceded by an integer identifier. Hence, the **string-definition**

```
IDSTITLE,                    "Sample program 1"
```

defines a string with an associated integer identifier, **IDSTITLE** (1000). When we examine the C code in the next section, you'll see how the resource string is loaded using the **IDSTITLE** symbolic reference.

The variables **load-option** and **mem-option** are both unused options in this program. **load-option** is an optional keyword:

Keyword	*Meaning*
PRELOAD	load resource immediately
LOADONCALL	load resource when called (default)

The variable **mem-option** specifies whether the resource is fixed or moveable in memory, and whether it is discardable. The keywords are:

Keyword	*Meaning*
FIXED	Resource remains fixed in memory
MOVEABLE	Resource can be moved by Windows
DISCARDABLE	Resource can be discarded if not needed

Several keywords can be used, provided the combination makes sense. For example, the default **mem-option** is MOVEABLE DISCARDABLE (both moveable and discardable).

4.4 THE C LANGUAGE SOURCE FILE: PGM1.C

```
/***************************************************************************/
/* Filename:     PGM1.C                                                   */
/*                                                                        */
/* Description:  PGM1.EXE source code                                     */
/*------------------------------------------------------------------------*/

#include "windows.h"
#include "pgm1.h"

  char                  szTitle[32];
  char                  szString1[64];
  int                   iString1Len;

  long FAR PASCAL       MainWndProc (HWND, unsigned, WORD, LONG);

BOOL MainInit (hInstance)
  HANDLE                hInstance;
  {
  PWNDCLASS             pMainClass;

  LoadString (hInstance, IDSTITLE, (LPSTR)szTitle, 32);
  iString1Len = LoadString (hInstance, IDSSTRING1, (LPSTR)szString1, 64);

  pMainClass = (PWNDCLASS)LocalAlloc (LPTR, sizeof(WNDCLASS));

  pMainClass->hCursor       = LoadCursor (NULL, IDC_ARROW);
  pMainClass->hIcon         = LoadIcon (NULL, IDI_APPLICATION);
  pMainClass->lpszMenuName  = (LPSTR)NULL;
  pMainClass->lpszClassName = (LPSTR)szTitle;
  pMainClass->hbrBackground = (HBRUSH)GetStockObject (WHITE_BRUSH);
  pMainClass->hInstance     = hInstance;
  pMainClass->style         = CS_HREDRAW | CS_VREDRAW;
  pMainClass->lpfnWndProc   = MainWndProc;

  if (!RegisterClass((LPWNDCLASS)pMainClass))
    return FALSE;

  LocalFree ((HANDLE)pMainClass);
  return TRUE;
  }


int PASCAL WinMain (hInstance, hPrevInstance, lpszCmdLine, cmdShow)
  HANDLE                hInstance;
  HANDLE                hPrevInstance;
  LPSTR                 lpszCmdLine;
  int                   cmdShow;
  {
  MSG                   msg;
  HWND                  hWnd;
  HMENU                 hMenu;

  if (!hPrevInstance)   /* Call init if this is the first instance
    {
    if (!MainInit (hInstance))
```

```
      return FALSE;
    }
  else                    /* Copy data from previous instance if not first*/
    {
    GetInstanceData (hPrevInstance, (PSTR)szTitle, 32);
    GetInstanceData (hPrevInstance, (PSTR)szString1, 64);
    GetInstanceData (hPrevInstance, (PSTR)&iString1Len, sizeof(int));
    }

  hWnd = CreateWindow  ((LPSTR)szTitle,
                        (LPSTR)szTitle,
                        WS_OVERLAPPEDWINDOW,
                        GetSystemMetrics (SM_CXSCREEN) / 4,      /*  x   */
                        GetSystemMetrics (SM_CYSCREEN) / 4,      /*  y   */
                        GetSystemMetrics (SM_CXSCREEN) / 2,      /* cx   */
                        GetSystemMetrics (SM_CYSCREEN) / 2,      /* cy   */
                        (HWND)NULL,                      /* no parent    */
                        (HMENU)NULL,             /* use class menu       */
                        (HANDLE)hInstance, /* handle to window instance */
                        (LPSTR)NULL);      /* no params to pass on      */

  ShowWindow (hWnd, cmdShow);
  UpdateWindow (hWnd);

  while (GetMessage((LPMSG)&msg, NULL, 0, 0))
    {
    TranslateMessage ((LPMSG)&msg);
    DispatchMessage ((LPMSG)&msg);
    }

  return (int)msg.wParam;
  }

long FAR PASCAL MainWndProc (hWnd, msg, wParam, lParam)
  HWND                  hWnd;
  unsigned              msg;
  WORD                  wParam;
  LONG                  lParam;
  {
  switch (msg)
    {
    case WM_DESTROY:
      PostQuitMessage (0);
      break;

    case WM_PAINT:
      {
      PAINTSTRUCT       ps;

      BeginPaint (hWnd, (LPPAINTSTRUCT)&ps);
      TextOut (ps.hdc, 10, 10, (LPSTR)szString1, iString1Len);
      EndPaint (hWnd, (LPPAINTSTRUCT)&ps);
      break;
      }
     default:
      return DefWindowProc (hWnd, msg, wParam, lParam);
      break;
    }
   return (0L);
   }

/*---------------------------------------------------------------------------*/
/* End of file:  PGM1.C                                                      */
/*****************************************************************************/
```

PGM1.C is the C language source file, which contains definitions required of every Windows application.

The first statement,

```
#include "WINDOWS.H"
```

includes WINDOWS.H, an ordinary C header file that is supplied with the Development Kit and contains definitions for all of Windows special constants, data types, data structures, and functions. WINDOWS.H should be included in every C language source file. (A helpful hint: If you ever encounter a discrepancy in any piece of Windows documentation, use WINDOWS.H as the final authority.)

4.4.1 A Close Look at the WinMain Function

When Windows loads PGM1, it gives control to PGM1's **WinMain** function. **WinMain** is PGM1's "executive," and controls all subsequent execution of the application.

The **WinMain** declaration has the form:

```
int PASCAL WinMain (hInstance,hPrevInstance,lpszCmdline,
                                                 cmdshow);

HANDLE          hInstance;
HANDLE          hPrevInstance;
LPSTR           lpszCmdLine;
int             cmdshow;
```

An occurrence of a program in the Windows environment is known as an *instance*. When PGM1 is loaded, it is assigned a unique instance number, or *handle*. **hInstance** is a handle to this instance of PGM1. **hPrevInstance** is the handle to the previous instance of PGM1, if one exists. Otherwise, the handle is NULL. In this chapter, we'll explain why you need to know the handle of a previous instance of your application.

lpszCmdLine is a long pointer to a null-terminated command line. The invoking program (usually the MS-DOS Executive) can pass parameters to the callee using this mechanism.

cmdShow is an integer value to be passed to a function called **ShowWindow**. We'll investigate **ShowWindow** later in this chapter.

4.4.2 Starting an Instance for the First Time

The first statements of **WinMain** look at **hPrevInstance** to see if this is the first instance of PGM1. If **hPrevInstance** is NULL, this is the first instance. For now, let's assume this is the first instance. For a program's first instance, the internal **MainInit** function is called.

MainInit is responsible for initializing the window class data structure and registering it with Windows. Upon completing its duties, it returns a BOOL value indicating success or failure.

The statement:

```
PWNDCLASS                    pMainClass;
```

defines a pointer to a data structure of type WNDCLASS. PGM1 fills in this structure with information about the application's window.

MainInit's first order of business is to load two string resources, using the **LoadString** function:

```
LoadString (hInstance, IDSTITLE, (LPSTR)szTitle, 32);
iString1Len = LoadString (hInstance, IDSSTRING1,
                          (LPSTR)szString1, 64);
```

hInstance is PGM1's instance handle. **IDSTITLE** is the string resource integer identifier that we defined in PGM1.H. **(LPSTR)szTitle** is a long pointer to a buffer that will receive the string, and **32** is the maximum number of characters to be copied into the buffer.

LoadString returns the actual number of characters copied into the buffer. If that number is zero, the string resource does not exist.

You can now see how **IDSTITLE** and **IDSSTRING1** relate to the .RC file: they are resource identifiers.

Next, **MainInit** asks for a local memory allocation for the WNDCLASS data structure, using the **LocalAlloc** function:

```
pMainClass = (PWNDCLASS)LocalAlloc (LPTR,
                          sizeof(WNDCLASS));
```

LocalAlloc allocates a number of bytes from the local heap as specified by the second parameter; in this case: **sizeof(WNDCLASS)**, or 26 bytes. **LPTR** is a bitwise conjunction (logical OR) of the two flags **LMEM_FIXED** and **LMEM_ZEROINIT**, specifying that this storage should be fixed in memory (non-moveable) and cleared with zeros.

LPTR can be found in WINDOWS.H, as can **LMEM_FIXED** and **LMEM_ZEROINIT**. If **LocalInit** is successful, it returns a handle to the allocated memory block that is cast as **PWNDCLASS**, which is a pointer to a window class data structure. Otherwise, the return value is NULL.

4.4.3 Defining a Window Class

To define a window class, a program must fill in the WNDCLASS data structure, found in WINDOWS.H. WNDCLASS contains the following fields:

```
WORD        style;
FARPROC     lpfnWndProc;
int         cbClsExtra;
int         cbWndExtra;
HANDLE      hInstance;
HICON       hIcon;
HCURSOR     hCursor;
HBRUSH      bBrBackground;
LPSTR       lpszMenuName;
LPSTR       lpszClassName;
```

The next step is to fill in these fields in preparation for class registration, using the pointing method ("->") of accessing the structure. The statement

```
HCURSOR          hCursor;
```

specifies the class cursor, and must be a handle to a cursor resource. The program acquires this handle with the **LoadCursor** function:

```
pMainClass->hCursor = LoadCursor (NULL, IDC_ARROW);
```

LoadCursor loads the cursor resource (specified by the second parameter) from the executable file associated with the handle specified in the first parameter. Since PGM1's resource script (.RC) file did not define any cursors, we specified a stock Windows cursor by setting the first parameter (the handle) to NULL and setting the second parameter to a flag, **IDC_ARROW**, that names the standard arrow cursor.

The statement

```
HICON          hIcon;
```

specifies the class icon and must be a handle to an icon resource. The program acquires this handle by using the **LoadIcon** function:

```
pMainClass->hIcon = LoadIcon (NULL, IDI_APPLICATION);
```

LoadIcon loads the icon resource (specified by the second parameter) from the executable file associated with the specified handle in the first parameter. Because PGM1's resource script file did not define any icons, we specified a stock Windows icon by setting the first parameter (the handle) to NULL and setting the second parameter to a flag, **IDI_APPLICATION**, that names a default application icon (a white box with a black border).

The statement

```
LPSTR          lpszMenuName;
```

specifies the resource name of a class menu and must be a long pointer to a null-terminated ASCII string. Because PGM1 defines no menus, it must supply a NULL:

```
pMainClass->lpszMenuName = (LPSTR)NULL;
```

The WNDCLASS field

```
LPSTR          lpszClassName;
```

specifies the name of the window's class, and is a long pointer to a null-terminated ASCII string. You'll recall that we did a **LoadString** on **IDSTITLE** into **szTitle**. The text we loaded from the resource file was "Sample Program 1," so PGM1 uses "Sample Program 1" as the class name:

```
pMainClass->lpszClassName = (LPSTR)szTitle;
```

The WNDCLASS field

```
HBRUSH         bBrBackground;
```

specifies the class background brush, and can be either a handle to a physical brush or a color value. PGM1 uses the handle method:

```
pMainClass->hbrBackground = (HBRUSH)GetStockObject
                                        (WHITE_BRUSH);
```

The Windows **GetStockObject** function retrieves a handle to one of several predefined stock pens, brushes, or fonts. PGM1 selects **WHITE_BRUSH**, which is exactly what it sounds like: a white brush.

The WNDCLASS field

```
HANDLE              hInstance;
```

specifies the class module. It must be an instance handle and cannot be NULL. PGM1 sets the field equal to the value given to it by the caller through the **WinMain** parameters:

```
pMainClass->hInstance = hInstance;
```

The WNDCLASS field

```
WORD                style;
```

specifies the class style, and

```
pMainClass->style = CS_HREDRAW | CS_VREDRAW;
```

tells Windows to redraw the entire window if the vertical or horizontal size changes.

The WNDCLASS field

```
FARPROC             lpfnWndProc;
```

specifies a long pointer to a window function. The statement

```
pMainClass->lpfnWndProc = MainWndProc;
```

sets **lpfnWndProc** to the window function **MainWndProc**.

The final two WNDCLASS fields

```
int                 cbClsExtra;
int                 cbWndExtra;
```

specify the number of bytes to allocate after the window class structure and the number of bytes to allocate after the window instance, respectively. PGM1 does not use these fields and leaves them equal to zero (remember, **LocalAlloc** set the entire structure to zero when it allocated the storage).

4.4.4 Registering the Window Class

Now that the program has defined the window class, it must register it with Windows via the **RegisterClass** function:

```
RegisterClass((LPWNDCLASS)pMainClass);
```

RegisterClass registers a window class that will be used by the Windows **CreateWindow** function later in the program. **RegisterClass** returns a BOOL value indicating success or failure. Therefore, the statement

```
if (!RegisterClass((LPWNDCLASS)pMainClass))
        return FALSE;
```

returns FALSE if **RegisterClass** fails.

Finally, if **RegisterClass** was successful, the **LocalFree** function is called to de-allocate the storage associated with **pMainClass:**

```
LocalFree ((HANDLE)pMainClass;
```

One might ask, "Why is the storage allocated by **LocalAlloc** not freed if **RegisterClass** fails?" The answer is that **WinMain** terminates immediately if **RegisterClass** fails, and a side effect of this termination is that local storage is automatically freed by Windows.

4.4.5 Starting a Second Instance

As noted earlier, **hPrevInstance** contains a NULL if this is the first occurrence of PGM1. Otherwise, it contains the handle of the previous instance. Let's now assume that **hPrevInstance** does not contain NULL.

When beginning a second instance of an application, it's preferable to retrieve information from the previous instance rather than reload it. To retrieve information, we use the Windows **GetInstanceData** function, which simply copies data from one instance to another. The statement

```
GetInstanceData (hPrevInstance, (PSTR)szTitle, 32);
```

copies **32** bytes from the previous instance of **szTitle** into this module. (**MainInit** already registered a window class for us, so we just needed to copy the strings.)

4.4.6 Creating a Window

PGM1 creates the window using the following function:

```
hWnd = CreateWindow ((LPSTR)szTitle,   /* lpClassName    */
   (LPSTR)szTitle,                     /* lpWindowName   */
   WS_OVERLAPPEDWINDOW,                /* dwStyle        */
   GetSystemMetrics (SM_CXSCREEN)/4,   /*  X             */
   GetSystemMetrics (SM_CXSCREEN)/4,   /*  Y             */
   GetSystemMetrics (SM_CXSCREEN)/2,   /* dX             */
   GetSystemMetrics (SM_CXSCREEN)/2,   /* dY             */
   (HWND)NULL,                         /* hWndParent     */
   (HMENU)NULL,                        /* hMenu          */
   (HANDLE)hInstance,                  /* hInstance      */
   (LPSTR)NULL);                       /* lpParam        */
```

The **CreateWindow** function is used to create overlapped, popup, and child windows. The code for PGM1 specifies the overlapped type. **CreateWindow** requires eleven parameters, which are described below:

1 **lpClassName** names the window class and is a long pointer to a null-terminated ASCII string. Remember, the **MainInit** procedure contained this statement:

```
pMainClass->lpszClassName = (LPSTR)szTitle;
```

This parameter constitutes the connection between the window to be created and the window class.

2 **lpWindowName** is also a long pointer to a null-terminated ASCII string and represents the window name. This window has a title bar where the window name is displayed as the caption.

3 **dwStyle** specifies the window style. It is a long unsigned integer and can be any combination of the available styles. PGM1 uses the **WS_OVERLAPPEDWINDOW** style, an overlapped window with a title bar, a system menu, and minimize and maximize boxes. (**WS_OVERLAPPEDWINDOW** can be found in WINDOWS.H.)

4–7 **X, Y, dX**, and **dY** specify the initial position and size of a window in device units (pixels). The **GetSystemMetrics** function returns information about the system metrics. PGM1 uses this function to return the height and width of the screen. PGM1 specifies that the window is to be one half the screen size and start one quarter from the top and left.

8 **hWndParent** is a handle to a parent window. We set this field to NULL for two reasons: PGM1's window has no parent, and this field must be set to NULL for overlapped windows.

9 **hMenu** is a handle to a menu to be used with the window. Because PGM1 has no menu, we use NULL.

10 **hInstance** is the instance handle passed to PGM1 by **WinMain.**

11 **lpParam** is a long pointer which is passed to the window function. This can point to anything the programmer wants to pass. In PGM1, we elected not to use it.

CreateWindow returns **hWnd**, a handle to the newly created window.

4.4.7 Displaying and Updating a Window

The next order of business is to display the window with the statement:

```
ShowWindow(hWnd, cmdShow);
```

The **ShowWindow** function displays the specified window **(hWnd)**. **cmdShow** indicates how Windows is to display it. Windows passes this information to the program through **WinMain**; it usually is **SHOW_OPENWINDOW,** which means to display an overlapped window for the first time.

Next, to ensure that the window's appearance is up-to-date, we use the statement

```
UpdateWindow(hWnd);
```

which forces Windows to call our window function with a paint command.

4.4.8 Handling Messages

At this point in our tour of PGM1.C, we've arrived at the code that performs **WinMain's** primary duty: pulling, translating, and dispatching messages to the window function.

Input events (actions from the keyboard, mouse, timer ticker, and so forth) generate messages. Windows places most messages in the application's message queue. The application then reads ("pulls") messages, translates them if necessary, and dispatches them to the appropriate window function.

The final part of **WinMain** contains the basic pull-translate-dispatch loop:

```
while (GetMessage((LPMSG)&msg, NULL, 0, 0))
        {
  TranslateMessage ((LPMSG)&msg);
  DispatchMessage ((LPMSG)&msg);
        }
  return (int)msg.wParam;
```

GetMessage returns the next message from the application's queue. If the queue is empty, **GetMessage** waits for a message to be placed there. While **GetMessage** waits, Windows allows other tasks to execute.

In PGM1, **(LPMSG)&msg** is a long pointer to **msg**, a message data structure of type MSG. (You may refer to WINDOWS.H to see the MSG construct.) **GetMessage** only gets messages associated with the window specified by the handle in the second parameter and within the range of the third and fourth parameters. However, if the second parameter is NULL, messages are retrieved for all windows belonging to the calling application. Also, if the third and fourth parameters are both zero, no filtering is performed and all messages are retrieved.

GetMessage returns a BOOL value of TRUE for all messages except **WM_QUIT,** for which it returns FALSE (zero). This process is the foundation of the **while** loop.

Windows utilizes "virtual key codes" for keyboard input as part of its strategy to guarantee device independence. In order to translate these codes into ANSI character values, a Windows application must use the **TranslateMessage** function. Because **TranslateMessage** has no effect on other types of messages, **WinMain** should always use this function to translate every message, not just virtual key messages.

DispatchMessage sends the translated message to the window function. For example, if the left mouse button is pressed, **DispatchMessage** sends **WM_LBUTTONDOWN** to the window function. The window function processes the message and returns to **DispatchMessage**. The **while** loop again calls **GetMessage** and the process starts all over again.

Once **GetMessage** pulls the **WM_QUIT** message, control drops out of the loop and into the **return** statement. Later on, we'll see how the window function processes **WM_QUIT**, where the exit code **msg.wParam** comes from, and how these all fit together.

4.4.9 The Window Function

The window function is much like an interrupt service routine: after the code is invoked, the application must be able to respond to a variety of situations, usually in an undetermined sequence. After **DispatchMessage** is called, Windows passes the message (two to four pieces of information) to the window function.

PGM1 defines **MainWndProc** as the window function. Recall that in defining the window class, PGM1 tied the window to the window function via:

```
pMainClass->lpfnWndProc = MainWndProc;
```

PGM1 now defines **MainWndProc:**

```
long FAR PASCAL MainWndProc (hWnd, msg, wParam, lParam)
        HWND            hWnd;
        unsigned        msg;
        WORD            wParam;
        LONG            lParam;
```

Windows always calls an application's procedures using the "far Pascal" calling convention. Therefore, the keywords **FAR** and **PASCAL** must be specified in the function declaration. Windows passes four parameters in a message: the first two (a window handle, **hWnd**, and a message, **msg**) are always valid; the last two (a WORD parameter, **wParam**, and a LONG parameter, **lParam**) contain message-specific information and are not always used.

MainWndProc is simply a common entry point for message processing. The first thing **MainWndProc** does is branch to the appropriate message-processing routine (**case**) based upon **msg**:

```
switch (msg);
```

PGM1 will handle only two of the many possible messages that it can (and will) receive. The balance will be handled by a default window function. The first case PGM1 will process is:

```
case WM_DESTROY:
  PostQuitMessage (0);
  break;
```

This message is issued when the user selects "Close" from the system menu. **PostQuitMessage** tells Windows that this instance wants to terminate. The return code is (**0**). Windows responds by returning FALSE to the next call to **GetMessage**, causing the **while** loop to terminate. **msg.wParam** contains the return code (**0**). The final return to Windows causes PGM1 to be released from memory.

The other **case** PGM1 will handle is:

```
case WM_PAINT:
      {
 PAINTSTRUCT                    ps;
 BeginPaint (hWnd, (LPPAINTSTRUCT)&ps);
 TextOut(ps.hdc, 10, 10, (LPSTR)szString1, iString1Len);
 EndPaint (hWnd, (LPPAINTSTRUCT)&ps);
 break;
 }
```

WM_PAINT is sent whenever Windows or the application wishes to repaint all or part of an application's window. It is usually sent by the **UpdateWindow** function.

BeginPaint prepares the window (specified by **hWnd**) for painting by filling in the **PAINTSTRUCT, ps**. It also issues a *handle to a display context*, or *HDC*.

EndPaint marks the end of painting, and returns the HDC to Windows for use in subsequent programs. A display context is a shared resource: as long as one application has it, no other application can use it. Therefore, an application should not "hold" an HDC, as there are only five display contexts in an entire Windows system.

PAINTSTRUCT contains information the window function uses to paint an application's window. (You can see a description of PAINTSTRUCT in WINDOWS.H.) The only field we'll examine in this example is **hdc**: handle to a display context.

TextOut is simply a text outputting routine. It sends the string, **szString1**, of length **iString1Len** to the specified display context, **ps.hdc**, at the specified coordinates, (**10,10**).

You should always remember that Windows has only five HDCs available for checkout. When you are finished using one, **return it**. (Every rule has an exception: a window can have a private display context. But for now, assume that DCs must be returned.)

PGM1 will receive many "WM_*xxx*" messages. We elected to handle only two. To deal with the balance, PGM1 uses the default Windows procedure **DefWindowProc**, which is invoked as follows:

```
default:
  return DefWindowProc (hWnd, msg, wParam, lParam);
```

The parameters are the same parameters passed to **MainWndProc** by Windows. **DefWindowProc** returns default values for all "WM_*xxx*" messages that were not trapped by **MainWndProc**.

4.5 CREATING AND USING YOUR OWN ICONS

The sample program presented in this chapter uses an application stock icon (**IDI_APPLICATION**). But you're not confined to using stock icons: if you want to create your own icon, you can easily incorporate it into the PGM1 files.

To create an icon, you'll use the Windows ICONEDIT utility, which lets you create an icon from scratch and save it as a file. Figure 4.2 illustrates an icon in the final stage of generation.

Figure 4.2

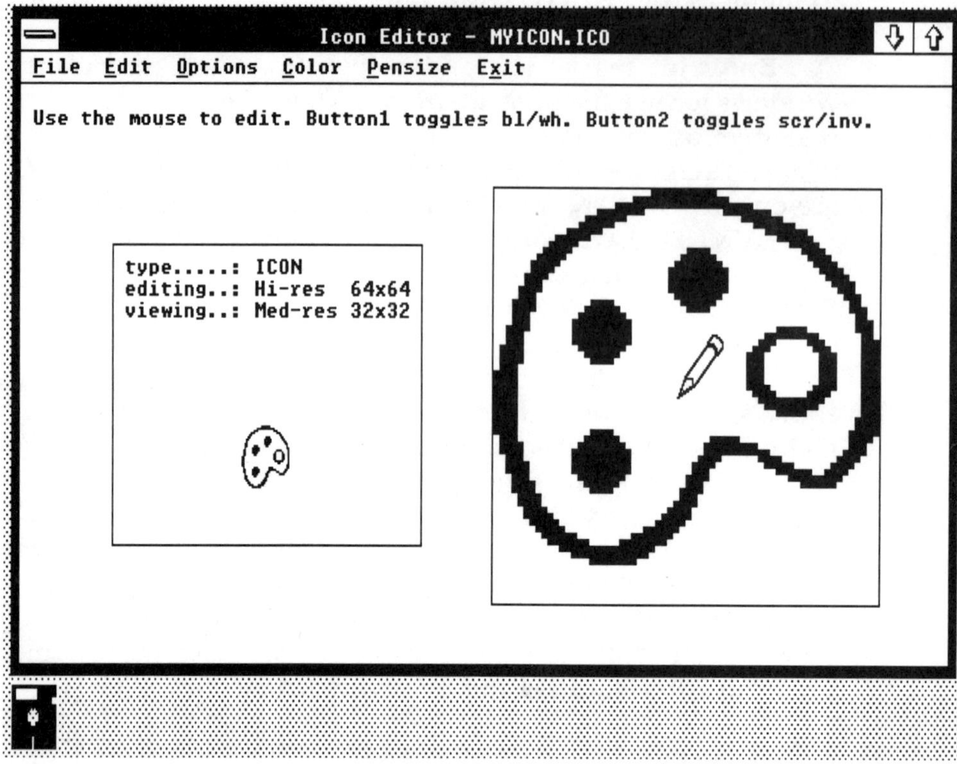

After creating and saving an icon, you'll define it with a constant integer expression in your application's header file. For example, you would add the following statement, which defines an icon named **MYICON**, to PGM1.H:

```
#define MYICON  1
```

MYICON symbolically represents the icon through the integer **1**. The integer selected must only be unique among the other resources.

An icon is a resource, so you'll also need to declare the icon in the program's .RC file. The declaration of the icon within the resource file might look like this:

```
MYICON  ICON    pgm1.ico
```

where ICON is the declaration of the statement type, and **pgm1.ico** is the filename assigned to the icon from the icon editor.

Finally, in the .C file, you must place a call to Windows to load your icon into the window class. To do this in PGM1, replace the statement that loaded the stock icon:

```
pMainClass->hIcon = LoadIcon (NULL, IDI_APPLICATION);
```

with:

```
 pMainClass->hIcon = LoadIcon (hInstance,
                               MAKEINTRESOURCE(MYICON));
```

Now, instead of loading a stock icon, the program will load the icon created with ICONEDIT. Figure 4.3 shows how, by selecting the "Minimize" option from the system menu, you can reduce the window to an icon. Figure 4.4 shows the new icon at the bottom of the screen.

Figure 4.3

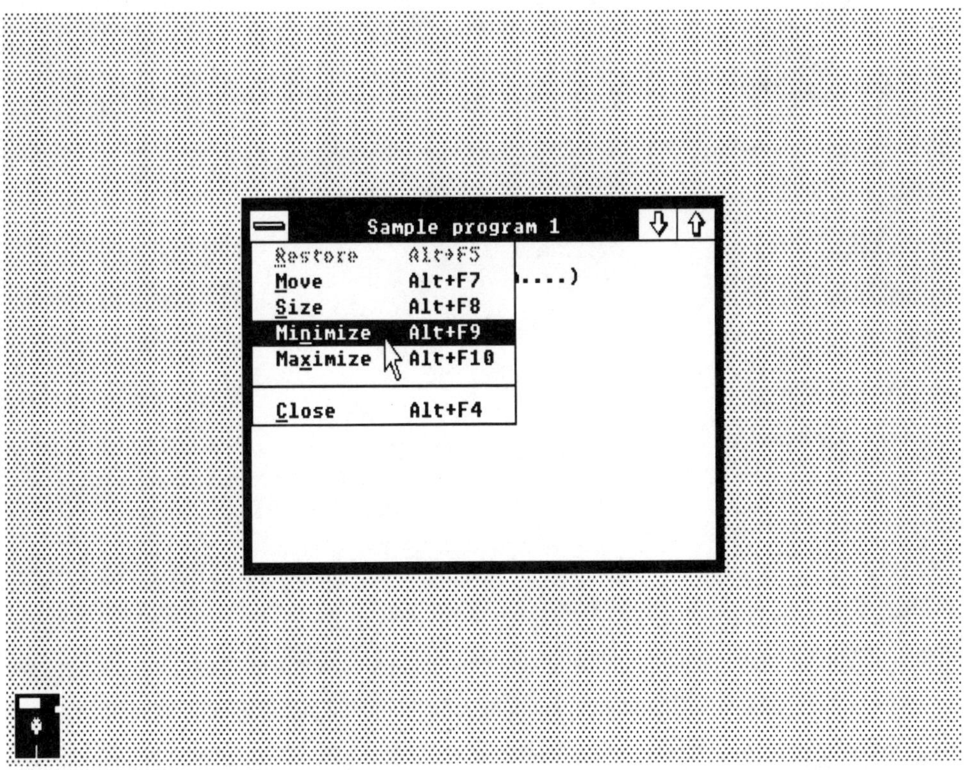

Figure 4.4

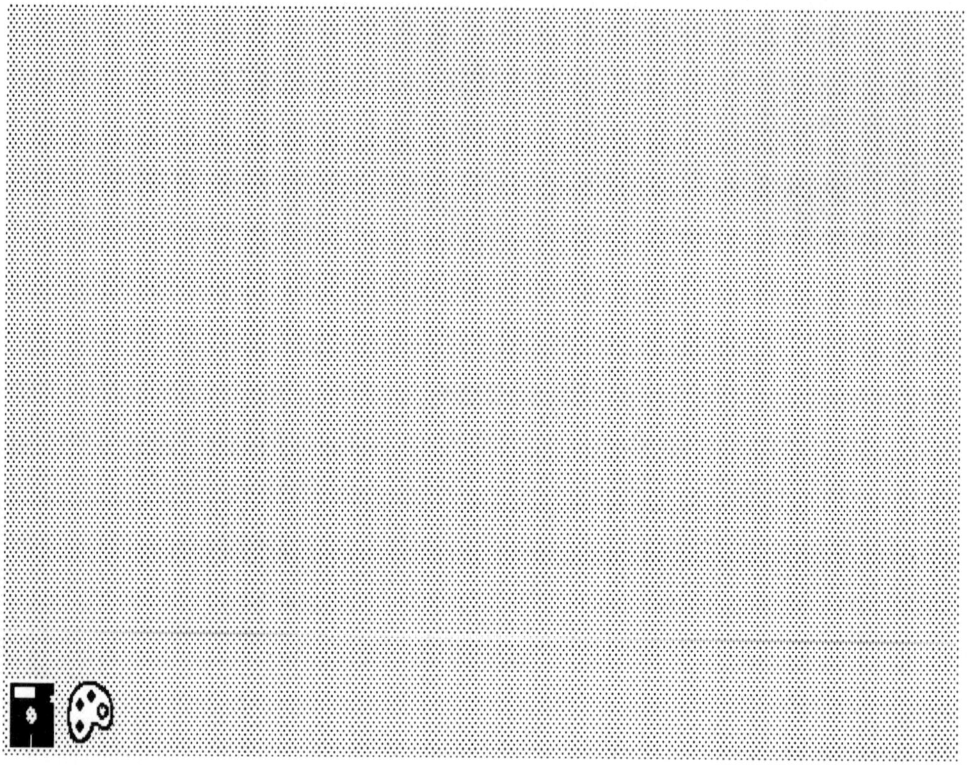

4.6 THE DEFINITION FILE: PGM1.DEF

```
;*****************************************************************:
; Filename:     PGM1.DEF                                          :
;                                                                 :
; Description:  Link definition file                              :
;-----------------------------------------------------------------:
NAME    PGM1

DESCRIPTION 'Sample program 1'

STUB    '..\WINSTUB.EXE'

CODE    MOVEABLE
DATA    MOVEABLE MULTIPLE

HEAPSIZE  128
STACKSIZE 4096

EXPORTS
    MainWndProc         @1

;-----------------------------------------------------------------:
; End of file:  PGM1.DEF                                          :
;*****************************************************************:
```

PGM1.DEF, the module definition or .DEF (pronounced "deaf") file, defines the application's contents and system requirements. The file's single-line statements describe attributes such as the module's name, code and data segment attributes, and exported routines.

The statement

```
NAME     PGM1
```

assigns the name **PGM1** to this module. The name is used to uniquely identify the module when importing and/or exporting functions. The statement

```
DESCRIPTION 'Sample program 1'
```

places the text into the .EXE file header. This can be useful for setting copyright information or serial numbers. The statement

```
STUB '..\WINSTUB.EXE'
```

identifies the stub DOS application program that is appended to the front of the application. A stub program should be executable under MS-DOS, and should either start Windows and the application, or at least inform users that this program requires Windows if they try to run the application directly from DOS.

The statement

```
CODE MOVEABLE
```

defines the code segment as MOVEABLE. The default is FIXED. The statement

```
DATA MOVEABLE MULTIPLE
```

defines the data segment as being MOVEABLE, and specifies that there is one segment for each instance (MULTIPLE). The default is FIXED MULTIPLE. The statement

```
HEAPSIZE 128
```

specifies that the application needs 128 bytes for its local heap. This is where storage is allocated from by **LocalInit**. The default is zero. The statement

```
STACKSIZE 4096
```

specifies that the application needs 4096 bytes of stack space. The default is zero or 4096, depending on whether or not the application makes function calls. The statement

```
EXPORTS
        MainWndProc                     @1
```

defines the name (**MainWndProc**) and ordinal number (**1**) of functions to be exported. Windows requires that all window functions be exported, with the exception of **WinMain**.

4.7 THE MAKE FILE: PGM1.

```
#***********************************************************************#
# Filename:     PGM1.                                                   #
#                                                                       #
# Description:  PGM1.EXE "MAKE" description file                        #
#-----------------------------------------------------------------------#

pgm1.obj: pgm1.c pgm1.h
    cl -d -c -AS -Gsw -Os -Zpe pgm1.c

pgm1.res: pgm1.rc pgm1.h
    rc -r pgm1.rc

pgm1.exe: pgm1.obj pgm1.res pgm1.def
    link4 pgm1,/align:16,/map,slibw,pgm1.def
    rc pgm1.res

#-----------------------------------------------------------------------#
# End of file:  PGM1.                                                   #
#***********************************************************************#
```

PGM1. contains the input instructions to the MAKE utility.

Once you have all your source files, you're ready to begin the "build" process. First, make sure the following development programs are accessible through your **PATH**= path:

Filename	*Description*
MAKE.EXE	Microsoft program maintenance utility
RC.EXE	Microsoft resource compiler
RCPP.EXE	Microsoft resource compiler preprocessor
CL.EXE	Microsoft C compiler
C1.EXE	Microsoft C compiler
C2.EXE	Microsoft C compiler
C3.EXE	Microsoft C compiler
LINK4.EXE	Microsoft Segmented-Executable Linker

Also, the following file must be available through the **INCLUDE**= environment statement:

Filename	*Description*
WINDOWS.H	Windows general header file

Finally, the following Microsoft C library files must be available through your **LIB**= environment statement:

Filename	*Description*
SLIBC.LIB	C runtime library
SLIBFA.LIB	Floating point math alternate library
SLIBFP.LIB	Floating point math library
SLIBW.LIB	Windows "application" libraries
SWINLIBC.LIB	Windows "library" libraries
EM.LIB	Model independent floating point library
LIBH.LIB	Model independent "compiler helper" functions

Enter the make file, PGM1. Then, at your development directory prompt, type:

```
MAKE PGM1
```

If all goes well, your screen should begin filling with compiler output similar to this:

```
Microsoft (R) Program Maintenance Utility  Version 4.02
Copyright (C) Microsoft Corp 1984, 1985, 1986.

make: target does not exist 'pgm1.obj'
        cl -d -c -AS -Gsw -Os -Zpe pgm1.c
Microsoft (R) C Compiler  Version 4.00
Copyright (C) Microsoft Corp 1984, 1985, 1986.

pgm1.c
P1 :   c1.exe -il D:\000333 -f pgm1.c -pc \:/ -Q 24242 -A
snd -Zp -Ze -Gs -I c:/INCLUDE -DM_I86 -DMSDOS -DM_I86SM -W1'
P2 :   c2.exe -il D:\000333 -CS -OS -GO -Gs -Gw -A snd -W1'
P3 :   c3.exe -il D:\000333 -Gw -FPi -Os -c pgm1.obj -A snd
-CC OsO'
make: target does not exist 'pgm1.res'
        rc -r pgm1.rc
Microsoft Windows Resource Compiler, V2.00

Creating PGM1.RES
RC: RCPP -E -D RC_INVOKED -f PGM1.RC -I C:\INCLUDE
```

```
PGM1.RC.
make: target does not exist 'pgm1.exe'
        link4 pgm1,/align:16,/map,slibw,pgm1.def

Microsoft (R) Segmented-Executable Linker Version 5.00.12
Copyright (C) Microsoft Corp 1984, 1985, 1986.

    rc pgm1.res
Microsoft Windows Resource Compiler, V2.00

Reading pgm1.res
..
Copying segment 1 (1843 bytes)
Copying segment 2 (106 bytes)
Resources will be aligned on 16 byte boundaries
Writing resource 63.6 (32 bytes)
Writing resource 64.6 (42 bytes)
```

If you made it this far, you're ready to run your program. If you didn't, you should see a message indicating where you went wrong. Check your listings, check your command line syntax, then try again.

Your development utilities will create a number of files:

Filename	*Description*
PGM1.OBJ	Object file created by C compiler
PGM1.RES	Binary file created by resource compiler
PGM1.MAP	Link map created by LINK4
PGM1.EXE	Application program created by LINK4

Assuming that your **PATH**= environment statement also points to your Windows program subdirectory, now you should be able to run Windows from this subdirectory. So, run your program, using the "Run" command from the MS-DOS Executive's File menu or double-clicking on your application's executable filename.

. . . .

Now you know the basics of starting an application, creating and displaying a main window, and processing messages. In the next chapter, you'll learn how to add menus to your application to give the user some control over the program.

5

CREATING MENUS AND PROCESSING MENU INPUT

- Introduction to PGM2
- The C Header File: PGM2.H
- The Resource Script File: PGM2.RC
- The C-Language Source File: PGM2.C
- The Definition File: PGM2.DEF
- The Make File: PGM2.

Menus are the principle means of user control in a Windows application. This chapter examines a sample program, **PGM2**, that adds menus to a main window and processes the input from menu items.

5.1 INTRODUCTION TO PGM2

PGM2 requires five source files:

PGM2.H	C language program header
PGM2.RC	Resource script file
PGM2.C	Code for PGM2
PGM2.DEF	Definition file (required by LINK4)
PGM2.	Input instructions to the MAKE utility

The source code to PGM2 is very similar in parts to PGM1. You may wish to copy PGM1's source files into the PGM2 directory and rename them so that you can use PGM1 as a "boilerplate," and just make the necessary changes to match the listings in this chapter.

Figure 5.1 illustrates the result of running PGM2. This window looks a lot like the the window displayed by PGM1, except for the addition of a menu bar with two items on it: "Beep. . ." and "Pick." "Beep's" ellipsis (. . .) indicates that a dialog box will be displayed when that menu item is chosen (a Windows style convention).

Figure 5.1

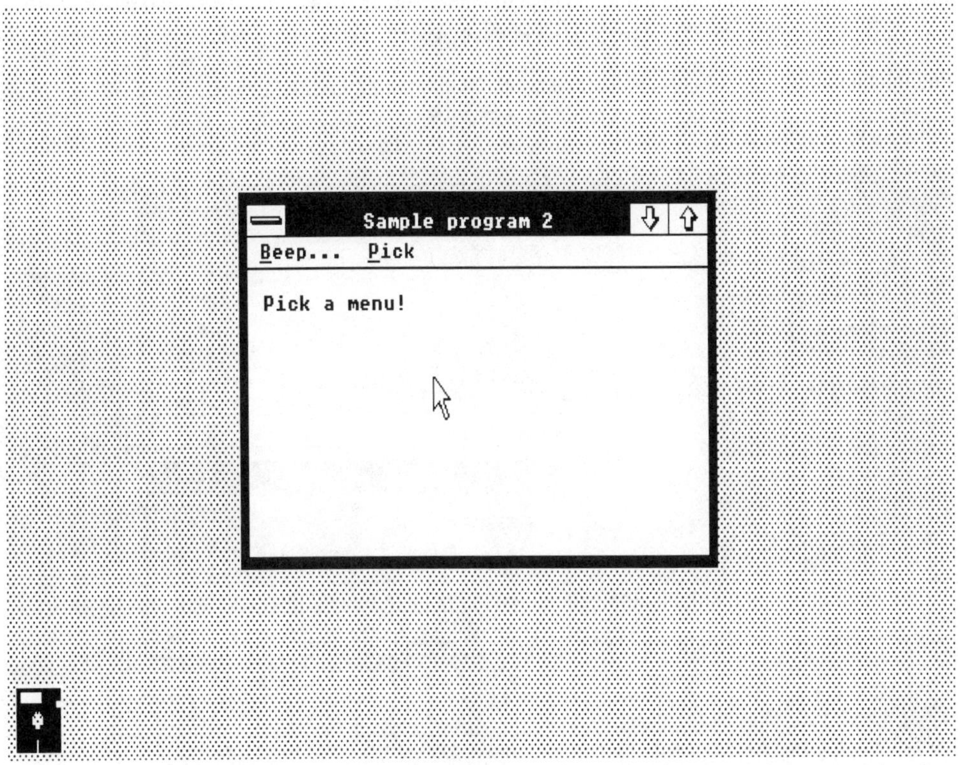

If the user selects "Beep. . .," PGM2 displays a dialog box, shown in Figure 5.2. The dialog box asks the question: "Want to hear a beep?" to which the user must respond "Yes" or "No."

Figure 5.2

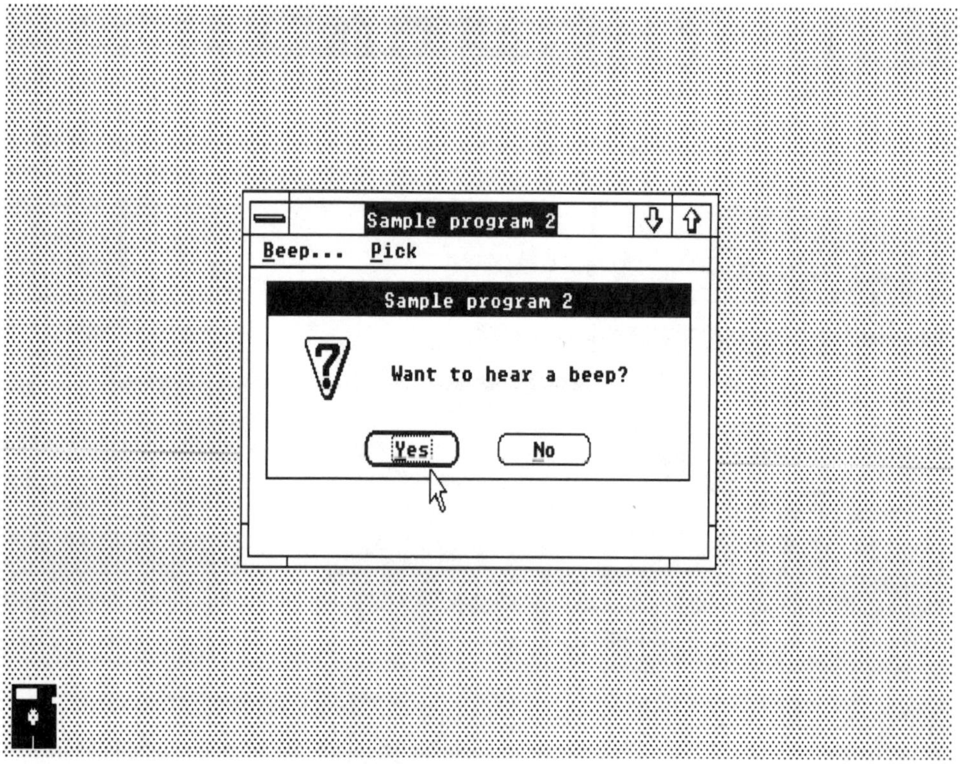

If the user selects "Pick" from the menu bar, Windows displays a pulldown menu as shown in Figure 5.3. This menu has three items: A, B, and C.

Figure 5.3

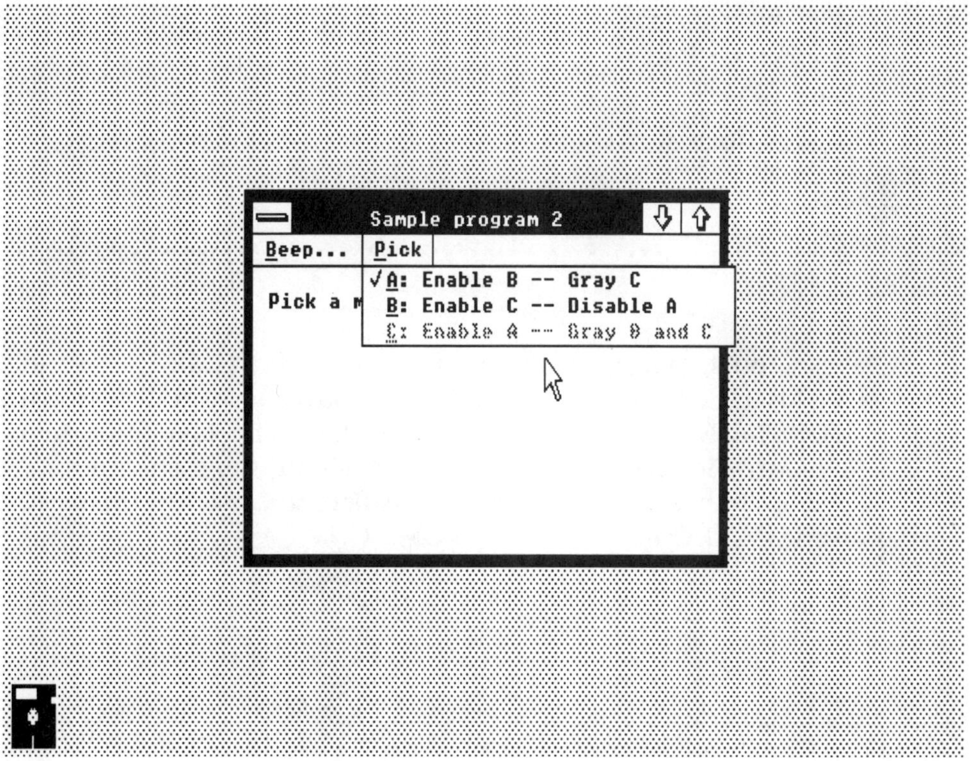

Initially, menu item A is checked and C is *grayed*. When an item is grayed, it cannot be selected by the user; it is disabled. Picking option B grays A and enables C. Selecting option C enables A and grays both B and C. Selecting option A returns the menu to the original state: B is enabled and C is grayed. You'll see the logic that controls this process as we examine PGM2.

The following sections show you the code in each of PGM2's files, followed by a detailed description of what the code in each file does.

5.2 THE C HEADER FILE: PGM2.H

```
/***************************************************************************/
/* Filename:      PGM2.H                                                 */
/*                                                                       */
/* Description:  PGM2.C  header file                                     */
/*-----------------------------------------------------------------------*/

#define IDSTITLE          1000    /* String table constants       */
#define IDSSTRING1        1010
#define IDSSTRING2        1020

#define MENU1             1310    /* Menu table constants         */
#define MENU2A            1321
#define MENU2B            1322
#define MENU2C            1323

/*-----------------------------------------------------------------------*/
/* End of file:  PGM2.H                                                  */
/***************************************************************************/
```

You'll notice that many parts of PGM2.H are identical to PGM1.H, except that a few things have been added. You'll recognize **IDSSTRING2** as a resource identifier. The last four items are also resource identifiers, similar to the string table constants. You'll soon see how these new resource identifiers are used to tie menu resources in PGM2.RC to the code in PGM2.C.

5.3 THE RESOURCE SCRIPT FILE: PGM2.RC

```
/************************************************************************/
/* Filename:     PGM2.RC                                                */
/*                                                                      */
/* Description:  PGM2.EXE resources                                     */
/*----------------------------------------------------------------------*/

#include "pgm2.h"

STRINGTABLE
BEGIN
    IDSTITLE,    "Sample program 2"
    IDSSTRING1, "Pick a menu!"
    IDSSTRING2, "Want to hear a beep?"
END

MainMenu MENU
BEGIN
    MENUITEM            "&Beep...",     MENU1
    POPUP               "&Pick"
    BEGIN
        MENUITEM        "&A: Enable B -- Gray C",       MENU2A, CHECKED
        MENUITEM        "&B: Enable C -- Disable A",    MENU2B
        MENUITEM        "&C: Enable A -- Gray B and C", MENU2C
    END
END

/*----------------------------------------------------------------------*/
/* End of file:  PGM2.RC                                                */
/************************************************************************/
```

PGM2.RC is similar to PGM1.RC, but another resource has been added. The MENU statement marks the beginning of a *menu resource*. A menu resource consists of a number of menu bar items and, optionally, popup menu items. Menu items are the names of the applications commands. The statement

```
MainMenu MENU
```

assigns the name **MainMenu** to the menu structure.

BEGIN and **END** statements bracket the menu, just as **BEGIN** and **END** bracket the STRINGTABLE statement.

MENUITEM defines an item to be placed on the menu bar and assigns the text a resource identifier. Thus:

```
MENUITEM "Beep...", MENU1
```

becomes our first menu item, which will be referred to as **MENU1**.

Following that, PGM2 defines a pulldown menu:

```
POPUP "Pick"
```

Text associated with the "popup" keyword is not assigned a resource identifier; it is merely displayed on the menu bar. When the user selects a pulldown menu, the menu items defined for the menu are displayed. These menu items are defined within **BEGIN** and **END** statements:

```
BEGIN
 MENUITEM "A: Enable B -- Gray C", MENU2A, CHECKED
 MENUITEM "B: Enable C -- Disable A", MENU2B
 MENUITEM "C: Enable A -- Gray B & C", MENU2C
END
```

MENUITEM text, id defines a menu item for a popup menu. Menu items can have check marks next to them to indicate a "selected" state. CHECKED indicates that the initial state of this item should be checked.

Whenever a user selects a menu item, the resource identification number is passed to Windows thru the **WM_COMMAND** message.

5.4 THE C-LANGUAGE SOURCE FILE: PGM2.C

```
/*************************************************************************/
/* Filename:      PGM2.C                                                 */
/*                                                                       */
/* Description:   PGM2.EXE source code                                   */
/*-----------------------------------------------------------------------*/

#include "windows.h"
#include "pgm2.h"

  char                szTitle[32];
  char                szString1[64];
  char                szString2[64];
  int                 iString1Len;
  int                 menu2           = MENU2A;
  int                 prevMenu2       = MENU2A;

  long FAR PASCAL     MainWndProc (HWND, unsigned, WORD, LONG);

BOOL MainInit (hInstance)
  HANDLE              hInstance;
  {
  PWNDCLASS           pMainClass;

  LoadString (hInstance, IDSTITLE, (LPSTR)szTitle, 32);
  iString1Len = LoadString (hInstance, IDSSTRING1, (LPSTR)szString1, 64);
  LoadString (hInstance, IDSSTRING2, (LPSTR)szString2, 64);
```

```
  pMainClass = (PWNDCLASS)LocalAlloc (LPTR, sizeof(WNDCLASS));

  pMainClass->hCursor       = LoadCursor (NULL, IDC_ARROW);
  pMainClass->hIcon         = LoadIcon (NULL, IDI_APPLICATION);
  pMainClass->lpszMenuName  = (LPSTR)"MainMenu";
  pMainClass->lpszClassName = (LPSTR)szTitle;
  pMainClass->hbrBackground = (HBRUSH)GetStockObject (WHITE_BRUSH);
  pMainClass->hInstance     = hInstance;
  pMainClass->style         = CS_HREDRAW | CS_VREDRAW;
  pMainClass->lpfnWndProc   = MainWndProc;

  if (!RegisterClass((LPWNDCLASS)pMainClass))
    return FALSE;

  LocalFree ((HANDLE)pMainClass);
  return TRUE;
  }


int PASCAL WinMain (hInstance, hPrevInstance, lpszCmdLine, cmdShow)
  HANDLE               hInstance;
  HANDLE               hPrevInstance;
  LPSTR                lpszCmdLine;
  int                  cmdShow;
  {
  MSG                  msg;
  HWND                 hWnd;
  HMENU                hMenu;


  if (!hPrevInstance)   /* Call init if this is the first instance      */
    {
    if (!MainInit (hInstance))
      return FALSE;
    }
  else                  /* Copy data from previous instance if not first*/
    {
    GetInstanceData (hPrevInstance, (PSTR)szTitle, 32);
    GetInstanceData (hPrevInstance, (PSTR)szString1, 64);
    GetInstanceData (hPrevInstance, (PSTR)szString2, 64);
    GetInstanceData (hPrevInstance, (PSTR)&iString1Len, sizeof(int));
    }

  hWnd = CreateWindow  ((LPSTR)szTitle,
                        (LPSTR)szTitle,
                        WS_OVERLAPPEDWINDOW,
                        GetSystemMetrics (SM_CXSCREEN) / 4,     /*  x   */
                        GetSystemMetrics (SM_CYSCREEN) / 4,     /*  y   */
                        GetSystemMetrics (SM_CXSCREEN) / 2,     /* cx   */
                        GetSystemMetrics (SM_CYSCREEN) / 2,     /* cy   */
                        (HWND)NULL,                       /* no parent    */
                        (HMENU)NULL,              /* use class menu       */
                        (HANDLE)hInstance, /* handle to window instance */
                        (LPSTR)NULL);      /* no params to pass on      */

  ShowWindow (hWnd, cmdShow);
  UpdateWindow (hWnd);

  while (GetMessage((LPMSG)&msg, NULL, 0, 0))
    {
    TranslateMessage ((LPMSG)&msg);
    DispatchMessage ((LPMSG)&msg);
    }

  return (int)msg.wParam;
  }
```

```
long FAR PASCAL MainWndProc (hWnd, msg, wParam, lParam)
  HWND                  hWnd;
  unsigned              msg;
  WORD                  wParam;
  LONG                  lParam;
  {
  switch (msg)
    {
    case WM_DESTROY:
      PostQuitMessage (0);
      break;

    case WM_PAINT:
      {
      PAINTSTRUCT       ps;

      BeginPaint (hWnd, (LPPAINTSTRUCT)&ps);


      TextOut (ps.hdc, 10, 10, (LPSTR)szString1, iString1Len);
      EndPaint (hWnd, (LPPAINTSTRUCT)&ps);
      break;
      }

    case WM_COMMAND:
      switch (wParam)
        {
        case MENU1:
          switch (MessageBox(hWnd, (LPSTR)szString2, (LPSTR)szTitle,
                MB_YESNO | MB_ICONQUESTION))
            {
            case IDYES:
              MessageBeep(0);
                                                    /* fall thru    */
            case IDNO:
              break;
            }
          break;

        case MENU2A:
        case MENU2B:
        case MENU2C:
          prevMenu2 = menu2;
          menu2 = wParam;
          break;
        }
      break;

    case WM_INITMENU:
      {
      HMENU     hMenu;

      hMenu = GetMenu (hWnd);
      CheckMenuItem (hMenu, prevMenu2, MF_UNCHECKED);
      CheckMenuItem (hMenu, menu2,  MF_CHECKED);

      switch (menu2)
        {
        case MENU2A:
          EnableMenuItem (hMenu, MENU2B, MF_ENABLED);
          EnableMenuItem (hMenu, MENU2C, MF_GRAYED);
          break;
```

```
        case MENU2B:
          EnableMenuItem (hMenu, MENU2A, MF_DISABLED);
          EnableMenuItem (hMenu, MENU2C, MF_ENABLED);
          break;

        case MENU2C:
          EnableMenuItem (hMenu, MENU2A, MF_ENABLED);
          EnableMenuItem (hMenu, MENU2B, MF_GRAYED);
          EnableMenuItem (hMenu, MENU2C, MF_GRAYED);
          break;
        }
      return (TRUE);
      }

    default:
      return DefWindowProc (hWnd, msg, wParam, lParam);
      break;
    }
  return (0L);
  }

/*---------------------------------------------------------------------*/
/* End of file:  PGM2.C                                                */
/***********************************************************************/
```

Only one significant change has been made to **WinMain** since you saw the previous version of this file in PGM1.C. The change was made to the following statement in the **MainInit** procedure:

```
pMainClass->lpszMenuName = (LPSTR)"MainMenu";
```

This statement defines "MainMenu" as the *class menu*, the default menu for a window. In PGM1, we specified NULL in this statement because the program did not use a menu bar. In PGM2 we want to associate the menu resource identified by the string **"MainMenu"** to **lpszMenuName**. The menu structure was assigned the name **MainMenu** in the .RC file. Once you have registered a class menu, each window of that class will use that menu unless you explicitly supply another handle when creating a window.

We didn't change the **hMenu** parameter of **CreateWindow** because we want to use the window's class menu.

5.4.1 Keeping Track of Checked Menu Items

There are two global variables at the program's top:

```
int     menu2           = MENU2A;
int     prevMenu2       = MENU2A;
```

These flags keep track of the state of the second menu, "Pick," and are both initialized to **MENU2A**. This code corresponds to the .RC file statement:

```
MENUITEM "A: Enable B -- Gray C", MENU2A, CHECKED
```

MENU2A is CHECKED. To keep track of that, PGM2 uses the global variable **menu2** and assigns it to the current **MENU2***x* value. **prevMenu2** contains the previous value of **menu2**.

5.4.2 Initializing a Menu

When the user moves the mouse pointer into the menu bar and presses a button, Windows sends a **WM_INITMENU** message to the window function, **MainWndProc**. Because this happens before any popup menus are displayed, this message signals a great opportunity to update the various menu items.

The statement **case WM_INITMENU:** first defines a local variable:

```
HMENU hMenu;
```

This is a handle to a menu resource. To address the menu, PGM2 uses the **GetMenu** function to retrieve this handle:

```
hMenu = GetMenu(hWnd);
```

GetMenu simply gets the handle to the menu of the specified window. From the earlier examination of PGM1, you already know about **hWnd**; the handle to the window passed to the program thru **MainWndProc**.

We use **CheckMenuItem** two ways: to check and un-check menu items. To use it, we must specify a handle to a window, a menu item identifier, and an operation. The statement

```
CheckMenuItem (hWnd, prevMenu2, MF_UNCHECKED);
```

removes the check mark associated with **prevMenu2**. Recall that we initially set **prevMenu2** equal to **MENU2A**. The statement

```
CheckMenuItem (hWnd, menu2, MF_CHECKED);
```

sets the check mark associated with **menu2**. Recall that **menu2** was initially set equal to **MENU2A**. The net effect of these statements is that the first time this routine is executed, it turns the check mark off, then back on. Subsequent executions turn off the previously checked menu item, and turn on the current one.

Next we want to enable/disable/gray menu items based upon the current value of **menu2**. This is accomplished via the Windows **EnableMenuItem** function. The first time through the routine, **menu2** is equal to **MENU2A**, so the **switch** falls into:

```
case MENU2A:
  EnableMenuItem (hMenu, MENU2B, MF_ENABLED);
  EnableMenuItem (hMenu, MENU2C, MF_GRAYED);
  break;
```

hMenu is the handle of the menu we want to address, **MENU2***x* is the menu item identifier, and **MF**_*xxxxxxx* is the operation flag. **MF_ENABLED** enables an item; **MF_GRAYED** grays (and disables) an item; and **MF_DISABLED** disables (but does not gray) an item.

5.4.3 Processing Menu Items

All menu items are referenced by an identifier (**MENU1, MENU2A**, etc). When a user selects a menu item, a **WM_COMMAND** message is sent to the **MainWndProc** window function. Contained in the **wParam** variable passed by Windows is, you guessed it, the menu identifier. So we **switch** on it:

```
switch (wParam)
```

5.4.3.1 Processing Popup Menu Items

The logic to update the state variables **prevMenu2** and **menu2** is quite simple; we set the entry point for all three menu items to the same place, and set the flags equal to the menu item selected:

```
case MENU2A:
case MENU2B:
case MENU2C:
  prevMenu2 = menu2;
  menu2 = wParam;
```

The menus are not updated until just before their display; that is, the check marks are not set/reset immediately when selected. A menu item is selected and we change the flag (**menu2**), yet the menu item remains unchecked (and unseen) until the next time the user displays the menu.

5.4.3.2 Processing a Stand-alone Menu Item

Remember that the menu item "Beep. . ." causes a message box to appear and display the question "Want to hear a beep?"

Just like selecting popup menu items, selecting a stand-alone menu item causes **MainWndProc** to get the message **WM_COMMAND** with **wParam** containing the menu identifier. In this case, the menu identifier is **MENU1**.

The following lines draw the "Beep. . . . message box:

```
switch (MessageBox(hWnd, (LPSTR)szString2,
        (LPSTR)szTitle, MB_YESNO | MB_ICONQUESTION))
  {
  case IDYES:
    MessageBeep(0);

  case IDNO:                          /* fall thru */
    break;
  }
break;
```

MessageBox is the function responsible for drawing the message box shown in Figure 5.2. **hWnd** is our old friend, the window handle. **(LPSTR)szString2** is a long pointer to a string to be placed inside the box. **(LPSTR) szTitle** is a long pointer to a string to be placed in the window's caption line. And **MB_YESNO** | **MB_ICONQUESTION** are two flags specifying "yes" and "no" response buttons and an icon that looks like a big question mark.

MessageBox draws the box, accepts a response from the user, and returns that answer to us. We simply **switch** on it. If the response is yes **(IDYES)**, PGM2 calls the **MessageBeep** function to generate the beep sound, then falls through to the **break**. The parameter (**0**) is a dummy, having no meaning whatsoever. If **MessageBox** returns no **(IDNO)**, PGM2 does nothing.

5.5 THE DEFINITION FILE: PGM2.DEF

```
;*****************************************************************:
; Filename:     PGM2.DEF                                          :
;                                                                 :
; Description:  Link definition file                              :
;-----------------------------------------------------------------:
NAME     PGM2

DESCRIPTION 'Sample program 2'

STUB     '..\WINSTUB.EXE'

CODE     MOVEABLE
DATA     MOVEABLE MULTIPLE

HEAPSIZE  128
STACKSIZE 4096

EXPORTS
    MainWndProc          @1

;-----------------------------------------------------------------:
; End of file:  PGM2.DEF                                          :
;*****************************************************************:
```

5.6 THE MAKE FILE: PGM2.

```
#*****************************************************************#
# Filename:     PGM2.                                             #
#                                                                 #
# Description:  PGM2.EXE "MAKE" description file                  #
#-----------------------------------------------------------------#

pgm2.obj: pgm2.c pgm2.h
    cl -d -c -AS -Gsw -Os -Zpe pgm2.c

pgm2.res: pgm2.rc pgm2.h
    rc -r pgm2.rc

pgm2.exe: pgm2.obj pgm2.res pgm2.def
    link4 pgm2,/align:16,/map,slibw,pgm2.def
    rc pgm2.res

#-----------------------------------------------------------------#
# End of file:  PGM2.                                             #
#*****************************************************************#
```

In this chapter, you've seen how to add menus to your application, how to process the input from menus, and how to draw a simple message box. In Chapter 6, you'll learn how to add accelerators to menus to speed up keyboard access, and how to create dialog boxes for additional user input.

6

CREATING DIALOG BOXES AND USING ACCELERATORS

- Introduction to PGM3
- The C Header File: PGM3.H
- The Resource Script File: PGM3.RC
- Adding Icons to Dialog Boxes
- The C Language Source Code: PGM3.C
- The Definition File: PGM3.DEF
- The Make File: PGM3.

When you need to gather information from the user, your program should display a dialog box with appropriate *controls* that can be used to enter text, choose options, and direct the actions of a command. A dialog box is a special popup window with its own *dialog function*, which Windows calls when it has messages for the dialog box.

In this chapter, you'll learn the basics of creating dialog boxes and associating accelerators with options in those boxes. As you learned in Chapter 1, "Basic Windows Concepts," accelerators (sometimes referred to as "fast path" keys) are keys that can be used to quickly select a command or dialog box option.

6.1 INTRODUCTION TO PGM3

PGM3 requires five source files:

PGM3.H	C language program header
PGM3.RC	Resource script file
PGM3.C	Code for PGM3
PGM3.DEF	Definition file (required by LINK4)
PGM3.	Input instructions to the MAKE utility

The source code to PGM3 is very similar in parts to PGM1. You may want to copy PGM1's source files into the PGM3 directory and rename them so that you can use PGM1 as a "boilerplate," and just make the necessary changes to match the listings in this chapter.

Figure 6.1 illustrates the result of running PGM3.

Figure 6.1

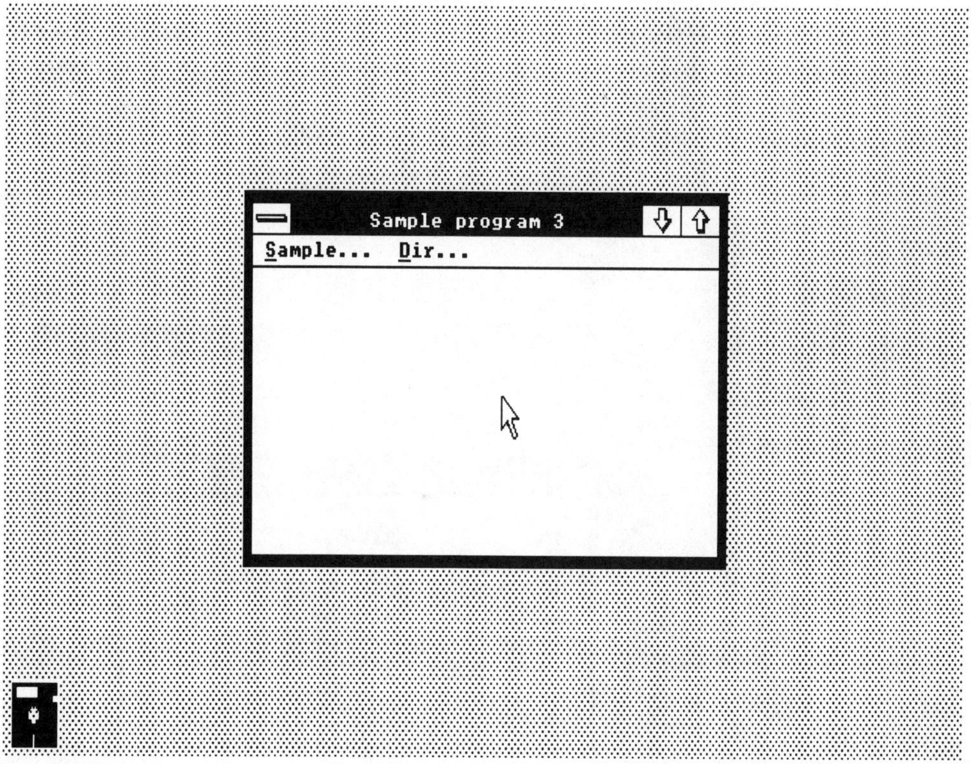

PGM3's menu bar has two menu items, "Sample . . ." and "Dir . . .", which are both followed by ellipses to indicate that dialog boxes will be displayed when those menu items are selected. But before examining the dialog boxes, let's look at the system menu, which is represented by the spacebar icon in the window's upper left corner.

Figure 6.2 illustrates what the user sees when the system menu is selected. We added a menu item, "About . . . ," to the bottom of the standard system menu. This menu item can be selected by two methods: by pointing to the item and clicking a mouse button, or by pressing the specified accelerator key, F1. Selecting "About . . ." displays a dialog box.

Figure 6.2

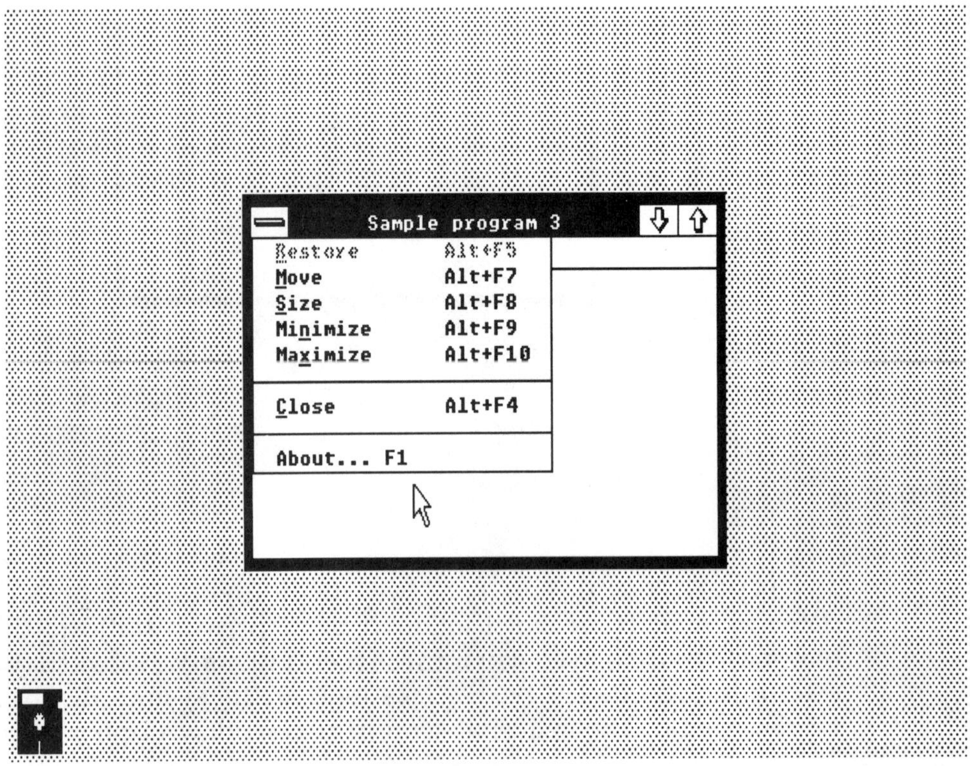

An "about" dialog box, an example of which is shown in Figure 6.3, is usually where the program title and copyright information is placed.

Figure 6.3

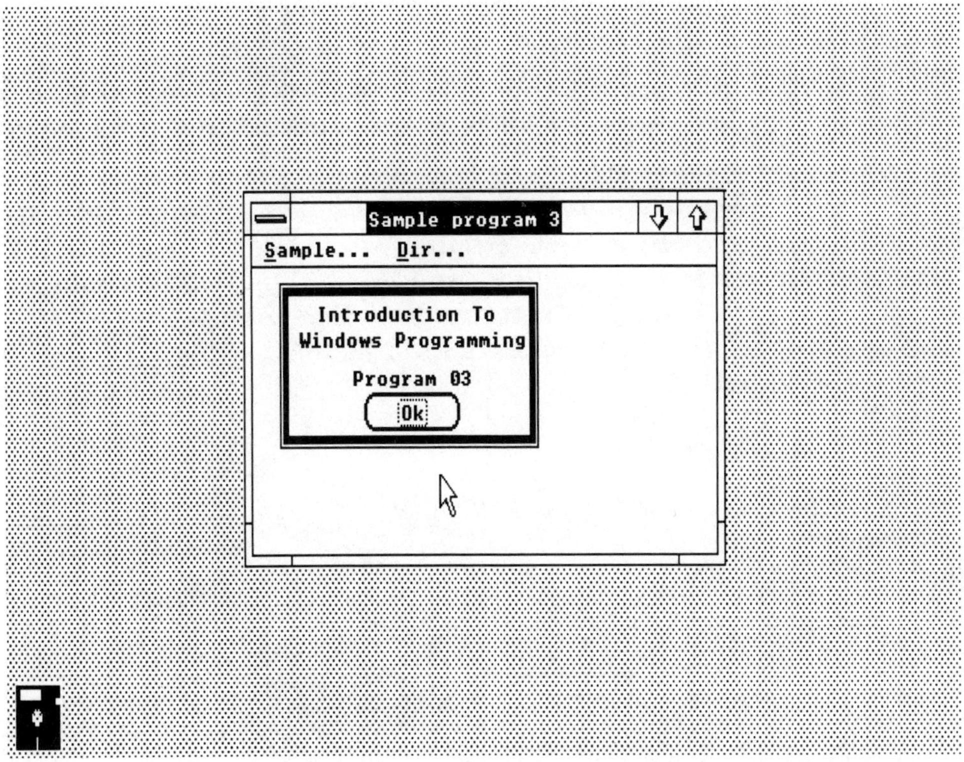

If the user selects "Sample. . ." from the menu bar, PGM3 displays the dialog box shown in Figure 6.4. A dialog box is a child window that usually contains a title bar and a number of *controls*. Controls are tiny child windows with predefined behavior; in other words, Microsoft has already written the window function for each type of control window. The dialog box in Figure 6.4 contains examples of all the standard Windows control types.

- A *list box* in the upper left corner contains European country names. A list box contains a number of strings; one or more strings can be selected by the user, depending on what the program allows.

- A *group box* in the lower left corner contains radio buttons. A *radio button* is simply an on/off switch, and a group box is a collection of a number of radio buttons. Only one radio button within a group can be "on" at a time.
- An *edit control box* in the upper right corner allows the entry of text, and is "active" when a flashing "I-beam" cursor is displayed within the rectangle.
- A *check box* is below the edit control, and like a radio button, it has two states: on and off. An X appears in a check box when it is "on."
- Three *push buttons* are in the lower right corner. "Defaults" returns all fields to a predetermined state. "Cancel" cancels any changes made in the dialog box. And "Accept" makes the changes indicated by the dialog box settings. Note that "Accept" has a heavier border than the other two buttons: this means that it's the default push button.

Figure 6.4

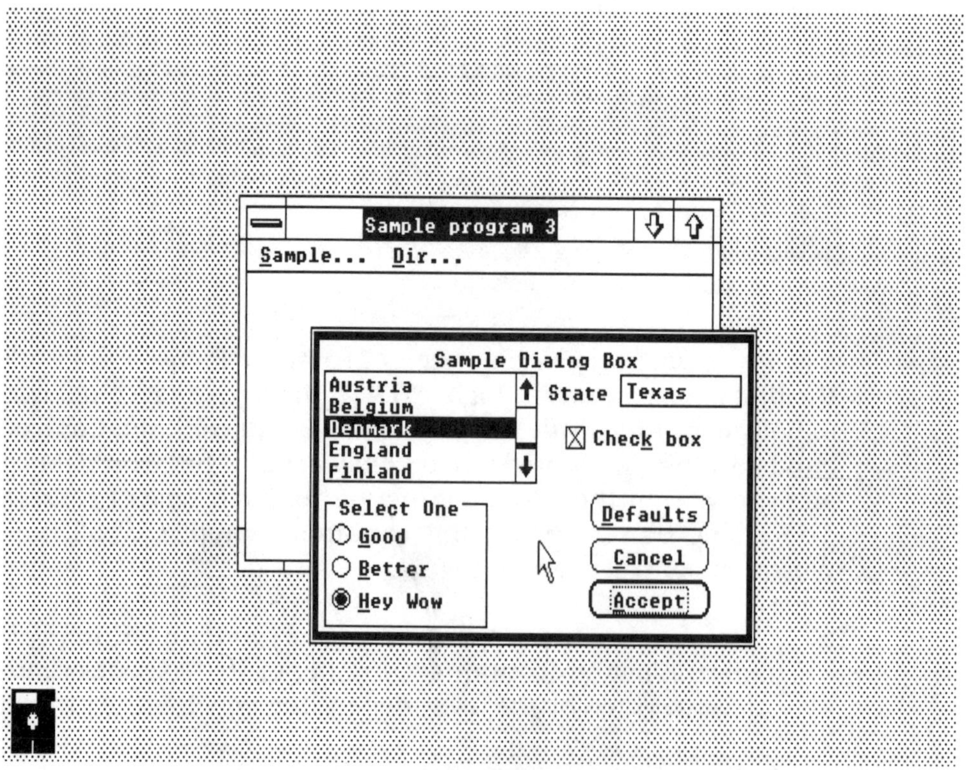

You'll see how a Windows application keeps track of all these dialog box controls as we examine PGM3.C in this chapter.

PGM3's third dialog box, shown in Figure 6.5, is displayed by selecting "Dir. . ." from the menu bar. This dialog box shows all files within a subdirectory, and allows the user to move around throughout the directories in the system. To change directories, the mouse user clicks on a directory and presses "Ok," or double-clicks when the mouse cursor is on a directory name. Keyboard users will tab to the list box, press the spacebar or direction keys to highlight an item, then press "Enter" to accept the default push button, "Ok."

Figure 6.5

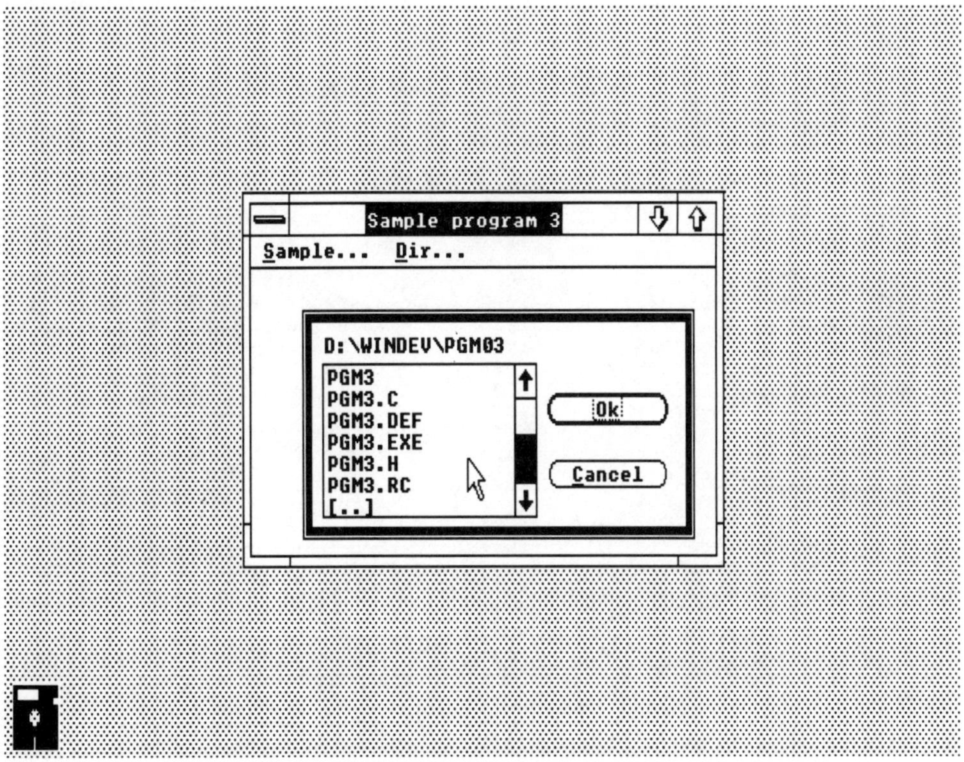

The basic procedure for creating a dialog box is:

1 Create a dialog box template with a text editor or with the Dialog Editor utility.

2 Create a dialog function to support the dialog box.

3 Export the dialog function.

You'll see how to do all of this in the following sections.

6.2 THE C HEADER FILE: PGM3.H

```
/*************************************************************************/
/* Filename:     PGM3.H                                                 */
/*                                                                       */
/* Description:  PGM3.C  header file                                    */
/*----------------------------------------------------------------------*/

#define IDSTITLE         1000     /* String table constants       */
#define IDSABOUT         1001

#define IDSRBGOOD        1010
#define IDSRBBETTER      1011
#define IDSRBBEST        1012
#define IDSDEFAULT       1013
#define IDSTEXT          1014
#define IDSCHECKBOX      1015
#define IDSLISTBOX       1016
#define IDSDIRBOX        1017
#define IDSPATH          1018

#define IDSSTR01         1021     /* The following 18 strings MUST be      */
#define IDSSTR02         1022     /* consecutive.  The reason is:          */
#define IDSSTR03         1023     /* when loading the stings, we will use */
#define IDSSTR04         1024     /* a "FOR-NEXT" loop where 'i' is an     */
#define IDSSTR05         1025     /* index off IDSSTR01.                   */
#define IDSSTR06         1026
#define IDSSTR07         1027
#define IDSSTR08         1028
#define IDSSTR09         1029
#define IDSSTR10         1030
#define IDSSTR11         1031
#define IDSSTR12         1032
#define IDSSTR13         1033
#define IDSSTR14         1034
#define IDSSTR15         1035
#define IDSSTR16         1036
#define IDSSTR17         1037
#define IDSSTR18         1038
#define CSTR             IDSSTR18 - IDSSTR01

#define MENU1            1040     /* Menu table constants         */
#define MENU2            1041
#define DIRDLGBOX        1042

/*----------------------------------------------------------------------*/
/* End of file:  PGM3.H                                                 */
/*************************************************************************/
```

You've learned that .H files contain constants, called resource identifiers, which are used to link resources in an .RC file with references in a .C source file.

PGM3.H is no different in design than PGM1.H or PGM2.H. There are simply more identifiers. The more resources you allocate to your program, the more identifiers you'll use.

PGM3.H does contain a "sleight of hand" that we should mention: the identifiers **IDSSTR01** through **IDSSTR18** *must* be consecutive, because the C code uses a **for-next** loop to load a number of strings associated with these identifiers. That means that many of the strings are never actually referenced by their identifier; instead, they are indexed off **IDSSTR01**.

6.3 THE RESOURCE SCRIPT FILE: PGM3.RC

```
/***************************************************************************/
/* Filename:     PGM3.RC                                                   */
/*                                                                         */
/* Description:  PGM3.EXE resources                                        */
/*-------------------------------------------------------------------------*/

#include "style.h"
#include "pgm3.h"

MainMenu MENU
BEGIN
    MENUITEM    "&Sample...",            MENU1
    MENUITEM    "&Dir...",               MENU2
END

STRINGTABLE
BEGIN
    IDSTITLE,    "Sample program 3"
    IDSABOUT,    "About... F1"
    IDSDEFAULT,  "Texas"
    IDSSTR01,    "Austria"
    IDSSTR02,    "Belgium"
    IDSSTR03,    "Denmark"
    IDSSTR04,    "England"
    IDSSTR05,    "Finland"
    IDSSTR06,    "France"
    IDSSTR07,    "Germany"
    IDSSTR08,    "Holland"
    IDSSTR09,    "Ireland"
    IDSSTR10,    "Italy"
    IDSSTR11,    "Lichtenstein"
    IDSSTR12,    "Luxembourg"
    IDSSTR13,    "Norway"
    IDSSTR14,    "Portugal"
    IDSSTR15,    "Scotland"
    IDSSTR16,    "Spain"
    IDSSTR17,    "Sweden"
    IDSSTR18,    "Switzerland"
END
```

```
acceltable ACCELERATORS
BEGIN
    VK_F1, IDSABOUT, VIRTKEY
    "^S",  MENU1
    "^D",  MENU2
END

About DIALOG 10, 10, 80, 52
STYLE WS_POPUP | WS_DLGFRAME
BEGIN
    CTEXT "Introduction To"                  -1,  9,  2, 60, 8
    CTEXT "Windows Programming"              -1,  3, 12, 76, 8
    CTEXT "Program 03"                       -1, 21, 26, 40, 8
    DEFPUSHBUTTON "Ok"                     IDOK, 25, 36, 32, 14, WS_GROUP
END

#define TABGRP      WS_TABSTOP | WS_GROUP
#define LBSTYLES    WS_VSCROLL | WS_BORDER | WS_VISIBLE | LBS_SORT | TABGRP

SampleDialog DIALOG 25,25,142,108
STYLE  WS_POPUP | WS_DLGFRAME
BEGIN
    CTEXT         "Sample Dialog Box",  -1,        38,  2, 68,  8
    LISTBOX                          IDSLISTBOX,    2, 12, 70, 40, LBSTYLES
    CTEXT         "State",       -1,               76, 14, 20,  8
    EDITTEXT                     IDSTEXT,         100, 12, 40, 12, TABGRP
    CHECKBOX      "Chec&k box", IDSCHECKBOX,      82, 28, 48, 15, TABGRP
    GROUPBOX      "Select One", -1,                2, 56, 54, 50, WS_GROUP
    RADIOBUTTON   "&Good",       IDSRBGOOD,         4, 66, 40, 12, TABGRP
    RADIOBUTTON   "&Better",     IDSRBBETTER,       4, 78, 40, 12
    RADIOBUTTON   "&Hey Wow",    IDSRBBEST,         4, 90, 40, 12
    PUSHBUTTON    "&Defaults",   IDSDEFAULT,       90, 56, 40, 14, TABGRP
    PUSHBUTTON    "&Cancel",     IDCANCEL,         90, 72, 40, 14, TABGRP
    DEFPUSHBUTTON "&Accept",     IDOK,             90, 88, 40, 14, TABGRP
END

DIRDLGBOX DIALOG 20, 20, 124, 76
STYLE WS_POPUP | WS_DLGFRAME
BEGIN
    LTEXT          "",           IDSPATH,    4,  4, 112,  8
    LISTBOX  IDSDIRBOX,   4, 16, 70, 56, LBS_STANDARD | WS_TABSTOP | WS_GROUP
    DEFPUSHBUTTON  "&Ok",        IDOK,      78, 26,  40, 12, WS_GROUP
    PUSHBUTTON     "&Cancel",    IDCANCEL,  78, 50,  40, 12, WS_GROUP
END

/*--------------------------------------------------------------------*/
/* End of file:  PGM3.RC                                              */
/**********************************************************************/
```

6.3.1 Including STYLE.H

The first notable addition to our resource file is:

```
#include "style.h"
```

STYLE.H, which is supplied with the Development Kit, contains definitions for some "style" arguments used in PGM3. For example, window styles such as **WS_POPUP** and **WS_DLGFRAME** are defined in this file. You'll need to include STYLE.H whenever a resource requires style parameters.

The string table has been expanded to include a few European country names, which will be loaded into a list box and displayed within the "Sample. . ." dialog box, allowing the user to select a country name.

6.3.2 Defining Accelerators

After the string table comes the statement:

```
acceltable ACCELERATORS
```

This is where we define our accelerators and make the logical connection between a key and an action. (In PGM3, pressing a key opens a dialog box.) The accelerators are bracketed between **BEGIN** and **END** statements. The basic form of an accelerator table entry is:

```
accelerator, ID [,type]
```

where *accelerator* is either a character enclosed in double quotes, or an integer representing an ASCII or virtual key. *ID* is an integer resource identifier. *type* is an optional parameter, required only if *accelerator* is an integer representing an ASCII or virtual key, in which case it takes the value ASCII or VIRTKEY. In our program,

```
VK_F1, IDSABOUT, VIRTKEY
```

assigns the identifier **IDSABOUT** to the virtual key **VK_F1** (found in WINDOWS.H). The statement

```
"^D", MENU2
```

assigns the key "^D", Control-D, to the identifier **MENU2**. The caret (^) means "control". "^" and "D" are two characters—not the ANSI character ^D (hexadecimal 04).

When the user strikes an accelerator, Windows sends a message to the window function, which processes the message as if the user had selected the menu item or option the accelerator is assigned to. For example, if the user pressed "F1" while running PGM3, the window function would process the resulting message as if the user had selected "About. . ." from the system menu.

6.3.3 Defining Dialog Boxes

Dialog boxes, like strings and menus, are resources. To create a dialog box, we define it using a number of dialog box-related statements. The first of these is the dialog statement:

```
name DIALOG x, y, width, height
```

name is either an integer resource ID or a unique ASCII string. PGM3 uses both methods: **About** and **SampleDialog** are strings; **DIRDLGBOX** is an integer that is defined in PGM3.H. It's preferable to use the integer method because Windows can locate integers more quickly than strings.

x and *y* are the box coordinates and are relative either to the window's upper left corner (if the dialog box is a child window) or the display's upper left corner (if the dialog box is a popup window).

The last two parameters specify the *width* and *height* of the dialog box. The units are a little strange: *width* is expressed in units equal to 1/4 of a character's width; *height* is expressed in units equal to 1/8 of a character's height. So the statement

```
About DIALOG 10, 10, 80, 52
```

defines a box named **About** located at (**10,10**) (although we have not yet defined whether the coordinates are absolute or relative) and is 20 characters wide (**80**/4) and 6.5 characters high (**52**/8). This system may seem awkward at first, but its reasoning will soon become clear. Dialog boxes deal with text. Because Windows functions on monitors with different resolutions, text that would appear large on one screen could appear tiny on another. Therefore, if you express units in relative terms, you don't need to worry about absolutes. You may want to refer to Figure 6.6 to see how coordinates and sites are computed.

The next statement:

```
STYLE WS_POPUP | WS_DLGFRAME
```

is optional within the DIALOG construct, and defines certain dialog box attributes. The parameters can be the window styles as defined for the **CreateWindow** function. In PGM3, this style statement defines the **About** dialog box as a popup window with a double border but no caption. If no style statement is given, the dialog box assumes the default values of **WS_POPUP** | **WS_BORDER** | **WS_SYSMENU** (a popup with a border and a system menu in the title bar).

Now, to define the contents of PGM3's dialog box. As always, **BEGIN** and **END** delimit the definitions. Definitions take the form of *control statements*. The general form of a control statement is:

```
type  text, ID, X, Y, width, height, [,style]
```

type is one of the following keywords: LTEXT, RTEXT, CTEXT, CHECKBOX, PUSHBUTTON, LISTBOX, GROUPBOX, DEFPUSHBUTTON, RADIOBUTTON, EDITTEXT, ICON, or CONTROL. The keyword defines the type of control this line describes.

text is an ASCII string to be displayed. *ID* is our old friend, the resource identifier, which was defined in the .H file. *X* and *Y* specify the upper left corner of the control field, and are relative to the upper left corner of the dialog box. *width* and *height* specify the control's size. As in the DIALOG statement, a control statement defines *width* in quarters of character widths and *height* in eighths of character heights (the so-called "quarters and eighths system").

style can define special style attributes (listed in the STYLE.H file) for the control. For example, a control can be a *tab stop*, meaning that when the user hits the tab key, the cursor stops at this control.

Let's examine the two types of control statements in the **About** dialog box definition. The first dialog box definition statement is:

```
CTEXT "Introduction To"  -1, 9, 2, 60, 8
```

CTEXT defines a "centered text control," which is simply a field containing text. Because we don't want to directly reference this field from within PGM3, the ID–**1** is used. This field is to be located at (**9,2**) relative to the dialog box's upper left corner. Because the text is 15 characters in length, we specify a *width* of 60 (15 * 4). Because the text is 1 character high, we specify a *height* of **8** (8 * 1).

The line

```
DEFPUSHBUTTON "Ok"  IDOK, 25, 36, 32, 14, WS_GROUP
```

defines a push button control, an "Ok" button, which is the default response. A push button is a rounded rectangle that contains text.

Mouse users can click on, or "push", this button when ready to continue. Keyboard users can tab to move the focus to a push button, then press "Enter" to select it. Pressing "Enter" while the focus is in the dialog box but not on a push button always selects the default push button. DEFPUSHBUTTON requests a push button with a heavy border, which signals the user that this is the default response. **IDOK** is a standard resource ID defined in WINDOWS.H. This push button is to be located at (**25, 36**) within the dialog box, and is to be **32** units in length and **14** units in height. Text is defaulted to center within a push button.

Users can move from control to control using the cursor keys or tab key, so **WS_GROUP** defines the first control of a group in which the user can move the cursor around. In this case, there is only one control field, **IDOK.**

When the user selects the "Ok" push button, a **WM_COMMAND** message is sent to the dialog function with **wParam** containing **IDOK**. On receiving **WM_COMMAND**, the dialog function closes the dialog box. You'll see exactly how this is done later in this chapter.

6.3.4 The Sample Dialog Box

The next dialog box we'll examine is defined in the line:

```
SampleDialog DIALOG 25, 25, 142, 108
```

This statement defines a box named **SampleDialog** that is to be located at (**25,25**) and is 35.5 characters wide (**142**/4) and 13.5 characters high (**108**/8). Figure 6.6 will help you understand these measurements.

The line

```
LISTBOX   IDSLISTBOX, 2, 12, 70, 40, LBSTYLES
```

defines a control of type LISTBOX. A list box contains a number of strings as defined by the application program. Later on, PGM3 will place the names of European countries in this list box (the names were also defined in this .RC file in the STRINGTABLE section).

Note that the LISTBOX statement has no **text** field. LISTBOX is a special case of the general control statement: the only difference is that the **text** field has been eliminated.

Figure 6.6

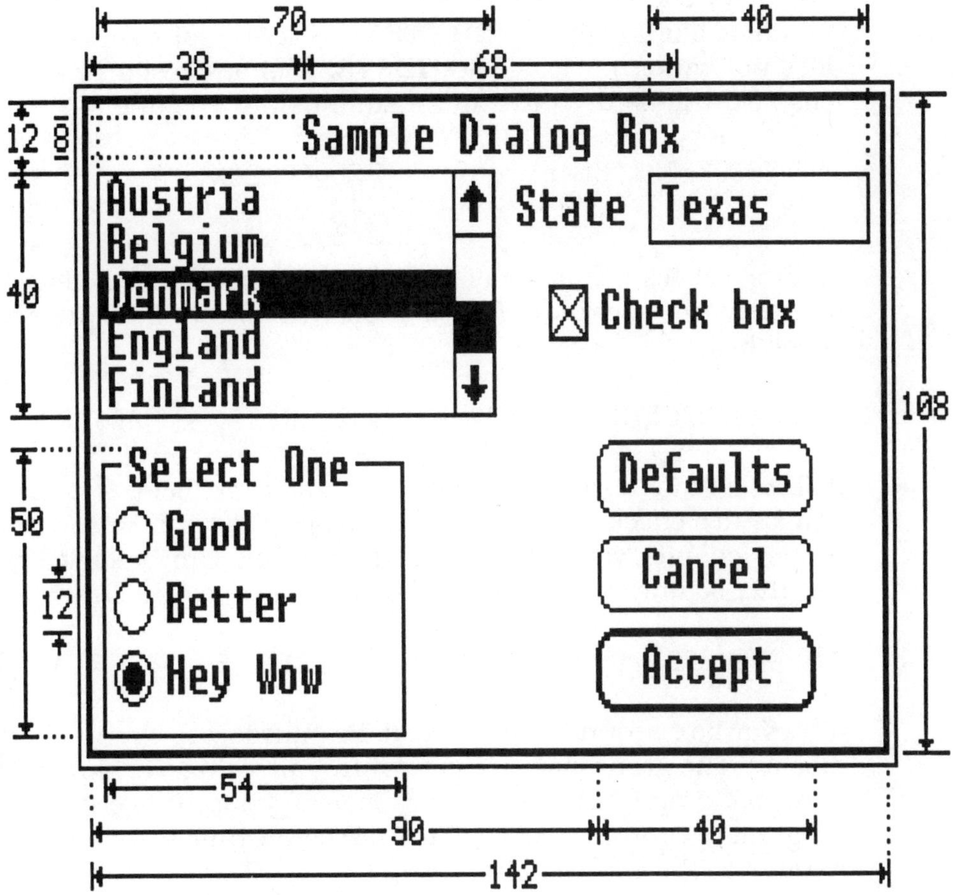

LBSTYLES (list box styles), defined just about the **SampleDialog** DIALOG statement, contains a number of style options for our list box: **WS_VSCROLL** specifies a vertical scroll bar; **WS_BORDER** specifies a border; **WS_VISIBLE** specifies that the list box will be displayed; **LBS_SORT** specifies that the entries will be sorted alphabetically; and **TABGRP** gives this control the attributes of both a tab stop and a group (**TABGRP** is "shorthand" for **WS_TABSTOP | WS_GROUP**).

The line

```
EDITTEXT  IDSTEXT, 100, 12, 40, 12, TABGRP
```

defines an edit control, which allows the user to enter and edit a text field. When the mouse user clicks the mouse button while the arrow cursor is in this field or the keyboard user tabs to the field, a blinking I-beam cursor appears.

Just like LISTBOX, EDITTEXT is a special case of control, and does not contain a **text** field. **IDSTEXT** is our resource ID. In PGM3, this field will be used to enter a state name. The line

```
CHECKBOX "Check Box", IDSCHECKBOX,
                                    82, 28, 48, 15, TABGRP
```

defines a check box, a small square that is either checked (with an "X") or empty (un-checked). Text is displayed to the immediate right of a check box.

```
RADIOBUTTON "Hey Wow", IDSRBBEST, 4, 90, 40, 12
```

defines a radio button, a small circle and a text field. A radio button is similar to a check box in that it is a toggle that is either on or off. Later in this chapter you'll see how radio buttons can be logically grouped together so only one can be "pressed" at a time. The line

```
GROUPBOX "Select One:", -1, 2, 56, 54, 50 WS_GROUP
```

draws a box around the three radio buttons to group them on the display. The group box doesn't control anything—it is merely a static item that graphically illustrates a logical group. It is entirely up to the program to control grouping. You'll see how this is accomplished when we look at the C code. The line

```
PUSHBUTTON "Defaults", IDSDEFAULT,
                                    90, 56, 40, 14, TABGRP
```

defines a simple push button. When the push button is "pressed," Windows sends a **WM_COMMAND** message to the dialog function with **wParam** containing the integer **IDSDEFAULT**. It will be up to our program to supply the default values. The line

```
DEFPUSHBUTTON "Accept", IDOK, 90, 56, 40, 14, TABGRP
```

defines another push button, but one with a heavy border to indicate to the user that this is the default push button.

6.3.5 The Directory Dialog Box

The remaining dialog box is defined in the line:

```
DIRDLGBOX DIALOG 20, 20, 124, 76
```

This **DIRDLGBOX** dialog box is slightly different from the two previous dialog box examples in that **DIRDLGBOX** is equated to an integer that was defined in PGM3.H. The dialog box contains a list box and two push buttons, "Ok" and "Cancel."

6.4 ADDING ICONS TO DIALOG BOXES

Most of the desktop applications packaged with Windows have an "About" dialog box containing that program's icon. How can you add an icon to a dialog box? Easy! Add the following statement to any dialog box description:

```
ICON          MYICON  -1,          x, y, 0, 0
```

MYICON is the symbolic name of the icon (this must be specified in your program's .H file). Because you'll never want to take action on the icon (as you would on a check box or radio button), code a **–1** in the ID field. The next two integers, **x** and **y**, specify the relative coordinates inside the dialog box to place the icon (you'll learn more about coordinates in Chapter 7). An icon is fixed in size, so code zeros in the next two width and height fields to remind yourself that these are not used.

Don't forget to include a statement specifying the icon's file, such as this one:

```
MYICON   ICON          pgm1.ico
```

6.5 THE C LANGUAGE SOURCE CODE: PGM3.C

```
/************************************************************************/
/* Filename:     PGM3.C                                                */
/*                                                                      */
/* Description:  PGM3.EXE source code                                  */
/*----------------------------------------------------------------------*/

#include "windows.h"
#include "pgm3.h"
```

```
  char                  szTitle[32];

  long FAR PASCAL       MainWndProc (HWND, unsigned, WORD, LONG);

  char                  szText[16];
  char                  szAbout[16];
  char                  szDefault[16];

  int                   fRadioButton    = IDSRBBEST;
  int                   fRadioButtonTemp;
  int                   iSel            = 2;
  HANDLE                hInst;
  HANDLE                hAccelTable;

  BOOL                  bCheckBox       = TRUE;

  FARPROC               lpprocAbout;
  FARPROC               lpprocSampleDlgProc;
  FARPROC               lpprocDirDlgProc;

BOOL FAR PASCAL About (hWnd, msg, wParam, lParam)
  HWND                  hWnd;
  unsigned              msg;
  WORD                  wParam;
  LONG                  lParam;
  {
  switch (msg)
    {
    case WM_COMMAND:
      EndDialog (hWnd, TRUE);
      return TRUE;

    case WM_INITDIALOG:
      return TRUE;

    default:
      return FALSE;
    }
  }

BOOL FAR PASCAL SampleDlgProc (hWnd, msg, wParam, lParam)
  HWND                  hWnd;
  unsigned              msg;
  WORD                  wParam;
  LONG                  lParam;
  {

  int                   i;
  char                  szTemp[16];

  switch (msg)
    {
    case WM_INITDIALOG:
      SetDlgItemText (hWnd, IDSTEXT, (LPSTR)szText);
      CheckDlgButton (hWnd, IDSCHECKBOX, bCheckBox);
      CheckRadioButton (hWnd, IDSRBGOOD, IDSRBBEST,
                (fRadioButtonTemp = fRadioButton));
      for (i=0; i<= CSTR; i++)
        {
        LoadString (hInst, IDSSTR01+i, (LPSTR)szTemp, 16);
        SendDlgItemMessage (hWnd, IDSLISTBOX, LB_ADDSTRING, 0,
                                        (LONG)(LPSTR)szTemp);
        }
      SendDlgItemMessage (hWnd, IDSLISTBOX, LB_SETCURSEL, iSel, 0L);
      return TRUE;
```

```
    case WM_COMMAND:
      switch (wParam)
        {
        case IDSDEFAULT:
          SetDlgItemText (hWnd, IDSTEXT, (LPSTR)szDefault);
          CheckDlgButton (hWnd, IDSCHECKBOX, TRUE);
          CheckRadioButton (hWnd, IDSRBGOOD, IDSRBBEST,
                (fRadioButtonTemp = IDSRBBEST));
          SendDlgItemMessage (hWnd, IDSLISTBOX, LB_SETCURSEL, 2, 0L);
          break;

        case IDOK:
          bCheckBox = IsDlgButtonChecked (hWnd, IDSCHECKBOX);
          fRadioButton = fRadioButtonTemp;
          szText[GetDlgItemText(hWnd, IDSTEXT, (LPSTR)szText, 16)] = '\0';
          iSel =  SendDlgItemMessage (hWnd, IDSLISTBOX,
                                              LB_GETCURSEL, 0, 0L);
                                                      /* fall thru */

        case IDCANCEL:
          EndDialog(hWnd, TRUE);
          break;

        case IDSCHECKBOX:
          CheckDlgButton(hWnd, IDSCHECKBOX,
                !IsDlgButtonChecked(hWnd, IDSCHECKBOX));
          break;

        case IDSRBGOOD:
        case IDSRBBETTER:
        case IDSRBBEST:
            CheckRadioButton(hWnd, IDSRBGOOD, IDSRBBEST,
                (fRadioButtonTemp = wParam));
            break;
        default:
            return FALSE;
        }
      break;  /* end of WM_COMMAND */

    default:
        return FALSE;
    }
  return TRUE;
  }

BOOL FAR PASCAL DirDlgProc (hWnd, msg, wParam, lParam)
  HWND                    hWnd;
  unsigned                msg;
  WORD                    wParam;
  LONG                    lParam;
  {
  char                    szAppName[16];
  char                    *szSearchFilespec = "*.*";
  char                    pStr1[64], pStr2[64];
  int                     i,      j;

  switch (msg)
    {
    case WM_INITDIALOG:
      {
      for (i=j=0; pStr1[i++]=szSearchFilespec[j++];);
      DlgDirList (hWnd, (LPSTR)pStr1, IDSDIRBOX, IDSPATH, 0x4037);
      break;
      }
```

```
    case WM_COMMAND:
      {
      switch (wParam)
        {
        case IDOK:
          if (DlgDirSelect (hWnd, (LPSTR)pStr2, IDSDIRBOX))
            {
            for (i=0; pStr1[i]=pStr2[i];i++);
            for (j=0; pStr1[i++]=szSearchFilespec[j++];);
            DlgDirList (hWnd, (LPSTR)pStr1, IDSDIRBOX, IDSPATH, 0x4037);
            break;
            }

        case IDCANCEL:
          EndDialog (hWnd, TRUE);
          break;

        case IDSDIRBOX:
          switch (HIWORD(lParam))
            {
            case 1:                    /* single click in listbox      */
              break;

            case 2:                    /* double click in listbox      */
              if (DlgDirSelect (hWnd, (LPSTR)pStr2, IDSDIRBOX))
                {
                for (i=0; pStr1[i]=pStr2[i];i++);
                for (j=0; pStr1[i++]=szSearchFilespec[j++];);
                DlgDirList (hWnd, (LPSTR)pStr1, IDSDIRBOX, IDSPATH, 0x4037);
                }
              break;
            }
          break;
        }
      break;
      }

    default:
      return FALSE;
    }
  return TRUE;
  }

BOOL MainInit (hInstance)
  HANDLE              hInstance;
  {
  PWNDCLASS           pMainClass;

  LoadString (hInstance, IDSTITLE, (LPSTR)szTitle, 32);
  LoadString (hInstance, IDSABOUT, (LPSTR)szAbout, 16);
  LoadString (hInstance, IDSDEFAULT, (LPSTR)szDefault, 16);
  LoadString (hInstance, IDSDEFAULT, (LPSTR)szText, 16);

  pMainClass = (PWNDCLASS)LocalAlloc (LPTR, sizeof(WNDCLASS));

  pMainClass->hCursor         = LoadCursor (NULL, IDC_ARROW);
  pMainClass->hIcon           = LoadIcon (NULL, IDI_APPLICATION);
  pMainClass->lpszMenuName    = (LPSTR)"MainMenu";
  pMainClass->lpszClassName   = (LPSTR)szTitle;
  pMainClass->hbrBackground   = (HBRUSH)GetStockObject (WHITE_BRUSH);
  pMainClass->hInstance       = hInstance;
  pMainClass->style           = CS_HREDRAW | CS_VREDRAW;
  pMainClass->lpfnWndProc     = MainWndProc;
```

```
  if (!RegisterClass((LPWNDCLASS)pMainClass))
    return FALSE;

  LocalFree ((HANDLE)pMainClass);
  return TRUE;
  }


int PASCAL WinMain (hInstance, hPrevInstance, lpszCmdLine, cmdShow)
  HANDLE              hInstance;
  HANDLE              hPrevInstance;
  LPSTR               lpszCmdLine;
  int                 cmdShow;
  {
  MSG                 msg;
  HWND                hWnd;
  HMENU               hMenu;

  if (!hPrevInstance)
    {
    if (!MainInit (hInstance))
      return FALSE;
    }
  else
    {
    GetInstanceData (hPrevInstance, (PSTR)szTitle, 32);
    GetInstanceData (hPrevInstance, (PSTR)szAbout, 16);
    }

  hWnd = CreateWindow  ((LPSTR)szTitle,
                        (LPSTR)szTitle,
                        WS_OVERLAPPEDWINDOW,
                        GetSystemMetrics (SM_CXSCREEN) / 4,      /*  x   */
                        GetSystemMetrics (SM_CYSCREEN) / 4,      /*  y   */
                        GetSystemMetrics (SM_CXSCREEN) / 2,      /* cx   */
                        GetSystemMetrics (SM_CYSCREEN) / 2,      /* cy   */
                        (HWND)NULL,                       /* no parent   */
                        (HMENU)NULL,              /* use class menu      */
                        (HANDLE)hInstance, /* handle to window instance */
                        (LPSTR)NULL);      /* no params to pass on      */

  hInst = hInstance;             /* Save instance handle for Dialog box  */

  lpprocAbout          = MakeProcInstance ((FARPROC)About, hInst);
  lpprocSampleDlgProc  = MakeProcInstance ((FARPROC)SampleDlgProc, hInst);
  lpprocDirDlgProc     = MakeProcInstance ((FARPROC)DirDlgProc, hInst);

                                 /* Plug "About..." into system menu     */

  hMenu = GetSystemMenu (hWnd, FALSE);
  ChangeMenu (hMenu, 0, NULL, 999, MF_APPEND | MF_SEPARATOR);
  ChangeMenu (hMenu, 0, (LPSTR)szAbout, IDSABOUT, MF_APPEND | MF_STRING);

  hAccelTable = LoadAccelerators (hInstance, (LPSTR) "acceltable");

  ShowWindow (hWnd, cmdShow);
  UpdateWindow (hWnd);

  while (GetMessage ((LPMSG)&msg, NULL, 0, 0))
    {
    if (TranslateAccelerator(hWnd, hAccelTable, (LPMSG)&msg) == 0)
      {
      TranslateMessage((LPMSG)&msg);
      DispatchMessage((LPMSG)&msg);
      }
    }
```

```
 FreeProcInstance (lpprocAbout);
 FreeProcInstance (lpprocSampleDlgProc);
 FreeProcInstance (lpprocDirDlgProc);

 return (int)msg.wParam;
 }


long FAR PASCAL MainWndProc (hWnd, msg, wParam, lParam)
  HWND                    hWnd;
  unsigned                msg;
  WORD                    wParam;
  LONG                    lParam;
  {
  switch (msg)
    {
    case WM_SYSCOMMAND:
      switch (wParam)
        {
        case IDSABOUT:
          DialogBox (hInst, (LPSTR)"About", hWnd, lpprocAbout);
          break;
        default:
          return DefWindowProc (hWnd, msg, wParam, lParam);
        }
      break;

    case WM_DESTROY:
      PostQuitMessage (0);
      break;

    case WM_COMMAND:
      switch (wParam)
        {
        case MENU1:
          DialogBox (hInst, (LPSTR)"SampleDialog", hWnd,
                                              lpprocSampleDlgProc);
          break;

        case MENU2:
          DialogBox (hInst, MAKEINTRESOURCE(DIRDLGBOX), hWnd,
                                              lpprocDirDlgProc);
          break;
        }
      break;

    default:
      return DefWindowProc (hWnd, msg, wParam, lParam);
      break;
    }
  return (0L);
  }

/*------------------------------------------------------------------------*/
/* End of file:  PGM3.C                                                    */
/**************************************************************************/
```

Several changes have been made in **WinMain** to accommodate the addition of accelerators and dialog boxes.

6.5.1 Binding a Dialog Box Function to a Data Segment

Remember that several instances of your program may be running simultaneously. Windows only needs one copy of the program—it's the same code, after all. The only *real* difference when the code executes is where the DS register points. For DS to be properly loaded, the function must be "bound" to a particular instance that it is running under.

Just like a main window, a dialog box has an associated function that will be called by Windows. To bind this function to the data segment of this instance, the function **MakeProcInstance** is used:

```
lpprocAbout = MakeProcInstance((FARPROC)About,
                                           hInstance);
```

The first parameter is a far pointer to a procedure that will be bound to the instance specified in the second parameter. Returned is a long pointer to a piece of prologue code that is executed before control is passed to the function. This prologue code is responsible for loading the data segment of the specified instance. Later, when PGM3 calls a function to display a dialog box, **lpprocAbout** will be passed to Windows. In this way, when Windows passes messages to the dialog function (**About**), the prologue code is executed and **About** addresses the correct data segment.

6.5.2 Changing the System Menu

Having a dialog function called **About** does us no good if we can't tell the world about it, so we attached it to a new item we'll put on the system menu. First, to access the system menu, we use this function to get the system menu's handle:

```
hMenu = GetSystemMenu (hWnd, FALSE);
```

hWnd is the window handle returned by **CreateWindow**, and FALSE (zero) means we want an identical copy of the menu.

Now that we have a system menu handle, we'll make changes using the Windows **ChangeMenu** function:

```
ChangeMenu (hMenu, 0, NULL, 999,
                         MF_APPEND | MF_SEPARATOR);
ChangeMenu (hMenu, 0, (LPSTR)szAbout,
                  IDSABOUT; MF_APPEND | MF_STRING);
```

ChangeMenu appends, inserts, deletes, or modifies menus. **hMenu** is our menu handle. The next parameter is an ID to a change item; however, since we are appending to the menu, we do not need to use this parameter, so it is set to zero.

The third parameter is a long pointer to a new item. Because the first **ChangeMenu** statement specifies a horizontal break (draws a horizontal line across the menu), this parameter is ignored. (Review figure 6.2.) In the second **ChangeMenu** statement, we use a long pointer to an ASCII string, **szAbout**, which was loaded earlier by **LoadString** and contains the text "About. . . F1".

The fourth parameter is an ID for the new item. Again, because our first **ChangeMenu** statement specifies a horizontal break, this parameter is ignored. In the second **ChangeMenu** statement, **IDSABOUT** is the same resource identifier that was used in **LoadString,** and will be the **wParam** of the Windows **WM_SYSCOMMAND** message that the **About** dialog box function will receive when a user presses the F1 key or selects "About. . . F1" from the system menu.

The last parameter specifies how the menu is to be changed. **MF_APPEND** means add to the end of the menu (append), **MF_SEPARATOR** specifies a horizontal break, and **MF_STRING** indicates that the third parameter is a long pointer to an ASCII string that will be added to the menu.

6.5.3 Initializing and Using Accelerators

You already know that you must load a resource before your program can use it, and that accelerators are resources defined in the .RC file. The following line loads an accelerator table and returns a handle to it:

```
hAccelTable = LoadAccelerators (hInstance,
                         (LPSTR) "acceltable");
```

The name given to the accelerator table in the .RC file is "acceltable," an ASCII string.

PGM3 uses the accelerator table in the get-translate-dispatch loop. When a message is retrieved using **GetMessage**, PGM3 calls **TranslateAccelerator** using

```
TranslateAccelerator (hWnd, hAccelTable, (LPMSG)&msg)
```

where **hWnd** is the window handle, **hAccelTable** is the handle to the accelerator table, and **msg** is the message data structure. **TranslateAccelerator** checks to see if the message is the result of the user pressing an accelerator (defined in the .RC file). If so, **TranslateAccelerator** immediately sends a message to the window function (in our case, **MainWndProc**). If not, **TranslateAccelerator** returns zero, and the program should call the Windows **TranslateMessage** and **DispatchMessage** functions. If a translation occurred, the message was already sent to **MainWndProc**: therefore **TranslateMessage** and **DispatchMessage** should not be called.

6.5.4 Freeing the Procedure Instance

The code for freeing a procedure instance comes next, so we'll discuss it here, even though we're not actually ready to quit at this point.

After receiving a message to quit, **WinMain** should use the function **FreeProcInstance** to disconnect the data segment from any connected procedure:

```
FreeProcInstance (lpprocAbout);
```

This releases the space occupied by the dialog box code and the associated prologue code that was installed by **MakeProcInstance. FreeProcInstance** returns no value.

6.5.5 Displaying Dialog Boxes

PGM3's **MainWndProc** handles three messages: **WM_DESTROY, WM_SYSCOMMAND,** and **WM_COMMAND**. You learned about **WM_DESTROY** in Chapter 4.

Remember that earlier in this program we changed the system menu by adding a horizontal break and the text "About. . . F1." At that time, we also associated the identifier **IDSABOUT** with the new menu item.

When the user selects a command from a system menu, Windows sends the window function a **WM_SYSCOMMAND** message. Don't confuse this with the **WM_COMMAND** message we've already studied: system menu messages go to **WM_SYSCOMMAND**, and other menu messages go to **WM_COMMAND**.

So, when the user selects "About. . . F1" from the system menu, Windows sends a **WM_SYSCOMMAND** message to the **MainWndProc**. **wParam** will contain the ID of the menu item that was selected, in this case, **IDSABOUT.**

```
case WM_SYSCOMMAND:
  switch (wParam)
    {
    case IDSABOUT:
      DialogBox (hInst, (LPSTR)"About",
                                      hWnd, lpprocAbout);
      break;
    default:
      return DefWindowProc (hwnd, msg, wParam, lParam);
    }
  break;
```

hInst is the handle to this instance (we saved it in **WinMain**). **(LPSTR)"About"** is a long pointer to an ASCII string and is the name of the dialog box to display. (You'll recall that we called the dialog box **About** in the .RC file.) **hWnd** is our old friend, the window handle. And **lpprocAbout** is a long pointer to a window procedure (actually, a long pointer to the window procedure's prologue code that binds the data segment to the code, as discussed in the previous section.)

That's all there is to displaying a dialog box. The **About** procedure will process commands until the dialog box is closed. At that time, control will resume at the **break** following the **DialogBox** function call.

PGM3 defines two more dialog boxes, which are both called in a similar way. When the user selects "Sample. . ." or "Dir. . ." from the menu bar, Windows sends **MainWndProc** a **WM_COMMAND** message with **wParam** corresponding to the selected menu item.

```
case MENU2:
 DialogBox (hInst, MAKEINTRESOURCE(DIRDLGBOX), hWnd,
                                    lpprocDirDlgBoxProc);
 break;
```

You'll note one minor difference: when we defined the dialog box (in the .RC file), we used an integer for the box name instead of an ASCII string. We called this integer **DIRDLGBOX** in the .H file. To reference the box, we use the macro MAKEINTRESOURCE. This macro converts an integer to a long pointer to a string, which is what **DialogBox** expects.

6.5.6 Processing Dialog Box Messages

A dialog box is a window in its own right, so it has its own processing procedure. Because PGM3 defines three dialog boxes, it needs three dialog box processing routines.

Recall that when Windows calls a routine in our module, it uses Pascal calling conventions for a "far" procedure. Therefore, we must explicitly tell the compiler to set up our routine in this manner. Windows will pass the same four arguments it passes to **MainWndProc: hWnd, msg, wParam,** and **lParam**.

6.5.7 Processing the About Dialog Box

The **About** dialog box is "about" as simple as they come. It processes only two of the messages Windows sends to it: **WM_COMMAND** and **WM_INITDIALOG.**

```
case WM_INITDIALOG:
  return TRUE;
```

Windows sends **WM_INITDIALOG** just prior to displaying the box on the system display. This gives us a chance to do any preprocessing we want to do. We'll use this opportunity in our other dialog boxes, but for the **About** dialog box, we only want to return TRUE.

WM_INITDIALOG passes one parameter in **wParam**: the handle of the first control item to be given the input focus, which is generally the first item with a **WS_TABSTOP** attribute. In this case, we have only one control item capable of accepting the input focus, **IDOK**, therefore **IDOK** is in **wParam**. Returning TRUE tells Windows to direct the input focus at the control item in **wParam**. Had we returned FALSE, we would have to manually set the focus.

```
case WM_COMMAND:
  EndDialog (hWnd, TRUE);
  return TRUE;
```

Windows passes a **WM_COMMAND** message when the user selects a menu item or when an accelerator keystroke is translated. Because we can get only one such message from **About (IDOK)**, we need not special case it:

```
case WM_COMMAND:
      switch (wParam)
        {
        case IDOK:
                 EndDialog (hWnd, TRUE);
                 return TRUE;
        }
```

The switch makes sense, but generates unnecessary code, because we will only get one **WM_COMMAND** message from this window, **IDOK**. We wrote it this way just to illustrate the switch on **wParam**. It could just as easily be written:

```
case WM_COMMAND:
  EndDialog (hWnd, TRUE);
  return TRUE;
```

EndDialog is called to inform Windows that we are done with this dialog box and would like it removed from the display. TRUE is the value returned to the calling dialog box function **DialogBox**. Note that the calling function does not use this information, although it could have. For example:

```
if (DialogBox(...))
```

would be true if **EndDialog** returns true.

We return FALSE (0) for all other messages, indicating that we did not process them.

6.5.8 Initializing the SampleDialog Box

Like the other dialog boxes, the **SampleDialog** box will handle only the two messages **WM_INITDIALOG** and **WM_COMMAND**. This box is much like the simple **About** box. You may wish to refer back to Figure 6.4 during this description.

Instead of simply returning TRUE for **WM_INITDIALOG,** we want to initialize the dialog box before it is displayed. Specifically, we want to:

1. Set the current value of **szText** in the edit control.
2. Check or "un-check" the check box as specified by the Boolean value **bCheckBox**.
3. Darken the selected radio button.
4. Place the names of some European countries in the list box.
5. Highlight the current selection in the list box.

We begin by setting the current value of **szText** in the edit control box. Back in **WinMain** we loaded the same string into **szText** and **szDefault**. To copy **szText** into the edit control, we use the following function:

```
SetDlgItemText (hWnd, IDSTEXT, (LPSTR)szText);
```

SetDlgItemText copies the string pointed to by the last parameter into the field specified by the second parameter. The first time through, the text "Texas" will be placed in the edit control.

Next, to check or un-check the check box as specified by the Boolean value **bCheckBox**, we use:

```
CheckDlgButton (hWnd, IDSCHECKBOX, bCheckBox);
```

If **bCheckBox** is TRUE, an "X" is placed in the check box; otherwise (FALSE), the "X" is removed.

To check the selected radio button, we use:

```
CheckRadioButton (hWnd, IDSRBGOOD, IDSRBBEST,
                  (fRadiobuttonTemp = fRadioButton));
```

This function is a little tricky. It first sets the temporary variable **fRadiobuttonTemp** equal to **fRadioButton**. We are going to allow the user to cancel any changes made, so we need to keep track of temporary states. Next, the value of **fRadioButton** (initially allocated as **IDSRBBEST**) is passed to the function. **CheckRadioButton** then checks the radio button of the last parameter and un-checks all others within the range specified by the second and third parameters. Note that **IDSRBGOOD, IDSRBBETTER,** and **IDSRBBEST** are consecutive. This is important because **CheckRadioButton** operates on all radio buttons within a range. This is the "real" logical grouping of radio buttons. As stated earlier, the .RC file statement GROUPBOX only graphically groups buttons. It's the range of the IDs that really groups them.

Setting the names of European countries in the list box is also a little tricky. Instead of expanding the loop into individual statements and using each resource ID explicitly, we'll index off **IDSSTR01**:

```
for (i=0; i<=CSTR; i++)
  {
  LoadString (hInst, IDSSTR01+i, (LPSTR)szTemp, 16);
  SendDlgItem Message (hWnd, IDSLISTBOX, LB_ADDSTRING,
                              0, (LONG)(LPSTR)szTemp);
  }
```

CSTR, defined in the .H file, is the number of strings to be loaded less one. You know what **LoadString** does. **SendDlgItemMessage** does exactly what its name implies: it sends a message to a dialog item. The message sent depends on the third parameter: in this case, we want to add a string to a list box, **IDSLISTBOX**. The string is located in **szTemp** (we just loaded it). The fourth parameter is not used by **LB_ADDSTRING**, so we set it to zero.

The final operation we want to perform in the initialization phase is to highlight a default, or current, selection in the list box. We arbitrarily set the initial selection, **iSel**, equal to two; this corresponds to the third list box entry. The statement

```
SendDlgItem Message (hWnd, IDSLISTBOX,
                              LB_SETCURSEL, iSel, 0)
```

sends the list box the command **LB_SETCURSEL,** which sets the current selection to **iSel**. For **LB_SETCURSEL**, the last parameter is not used, so we set it to 0.

6.5.9 Processing the SampleDialog Box

Let's now assume our second dialog box, **SampleDialog,** is on the system display. At this point, the user can do a number of things for amusement:

1 Select an item from the list box.
2 Scroll the list box items up and down.
3 Select one of the radio buttons.
4 Type text in the edit control.
5 Check or un-check the check box.
6 Set all items back to the defaults.
7 Cancel the operation.
8 Accept the current settings.

Let's examine each of these operations individually. The list box operations are the easiest, because in this particular case, Windows will do everything for us. Windows handles the selection of an item and the scrolling–we don't have to worry about it.

The edit control is also handled by Windows—all we need to do is set it (which we already did), and read it later when the "Accept" button is pressed.

Because the radio buttons are mutually exclusive, we want only one selected at a time. When the user "pushes" one, we will get a **WM_COMMAND** message with **wParam** containing **IDSRBGOOD, IDSRBBETTER,** or **IDSRBBEST**. So we group the radio buttons together as follows:

```
case IDSRBGOOD:
case IDSRBBETTER:
case IDSRBBEST:
  CheckRadioButton (hWnd, IDSRBGOOD, IDSRBBEST,
                          fRadioButtonTemp = wParam));
  break;
```

You already know how **CheckRadioButton** works: it checks the control specified by the last parameter and un-checks the others within the range of the second and third parameters. So the above lines do two things:

1 Set the temporary variable equal to the selected button.

2 Display the selected button as "on" and turn the other "off". (Remember that we are going to allow a "Cancel" operation, so all changes must be temporary until the "Accept" button is pushed.)

Processing the check box is a cinch: if it is checked, we un-check it; if it is not checked, we check it:

```
case IDSCHECKBOX:
  CheckDlgButton (hWnd, IDSCHECKBOX,
            !IsDlgButtonChecked (hWnd, IDSCHECKBOX));
break;
```

IsDlgButtonChecked returns a Boolean value describing the state of the check box: TRUE or FALSE. So, **!IsDlgButtonChecked** inverts the response, and feeds it to **CheckDlgButton** (you already know what that does).

Next we are going to look at the "Defaults" push button. We'll define this button to:

1 Set the edit control to the string "Texas."
2 Set the checkbox "on."
3 Select the "Hey Wow" radio button.
4 Select the third list box item ("Denmark").

To set the edit control to the string "Texas", we use the **SetDlgItemText** function, just as we did in the initialization routine, except that we point to the string **szDefault**. (Again, note **szDefault** was loaded by **WinMain**.) To set the check box "on", we use **CheckDlgButton** with TRUE. To select the "Hey Wow" radio button, we use **CheckRadioButton**. And finally, to select the third list box item, we use **SendDlgItemMessage** with the command **LB_SETCURSEL**. We have used all of these functions in previous chapters.

After selecting options or entering text in the dialog box, the user will select either "Accept" or "Cancel". If "Accept" is selected, we must:

1 Determine the current state of the check box.
2 Get the current radio button.
3 Fetch the text from the edit control.
4 Determine the current selection in the list box.

To determine the current state of the check box, we again use the function **IsDlgButtonChecked:**

```
bCheckBox = IsDlgButtonChecked (hWnd, IDSCHECKBOX);
```

The next time this dialog box is displayed, the initialization routine will correctly set the check box state.

To get the current radio button, we simply copy the temporary variable value into the actual value:

```
fRadioButton = fRadioButtonTemp;
```

Fetching the text from the edit control is a slightly tricky operation:

```
szText[ GetDlgItemText(hWnd, IDSTEXT,
                       (LPSTR)szText, 16) ] = '/0';
```

GetDlgItemText gets the text associated with the edit control **IDSTEXT** (of maximum length **16**), places it in **szText**, and returns the number of characters placed in **szText**. We use that number as an index into **szText** and store a NULL character there, thus completing the ASCII string.

To determine the current selection from the list box, we use the following line:

```
iSel = SendDlgItemMessage (hWnd, IDSLISTBOX,
                           LB_GETCURSEL, iSel, 0);
```

where **LB_GETCURSEL** is the command to get the current selection. Returned is the index of the current selection. We store the index back into **iSel** for use the next time the box is displayed. Now the program falls through to the "Cancel" logic.

If the user selects "Cancel," the dialog box is taken down via **EndDialog**. Any work done in the box is forgotten.

6.5.10 Initializing the DirDialog Box

To initialize the directory dialog box, we need to do two things: set up a file search specification, and tell Windows to search for matching files and place them in a list box. Let's begin by establishing a search specification:

```
for (i=j=0; pStr1[i++]=szSearchFilespec[j++];);
```

This statement copies the default search file specification (*.*) into the string **pStr1**. Next we need to get Windows to search for a match and fill the list box. To do so, we use this statement:

```
DlgDirList (hWnd, (LPSTR)pStr1, IDSDIRBOX, IDSPATH,
                                               0x4037);
```

pStr1 is the search specification, **IDSDIRBOX** is the list box resource ID, and **IDSPATH** is a field in which Windows will place the current path for display. The last parameter allows for inclusion/exclusion of certain types of files. It is an integer whose bits are defined as follows:

Hex value	*Meaning*
0001	Read only file
0002	Hidden file
0004	System file
0010	Subdirectory
0020	Archive file
4000	Drives
8000	Exclusive

Given these definitions, the value **0x4037** combined with the search specification "*.*" tells Windows to search for all files that are normal, read only, hidden, system, or archive, and include subdirectory names and other system drives. The last bit, "exclusive," tells Windows to use only the specified attribute. For example, **0x8004** would mean "search for only system files that match '*.*'."

6.5.11 Processing the DirDialog Box

In the previous **SampleDialog** box, we elected to do nothing with the list box. In the **DirDialog** box, we'll intercept the list box messages from Windows and do something with them.

Whenever the user selects an item in the list box, we get a **IDSDIRBOX** message thru **WM_COMMAND**. The high word of **lParam** will contain a one (1) for a single click, or a two (2) for a double click. We don't care about the single click, but we want to pay attention to the double click:

```
case IDSDIRBOX:
  switch (HIWORD(lParam))
    {
    case 1:              /* single click case */
      break;
    case 2:
      if (DlgDirSelect (hWnd, (LPSTR)pStr2, IDSDIRBOX))
        {
        for (i=0; pStr1[i] = pstr2[i]; i++);
        for (j=0; pStr1[i++] = szSearchFilespec[j++];);
        DlgDirList (hWnd, (LPSTR)pStr1, IDSDIRBOX,
                                    IDSPATH, 0x04037);
        }
      break;
    }
  break;
```

HIWORD is a macro that retrieves the high word from a long (double word) integer. **DlgDirSelect** gets the current selection and copies it into the specified space. In our example, **pStr2** will contain the selected filename. If a drive or directory was selected, **pStr2** will contain a ready-to-be-used path. **DlgDirSelect** returns TRUE if a drive or directory was selected. We use this in our code structure, placing the function within an **if** statement. If the user selects a drive or directory, we want to reload the list box and display it again.

There is only one difference between the double click logic and **IDOK**. In the **IDOK** logic, if **DlgDirSelect** does not find a drive or directory, it falls into **IDCANCEL** and closes the dialog box. In the double click logic, nothing happens.

6.6 THE DEFINITION FILE: PGM3.DEF

```
;*****************************************************************:
; Filename:      PGM3.DEF                                          :
;                                                                  :
; Description:  Link definition file                               :
;-----------------------------------------------------------------:
NAME    PGM3

DESCRIPTION 'Sample program 3'

STUB    '..\WINSTUB.EXE'

CODE    MOVEABLE
DATA    MOVEABLE MULTIPLE

HEAPSIZE  128
STACKSIZE 4096

EXPORTS
    MainWndProc          @1
    About                @2
    SampleDlgProc        @3
    DirDlgProc           @4

;-----------------------------------------------------------------:
; End of file:  PGM3.DEF                                           :
;*****************************************************************:
```

Because our program has added three new procedures that Windows will call, we must export them to make them available for calling:

```
Exports:
        MainWndProc                    @1
        About                          @2
        SampleDlgProc                  @3
        DirDlgProc                     @4
```

6.7 THE MAKE FILE: PGM3.

```
#*********************************************************************#
# Filename:     PGM3.                                                 #
#                                                                     #
# Description:  PGM3.EXE "MAKE" description file                      #
#---------------------------------------------------------------------#

pgm3.obj: pgm3.c pgm3.h
    cl -d -c -AS -Gsw -Os -Zpe pgm3.c

pgm3.res: pgm3.rc pgm3.h
    rc -r pgm3.rc

pgm3.exe: pgm3.obj pgm3.res pgm3.def
    link4 pgm3,/align:16,/map,slibw,pgm3.def
    rc pgm3.res

#---------------------------------------------------------------------#
# End of file:  PGM3.                                                 #
#*********************************************************************#
```

. . . .

In this chapter, you've learned how to link accelerators with menu items, how to create dialog boxes and specify options for them, and how to add a menu item to the system menu. In Chapter 7, you'll learn about Windows coordinate systems so that you can specify exactly where to put windows and the objects in them.

7

INTRODUCTION TO GDI

- GDI Coordinate Systems and Mapping Modes
- Introduction to PGM4
- The C Header File: PGM4.H
- The Resource Script File: PGM4.RC
- The C-Language Source File: PGM4.C
- The Module Definition File: PGM4.DEF
- The Make File: PGM4.

By studying PGM4, the program presented in this chapter, you'll learn the basic functions of the Windows Graphics Device Interface (GDI).

7.1 GDI COORDINATE SYSTEMS AND MAPPING MODES

To achieve device independence in its graphic operations, the Windows Graphic Device Interface (GDI) uses a set of transformation equations that map *logical coordinates* to actual *physical coordinates* and vice versa. Logical coordinates are always inside the client area of a window. No matter where the window is on the display, the logical coordinates will never move, because they are relative to the window frame. Physical coordinates, on the other hand, are actually device-specific numbers.

References are usually in logical coordinates, although sometimes device units are used. Coordinate transformation functions are provided by Windows. You control these functions through the use of *mapping modes*.

Windows defines eight mapping modes. These modes are grouped into three categories:

- Completely constrained
- Partially constrained
- Unconstrained

The constraint imposed is that of scale. In completely constrained modes, the scales of both X and Y are fixed and cannot be changed. In the partially constrained mode, the X and Y units are maintained so that X and Y appear the same length (1:1), no matter what display device is used. In the unconstrained mode, you have complete control over how your coordinate system is defined.

Before attempting to explain the mapping modes and their respective logical coordinates, let's look at physical, or device, coordinates. Figure 7.1 illustrates the composition of physical coordinates. The upper left corner of the window's client area is (0,0). From the origin, proceeding to the right is positive X, and proceeding down is positive Y. The units are always in pixels, or pels.

Figure 7.1

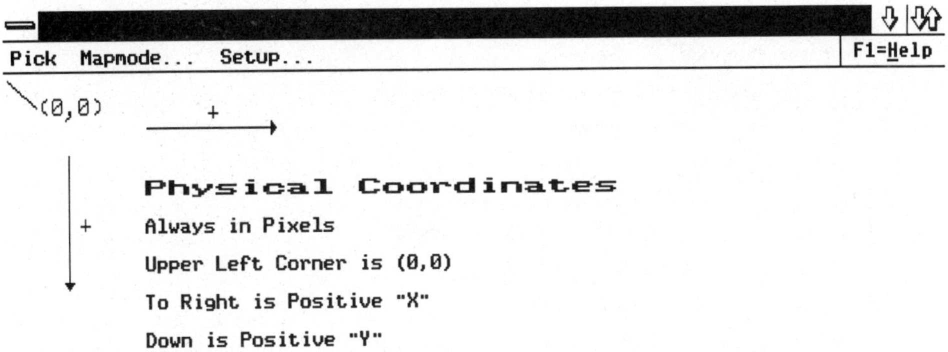

7.1.1 Completely Constrained Mapping Modes

Windows defines six completely constrained mapping modes:

MM_TEXT
MM_LOMETRIC
MM_LOENGLISH
MM_TWIPS
MM_HIMETRIC
MM_HIENGLISH

The units of **MM_TEXT** are identical to the device's physical units: pixels. Thus, if the client area has 640 x 162 pixels, the window's lower right corner will be (639,161).

Figure 7.2 illustrates the other five mapping modes and their units and relationships. The upper left corner of the window is (0,0). In **MM_LOMETRIC** mode, for example, one unit equals one tenth of a millimeter; so 1000 units equals 10 centimeters on the display surface.

Figure 7.2

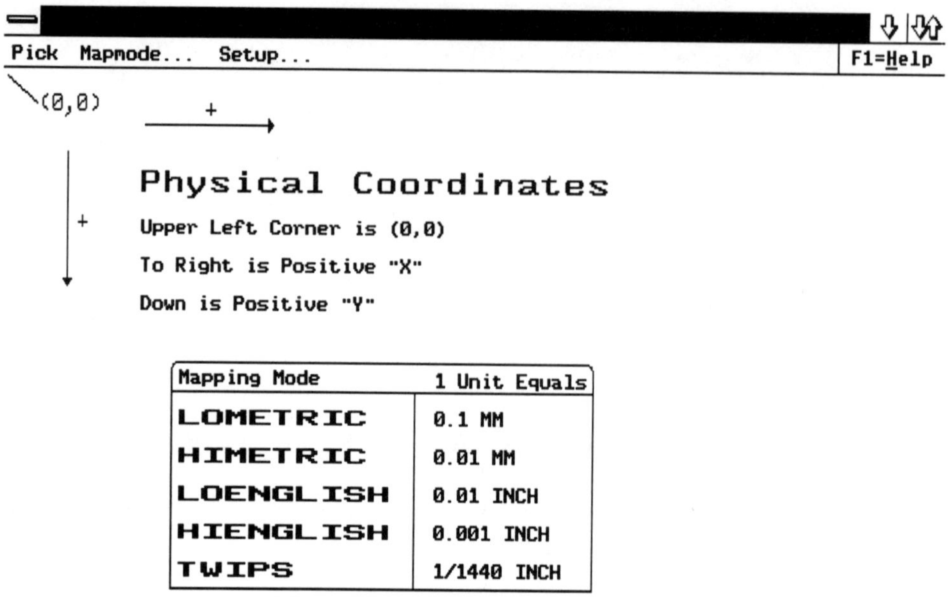

7.1.2 Unconstrained Mapping Mode: ANISOTROPIC

If you choose the **MM_ANISOTROPIC** mapping mode, GDI gives you complete control of the coordinate system in the window. You'll soon see that if you want the lower right corner of your window to be (0,0) and the upper left corner to be (2000,–5000), you need only say so.

Figure 7.3 shows the limits of the logical coordinate system. You must create a rectangle by specifying the upper left and lower right corners within these limits. This space will be completely within the client area of the window.

When you have selected a rectangle, you must lock down the logical window's *origin* and *extent*. The origin is the upper left corner of the rectangle, and the extent is the number of units in the X and Y direction required to get to the second point.

Next, you must specify the *viewport*. The viewport describes how the window is mapped onto the device. If you want your logical coordinate system to be mapped exactly into the client area you must ask Windows to provide the size of your client area, then return that information as the extent of the viewport. This will become much clearer after we examine a few examples in this chapter.

Figure 7.3

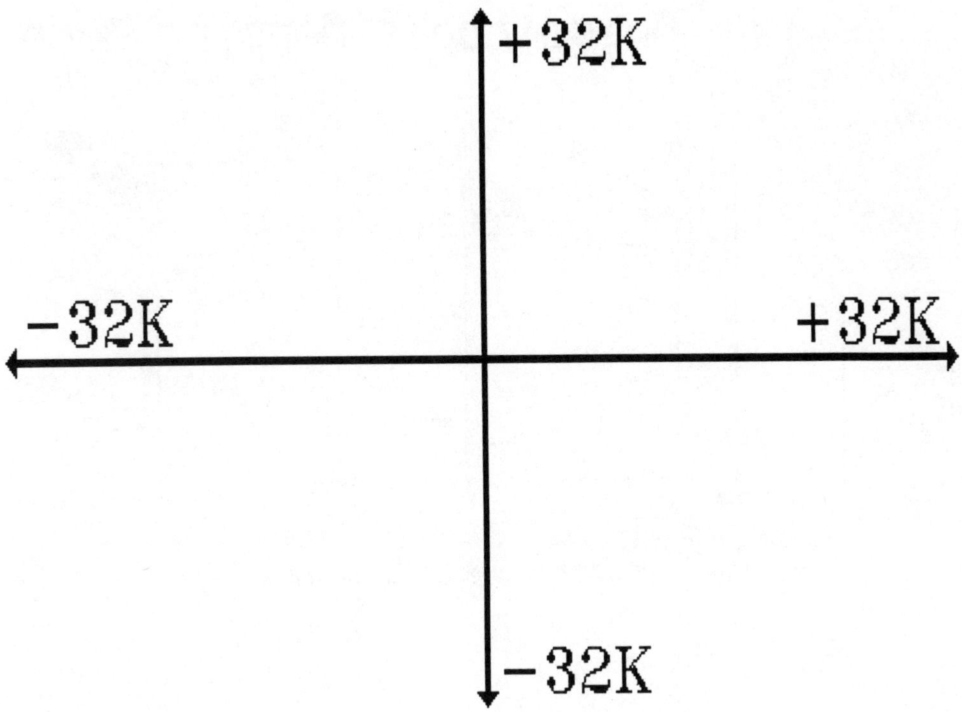

Figure 7.4 illustrates how to set up a coordinate system as shown in the window's client area: the origin is in the upper left corner and the lower right corner is (640, 200). The window origin is set at (0,0) and the extent is (640,200). The viewport origin is set to (0,0) and the extent to whatever Windows specifies as the physical coordinate of the lower right corner; in this case (640,162).

Figure 7.5 illustrates how you can turn the coordinate system of Figure 7.4 upside down by simply making adjustments to the window origin and extents. Here, the upper left corner is (640,0) and the lower right is (0,200); consequently, the window extent is (–640,200).

Figure 7.6 illustrates an example of placing the logical origin in the center of the window. The window origin is placed at (–150,75) and the lower right corner at (100,–150) for an extent of (250,–225). It couldn't be any easier!

Figure 7.4

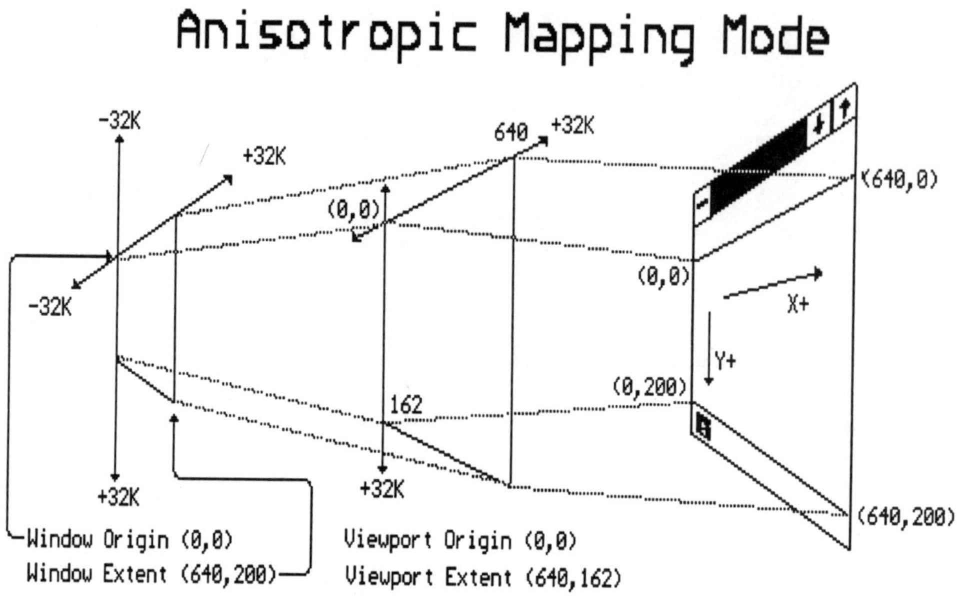

Figure 7.5

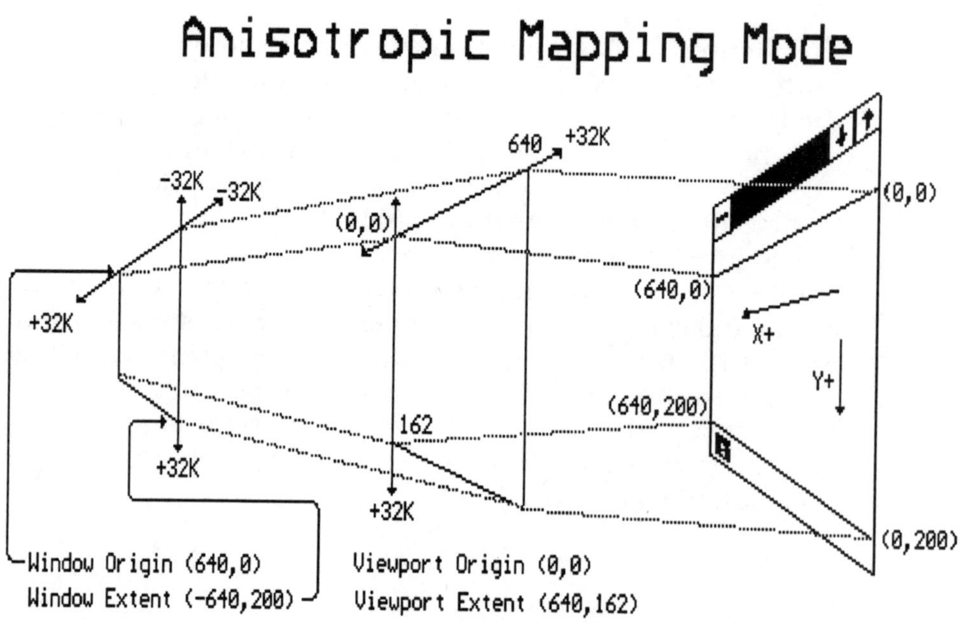

Figure 7.6

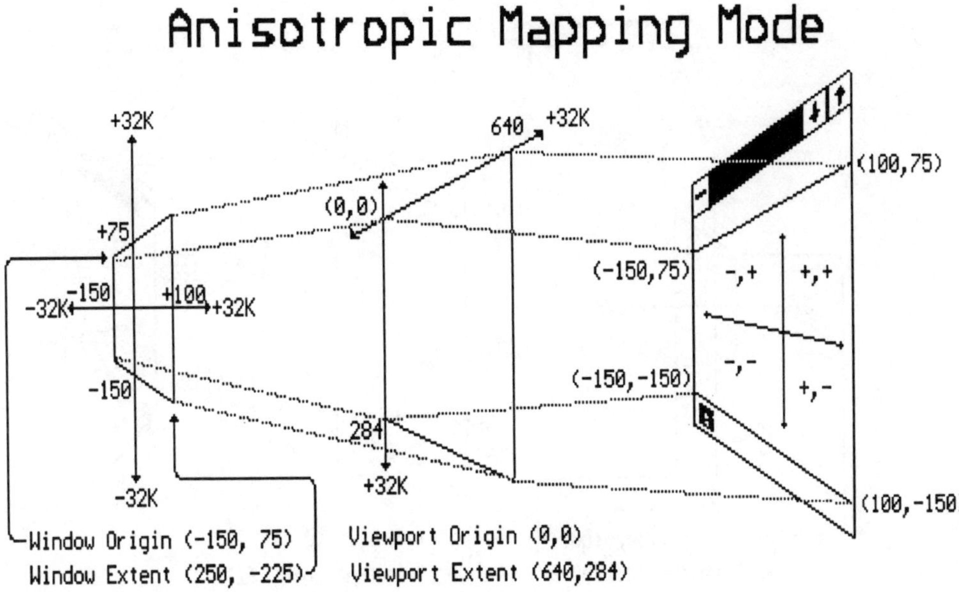

7.1.3 Partially Constrained Mapping Mode: ISOTROPIC

MM_ISOTROPIC is called a partially constrained mapping mode, because GDI constrains one of the axes to maintain a one-to-one correspondence in the units; that is, the physical length of one unit in one direction equals the physical length of one unit in the other direction. Thus, a square looks like a square instead of a rectangle.

Figure 7.7 illustrates how GDI constrains a specification. In this example, we state that we want an origin of (100,–100) and an extent of (–200,200). In anisotropic mode, the lower right corner is (–100,100) but in isotropic mode, it is (–299,100), because GDI has constrained the X scale so that units in the X direction equal units in the Y direction.

Figure 7.8 illustrates another example of “flipping” the coordinate system by making adjustments on the viewport origin and extent.

Figure 7.9 illustrates how you can preserve a window's logical coordinates by making adjustments in the viewport, even if the window has changed sizes.

Figure 7.7

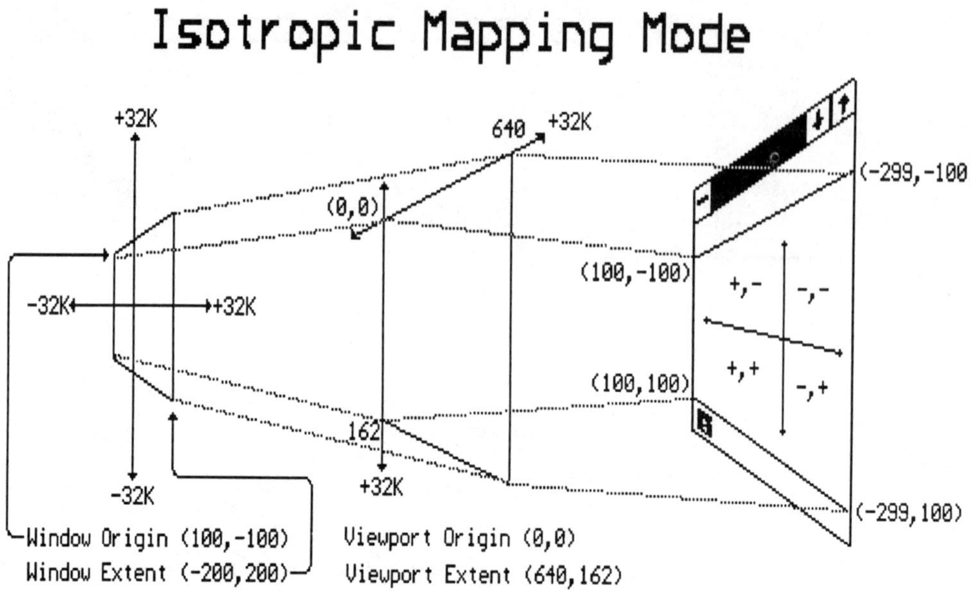

Figure 7.8

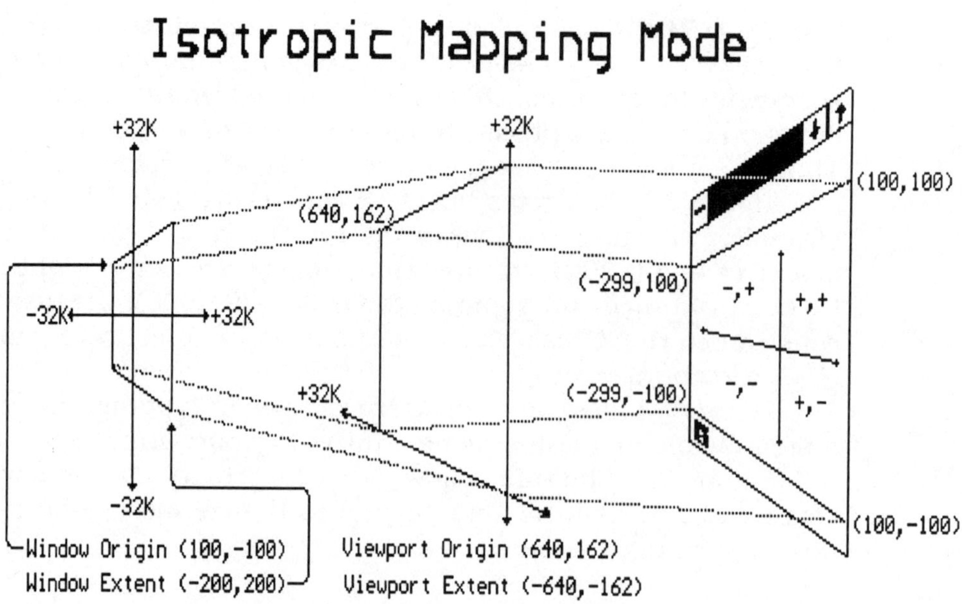

Figure 7.9

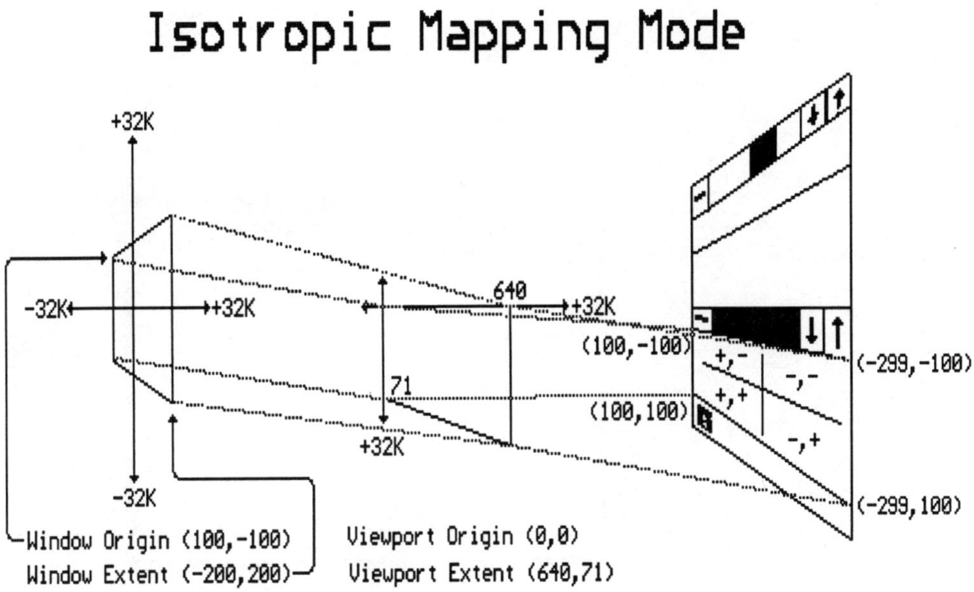

7.2 INTRODUCTION TO PGM4

PGM4 requires five source files:

PGM4.H	C language program header
PGM4.RC	Resource script file
PGM4.C	C program code
PGM4.DEF	Module definition file
PGM4.	Input instructions to the MAKE utility

Figure 7.10 illustrates PGM4's main window. PGM4's menu bar has three items, "Pick," "Mapmode. . .," and "Setup. . ." Selecting "Pick" displays a menu of eight geometric figure names: **Line, Polyline, Rectangle, RoundRect, Polygon, Ellipse, Arc,** and **Pie.**

As Figure 7.11 shows, selecting "Mapmode. . ." displays a dialog box that allows you to select one of eight mapping modes.

Figure 7.10

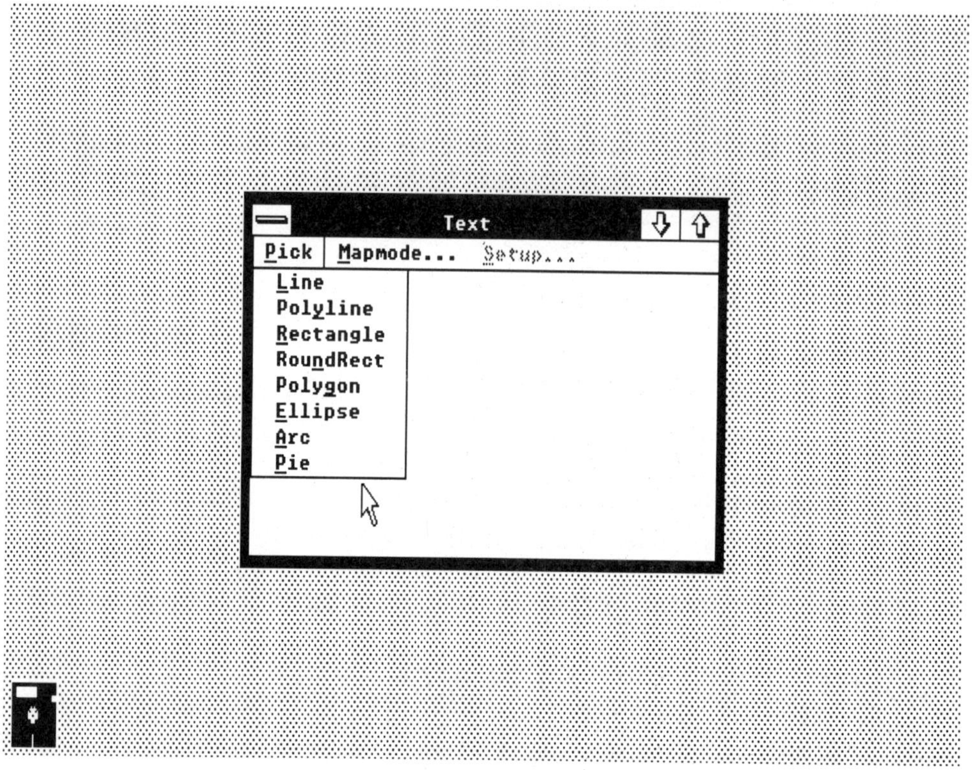

Figure 7.11

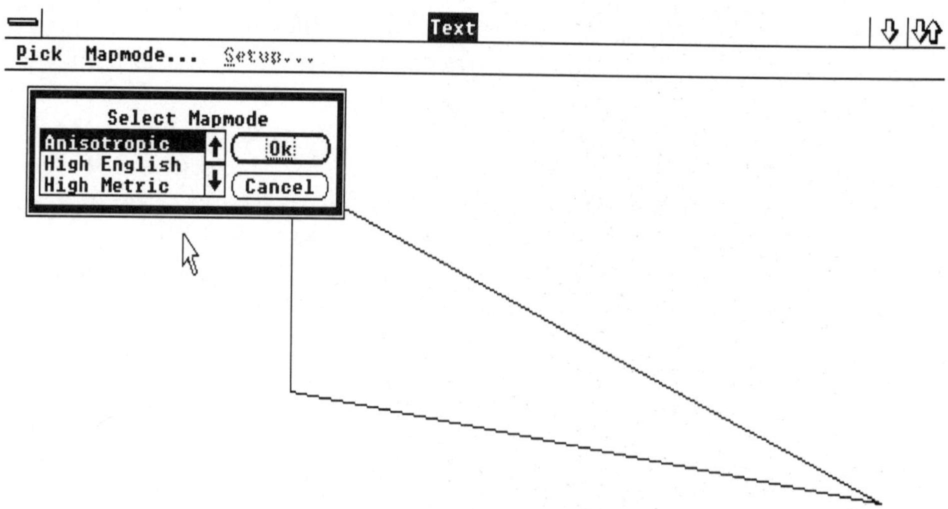

As Figure 7.12 shows, selecting "Setup. . ." allows you to change the window and viewport origins and extents. "Setup. . ." can only be selected when the map mode is ANISOTROPIC or ISOTROPIC.

Figure 7.12

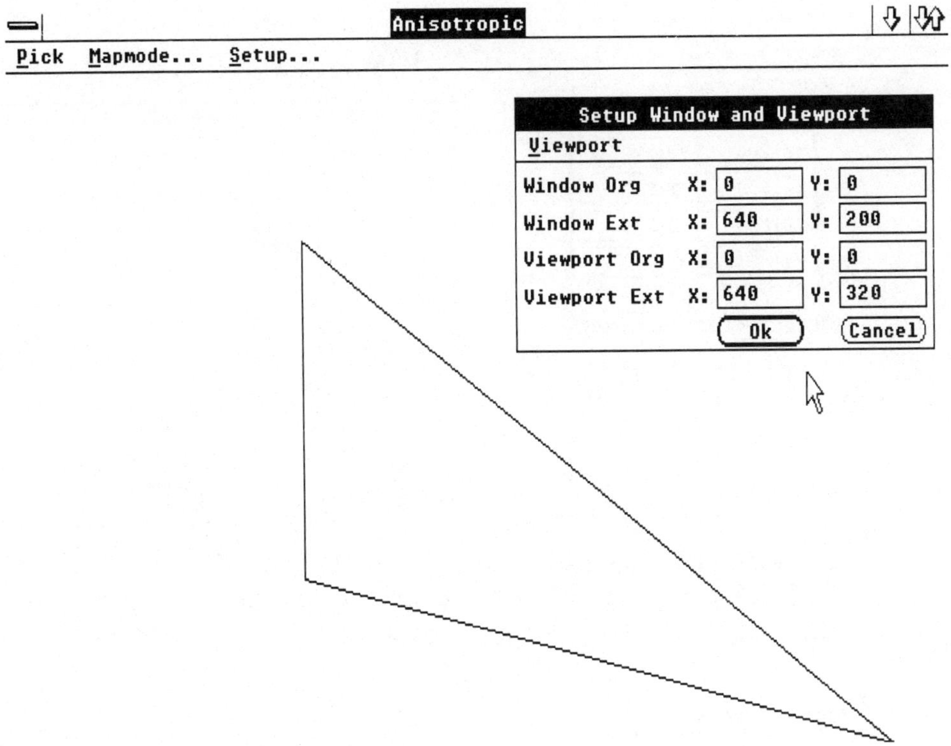

When the user selects one of the "Pick" items, a dialog box appears, as shown in Figure 7.13. The user is then expected to enter from two to four coordinates, depending on the shape selected. Pressing the "Ok" button causes the shape to be drawn.

Figure 7.13

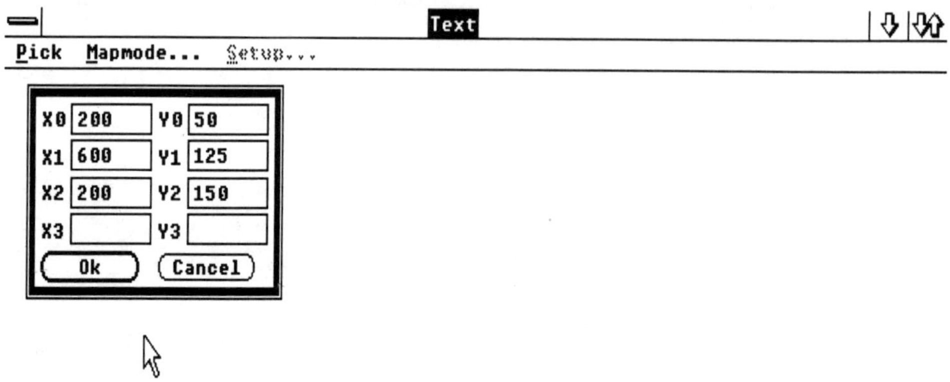

Initially, this program is in text mode. Figures 7.14, 7.15, and 7.16 illustrate the difference in selecting among the text, isotropic and anisotropic modes (using the supplied default values).

Figure 7.14

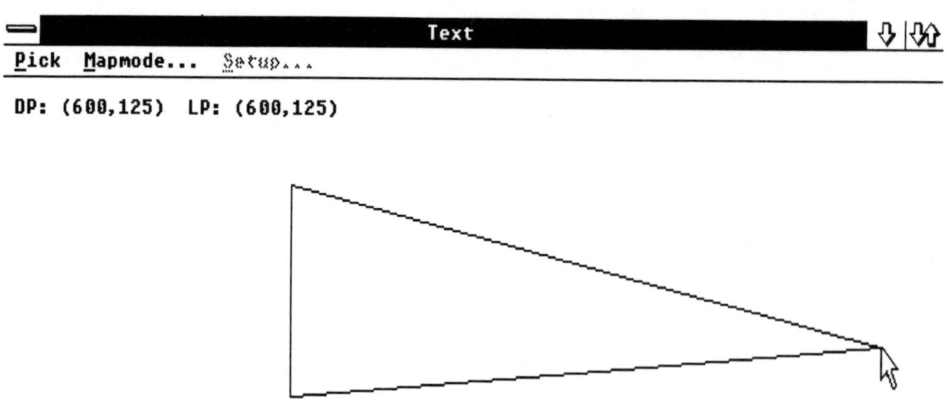

Figure 7.15

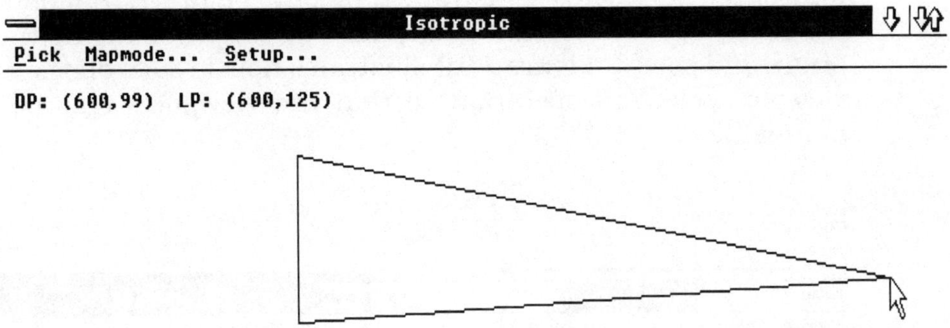

Figure 7.16

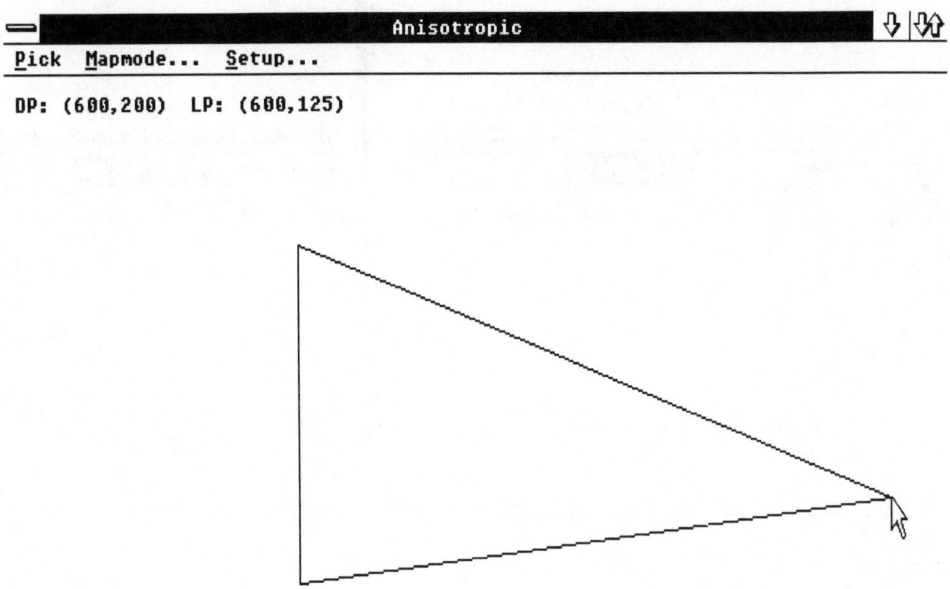

Figure 7.17 illustrates the difference in scaling of a triangle in four of the completely constrained modes. Figure 7.18 illustrates how the coordinate system can be inverted by simply changing the window origin and extent. Figure 7.19 illustrates how to turn off the automatic viewport selection operation so that the viewports may be adjusted manually.

Figure 7.17

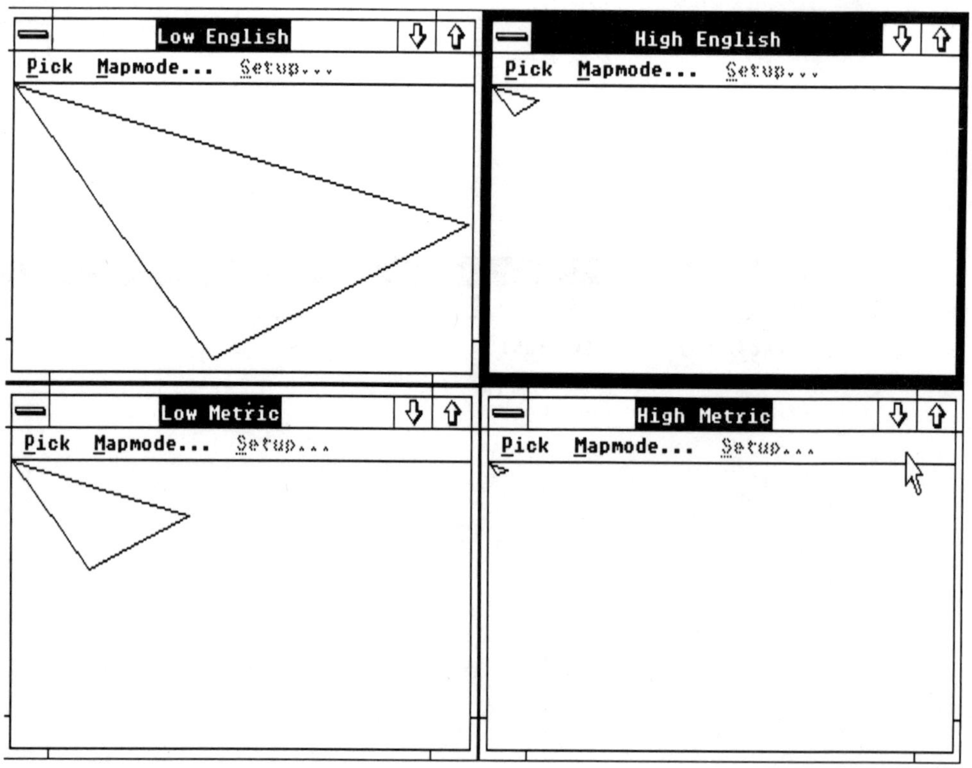

Figure 7.18

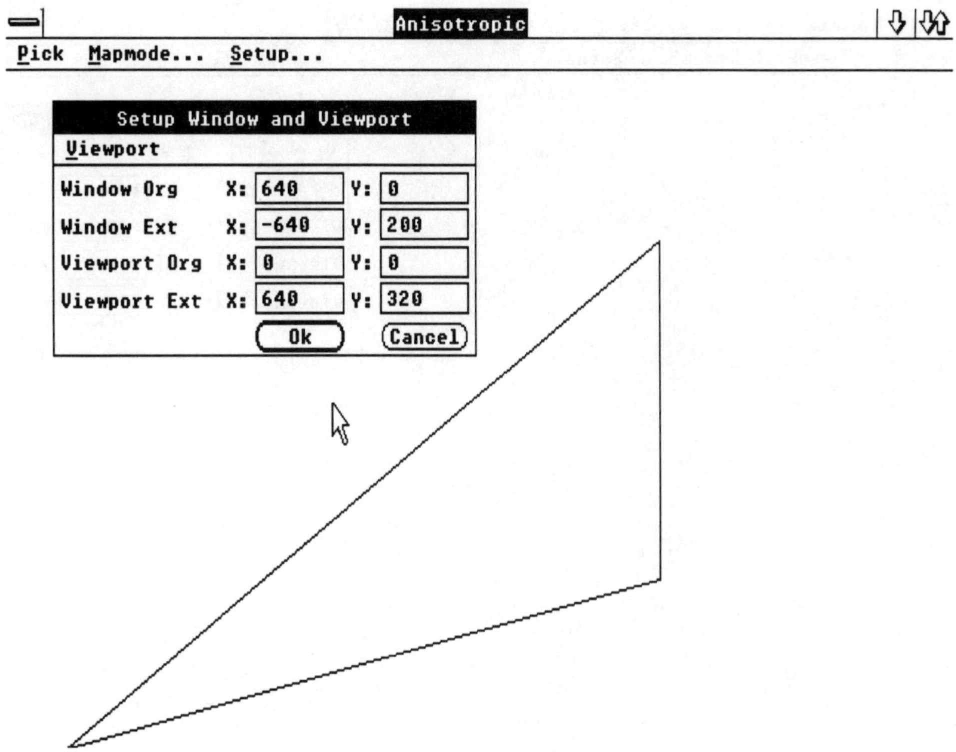
Anisotropic
Pick Mapmode... Setup...
Setup Window and Viewport
Viewport
Window Org X: 640 Y: 0
Window Ext X: -640 Y: 200
Viewport Org X: 0 Y: 0
Viewport Ext X: 640 Y: 320
Ok
Cancel

Figure 7.19

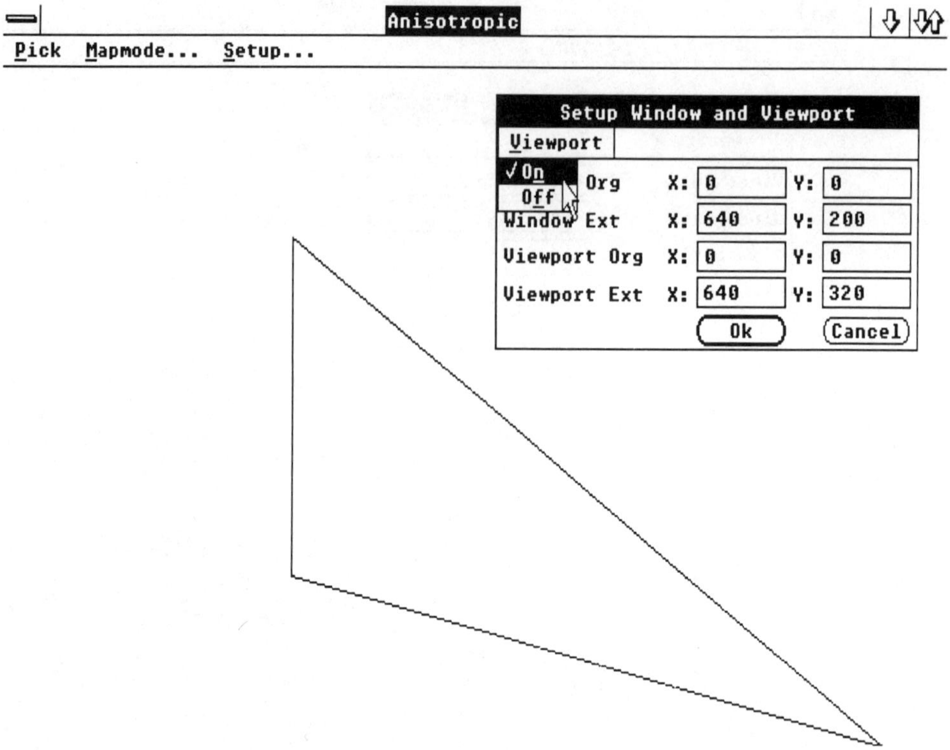
Anisotropic
Pick Mapmode... Setup...
Setup Window and Viewport
Viewport
✓On
Off
Org X: 0 Y: 0
Window Ext X: 640 Y: 200
Viewport Org X: 0 Y: 0
Viewport Ext X: 640 Y: 320
Ok
Cancel

Figures 7.20, 7.21, and 7.22 illustrate how, by adjusting only the viewport origins and extents, you can alter the coordinate system of your particular window. In all three examples, the arrow points to the same logical point.

Figure 7.20

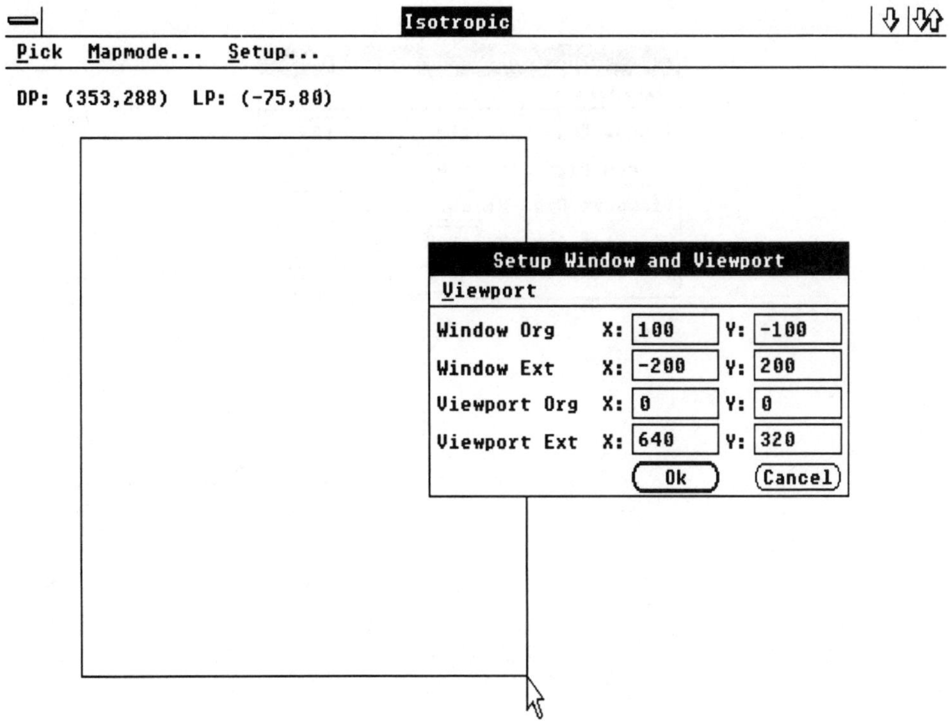

Figure 7.21

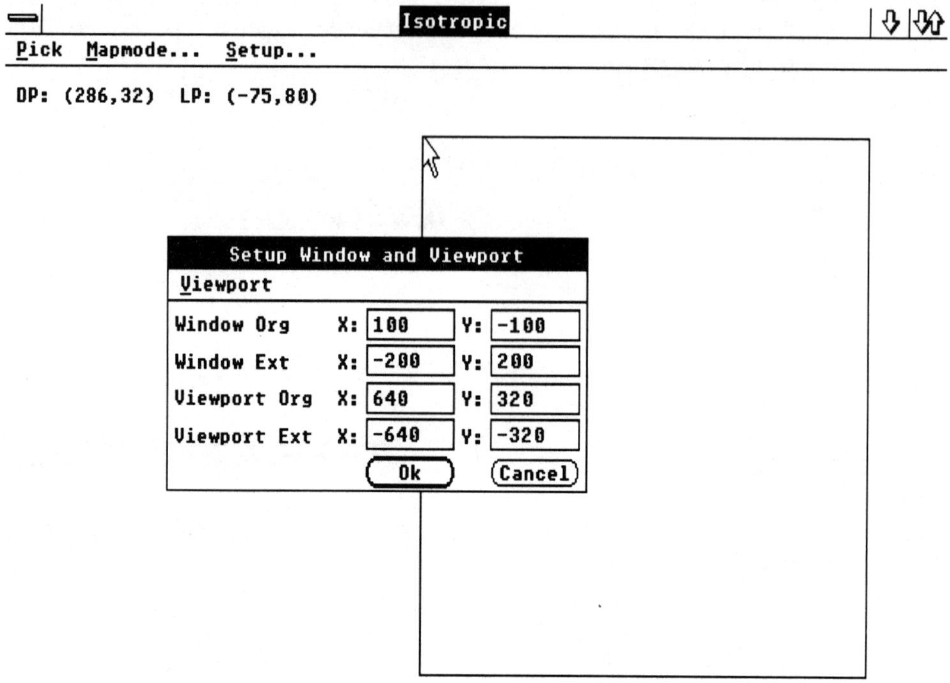
Isotropic
Pick Mapmode... Setup...
DP: (286,32) LP: (-75,80)
Setup Window and Viewport
Viewport
Window Org X: 100 Y: -100
Window Ext X: -200 Y: 200
Viewport Org X: 640 Y: 320
Viewport Ext X: -640 Y: -320
Ok
Cancel

Figure 7.22

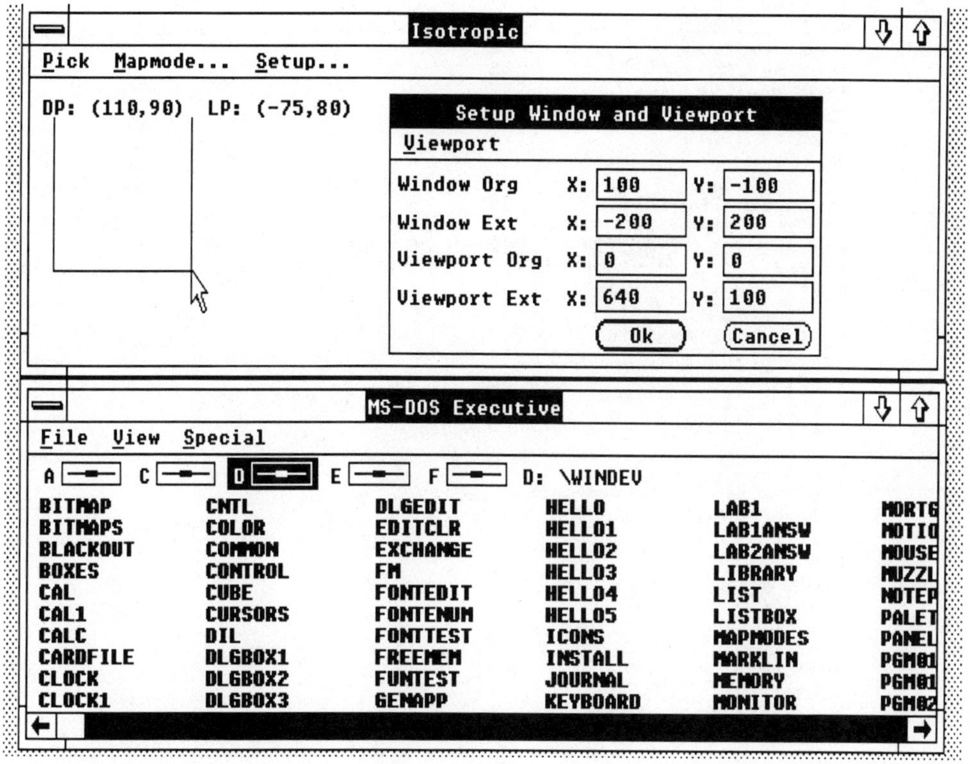

7.3 THE C HEADER FILE: PGM4.H

```
/*************************************************************************/
/* Filename:     PGM4.H                                                  */
/*                                                                       */
/* Description:  PGM4.C  header file                                     */
/*-----------------------------------------------------------------------*/

#define IDSSTRA         1010
#define IDSSTRB         1011

#define IDDMAPMODE      1100
#define IDDLINE         1110
#define IDDPOLYLINE     1120
#define IDDRECTANGLE    1130
#define IDDROUNDRECT    1140
#define IDDPOLYGON      1150
#define IDDELLIPSE      1160
#define IDDARC          1170
#define IDDPIE          1180
```

```
#define COORDSDLGBOX    1200
#define IDDX0           1201
#define IDDY0           1202
#define IDDX1           1203
#define IDDY1           1204
#define IDDX2           1205
#define IDDY2           1206
#define IDDX3           1207
#define IDDY3           1208


#define MAPMODEDLGBOX   1300
#define IDSANISOTROPIC  1301    /* The following 8 strings MUST be      */
#define IDSHIENGLISH    1302    /* consecutive.  The reason is:         */
#define IDSHIMETRIC     1303    /* when loading the stings, we will use */
#define IDSISOTROPIC    1304    /* a "FOR-NEXT" loop where 'i' is an    */
#define IDSLOENGLISH    1305    /* index off IDSANISOTROPIC             */
#define IDSLOMETRIC     1306
#define IDSTEXT         1307
#define IDSTWIPS        1308
#define CSTR            IDSTWIPS - IDSANISOTROPIC
#define IDSMAPMODEBOX   1309

#define SETUPDLGBOX     1310
#define IDWINORGX       1311
#define IDWINORGY       1312
#define IDWINEXTX       1313
#define IDWINEXTY       1314
#define IDVIEWORGX      1315
#define IDVIEWORGY      1316
#define IDVIEWEXTX      1317
#define IDVIEWEXTY      1318
#define IDDSETUP        1319
#define IDDLGMENU1A     1320
#define IDDLGMENU1B     1321
#define IDDSIZEMSG      1322

/*-------------------------------------------------------------------*/
/* End of file:  PGM4.H                                              */
/*********************************************************************/
```

7.4 THE RESOURCE SCRIPT FILE: PGM4.RC

```
/*********************************************************************/
/* Filename:     PGM4.RC                                             */
/*                                                                   */
/* Description:  PGM4.EXE resources                                  */
/*-------------------------------------------------------------------*/

#include "style.h"
#include "pgm4.h"

#define TABGRP      WS_TABSTOP | WS_GROUP

STRINGTABLE
BEGIN
    IDSSTRA,            "DP: ("
    IDSSTRB,            ")  LP: ("
    IDSANISOTROPIC      "Anisotropic"
```

```
    IDSHIENGLISH        "High English"
    IDSHIMETRIC         "High Metric"
    IDSISOTROPIC        "Isotropic"
    IDSLOENGLISH        "Low English"
    IDSLOMETRIC         "Low Metric"
    IDSTEXT             "Text"
    IDSTWIPS            "Twips"
END

MainMenu MENU
BEGIN
    POPUP               "&Pick"
    BEGIN
        MENUITEM        "&Line",                 IDDLINE
        MENUITEM        "&Pol&yline",            IDDPOLYLINE
        MENUITEM        "&Rectangle",            IDDRECTANGLE
        MENUITEM        "Rou&ndRect",            IDDROUNDRECT
        MENUITEM        "Poly&gon",              IDDPOLYGON
        MENUITEM        "&Ellipse",              IDDELLIPSE
        MENUITEM        "&Arc",                  IDDARC
        MENUITEM        "&Pie",                  IDDPIE
    END
    MENUITEM            "&Mapmode...",           IDDMAPMODE
    MENUITEM            "&Setup...",             IDDSETUP
END

COORDSDLGBOX DIALOG 10, 10, 82, 72
STYLE WS_POPUP| WS_DLGFRAME
BEGIN
    CTEXT "X0"          -1,               2,  4,  8,  8
    EDITTEXT            IDDX0,           12,  2, 28, 12, TABGRP
    CTEXT "Y0"          -1,              42,  4,  8,  8
    EDITTEXT            IDDY0,           52,  2, 28, 12, TABGRP
    CTEXT "X1"          -1,               2, 18,  8,  8
    EDITTEXT            IDDX1,           12, 16, 28, 12, TABGRP
    CTEXT "Y1"          -1,              42, 18,  8,  8
    EDITTEXT            IDDY1,           52, 16, 28, 12, TABGRP
    CTEXT "X2"          -1,               2, 32,  8,  8
    EDITTEXT            IDDX2,           12, 30, 28, 12, TABGRP
    CTEXT "Y2"          -1,              42, 32,  8,  8
    EDITTEXT            IDDY2,           52, 30, 28, 12, TABGRP
    CTEXT "X3"          -1,               2, 46,  8,  8
    EDITTEXT            IDDX3,           12, 44, 28, 12, TABGRP
    CTEXT "Y3"          -1,              42, 46,  8,  8
    EDITTEXT            IDDY3,           52, 44, 28, 12, TABGRP
    DEFPUSHBUTTON "Ok",     IDOK,         2, 58, 34, 12, TABGRP
    PUSHBUTTON    "Cancel", IDCANCEL,    42, 58, 34, 12, TABGRP
END

#define LBSTYLES    WS_VSCROLL | WS_BORDER | WS_VISIBLE | LBS_SORT | TABGRP

MAPMODEDLGBOX DIALOG 10, 10, 104, 40
STYLE WS_POPUP| WS_DLGFRAME
BEGIN
    CTEXT "Select Mapmode"      -1,              25,  2,  56,  8
    LISTBOX                     IDSMAPMODEBOX,    2, 12,  64, 26, LBSTYLES
    DEFPUSHBUTTON  "Ok",        IDOK,            68, 12,  34, 12, TABGRP
    PUSHBUTTON     "Cancel",    IDCANCEL,        68, 26,  34, 12, TABGRP
END

DlgMenu MENU
BEGIN
    POPUP "&Viewport"
    BEGIN
```

```
        MENUITEM        "O&n",          IDDLGMENU1A,    CHECKED
        MENUITEM        "O&ff",         IDDLGMENU1B
    END
END


SETUPDLGBOX DIALOG 400, 20, 142, 72
STYLE WS_POPUP | WS_CAPTION
CAPTION "Setup Window and Viewport"
MENU DlgMenu
BEGIN
    CTEXT "Window Org    X:", -1,            2, 04, 64,  8
    EDITTEXT                  IDWINORGX,   68, 02, 30, 12, TABGRP
    CTEXT "Y:",               -1,         100, 04,  8,  8
    EDITTEXT                  IDWINORGY, 110, 02, 30, 12, TABGRP
    CTEXT "Window Ext    X:", -1,            2, 18, 64,  8
    EDITTEXT                  IDWINEXTX,   68, 16, 30, 12, TABGRP
    CTEXT "Y:",               -1,         100, 18,  8,  8
    EDITTEXT                  IDWINEXTY, 110, 16, 30, 12, TABGRP
    CTEXT "Viewport Org  X:", -1,            2, 32, 64,  8
    EDITTEXT                  IDVIEWORGX, 68, 30, 30, 12, TABGRP
    CTEXT "Y:",               -1,         100, 32,  8,  8
    EDITTEXT                  IDVIEWORGY,110, 30, 30, 12, TABGRP
    CTEXT "Viewport Ext  X:", -1,            2, 46, 64,  8
    EDITTEXT                  IDVIEWEXTX, 68, 44, 30, 12, TABGRP
    CTEXT "Y:",               -1,         100, 46,  8,  8
    EDITTEXT                  IDVIEWEXTY,110, 44, 30, 12, TABGRP
    DEFPUSHBUTTON "Ok",       IDOK,         68, 58, 30, 12, TABGRP
    PUSHBUTTON    "Cancel",   IDCANCEL,   110, 58, 30, 12, TABGRP
END
/*-------------------------------------------------------------------*/
/* End of file:  PGM4.RC                                             */
/*********************************************************************/
```

7.5 THE C-LANGUAGE SOURCE FILE: PGM4.C

```
/*********************************************************************/
/* Filename:     PGM4.C                                              */
/*                                                                   */
/* Description:  PGM4.EXE source code                                */
/*-------------------------------------------------------------------*/

#include "windows.h"
#include "pgm4.h"

  BOOL                  SetupDlgBoxFlag = TRUE;
  BOOL                  SetupDlgBoxUp = FALSE;
  HWND                  SetupDlgBoxhWnd;
  int                   i;
  char                  szTemp[16];
  char                  szString[64];
  char                  szstringA[16];
  char                  szstringB[16];
  char                  szstringC[17];
  char                  szMMode[CSTR+1][16];

  HANDLE                hInst;

  int                   option          = 0;
  int                   prevOption      = 0;
```

```
  FARPROC               lpprocCoordsDlgBox;
  FARPROC               lpprocMapModeDlg;
  FARPROC               lpprocSetupDlgBox;

  int                   iSel                    = 6;            /* text */
  int                   mapMode                 = MM_TEXT;

  POINT                 Points[4] = {200, 50, 600, 200, 200, 150, 500, 200};
  RECT                  myRect;

  int                   WinOrgX         = 0;
  int                   WinOrgY         = 0;
  int                   WinExtX         = 640;
  int                   WinExtY         = 200;
  int                   ViewOrgX        = 0;
  int                   ViewOrgY        = 0;
  int                   ViewExtX        = 640;
  int                   ViewExtY        = 200;

  long FAR PASCAL       MainWndProc (HWND, unsigned, WORD, LONG);

typedef BOOL FAR * LPBOOL;

BOOL FAR PASCAL MapModeDlgProc (hWnd, msg, wParam, lParam)
  HWND                  hWnd;
  unsigned              msg;
  WORD                  wParam;
  LONG                  lParam;
  {
  char                  szTemp[16];
  switch (msg)
    {
    case WM_INITDIALOG:
      for (i=0; i<= CSTR; i++)
        SendDlgItemMessage (hWnd, IDSMAPMODEBOX, LB_ADDSTRING, 0,
                                           (LONG)(LPSTR)szMMode[i]);
      SendDlgItemMessage (hWnd, IDSMAPMODEBOX, LB_SETCURSEL, iSel, 0L);
      return TRUE;

    case WM_COMMAND:
      switch (wParam)
        {
        case IDOK:
          iSel =  SendDlgItemMessage (hWnd, IDSMAPMODEBOX,
                                           LB_GETCURSEL, 0, 0L);
          switch (iSel)
            {
            case 0:
              mapMode = MM_ANISOTROPIC;
              break;

            case 1:
              mapMode = MM_HIENGLISH;
              break;

            case 2:
              mapMode = MM_HIMETRIC;
              break;

            case 3:
              mapMode = MM_ISOTROPIC;
              break;
```

```
            case 4:
              mapMode = MM_LOENGLISH;
              break;

            case 5:
              mapMode = MM_LOMETRIC;
              break;

            case 6:
              mapMode = MM_TEXT;
              break;

            case 7:
              mapMode = MM_TWIPS;
              break;
            }

          EndDialog(hWnd, TRUE);
          break;

        case IDCANCEL:
          EndDialog(hWnd, FALSE);
          break;
        }
      break;  /* end of WM_COMMAND */

    default:
        return FALSE;
    }
  return TRUE;
  }


BOOL FAR PASCAL SetupDlgBoxProc (hWnd, msg, wParam, lParam)
  HWND                   hWnd;
  unsigned               msg;
  WORD                   wParam;
  LONG                   lParam;
  {
  int                    TempWinOrgX,          TempWinOrgY;
  int                    TempWinExtX,          TempWinExtY;
  int                    TempViewOrgX,         TempViewOrgY;
  int                    TempViewExtX,         TempViewExtY;

  BOOL                   fValOK;
  BOOL                   fValOKsum;

  SetupDlgBoxhWnd = hWnd;
  switch (msg)
    {
    case WM_INITDIALOG:
      SetupDlgBoxUp = TRUE;
      SetDlgItemInt (hWnd, IDWINORGX,  WinOrgX,  TRUE);
      SetDlgItemInt (hWnd, IDWINORGY,  WinOrgY,  TRUE);
      SetDlgItemInt (hWnd, IDWINEXTX,  WinExtX,  TRUE);
      SetDlgItemInt (hWnd, IDWINEXTY,  WinExtY,  TRUE);
      if (SetupDlgBoxFlag)
        {
        SetDlgItemInt (hWnd, IDVIEWORGX, myRect.left, TRUE);
        SetDlgItemInt (hWnd, IDVIEWORGY, myRect.top, TRUE);
        SetDlgItemInt (hWnd, IDVIEWEXTX, myRect.right, TRUE);
        SetDlgItemInt (hWnd, IDVIEWEXTY, myRect.bottom, TRUE);
        }
```

```
  else
    {
    SetDlgItemInt (hWnd, IDVIEWORGX, ViewOrgX, TRUE);
    SetDlgItemInt (hWnd, IDVIEWORGY, ViewOrgY, TRUE);
    SetDlgItemInt (hWnd, IDVIEWEXTX, ViewExtX, TRUE);
    SetDlgItemInt (hWnd, IDVIEWEXTY, ViewExtY, TRUE);
    }
  break;

case WM_INITMENU:
  {
  HMENU     hMenu = GetMenu (hWnd);
  CheckMenuItem (hMenu, IDDLGMENU1A,
                    SetupDlgBoxFlag ? MF_CHECKED : MF_UNCHECKED);
  CheckMenuItem (hMenu, IDDLGMENU1B,
                    SetupDlgBoxFlag ? MF_UNCHECKED : MF_CHECKED);
  break;
  }

case WM_COMMAND:
  switch (wParam)
    {
    case IDOK:
      fValOKsum = FALSE;
      TempWinOrgX = GetDlgItemInt(hWnd,IDWINORGX,  (LPBOOL)&fValOK,TRUE);
      fValOKsum  |= ((fValOK==TRUE) ? 0 : 1);
      TempWinOrgY = GetDlgItemInt(hWnd,IDWINORGY,  (LPBOOL)&fValOK,TRUE);
      fValOKsum  |= ((fValOK==TRUE) ? 0 : 1);
      TempWinExtX = GetDlgItemInt(hWnd,IDWINEXTX,  (LPBOOL)&fValOK,TRUE);
      fValOKsum  |= ((fValOK==TRUE) ? 0 : 1);
      TempWinExtY = GetDlgItemInt(hWnd,IDWINEXTY,  (LPBOOL)&fValOK,TRUE);
      fValOKsum  |= ((fValOK==TRUE) ? 0 : 1);
      TempViewOrgX =GetDlgItemInt(hWnd,IDVIEWORGX,(LPBOOL)&fValOK,TRUE);
      fValOKsum  |= ((fValOK==TRUE) ? 0 : 1);
      TempViewOrgY =GetDlgItemInt(hWnd,IDVIEWORGY,(LPBOOL)&fValOK,TRUE);
      fValOKsum  |= ((fValOK==TRUE) ? 0 : 1);
      TempViewExtX =GetDlgItemInt(hWnd,IDVIEWEXTX,(LPBOOL)&fValOK,TRUE);
      fValOKsum  |= ((fValOK==TRUE) ? 0 : 1);
      TempViewExtY =GetDlgItemInt(hWnd,IDVIEWEXTY,(LPBOOL)&fValOK,TRUE);
      fValOKsum  |= ((fValOK==TRUE) ? 0 : 1);

      if (fValOKsum)
        {
        MessageBeep(0);
        break;
        }

      WinOrgX  = TempWinOrgX;
      WinOrgY  = TempWinOrgY;
      WinExtX  = TempWinExtX;
      WinExtY  = TempWinExtY;
      ViewOrgX = TempViewOrgX;
      ViewOrgY = TempViewOrgY;
      ViewExtX = TempViewExtX;
      ViewExtY = TempViewExtY;

      EndDialog(hWnd, TRUE);
      break;

    case IDCANCEL:
      EndDialog(hWnd, FALSE);
      break;
```

```
        case IDDLGMENU1A:
          SetupDlgBoxFlag = TRUE;                /* fall thru */

        case IDDSIZEMSG:
          SetDlgItemInt (hWnd, IDVIEWORGX, myRect.left, TRUE);
          SetDlgItemInt (hWnd, IDVIEWORGY, myRect.top, TRUE);
          SetDlgItemInt (hWnd, IDVIEWEXTX, myRect.right, TRUE);
          SetDlgItemInt (hWnd, IDVIEWEXTY, myRect.bottom, TRUE);
          break;

        case IDDLGMENU1B:
          SetupDlgBoxFlag = FALSE;
          break;
        }
      break;

    case WM_DESTROY:
      SetupDlgBoxUp = FALSE;
      break;

    default:
      return FALSE;
    }
  return TRUE;
  }

BOOL FAR PASCAL CoordsDlgBoxProc (hWnd, msg, wParam, lParam)
  HWND          hWnd;
  unsigned      msg;
  WORD          wParam;
  LONG          lParam;
  {
  int           TempX1,          TempY1,          TempX3,          TempY3;
  int           TempX2,          TempY2,          TempX4,          TempY4;

  BOOL          fValOK;
  BOOL          fValOKsum;

  switch (msg)
    {
    case WM_INITDIALOG:
      switch (option)
        {
        case IDDPOLYLINE:
        case IDDARC:
        case IDDPIE:
          SetDlgItemInt(hWnd, IDDX3, Points[3].x, TRUE);
          SetDlgItemInt(hWnd, IDDY3, Points[3].y, TRUE);
        case IDDPOLYGON:
        case IDDROUNDRECT:
          SetDlgItemInt(hWnd, IDDX2, Points[2].x, TRUE);
          SetDlgItemInt(hWnd, IDDY2, Points[2].y, TRUE);
        case IDDLINE:
        case IDDRECTANGLE:
        case IDDELLIPSE:
          SetDlgItemInt(hWnd, IDDX1, Points[1].x, TRUE);
          SetDlgItemInt(hWnd, IDDY1, Points[1].y, TRUE);
          SetDlgItemInt(hWnd, IDDX0, Points[0].x, TRUE);
          SetDlgItemInt(hWnd, IDDY0, Points[0].y, TRUE);
        }
        break;
```

```
case WM_COMMAND:
  switch (wParam)
    {
    case IDOK:
      fValOKsum = FALSE;
      switch (option)
        {
        case IDDPOLYLINE:
        case IDDARC:
        case IDDPIE:
          TempX4 = GetDlgItemInt(hWnd, IDDX3, (LPBOOL)&fValOK, TRUE);
          fValOKsum |= ((fValOK==TRUE) ? 0 : 1);
          TempY4 = GetDlgItemInt(hWnd, IDDY3, (LPBOOL)&fValOK, TRUE);
          fValOKsum |= ((fValOK==TRUE) ? 0 : 1);
        case IDDPOLYGON:
        case IDDROUNDRECT:
          TempX3 = GetDlgItemInt(hWnd, IDDX2, (LPBOOL)&fValOK, TRUE);
          fValOKsum |= ((fValOK==TRUE) ? 0 : 1);
          TempY3 = GetDlgItemInt(hWnd, IDDY2, (LPBOOL)&fValOK, TRUE);
          fValOKsum |= ((fValOK==TRUE) ? 0 : 1);
        case IDDLINE:
        case IDDRECTANGLE:
        case IDDELLIPSE:
          TempX2 = GetDlgItemInt(hWnd, IDDX1, (LPBOOL)&fValOK, TRUE);
          fValOKsum |= ((fValOK==TRUE) ? 0 : 1);
          TempY2 = GetDlgItemInt(hWnd, IDDY1, (LPBOOL)&fValOK, TRUE);
          fValOKsum |= ((fValOK==TRUE) ? 0 : 1);
          TempX1 = GetDlgItemInt(hWnd, IDDX0, (LPBOOL)&fValOK, TRUE);
          fValOKsum |= ((fValOK==TRUE) ? 0 : 1);
          TempY1 = GetDlgItemInt(hWnd, IDDY0, (LPBOOL)&fValOK, TRUE);
          fValOKsum |= ((fValOK==TRUE) ? 0 : 1);
        }
      if (fValOKsum)
        {
        MessageBeep(0);
        break;
        }

      switch (option)
        {
        case IDDPOLYLINE:
        case IDDARC:
        case IDDPIE:
          Points[3].x = TempX4;
          Points[3].y = TempY4;
        case IDDPOLYGON:
        case IDDROUNDRECT:
          Points[2].x = TempX3;
          Points[2].y = TempY3;
        case IDDLINE:
        case IDDRECTANGLE:
        case IDDELLIPSE:
          Points[1].x = TempX2;
          Points[1].y = TempY2;
          Points[0].x = TempX1;
          Points[0].y = TempY1;
        }
      EndDialog(hWnd, TRUE);
      break;

    case IDCANCEL:
      option = 0;
      EndDialog(hWnd, FALSE);
      break;
```

```
      }
      break;

    default:
      return FALSE;
    }
  return TRUE;
  }

paintProc (hDC)
  HDC                   hDC;
  {
  HPEN                  hPenOld;
  HBRUSH                hBrushOld;

  SetMapMode (hDC, mapMode);
  if ((mapMode == MM_ISOTROPIC)
   || (mapMode == MM_ANISOTROPIC))
    {
    SetWindowOrg (hDC, WinOrgX, WinOrgY);
    SetWindowExt (hDC, WinExtX, WinExtY);
    SetViewportOrg (hDC, ViewOrgX, ViewOrgY);
    SetViewportExt (hDC, ViewExtX, ViewExtY);
    }

  hPenOld = SelectObject (hDC, GetStockObject (BLACK_PEN));
  hBrushOld = SelectObject (hDC, GetStockObject(NULL_BRUSH));
  switch (option)
    {
    case IDDLINE:
      MoveTo (hDC, Points[0].x, Points[0].y);
      LineTo (hDC, Points[1].x, Points[1].y);
      break;

    case IDDPOLYLINE:
      Polyline (hDC, (LPPOINT)Points, 4);
      break;

    case IDDRECTANGLE:
      Rectangle (hDC, Points[0].x, Points[0].y, Points[1].x, Points[1].y);
      break;

    case IDDROUNDRECT:
      RoundRect (hDC, Points[0].x, Points[0].y, Points[1].x, Points[1].y,
                      Points[2].x, Points[2].y);
      break;

    case IDDPOLYGON:
      Polygon (hDC, (LPPOINT)Points, 3);
      break;

    case IDDELLIPSE:
      Ellipse (hDC, Points[0].x, Points[0].y, Points[1].x, Points[1].y);
      break;

    case IDDARC:
      Arc (hDC,Points[0].x, Points[0].y, Points[1].x, Points[1].y,
               Points[2].x, Points[2].y, Points[3].x, Points[3].y);
      break;

    case IDDPIE:
      Pie (hDC, Points[0].x, Points[0].y, Points[1].x, Points[1].y,
                Points[2].x, Points[2].y, Points[3].x, Points[3].y);
      break;
```

```
    }
  SelectObject (hDC, hBrushOld);
  SelectObject (hDC, hPenOld);
  }

BOOL MainInit (hInstance)
  HANDLE              hInstance;
  {
  PWNDCLASS           pMainClass;

  LoadString (hInstance, IDSSTRA, (LPSTR)szstringA, 16);
  LoadString (hInstance, IDSSTRB, (LPSTR)szstringB, 16);
  for (i=0; i<= CSTR; i++)
    LoadString (hInstance, IDSANISOTROPIC+i, (LPSTR)szMMode[i], 16);

  pMainClass = (PWNDCLASS)LocalAlloc (LPTR, sizeof(WNDCLASS));

  pMainClass->hCursor         = LoadCursor (NULL, IDC_ARROW);
  pMainClass->hIcon           = LoadIcon (NULL, IDI_APPLICATION);
  pMainClass->lpszMenuName    = (LPSTR)"MainMenu";
  pMainClass->lpszClassName   = (LPSTR)"mMode";
  pMainClass->hbrBackground   = (HBRUSH)GetStockObject (WHITE_BRUSH);
  pMainClass->hInstance       = hInstance;
  pMainClass->style           = CS_HREDRAW | CS_VREDRAW;
  pMainClass->lpfnWndProc     = MainWndProc;

  if (!RegisterClass((LPWNDCLASS)pMainClass))
    return FALSE;

  LocalFree ((HANDLE)pMainClass);
  return TRUE;
  }

int PASCAL WinMain (hInstance, hPrevInstance, lpszCmdLine, cmdShow)
  HANDLE              hInstance;
  HANDLE              hPrevInstance;
  LPSTR               lpszCmdLine;
  int                 cmdShow;
  {
  MSG                 msg;
  HWND                hWnd;

  if (!hPrevInstance)
    {
    if (!MainInit (hInstance))
      return FALSE;
    }
  else
    {
    GetInstanceData (hPrevInstance, (PSTR)szstringA, 16);
    GetInstanceData (hPrevInstance, (PSTR)szstringB, 16);
    for (i=0; i<= CSTR; i++)
      GetInstanceData (hPrevInstance, (PSTR)szMMode[i], 16);
    }
  hWnd = CreateWindow  ((LPSTR)"mMode", (LPSTR)"", WS_OVERLAPPEDWINDOW,
    GetSystemMetrics (SM_CXSCREEN) / 4, GetSystemMetrics (SM_CYSCREEN) / 4,
    GetSystemMetrics (SM_CXSCREEN) / 2, GetSystemMetrics (SM_CYSCREEN) / 2,
    (HWND)NULL, (HMENU)NULL, (HANDLE)hInstance,  (LPSTR)NULL);
  hInst = hInstance;

  lpprocCoordsDlgBox =MakeProcInstance((FARPROC)CoordsDlgBoxProc,hInstance);
  lpprocMapModeDlg = MakeProcInstance((FARPROC)MapModeDlgProc, hInstance);
  lpprocSetupDlgBox = MakeProcInstance((FARPROC)SetupDlgBoxProc, hInstance);
```

```
  ShowWindow (hWnd, cmdShow);
  UpdateWindow (hWnd);

  while (GetMessage((LPMSG)&msg, NULL, 0, 0))
    {
    TranslateMessage ((LPMSG)&msg);
    DispatchMessage ((LPMSG)&msg);
    }

  FreeProcInstance (lpprocCoordsDlgBox);
  FreeProcInstance (lpprocMapModeDlg);
  FreeProcInstance (lpprocSetupDlgBox);

  return (int)msg.wParam;
  }

long FAR PASCAL MainWndProc (hWnd, msg, wParam, lParam)
  HWND                  hWnd;
  unsigned              msg;
  WORD                  wParam;
  LONG                  lParam;
  {
  switch (msg)
    {
    case WM_CREATE:
      {
      HMENU     hMenu = GetMenu (hWnd);
      EnableMenuItem (hMenu, IDDSETUP, MF_GRAYED);
      SetWindowText (hWnd, (LPSTR)szMMode[iSel]);
      break;
      }

    case WM_DESTROY:
      PostQuitMessage (0);
      break;

    case WM_PAINT:
      {
      PAINTSTRUCT ps;

      BeginPaint (hWnd, (LPPAINTSTRUCT)&ps);
      paintProc (ps.hdc);
      EndPaint (hWnd, (LPPAINTSTRUCT)&ps);
      break;
      }

    case WM_COMMAND:
      {
      switch (wParam)
        {
        case IDDMAPMODE:
          if (DialogBox(hInst, MAKEINTRESOURCE(MAPMODEDLGBOX),
                                            hWnd, lpprocMapModeDlg))
            {
            HMENU       hMenu = GetMenu (hWnd);
            InvalidateRect (hWnd, (LPRECT)NULL, TRUE);
            if ((mapMcde == MM_ISOTROPIC)
             || (mapMode == MM_ANISOTROPIC))
              EnableMenuItem (hMenu, IDDSETUP, MF_ENABLED);
            else
              EnableMenuItem (hMenu, IDDSETUP, MF_GRAYED);
            SetWindowText (hWnd, (LPSTR)szMMode[iSel]);
            DrawMenuBar(hWnd);
            }
          break;
```

```
    case IDDSETUP:
      if (DialogBox(hInst, MAKEINTRESOURCE(SETUPDLGBOX),
                                         hWnd, lpprocSetupDlgBox))
        InvalidateRect (hWnd, (LPRECT)NULL, TRUE);
      break;

    default:
      option = wParam;
      DialogBox(hInst, MAKEINTRESOURCE(COORDSDLGBOX),
                                         hWnd, lpprocCoordsDlgBox);
      InvalidateRect (hWnd, (LPRECT)NULL, TRUE);
      break;
    }
  break;
  }

case WM_SIZE:
  {
  HDC   hDC = GetDC (hWnd);
  SetMapMode(hDC, MM_TEXT);
  SetWindowOrg(hDC, 0, 0);
  SetViewportOrg(hDC, 0, 0);
  ReleaseDC(hWnd, hDC);
  GetClientRect(hWnd, (LPRECT)&myRect);
  if (SetupDlgBoxFlag)
    {
    ViewOrgX = myRect.left;
    ViewOrgY = myRect.top;
    ViewExtX = myRect.right;
    ViewExtY = myRect.bottom;
    if (SetupDlgBoxUp)
      SendMessage (SetupDlgBoxhWnd, WM_COMMAND, IDDSIZEMSG, (LONG)NULL);
    }
  }

case WM_INITMENU:
  {
  HMENU     hMenu = GetMenu (hWnd);
  if (prevOption)
    CheckMenuItem (hMenu, prevOption, MF_UNCHECKED);
  if (option)
    CheckMenuItem (hMenu, (prevOption = option), MF_CHECKED);
  break;
  }

case WM_MOUSEMOVE:
  {
  int       i,      j;
  POINT     point;
  HDC       hDC;
  RECT      Rect;

  if (!(wParam & MK_LBUTTON))
    {
    point   = MAKEPOINT(lParam);            /* click info in lParam */
    hDC = GetDC (hWnd);
    SetMapMode (hDC, mapMode);
    if ((mapMode == MM_ISOTROPIC)
     || (mapMode == MM_ANISOTROPIC))
      {
      SetWindowOrg (hDC, WinOrgX, WinOrgY);
      SetWindowExt (hDC, WinExtX, WinExtY);
      SetViewportOrg (hDC, ViewOrgX, ViewOrgY);
      SetViewportExt (hDC, ViewExtX, ViewExtY);
      }
```

```
        for (i=0; szString[i] = szstringA[i]; i++);       /* "DP: ("      */
        itoa (point.x, szstringC, 10);
        for (j=0; szString[i] = szstringC[j++]; i++);    /* device pt "X"*/
        szString[i++] = ',';
        itoa (point.y, szstringC, 10);
        for (j=0; szString[i] = szstringC[j++]; i++);    /* device pt "Y"*/
        DPtoLP (hDC, (LPPOINT) &point, 1);
        for (j=0; szString[i] = szstringB[j]; i++, j++);/* ")  LP: ("  */
        itoa (point.x, szstringC, 10);
        for (j=0; szString[i] = szstringC[j++]; i++);    /* logical pt "X" */
        szString[i++] = ',';
        itoa (point.y, szstringC, 10);
        for (j=0; szString[i] = szstringC[j++]; i++);    /* locical pt "Y" */
        szString[i++] = ')';
        for (; i<64; i++)
          szString[i] = ' ';
        SetMapMode(hDC, MM_TEXT);
        SetWindowOrg(hDC, 0, 0);
        SetViewportOrg(hDC, 0, 0);
        GetClientRect(hWnd, (LPRECT)&Rect);
        TextOut(hDC, Rect.left+8, Rect.top+8, (LPSTR)szString, 64);
        ReleaseDC(hWnd, hDC);
        }
      break;
      }

    default:
      return DefWindowProc (hWnd, msg, wParam, lParam);
      break;
    }
  return (0L);
  }

/*----------------------------------------------------------------------*/
/* End of file:  PGM4.C                                                 */
/************************************************************************/
```

7.5.1 Additions to MainWndProc

Windows sends the message **WM_CREATE** when the **CreateWindow** function is called. The window has not been made visible when this message is received, thereby allowing the application to do any initialization it requires.

```
case WM_CREATE:
{
HMENU hMenu = GetMenu (hWnd);
EnableMenuItem (hMenu, IDDSETUP, MF_GRAYED);
SetWindowText (hWnd, (LPSTR)szMMode[iSel]);
break;
}
```

You have seen examples of the first two lines in previous chapters. They get a handle to the menu and gray the menu item **IDDSETUP**.

The third statement, **SetWindowText**, is new. It sets the window's title to the string pointed to by **szMMode[iSel]**. When PGM4 begins, **iSel** equals 6, which, when used as an index into the array of strings **szMMode**, points to "Text". (**szMMode** was loaded by **WinMain**.) Thus, the string "Text" is placed in the title bar.

```
case WM_MOUSEMOVE:
  {
  POINT    point;
  HDC      hDC;
  if (!(wParam & MK_LBUTTON))
    {
    point = MAKEPOINT(lParam);
    hDC = GetDC (hWnd);
    SetMapMode (hDC, mapMode);
    if ((mapMode == MM_ISOTROPIC)
      || (mapMode == MM_ANISOTROPIC))
      {
      SetWindowOrg (hDC, WinOrgX, WinOrgY);
      SetWindowExt (hDC, WinExtX, WinExtY);
      SetViewportOrg (hDC, ViewOrgX, ViewOrgY);
      SetViewportExt (hDC, ViewExtX, ViewExtY);
      }
      ...
     DPtoLP (hDC, (LPPOINT) &point, 1);
      ...
       SetMapMode(hDC, MM_TEXT);
       TextOut(hDC, 10, 10, (LPSTR)szString, 64);
       ReleaseDC(hWnd, hDC);
       }
       break;
       }
```

Windows sends a **WM_MOUSEMOVE** message whenever the user moves the mouse. Various bits of **wParam** will be set if corresponding virtual keys are down. The flags are:

MK_LBUTTON	Left button is down
MK_MBUTTON	Middle button is down
MK_RBUTTON	Right button is down
MK_SHIFT	Shift key is down
MK_CONTROL	Control key is down

lParam contains the mouse's X and Y coordinates relative to the window's upper left corner. The low word contains X; the high word contains Y. The MAKEPOINT macro is used to convert **lParam** into a POINT. POINT is a simple data structure, and is defined in WINDOWS.H:

```
typedef struct {
  int x;
  int y;
  } POINT;
```

After securing the mouse point, we need to get a DC (display context). For **WM_PAINT**, the **BeginPaint** function does it for us, as you've seen in Chapter 4. Here, we are on our own, so we must do it by using the **GetDC** function. **GetDC** returns with a number of default attributes; among them is the current mapping mode, which is set to **MM_TEXT**. To use the conversion function **DPtoLP** (converts display point to logical point), we need to set the current map mode and, if applicable, the window and viewport origins and extents.

SetMapMode sets the mapping mode for the specified display context **hDC. SetWindowOrg** and **SetWindowExt** set the window origin and extents for the specified DC. **SetViewportOrg** and **SetViewportExt** set the viewport origin and extents for the specified DC. The window and viewport functions are meaningless in modes other than ANISOTROPIC and ISOTROPIC.

DPtoLP converts device points into logical points and depends on the mapping mode of the specified DC. The second parameter is a long pointer to an array of points to be converted. The third parameter specifies the array size.

The second **SetMapMode** statement allows us to output the text at the same place no matter which mapping mode is used for drawing the geometric figures.

Finally, we are through with the DC, so we return it to Windows using the **ReleaseDC** function.

WM_COMMAND is called whenever the user selects one of the command line items. We switch on **wParam** to trap **IDDMAPMODE** and **IDDSETUP**. Other than that, we don't care which menu item was selected because we're going to perform the following tasks for all items:

1. Save **wParam** (the selected menu item resource ID such as **IDDLINE** or **IDDPOLYGON**).
2. Display a dialog box and get coordinates for the selected object.
3. Force a repainting of the window.

To perform these tasks, we use the following lines:

```
default:
  option = wParam;
  DialogBox (hInst, MAKEINTRESOURCE(COORDSDLGBOX),
                                  hWnd, lpprocCoordsDlgBox);
  InvalidateRect (hWnd, (LPRECT)NULL, TRUE);
  break;
```

Note that **DialogBox** specifies **lpprocCoordsDlgBox** to be used as the dialog function. Later on you'll see how that function uses the global variable **option.**

InvalidateRect queues a request to repaint our window. The parameters NULL and TRUE indicate that we want the entire window erased, then repainted. Eventually, the following events will occur:

1. Processing of the **WM_COMMAND** message will return to Windows (via **break;**).
2. Windows will return to the **DispatchMessage** function in **WinMain**.
3. **WinMain** will continue in the **while** loop with **GetMessage**.
4. **GetMessage** will get the paint message posted by **InvalidateRect.**
5. **DispatchMessage** will send a **WM_PAINT** message to **MainWndProc.**
6. **MainWndProc** will switch to case **WM_PAINT:** for processing.

The two cases we specifically test for in **WM_COMMAND** are **IDDMAPMODE** and **IDDSETUP. IDDMAPMODE** is responsible for putting up a dialog box to let the user specify a map mode. **IDDSETUP** is the dialog box that gets the parameters for setting the window and viewport origins and extents.

We start off with the conditional

```
case IDDMAPMODE:
  if (DialogBox(...) {
```

which can be translated into "If the user selected a map mode. . ."

You'll see how the TRUE/FALSE return gets set from the dialog box call when we examine the **MapModeDlgProc** function. If the call returns true, the global variable **mapMode** will contain the selected mapping mode. We have seen all the functions in the **IDDMAPMODE** case with the exception of one. The logic is:

1. Force Windows to repaint the client area.
2. If map mode is ISOTROPIC or ANISOTROPIC, enable the menu option **IDDSETUP**, else disable the option. This is done because the window and viewport origin and extent functions are meaningless in anything other than those two mapping modes.
3. Set the title bar to the current map mode.
4. Redraw the menu bar, using the new function:

   ```
   DrawMenuBar (hWnd);
   ```

DrawMenuBar (hWnd) simply directs Windows to redraw the menu bar. Windows doesn't automatically update the menu bar as a result of the **EnableMenuItem** call, so we must do it manually.

The final case **WM_COMMAND** must process is **IDDSETUP**. This logic puts up a dialog box, then forces Windows to repaint the client area of our window. The dialog box is responsible for getting specific information about the window and viewport origin and extent. We'll examine the **SetupDlgBoxProc** shortly.

7.5.2 Drawing Geometric Shapes: paintProc

PGM1.C first presented the Windows message **WM_PAINT**. We receive this message whenever the window needs to be repainted. In response, we make the required **BeginPaint** and **EndPaint** calls. Between the two, we call **paintProc**, PGM4's internal procedure that is responsible for drawing the geometric shapes.

```
case WM_PAINT:
     {
     PAINTSTRUCT ps;

     BeginPaint (hWnd, (LPPAINTSTRUCT)&ps);
     paintProc (ps.hdc);
     EndPaint (hWnd, (LPPAINTSTRUCT)&ps);
     break;
     }
```

Recall from PGM1 that **BeginPaint** prepares the window (specified by **hWnd**) for painting by filling in the **PAINTSTRUCT, ps. PAINTSTRUCT** is formally defined in WINDOWS.H. We will pass to **paintProc** the value of **hDC**, the display context. (**paintProc** was not placed in the **WM_PAINT** in-line code in order to keep **MainWndProc** from getting too large for the compiler's post-optimizer).

```
paintProc (hDC)
  {
  HDC hDC;
```

Following the formal function declaration are two variable definitions and two statements:

```
HPEN     hPenOld;
HBRUSH   hBrushOld;

hPenOld = SelectObject (hDC, GetStockObject
                                        (BLACK_PEN));
hBrushOld = SelectObject (hDC, GetStockObject
                                        (NULL_BRUSH));
```

HPEN and **HBRUSH** define the storage locations for the handles returned by the **SelectObject** function. **GetStockObject** returns a handle for a predefined object. In our case, we want a black pen and a null (invisible) brush. **SelectObject** associates a display context and an object handle. Thus, the first statement associates our display context (DC) and the stock object black pen handle that was returned by

GetStockObject. Returned is the handle to the old object; we will save this for later.

A DC can have several objects selected at one time, but only one from each type: pen, brush, font, bitmap, and region. In our example, we select a pen and a brush.

To set the current map mode, we use the Windows function:

```
SetMapMode (hDC, mapMode);
```

hDC is the display context handle (assigned by **BeginPaint** and passed to **paintProc**). **mapMode** is the current mapping mode and equals **MM_TEXT** when the program begins.

If the mapping mode is **MM_ISOTROPIC** or **MM_ANISOTROPIC**, we will need to set the window and viewport origins and extents. To do so, we use the following four functions:

```
SetWindowOrg (hDC, WinOrgX, WinOrgY);
SetWindowExt (hDC, WinExtX, WinExtY);
SetViewportOrg (hDC, ViewOrgX, ViewOrgY);
SetViewportExt (hDC, ViewExtX, ViewExtY);
```

These functions do exactly what they sound like they do: they set the window and viewport origins and extents. The calling order of the above functions is very important in **MM_ISOTROPIC** mode. The viewport is adjusted so that the window can fit inside of it.

When you call **SetWindowExt** first, the old viewport is adjusted to meet the condition. Then, a call to **SetViewportExt** adjusts the new viewport to meet the condition and thereby cancels the first adjustment. Therefore, when in **MM_ISOTROPIC** mode, you should call **SetWindowExt** before calling **SetViewportExt**.

Recall in **WM_COMMAND** we saved **wParam**, the menu item selected by the user, in **option**. We are now going to branch on it:

```
switch (option)
```

Our first **case** is:

```
case IDDLINE:
  MoveTo (hDC, Points[0].x, Points[0].y);
  LineTo (hDC, Points[1].x, Points[1].y);
  break;
```

These two functions simply move to a point and draw a line from there to some other point.

```
case IDDPOLYLINE:
  Polyline (hDC, (LPPOINT)Points, 4);
  break;
```

Polyline draws a number of lines from one to another. Passed to the function is an array of points and the number of points in that array. **Polyline** moves to the first point and draws lines from point to point. The above statement could be reproduced using the following function calls:

```
MoveTo (hDC, Points[0].x, Points[0].y);
LineTo (hDC, Points[1].x, Points[1].y);
LineTo (hDC, Points[2].x, Points[2].y);
LineTo (hDC, Points[3].x, Points[3].y);
```

The next **case** is:

```
case IDDRECTANGLE:
  Rectangle (hDC, Points[0].x, Points[0].y,
                        Points[1].x, Points[1].y);
  break;
```

Rectangle simply draws a rectangle using the two specified points as opposite corners.

```
case IDDROUNDRECT:
  RoundRect (hDC, Points[0].x, Points[0].y,
                    Points[1].x, Points[1].y,
                    Points[2].x, Points[2].y);
  break;
```

RoundRect is similar to **Rectangle**, except that the last argument specifies how much of the line to round off.

```
case IDDPOLYGON:
  Polygon (hDC, (LPPOINT)Points, 3);
  break;
```

Polygon is similar to **Polyline**, except that the last point and the first point are connected. Thus, the figure drawn by the above function call could also be drawn with:

```
MoveTo (hDC, Points[0].x, Points[0].y);
LineTo (hDC, Points[1].x, Points[1].y);
LineTo (hDC, Points[2].x, Points[2].y);
LineTo (hDC, Points[0].x, Points[0].y);
```

The next **case** is:

```
case IDDELLIPSE:
  Ellipse (hDC, Points[0].x, Points[0].y,
                        Points[1].x, Points[1].y);
  break;
```

Ellipse draws an ellipse using the specified points as a bounding rectangle.

```
case IDDARC:
  Arc (hDC, Points[0].x, Points[0].y,
                Points[1].x, Points[1].y,
                Points[2].x, Points[2].y,
                Points[3].x, Points[3].y);
  break;
```

Arc draws an elliptical arc. The center of the arc is the center of the bounding rectangle specified by the first two points. The third point specifies where the arc starts; the fourth point specifies where the arc ends.

```
case IDDPIE:
  Pie (hDC, Points[0].x, Points[0].y,
                Points[1].x, Points[1].y,
                Points[2].x, Points[2].y,
                Points[3].x, Points[3].y);
  break;
```

Pie is similar to **Arc** except that the ends of the arc and the center are connected by lines, creating a pie shape.

```
SelectObject (hDC, hBrushOld);
SelectObject (hDC, hPenOld);
```

Earlier, when we selected our pen and brush, we saved the old pen and old brush handle. This is *extremely* important. The act of selection "locks" an item (pen or brush) into a memory address. It also "unlocks" the previous selection. When we are done, we need to unlock our objects so they can move about in memory; thereby not creating any memory "roadblocks." This completes **paintProc**. Control returns to **WM_PAINT** where **EndPaint** will be called to complete paint processing.

7.5.3 Fetching Coordinates: CoordsDlgBoxProc

CoordsDlgBoxProc is called by the default logic of **MainWndProc WM_COMMAND**. This procedure is responsible for fetching the coordinates of the various points for whatever geometric object was selected from the "Pick" menu.

7.5.4 Trapping WM_INITDIALOG

Before our dialog box is displayed, we want to do a little preprocessing. To do so, we need to trap the **WM_INITDIALOG** message. Recall that before calling the **DialogBox** function, we saved **wParam** in **option** where **wParam** was the ID of the selected "Pick" menu item. We are now going to use that information:

```
switch (option) {
```

Our cases will, of course, be the menu item IDs such as **IDDPOLYLINE, IDDROUNDRECT** or **IDDELLIPSE**. Three of the geometric shapes use four points, two use three points, and three use two points. We can set up the logic such that the four-point figures can fall into the three-point logic, and the three-point figures can fall into the two-point logic.

The statement

```
SetDlgItemInt (hWnd, IDDX0, Points[0].x, TRUE);
```

sets an integer value into a dialog item. TRUE indicates the integer is signed. Thus, the EDITTEXT field

```
EDITTEXT      IDDX0, 12,2,28,12, WS_TABSTOP | WS_GROUP
```

will have a default value when the dialog box is displayed.

7.5.5 Setting Up Temporary Variables for Dialog Boxes

Because all users make mistakes—such as typing a letter instead of a number—and because users may choose to cancel instead of carrying out the operations specified in a dialog box, we must set up some temporary variables to work in.

Upon receipt of "Ok," we will examine each of the EDITTEXT fields for valid integer values with the Windows function **GetDlgItemInt:**

```
TempX4 = GetDlgItemInt (hWnd, IDDX3,
                         (LPBOOL)&fValOK, TRUE);
```

This function fetches the signed (TRUE) integer from the field **IDDX3** and places a Boolean value in **fValOK**. If **fValOK** is true, the returned value that is stored in **TempX4** contains a valid number.

Once all the values are collected, a test is done on the summation of all the **fValOK** responses to see if any invalid numbers were retrieved. If so, the speaker beeps and control is returned to the dialog box for further input. If all is okay, the temporary variables are committed to the global variables for use by **paintProc.**

7.5.6 Selecting a Mapping Mode: MapModeDlgProc

MapModeDlgProc is called by the **IDDMAPMODE** logic of **MainWndProc WM_COMMAND**. This procedure allows the user to select a mapping mode from a list box.

7.5.7 Using WM_INITDIALOG

Before the dialog box is displayed, we want to initialize the list box with the names of the various mapping modes:

```
for (i=0; i<=CSTR; i++)
SendDlgItemMessage (hWnd, IDSMAPMODEBOX, LB_ADDSTRING,
                              0, LONG)(LPSTR)szMMode[i]);
```

We want to copy all eight strings into the list box. The **SendDlgItemMessage** function sends to **IDSMAPMODEBOX** the string pointed to by **szMMode[i]**. **LB_ADDSTRING** is the subcommand that instructs **SendDlgItemMessage** to add this string to the list box. The **0** is simply a placeholder for an unused parameter.

```
SendDlgItemMessage (hWnd, IDSMAPMODEBOX, LB_SETCURSEL,
                                          iSel, 0L);
```

This variation sends the subcommand **LB_SETCURSEL**, which sets the current selection. The arguments are the list box name and **iSel**, the current selection value. The long zero is simply a placeholder.

7.5.8 Checking List Box Selections

PGM4 traps only "Ok" and "Cancel". If the user selects "Ok," then we'll need to ask Windows what the user selected from the list box. (Isn't this great? Windows does all the dirty work for us!)

```
iSel = SendDlgItemMessage (hWnd, IDSMAPMODEBOX,
                           LB_GETCURSEL, 0, 0L);
```

This is just the opposite of **LB_SETCURSEL**; it gets the current selection and we place that value into our global variable **iSel**.

We now want to switch on **iSel** to translate the list box index value (0–7) to a Windows map mode value as defined in WINDOWS.H.

```
switch (iSel)
  {
  case 0:
    mapMode = MM_ANISOTROPIC;
    break;
  case 1:
    ...
  }
```

If the user selects "Ok," we'll end the dialog with TRUE so that the **MainWndProc WM_COMMAND IDDMAPMODE** logic can go about its business of changing the title line, graying the menu line, and so on:

```
EndDialog (hWnd, TRUE);
break;
```

If the user selects "Cancel," we'll return FALSE to avert the logic described above:

```
case IDCANCEL:
EndDialog (hWnd, FALSE);
break;
```

7.5.9 Specifying Window and Viewport Origins and Extents: SetupDlgBoxProc

SetupDlgBoxProc is called by the **IDDSETUP** logic of **MainWndProc WM_COMMAND**. This procedure allows the user to specify exactly what the window and viewport origins and extents are. Note that this logic can be invoked only if the mapping mode is ISOTROPIC or ANISOTROPIC because the menu will be grayed if one of these modes is not selected (one cannot select a grayed item).

At this point, we must take into consideration what might be going on in other parts of the Windows environment. Just because we have a dialog box up doesn't mean that someone cannot be using another part of the screen in another window (ours may not be the only window displayed). It is possible for our window to be resized while our dialog box is up: for example, if the user changes the size of another window, our window will be automatically resized. This implies that the default values for the viewport origin and extent can change (the default values contain the physical size of our window's client area).

So, we want to do this: if our window's size changes while this dialog box is being displayed, we want to send our dialog box logic (the **SetupDlgBoxProc**) a message saying that the main window has been resized and requesting the new size of the client area. Therefore, we begin our procedure with the statements:

```
SetupDlgBoxhWnd = hWnd;
switch (msg) {
case WM_INITDIALOG:
SetupDlgBoxUp = TRUE;
```

This establishes the two global variables **SetupDlgBoxhWnd** and **SetupDlgBoxUp**. When our main window is resized, **MainWndProc** case **WM_SIZE** computes the size of the new client area; if this dialog box is up, it sends a message to the **SetupDlgBoxProc** procedure:

```
SendMessage(SetupDlgBoxhWnd, WM_COMMAND, IDDSIZEMSG,
                                          (LONG)NULL);
```

The parameters are of the form (**hWnd**, message, **wParam, lParam**). The window handle (**hWnd**) is our global variable **SetupDlgBoxhWnd**, the window handle from the dialog box procedure. *message* is the message we want to send: **WM_COMMAND. wParam** is what **WM_COMMAND** switches on, so we send it **IDDSIZEMSG**, indicating that a window has changed size.

Soon we'll examine the size logic for both **MainWndProc** and **SetupDlgBoxProc**. First, let's go back to the dialog box's initialization code.

We have already looked at the first line, so let's examine the next one:

```
SendDlgItemInt (hWnd, IDWINORGX, WinOrgX, TRUE);
```

This statement is just like the one we used in **CoordsDlgBoxProc**. It sets a dialog box field to a value. Specifically, it sets the field named **IDWINORGX** to the integer (TRUE) value **WinOrgX**.

If we want automatic sizing of the viewport (**SetupDlgBoxFlag** = TRUE) the first group of **SetDlgItemInt** statements is used; otherwise, the second group is executed.

As always, **WM_INITMENU** is called whenever the user selects a menu item. This little piece of code simply checks the current selection.

Just like **CoordsDlgBoxProc**, this dialog box has only two pushbuttons, "Ok" and "Cancel." If "Ok" is chosen, we need to read the EDITTEXT fields and save the values in temporary storage. If all values are valid, we commit them to working global variables and end the dialog, otherwise we "break."

Now, let's tidy up this sizing business. If the window gets sized, Windows sends **MainWndProc** a **WM_SIZE** message. In turn, we compute the size (in pixels—remember **MM_TEXT** uses pixels) of our new client area. To get the client area size, we use the Windows function:

```
GetClientRect (hWnd, (LPRECT)&myRect);
```

This function fills in the structure pointed to by the second parameter with the client rectangle size.

If the **SETUPDLGBOX Viewport** menu selection is set to "On" (automatic setting of the viewport—**SetupDlgBoxFlag** = TRUE), then we'll commit the new values to global variables. Furthermore, if the dialog box is currently being displayed (**SetupDlgBoxUp** = TRUE), then we want to **SendMessage** to **SetupDlgBoxProc** so that it knows about the sizing event.

Finally, upon receipt of the sizing message, **SetupDlgBoxProc WM_COMMAND IDDSIZEMSG** sets the new values of the viewport origin and extent to the EDITTEXT fields.

7.6 THE MODULE DEFINITION FILE: PGM4.DEF

```
;*************************************************************:
; Filename:     PGM4.DEF                                      :
;                                                             :
; Description:  Link definition file                          :
;-------------------------------------------------------------:
NAME    PGM4

DESCRIPTION 'Sample program 4'

STUB    '..\WINSTUB.EXE'

CODE    MOVEABLE
DATA    MOVEABLE MULTIPLE

HEAPSIZE  128
STACKSIZE 4096

EXPORTS
    MainWndProc          @1
    CoordsDlgBoxProc     @2
    MapModeDlgProc       @3
    SetupDlgBoxProc      @4

;-------------------------------------------------------------:
; End of file:  PGM4.DEF                                      :
;*************************************************************:
```

7.7 THE MAKE FILE: PGM4.

```
#*********************************************************************#
# Filename:     PGM4.                                                 #
#                                                                     #
# Description:  PGM4.EXE "MAKE" description file                      #
#---------------------------------------------------------------------#

pgm4.obj: pgm4.c pgm4.h
    cl -d -c -AS -Gsw -Os -Zpe pgm4.c

pgm4.res: pgm4.rc pgm4.h
    rc -r pgm4.rc

pgm4.exe: pgm4.obj pgm4.res pgm4.def
    link4 pgm4,/align:16,/map,slibw,pgm4.def
    rc pgm4.res

#---------------------------------------------------------------------#
# End of file:  PGM4.                                                 #
#*********************************************************************#
```

When you start this program, Windows will shrink the MS-DOS Executive to its disk icon. Select “Mapmode. . .” and pick either ANISOTROPIC or ISOTROPIC. Then select “Setup.” Note the default values given to the viewport. Now, without closing this dialog box, pick up the “disk” icon and place it halfway up the screen on the far right side, forcing a vertical split (resizing our program’s client area). Note how the viewport values change.

. . . .

In this chapter, you’ve been introduced to the basic ideas that GDI uses to locate objects on the screen. In Chapter 8, you’ll learn about GDI bitmaps and cursor functions.

8

GDI BITMAPS AND CURSOR FUNCTIONS

- Introduction To PGM5
- The C Language Source File: PGM5.C
- The Module Definition File: PGM5.DEF
- The Make File: PGM5.

This chapter introduces you to the Windows Graphics Device Interface (GDI) bitmap and cursor functions. You'll see how to create a display context, how to create a bitmap, and how to write to the bitmap, all while the bitmap is in "background" memory. You'll also see how a bitmap is transferred onto the system display on demand.

8.1 INTRODUCTION TO PGM5

PGM5 requires only three source files:

PGM5.C	C program code
PGM5.DEF	Module definition file
PGM5.	Input instructions to the MAKE utility

Note the absence of a header file (.H) and a resource script (.RC) file. Because this program has no menus and does not use a significant number of strings, we can use only the .C, .DEF, and MAKE files.

The results of PGM5 should look similar to Figure 8.1. You'll see a 10-by-10 grid that almost completely fills the window either from top to bottom or left to right. This program finds the biggest square in the window: on most screens, the grid will extend from top to bottom.

Figure 8.1

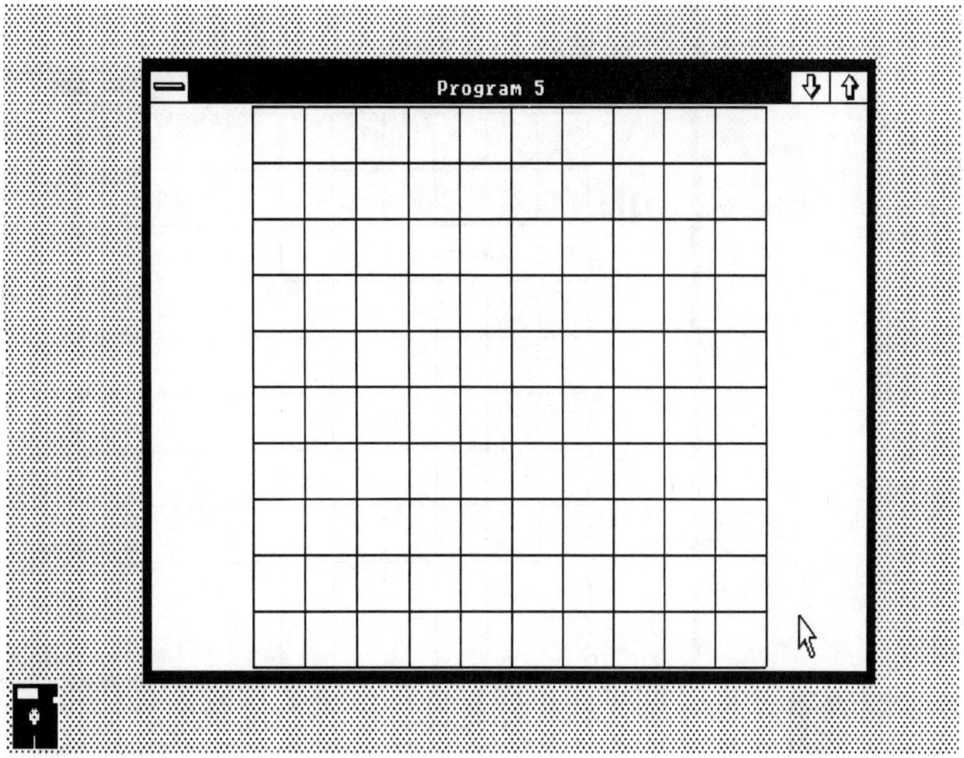

The arrow cursor can be moved into any of the 100 squares within the grid. If the user holds down the left mouse button, the arrow cursor changes to a cross-hair cursor (shown in Figure 8.2) and cursor movement is confined to the dimensions of the grid. (The process of confining an object to a specific area is called *clipping*.) When the user releases the mouse button, a geometrical figure (shown in Figure 8.3) appears in the square the cursor is located in. If the user presses and releases the left mouse button in a square with a geometrical figure, this erases the figure.

Figure 8.2

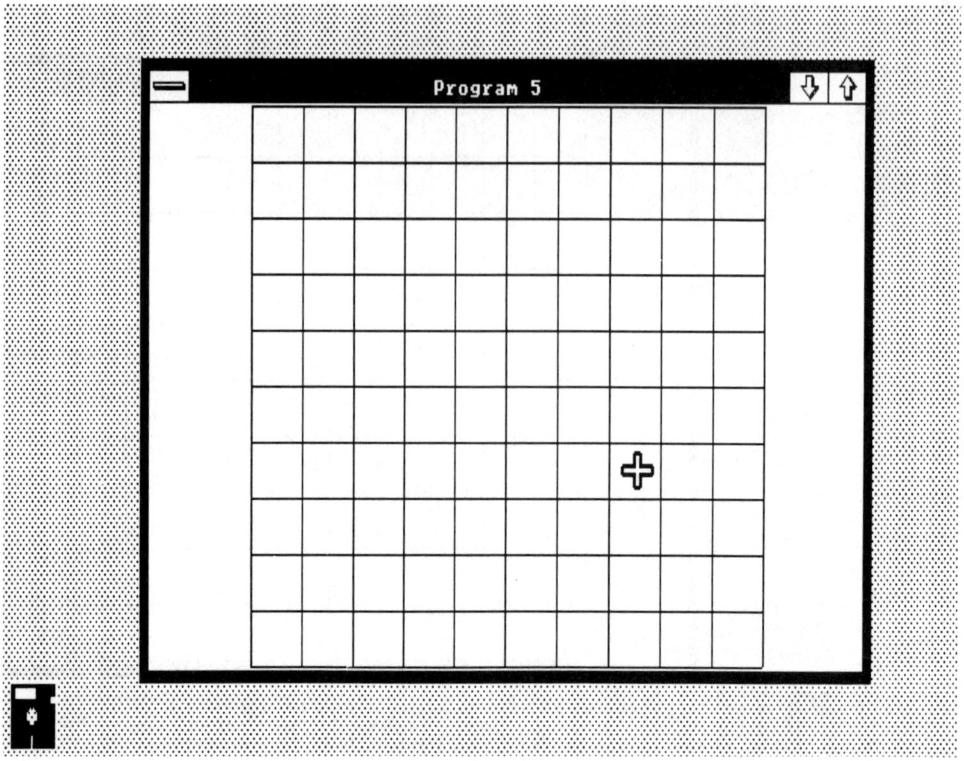

Figure 8.3

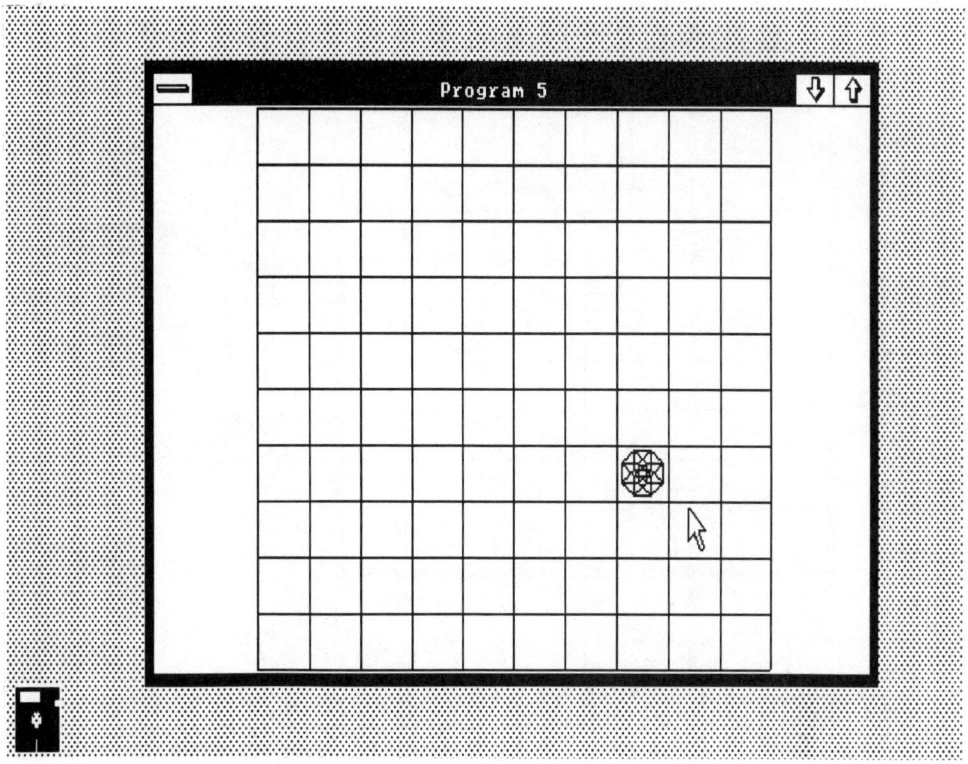

If PGM5's window changes size (for example, if several windows were opened simultaneously) the grid in PGM5's window remains proportional and fills the window as completely as possible, as shown in Figure 8.4. To achieve this, PGM5 does not switch into **MM_ISOTROPIC** mode, but rather uses an *aspect ratio* computation based upon the physical display size, the number of pixels in the X and Y directions, and the window, or client area, size. When PGM5's window changes size, so does the geometrical figure. This is accomplished by using a bitmap.

Figure 8.4

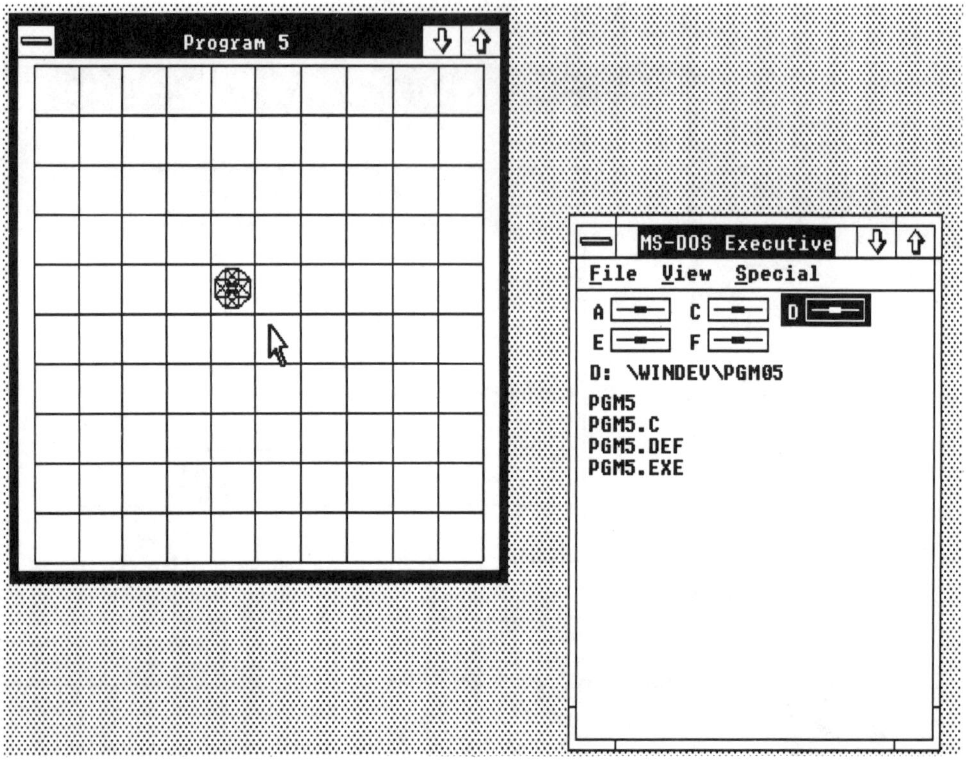

You'll see how PGM5 handles resizing windows and the objects within them, changing cursors, and drawing bitmaps in the following section.

8.2 THE C LANGUAGE SOURCE FILE: PGM5.C

```
/*************************************************************************/
/* Filename:     PGM5.C                                                  */
/*                                                                       */
/* Description:  PGM5.EXE source code                                   */
/*-----------------------------------------------------------------------*/

#include "windows.h"

  float                  aspect;                /* aspect ratio          */
  int                    bitspixel;             /* # bits/pixel display */
  int                    brdHeight;
  RECT                   brdRect;
  int                    brdWidth;
  HCURSOR                cursorArrow;           /* handle to arrow cur   */
  HCURSOR                cursorCross;           /* handle to cross cur   */
  int                    fromLeft;
  int                    fromTop;
  HANDLE                 hInst;
  HBRUSH                 hBrushColorWindow;
  HBRUSH                 hBrushOld;
  HANDLE                 hInst;
  HPEN                   hPenColorWindowText;
  HPEN                   hPenOld;
  HDC                    hPieceDC;
  HBITMAP                hBitmapOld;
  HBITMAP                hPieceBitmap;
  int                    i;
  BOOL                   leftButtonDownOnBoard;
  BOOL                   madeBitmaps = FALSE;
  long FAR PASCAL        MainWndProc (HWND, unsigned, WORD, LONG);
  HCURSOR                oldCursor;             /* handle to old cursor */
  POINT                  piece;
  RECT                   pieceRect;
  int                    pieceX;
  int                    pieceY;
  int                    planes;                /* # color planes        */
  PWNDCLASS              pMainClass;
  POINT                  point;
  int                    pointX;
  int                    pointY;

int PASCAL WinMain (hInstance, hPrevInstance, lpszCmdLine, cmdShow)
  HANDLE                 hInstance;
  HANDLE                 hPrevInstance;
  LPSTR                  lpszCmdLine;
  int                    cmdShow;
  {
  MSG                    msg;
  HWND                   hWnd;

  if (hPrevInstance)
    return FALSE;

  pMainClass = (PWNDCLASS)LocalAlloc (LPTR, sizeof(WNDCLASS));
  pMainClass->hCursor        = NULL;
  pMainClass->hIcon          = LoadIcon (NULL, IDI_APPLICATION);
  pMainClass->lpszMenuName   = (LPSTR)NULL;
  pMainClass->lpszClassName  = (LPSTR)"PGM5";
```

```
  pMainClass->hbrBackground   =
        hBrushColorWindow     = CreateSolidBrush (GetSysColor(COLOR_WINDOW));
  pMainClass->hInstance       = hInstance;
  pMainClass->style           = CS_HREDRAW | CS_VREDRAW;
  pMainClass->lpfnWndProc     = MainWndProc;

  if (!RegisterClass((LPWNDCLASS)pMainClass))
    return FALSE;
  LocalFree ((HANDLE)pMainClass);

  hWnd = CreateWindow  ((LPSTR)"PGM5", (LPSTR)"Program 5",
    WS_OVERLAPPEDWINDOW,
    GetSystemMetrics (SM_CXSCREEN) / 4, GetSystemMetrics (SM_CYSCREEN) / 4,
    GetSystemMetrics (SM_CXSCREEN) / 2, GetSystemMetrics (SM_CYSCREEN) / 2,
    (HWND)NULL, (HMENU)NULL, (HANDLE)hInstance, (LPSTR)NULL);
  hInst = hInstance;

  ShowWindow (hWnd, cmdShow);
  UpdateWindow (hWnd);

  while (GetMessage ((LPMSG)&msg, NULL, 0, 0))
    {
    TranslateMessage((LPMSG)&msg);
    DispatchMessage((LPMSG)&msg);
    }
  return (int)msg.wParam;
  }
/*-----------------------------------------------------------------*/
/* Procedures which make up the window class.                      */
/*-----------------------------------------------------------------*/
long FAR PASCAL MainWndProc(hWnd, message, wParam, lParam)
  HWND          hWnd;
  unsigned      message;
  WORD          wParam;
  LONG          lParam;
  {
  PAINTSTRUCT   ps;
  HDC           hDC;

  switch (message)
    {
    case WM_CREATE:
      hDC = GetDC (hWnd);
      aspect = (float)(((long) GetDeviceCaps (hDC, HORZRES)*100) /
                    (long) GetDeviceCaps (hDC, HORZSIZE)) /
                    (float)((((long) GetDeviceCaps (hDC, VERTRES)*100) /
                    (long) GetDeviceCaps (hDC, VERTSIZE));
      planes = GetDeviceCaps (hDC, PLANES);
      bitspixel = GetDeviceCaps (hDC, BITSPIXEL);
      ReleaseDC (hWnd, hDC);
      cursorArrow  = LoadCursor (NULL, IDC_ARROW);
      cursorCross  = LoadCursor (NULL, IDC_CROSS);
      SetCursor (oldCursor = cursorArrow);
      hPenColorWindowText = CreatePen (0, 1, GetSysColor(COLOR_WINDOWTEXT));
      break;

    case WM_SIZE:
      SizeProc (hWnd, wParam, lParam);
      break;

    case WM_PAINT:
      BeginPaint (hWnd, (LPPAINTSTRUCT)&ps);
```

```
    hPenOld = SelectObject (ps.hdc, hPenColorWindowText);
    for (i=0; i<=10; i++)
      {
      MoveTo (ps.hdc, fromLeft,           fromTop+(i*pieceY));
      LineTo (ps.hdc, fromLeft+brdWidth, fromTop+(i*pieceY));
      MoveTo (ps.hdc, fromLeft+i*pieceX, fromTop);
      LineTo (ps.hdc, fromLeft+i*pieceX, fromTop+brdHeight);
      }
    SelectObject (ps.hdc, hPenOld);
    EndPaint (hWnd, (LPPAINTSTRUCT)&ps);
    break;

  case WM_DESTROY:
    DeleteObject (hBrushColorWindow);
    DeleteObject (hPenColorWindowText);
    DeleteDC (hPieceDC);
    DeleteObject (hPieceBitmap);
    PostQuitMessage(0);
    break;

  case WM_ERASEBKGND:
    {
    RECT rect;
    GetClientRect (hWnd, (LPRECT)&rect);
    hBrushOld = SelectObject ((HDC)wParam, hBrushColorWindow);
    FillRect ((HDC)wParam, (LPRECT)&rect, hBrushColorWindow);
    SelectObject ((HDC)wParam, hBrushOld);
    break;
    }

  case WM_LBUTTONUP:
    pointX = LOWORD (lParam);
    pointY = HIWORD (lParam);
    if (leftButtonDownOnBoard)
      {
      SetCursor (oldCursor);
      ClipCursor (NULL);
      piece.x = fromLeft + (pointX-fromLeft)/pieceX*pieceX;
      piece.y = fromTop  + (pointY-fromTop)/pieceY*pieceY;
      hDC = GetDC (hWnd);
      hBitmapOld = SelectObject (hPieceDC, hPieceBitmap);
      BitBlt (hDC, piece.x, piece.y, pieceX, pieceY,
                            hPieceDC, 0, 0, SRCCOPY);
      SelectObject (hPieceDC, hBitmapOld);
      ReleaseDC (hWnd, hDC);
      }
    break;

  case WM_LBUTTONDOWN:
    pointX = LOWORD (lParam);
    pointY = HIWORD (lParam);
    if ((pointX >= fromLeft)
     && (pointX <= fromLeft+brdWidth)
     && (pointY >= fromTop)
     && (pointY <= fromTop+brdHeight))
      {
      leftButtonDownOnBoard = TRUE;
      oldCursor = SetCursor (cursorCross);

    point.x = fromLeft;
    point.y = fromTop;
    ClientToScreen (hWnd, (LPPOINT) &point);
    brdRect.left = point.x;
```

```
            brdRect.top = point.y;

            point.x = fromLeft+brdWidth;
            point.y = fromTop+brdHeight;
            ClientToScreen (hWnd, (LPPOINT) &point);
            brdRect.right = point.x-1;
            brdRect.bottom = point.y-1;

            ClipCursor ((LPRECT)&brdRect);

            piece.x = fromLeft + (pointX-fromLeft)/pieceX*pieceX;
            piece.y = fromTop  + (pointY-fromTop)/pieceY*pieceY;
            hDC = GetDC (hWnd);
            hBitmapOld = SelectObject (hPieceDC, hPieceBitmap);
            BitBlt (hDC, piece.x, piece.y, pieceX, pieceY,
                                hPieceDC, pieceX, 0, SRCCOPY);
            SelectObject (hPieceDC, hBitmapOld);
            ReleaseDC (hWnd, hDC);
            }
          else
            leftButtonDownOnBoard = FALSE;
          break;

        default:
          return (DefWindowProc (hWnd, message, wParam, lParam));
          break;
        }
      return (0L);
      }

    SizeProc (hWnd, wParam, lParam)
      HWND          hWnd;
      WORD          wParam;
      LONG          lParam;
      {
      POINT         q[33];
      HDC           hDC     = GetDC (hWnd);
      int           wHeight = HIWORD(lParam);
      int           wWidth  = LOWORD(lParam);

      if (madeBitmaps == TRUE)
        {
        DeleteDC (hPieceDC);
        DeleteObject (hPieceBitmap);
        }

      if (wWidth > wHeight * aspect)
        pieceY = wHeight / 10;              /* height limits        */
      else
        pieceY = wWidth / 10 / aspect;      /* width limits         */

      if (!pieceY)
        pieceY++;

      pieceX = pieceY * aspect;

      brdWidth    = pieceX * 10;
      fromLeft    = (wWidth - brdWidth) / 2;
      brdHeight   = pieceY * 10;
      fromTop     = (wHeight - brdHeight) / 2;

      hPieceDC = CreateCompatibleDC (hDC);
```

```
hPieceBitmap = CreateBitmap (pieceX*2, pieceY, planes, bitspixel, 0L);

hBitmapOld = SelectObject (hPieceDC, hPieceBitmap);
SetRect ((LPRECT)&(pieceRect), 0, 0, pieceX*2, pieceY);
FillRect (hPieceDC, (LPRECT)&pieceRect, hBrushColorWindow);

hPenOld = SelectObject (hPieceDC, hPenColorWindowText);
MoveTo (hPieceDC, 0,        pieceY);
LineTo (hPieceDC, 0,        0);
LineTo (hPieceDC, pieceX*2, 0);
MoveTo (hPieceDC, pieceX,   0);
LineTo (hPieceDC, pieceX, pieceY);

q[5].x  = q[6].x  = q[10].x = q[21].x =               pieceX * 0.1;
q[4].x  = q[7].x  = q[9].x  = q[22].x =
q[23].x = q[27].x = q[28].x = q[30].x =               pieceX * 0.3334;
q[11].x = q[12].x = q[20].x = q[25].x =               pieceX * 0.4330;
q[8].x  = q[15].x = q[16].x = q[29].x =               pieceX * 0.5670;
q[0].x  = q[3].x  = q[13].x = q[18].x =
q[19].x = q[24].x = q[26].x = q[31].x = q[32].x =     pieceX * 0.6666;
q[1].x  = q[2].x  = q[14].x = q[17].x =               pieceX * 0.9;
q[0].y  = q[7].y  = q[23].y = q[24].y = q[32].y =     pieceY * 0.1;
q[1].y  = q[6].y  = q[8].y  = q[10].y =
q[11].y = q[16].y = q[17].y = q[25].y =               pieceY * 0.3334;
q[13].y = q[22].y = q[30].y = q[31].y =               pieceY * 0.4330;
q[9].y  = q[18].y = q[26].y = q[27].y =               pieceY * 0.5670;
q[2].y  = q[5].y  = q[12].y = q[14].y =
q[15].y = q[20].y = q[21].y = q[29].y =               pieceY * 0.6666;
q[3].y  = q[4].y  = q[19].y = q[28].y =               pieceY * 0.9;

Polyline (hPieceDC, (LPPOINT)q, 33);

SelectObject (hPieceDC, hBitmapOld);
SelectObject (hPieceDC, hPenOld);

madeBitmaps = TRUE;
ReleaseDC (hWnd, hDC);
}

/*------------------------------------------------------------------------*/
/* End of file:  PGM5.C                                                   */
/**************************************************************************/
```

The first thing you'll notice about PGM5.C is the large number of global variables declared at the beginning of the program. Most of these variables are types that you've already seen in previous chapters.

By now, you'll easily recognize the handle from the WINDOWS.H file:

```
typedef WORD    HANDLE;
```

Next, several new handles are introduced, and several old handles are reintroduced. All these handles can be found in WINDOWS.H.

```
typedef   HANDLE HBITMAP;   /* handle to a bitmap */
typedef   HANDLE HBRUSH;    /* handle to a brush  */
typedef   HANDLE HCURSOR;   /* handle to a cursor */
typedef   HANDLE HDC;       /* handle to a DC     */
typedef   HANDLE HPEN;      /* handle to a pen    */
```

Next are two familiar data structures from the WINDOWS.H file: RECT and POINT. RECT is a rectangle and POINT is a point.

```
typedef         struct {
        int     left;
        int     top;
        int     right;
        int     bottom;
}               RECT;
```

```
typedef         struct {
        int     x;
        int     y;
}               POINT;
```

8.2.1 Preprocessing Before Displaying a Window

Windows sends **MainWndProc** a **WM_CREATE** message before the window is displayed. Upon receiving this message, we want to do a few tasks before displaying the window:

1. Compute an aspect ratio.
2. Get information about the environment the program is running in.
3. Get several stock cursors.
4. Create a pen the color of our background.

Let's look at this aspect ratio concept for a moment. Pixels (and logical units in the case of **MM_TEXT** mode) are usually wider than they are high. Therefore, a "logical" square may not appear square on the display screen. To compensate for this, we can do one of two things: (1) select **MM_ISOTROPIC** mode, or (2) compute the aspect ratio ourselves. In PGM5, we'll compute the aspect ratio.

After getting a DC handle, we use the Windows function **GetDeviceCaps** to get information about the type of display adapter the program is running on. Using this data, we can compute an aspect ratio that will enable us to visually proportion X to Y. Figure 8.5 illustrates how to compute the aspect ratio. In actuality, we will multiply the two numerators by 100 to achieve a greater accuracy.

Figure 8.5

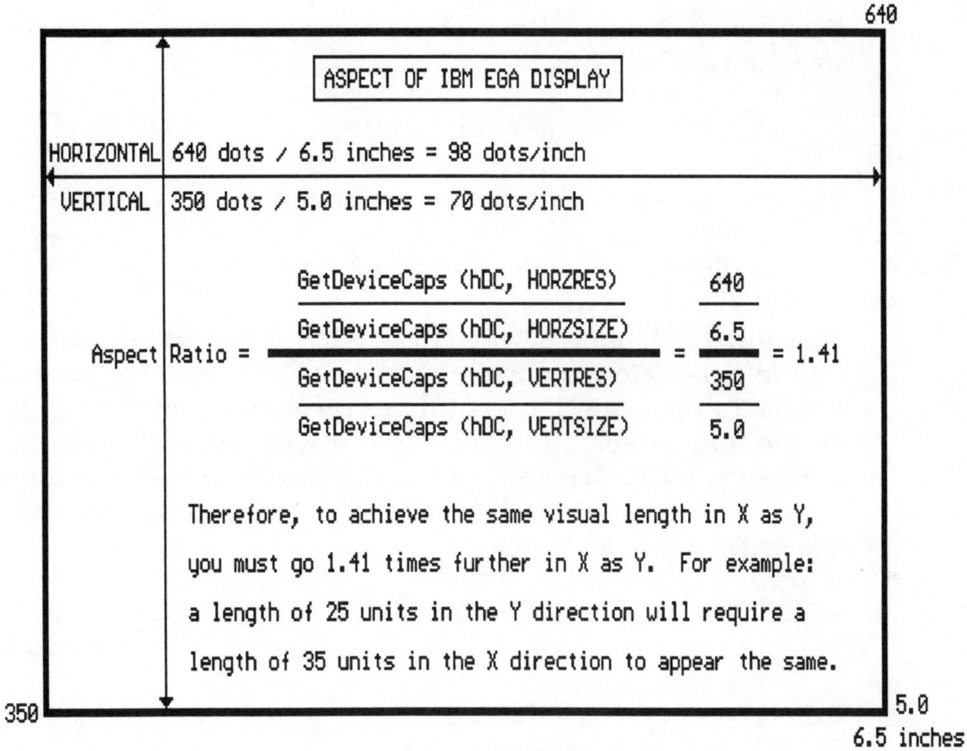

Several things will remain constant throughout the execution of this program: the number of video planes, number of bits per pixel, stock items such as arrow and cross cursors, etc. Bearing that in mind, we'll establish a few variables and handles now so that we don't have to do it again:

```
planes      = GetDeviceCaps (hDC, PLANES);
bitspixel   = GetDeviceCaps (hDC, BITSPIXEL)
```

planes is the number of color planes the device has, and **bitspixel** is the number of bits it takes to represent one pixel. These "bits" of information will be useful later on when we create our bitmap.

Next, we want to initialize the cursor. In previous chapters, we specified a cursor in the class structure:

```
pMainClass->hCursor = LoadCursor (NULL, IDC_ARROW);
```

Because we want to control the cursor ourselves, in this program we use the following line:

```
pMainClass->hCursor = NULL;
```

and use the following function in the initialization code:

```
SetCursor (oldCursor = cursorArrow);
```

This function changes (when necessary) the cursor to the one specified by the parameter: a cursor handle. In this case, we are passing the handle to the arrow cursor, and at the same time, saving that handle as the "old cursor." To complete the **WM_CREATE** code, we need to create a pen that has the color of the text used in the window area. To do this, we make two calls: one to fetch the color and another to create the pen:

```
hPenColorWindowText = CreatePen (0, 1, GetSysColor
                                  (COLORWINDOWTEXT));
```

CreatePen requires three arguments: *style*, *width*, and *color*. *Style* is an option from the following table:

#	*Style*
0	Solid
1	Dash
2	Dot
3	Dash and dot
4	Dash and two dots
5	Null

We selected "0" to get a solid brush. *Width* is specified in logical units: we want a brush with a width of 1. Because we are using the text mapping mode, one logical unit equals one pixel; therefore, we select the value "1." **GetSysColor** returns an RGB color (long integer), and we pass this value along to **CreatePen.**

8.2.2 Handling Size Changes for a Window

PGM5 receives a **WM_SIZE** message whenever its window changes size. This always happens at least once, when the window is created. It also happens when the user resizes the window using the minimize or maximize boxes or the commands on the system menu.

When we receive the **WM_SIZE** message, we want to:

1. Delete any previous bitmaps and DCs.
2. Compute the height and width of the grid cells.
3. Compute the height and width of the grid (10 cells).
4. Compute the distance from the window's upper left corner to the upper left corner of the grid.
5. Compute the coordinates of the upper left and lower right corners of the grid.
6. Create a memory display context that is compatible with the window's display context.
7. Create a bitmap.
8. Clear the bitmap to the background color.
9. Draw a "complicated" figure within the bitmap.

WM_SIZE will pass the client area's size in **lParam**. We use the macros LOWORD and HIWORD to pick out the width and height:

```
int     wHeight     = HIWORD (lParam);
int     wWidth      = LOWORD (lParam);
```

If this is not the first time through **WM_SIZE**, we need to delete any bitmaps and DCs that we have already created, thereby releasing the associated storage:

```
DeleteDC (hPieceDC);
DeleteObject (hPieceBitmap);
```

hPieceDC and **hPieceBitmap** are handles to a display context and to a bitmap, respectively.

Now we need to decide whether or not the width is greater than the height times the aspect ratio, in order to decide how to limit the cell size. Referring to Figure 8.5, let's suppose our window is 640 pixels wide by 350 pixels high. 640 "X-size" pixels would equal 350 times 1.41, or 493.5 "Y-size" pixels. Because 640 is greater than 493, we know that Y is the limiting factor: a length of 350 in the Y direction is shorter in appearance than 640 in the X. Therefore, the size of our cell in the Y direction is the integer portion of the division of the window height by ten (the number of cells in Y).

Had X been the limiting factor (meaning the width is smaller in appearance than the height), we would divide the width by 10, then divide that by the aspect to get Y.

The width of a cell is equal to the height times the aspect:

```
pieceX = pieceY * aspectYX;
```

Next, we want to create a compatible memory display context and a bitmap associated with that DC:

```
hPieceDC = CreateCompatibleDC (hDC);
hPieceBitmap = CreateBitmap (pieceX*2, pieceY,
                              planes, bitspixel, 0L);
```

CreateCompatibleDC creates a memory DC (display context) that is compatible with the system display context (**hDC**). We will use this memory DC to prepare an image for actual display. **CreateBitmap** sets aside an area of memory that we will use as a bitmap. This bitmap is **pieceX*2** pixels wide, **pieceY** pixels high, has **planes** planes, **bitspixel** bits per pixel, and is uninitialized (**0L**).

Figure 8.6 illustrates a bitmap that is **pieceX*2** wide and **pieceY** high. We have selected **pieceX*2** because we want to represent two cells: one with a geometric figure and one without. When the user presses the left mouse button, we'll transfer the blank bitmap onto the screen, thereby erasing the figure. When the user releases the button, we'll transfer the bitmap with the figure into the cell on the screen.

Figure 8.6

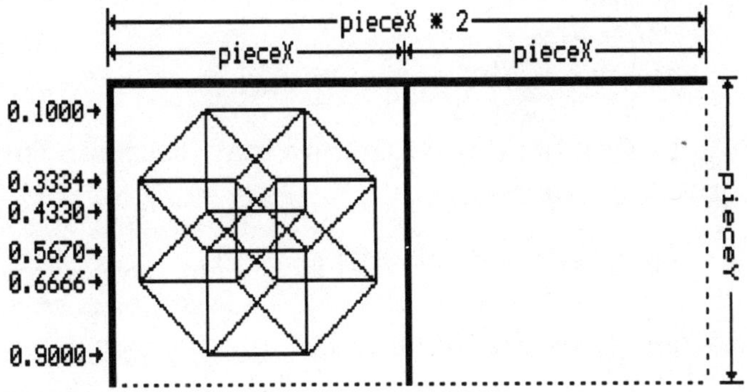

But right now, we only have a bitmap, so let's initialize and draw in it. As we have done before, we must select our tools. Before, however, we always used **hDC** as our display context because we wanted to draw on the screen in our window. Now, we want to draw in our memory display context, so we connect the newly formed display context, **hPieceDC**, with the new bitmap, **hPieceBitmap:**

```
hBitmapOld = SelectObject (hPieceDC, hPieceBitmap);
```

Next we want to fill the bitmap with the color of the window, so we set a rectangle and fill it:

```
SetRect ((LPRECT)&(pieceRect), 0, 0, pieceX*2, pieceY);
FillRect (hPieceDC, (LPRECT)&pieceRect,
                                        hBrushColorWindow);
```

Later, when we transfer bits from this bitmap to our actual display, we will be transferring a complete cell, i.e., **pieceX** by **pieceY** pixels. This implies that the grid will be overwritten. So, we simply duplicate the top and left lines in our bitmap:

```
hPenOld = SelectObject (hPieceDC, hPenColorWindowText);
MoveTo (hPieceDC, 0,            pieceY);
LineTo (hPieceDC, 0,            0);
LineTo (hPieceDC, pieceX*2,     0);
MoveTo (hPieceDC, pieceX,       0);
LineTo (hPieceDC, pieceX,       pieceY);
```

Next, we'll initialize an array with the various points of our "complicated" geometric figure:

```
q[5].x = q[6].x = q[10].x = q[21].x = pieceX * 0.1;
```

The points are set in such an order that we may issue the **Polyline** call to draw the figure:

```
Polyline (hPieceDC, (LPPOINT)q, 33);
```

We are done for now with the memory DC and the pen, so we release them:

```
SelectObject (hPieceDC, hBitmapOld);
SelectObject (hPieceDC, hPenOld);
```

And finally, we set the Boolean variable **madeBitmaps** to TRUE. Any subsequent calls to **WM_SIZE** will cause these bitmaps to be deleted before new ones are created. Remember that **pieceX** and **pieceY** are size-dependent, therefore our bitmap is also dependent:

```
madeBitmaps = TRUE;
```

8.2.3 Painting in a Window

The processing of **WM_PAINT** message is simple. As usual, we call **BeginPaint** and **EndPaint**. It is within the **WM_PAINT** procedure that we will draw the 10-by-10 grid. Because we will be using **LineTo** (which uses the "current pen" to draw), we need to select a pen:

```
hPenOld = SelectObject (ps.hdc, hPenColorWindowText);
```

Following the pen selection, the program enters a loop that draws 10 vertical and 10 horizontal lines. The variables **fromLeft** and **fromTop** represent the distance from the left and top of the window to draw the first line. **brdWidth** and **brdHeight** are the board's width and height in logical units (pixels). All four of these values were computed during processing of **WM_SIZE**.

As always, we must release our object:

```
SelectObject (ps.hdc, hPenOld),
```

8.2.4 Erasing the Background

Just for fun, let's process **WM_ERASEBKGRND** (erase background) ourselves (**DefWindowProc** usually does it). If you know you won't need an erased background, you can trap this out. For example, if you are filling the entire screen, why erase?

Erasing the background involves four simple calls:

```
GetClientRect (hWnd, (LPRECT)&rect);
hBrushOld = SelectObject ((HDC)wParam,
                                    hBrushColorWindow);
FillRect ((HDC)wParam, (LPRECT)&rect,
                                    hBrushColorWindow);
SelectObject (HDC), hBrushOld);
```

GetClientRect gets the rectangle associated with the client area of our window. **SelectObject** associates the display context handle supplied in **wParam** with the brush that we specified, which is the same color as the window background. **FillRect** flood-fills the area with the color of the brush.

8.2.5 Changing and Clipping the Cursor

When the user presses the left mouse button, **MainWndProc** will get a **WM_LBUTTONDOWN** message. **lParam** will contain the logical coordinates of the position of the cursor when the event occurred:

```
pointX = LOWORD (lParam);
pointY = HIWORD (lParam);
```

If the cursor was inside the 10-by-10 grid when the button was pressed, we want to do some processing. First, we want to set a Boolean flag indicating that the button was pressed while the cursor was within the grid boundaries:

```
leftButtonDownOnBoard = TRUE;
```

This flag will be used in the processing of the "button up" logic. Next, we change the cursor to a cross:

```
oldCursor = SetCursor (cursorCross);
```

During initialization we retrieved handles to two cursors: the arrow and cross. **OldCursor** is the handle to the previous cursor. After changing the cursor, we want to clip it to the confines of the grid. We compute the exact location on the screen to clip the cursor to, and place this information into a **RECT** (rectangle) data structure:

```
point.x                               = fromLeft;
point.y                               = fromTop;
ClientToScreen (hWnd, (LPPOINT) &point);
brdRect.left                          = point.x;
brdRect.top                           = point.y;
```

ClientToScreen converts logical to physical coordinates. We pass it the grid's top and left sides and it returns that information in actual display coordinates. We'll repeat this procedure for the right and bottom sides.

We now use those coordinates to do the clipping:

```
ClipCursor ((LPRECT)&brdRect);
```

To transfer the memory display context bitmap to the screen, we need to know the coordinates of the upper left corner of the cell that the cursor is in. This is simply:

```
piece.x = fromLeft + (pointX-fromLeft)/pieceX*pieceX;
piece.y = fromTop  + (pointY-fromTop)/pieceY*pieceY;
```

All of this preparation leads up to the main event: the bitmap or bit block transfer (**BitBlt**):

```
hDC = GetDC (hWnd);
BitBlt (hDC, piece.x, piece.y, pieceX, pieceY,
                          hPieceDC, pieceX, 0, SRCCOPY);
ReleaseDC (hWnd, hDC);
```

BitBlt transfers a bitmap from one DC to another or from one area within a DC to another area within the DC. In this case, we are transferring the bitmap associated with **hPieceDC** from the starting coordinates (**pieceX, 0**). This is the blank bitmap shown in Figure 8.6. We'll move (**pieceX, pieceY**) bits to the coordinates (**piece.x, piece.y**) within the bitmap associated with **hDC. SRCCOPY** is called a *raster code* and performs a straight transfer, overwriting any bits that may have been there.

8.2.6 "Unclipping" the Cursor

The logic for **WM_LBUTTONUP** is much like **WM_LBUTTONDOWN** except that it's reversed. After getting the event point and verifying that we had processed **WM_LBUTTONDOWN** as being within the confines of the grid, we want to return the cursor to the **oldCursor** (arrow):

```
SetCursor (oldCursor);
```

Clipping the cursor to NULL "unclips" it, allowing it to move freely about the screen:

```
ClipCursor (NULL);
```

After computing the coordinates of the cell's upper left corner, we transfer our bit block containing the geometrical figure:

```
BitBlt (hDC, piece.x, piece.y, pieceX, pieceY,
                              hPieceDC, 0, 0, SRCCOPY);
```

The only difference between this bit block transfer and the one we used for **WM_LBUTTONDOWN** is that we will use the left half of the bitmap, i.e., the part that contains the figure. Note that our source's starting coordinates are (**0, 0**), or the upper left corner of the memory bitmap.

8.2.7 Deleting Tools

Before exiting, we tidy up by deleting our tools:

```
DeleteObject (hBrushColorWindow);
DeleteObject (hPenColorWindowText);
DeleteDC (hPieceDC);
DeleteObject (hPieceBitmap);
```

We must delete anything we create in order to de-allocate the associated storage.

8.3 THE MODULE DEFINITION FILE: PGM5.DEF

```
;******************************************************************;
; Filename:     PGM5.DEF                                           ;
;                                                                  ;
; Description:  Link definition file                               ;
;------------------------------------------------------------------;
NAME     PGM5

DESCRIPTION 'Sample program 5'

STUB     '..\WINSTUB.EXE'

CODE     MOVEABLE
DATA     FIXED MULTIPLE

HEAPSIZE  1024
STACKSIZE 4096

EXPORTS
    MainWndProc         @1
;------------------------------------------------------------------;
; End of file:  PGM5.DEF                                           ;
;******************************************************************;
```

8.4 THE MAKE FILE: PGM5.

```
#***********************************************************************#
# Filename:     PGM5.                                                   #
#                                                                       #
# Description:  PGM5.EXE "MAKE" description file                        #
#-----------------------------------------------------------------------#

pgm5.obj: pgm5.c
    cl -d -c -AS -Gsw -Os -FPa -Zpe pgm5.c

pgm5.exe: pgm5.obj pgm5.def
    link4 pgm5, /align:16, nul, slibw, pgm5.def

#-----------------------------------------------------------------------#
# End of file:  PGM5.                                                   #
#***********************************************************************#
```

. . . .

In this chapter, you've learned how to create, display, and remove bitmaps, how to change objects within a window when the window changes size, how to change cursors, and how to clip cursors. In Chapter 9, you'll learn to create and manage child windows and popup windows.

9

WORKING WITH POPUP WINDOWS

- Introduction to Child and Popup Windows
- Introduction to PGM6
- The C Language Source File: PGM5.C
- The Module Definition File: PGM6.DEF
- The Make File: PGM6.

So far, all the sample programs in this book have dealt only with overlapped windows, the windows normally used as the main windows of applications. In this chapter, you'll see how child windows and popup windows are created and managed.

9.1 INTRODUCTION TO CHILD AND POPUP WINDOWS

Child windows and popup windows behave much the same way overlapped windows do. They have their own window functions, and they can have all of the attributes of overlapped windows (title bar, menu bar, minimize and maximize boxes, scroll bars, etc.). Figure 9.1 illustrates a typical popup window.

Figure 9.1

The primary difference between popups and child windows is that they use different coordinates. Popups use screen coordinates and child windows use logical coordinates, relative to (0,0) in the parent window's client area. Thus a popup window can appear anywhere on the screen, but a child window is generally restricted to the parent's window.

Because popup windows and child windows are so closely related, in this chapter we will study only popup windows. Chapter 10 describes the use of multiple child windows.

As stated above, a popup window can take on any number of attributes. Furthermore, an application can have any number of popup windows open at once. For example, the MS-DOS Executive is a conglomeration of numerous child windows: the disk drive icons are borderless windows, as is each of the columns of filenames. The user does not perceive these as separate windows because they are borderless, but the separate windows make it easier to manage the MS-DOS Executive display.

9.2 INTRODUCTION TO PGM6

PGM6 requires three files:

PGM6.C	C program code
PGM6.DEF	Module definition file
PGM6.	Input instructions to the MAKE utility

Figure 9.1 illustrates what you'll see when you start PGM6. Instead of the normal overlapped window, a popup window is displayed. For the sake of simplicity, PGM6's popup window does nothing spectacular. If you want to see something in the client area, you can easily add code to case **WM_PAINT.**

Figure 9.2

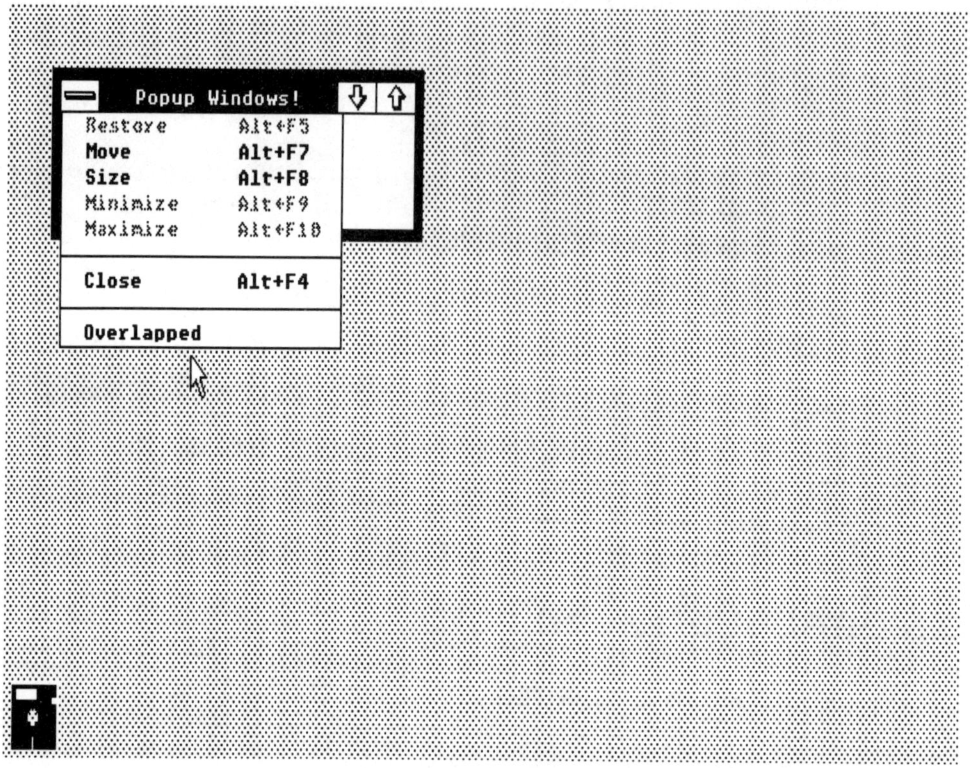

Figure 9.2 illustrates PGM6's system menu. Note that "Minimize" and "Maximize" have been grayed by Windows; they cannot be selected. We have also added a menu item called "Overlapped," which changes the original popup window into an overlapped window, shown in Figure 9.3.

Figure 9.3

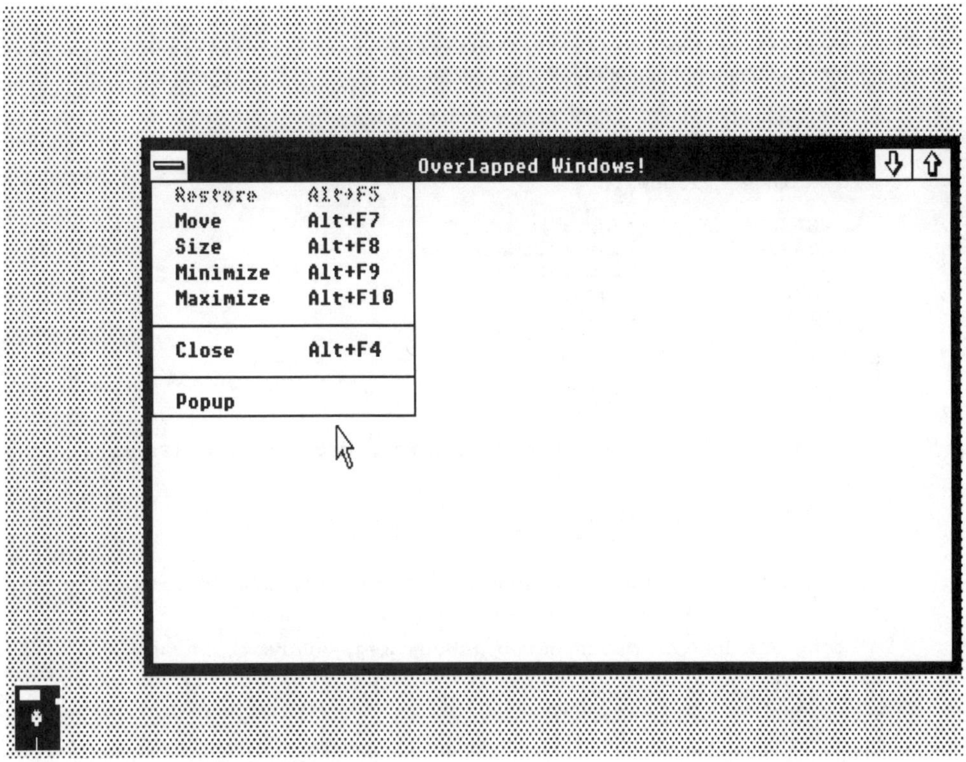

When the overlapped window is displayed, “Minimize” and “Maximize” are enabled to allow the user to reduce the window to an icon or maximize the window. The “Overlapped” menu item is replaced by “Popup,” which allows the user to change the window back into a popup window.

9.3 THE C LANGUAGE SOURCE FILE: PGM5.C

```
/**************************************************************************/
/* Filename:     PGM6.C                                                   */
/*                                                                        */
/* Description:  PGM6.EXE source code                                     */
/*------------------------------------------------------------------------*/

#include "windows.h"

  HANDLE        hInst;
  FARPROC       lpDefaultWndProc;
  long          WindowStyle            = WS_POPUP;
  HMENU         hMenu;
  int           PopupX                 = 30;
  int           PopupY                 = 30;
  int           PopupW                 = 240;
  int           PopupH                 = 70;
  RECT          rect;

long FAR PASCAL DefaultWndProc (hWnd, msg, wParam, lParam)
  HWND          hWnd;
  int           msg;
  WORD          wParam;
  LONG          lParam;
  {
  return (DefWindowProc (hWnd, msg, wParam, lParam));
  }

long FAR PASCAL MainWndProc (hWnd, msg, wParam, lParam)
  HWND          hWnd;
  unsigned      msg;
  WORD          wParam;
  LONG          lParam;
  {
  switch (msg)
    {
    case WM_SYSCOMMAND:
      switch (wParam)
        {
        case 1000:
          SetWindowLong (hWnd, GWL_WNDPROC, (LONG)lpDefaultWndProc);
          DestroyWindow (hWnd);
          if (WindowStyle == WS_POPUP)
            {
            WindowStyle = WS_OVERLAPPED;
            hWnd = CreateWindow ((LPSTR)"PGM6",
                                 (LPSTR)"Overlapped Windows!",
                                 WS_OVERLAPPEDWINDOW,
                                 GetSystemMetrics (SM_CXSCREEN) / 4,
                                 GetSystemMetrics (SM_CYSCREEN) / 4,
                                 GetSystemMetrics (SM_CXSCREEN) / 2,
                                 GetSystemMetrics (SM_CYSCREEN) / 2,
                                 NULL, NULL, hInst, (LPSTR)NULL);
            }
          else
            {
```

```
          WindowStyle = WS_POPUP;
          hWnd = CreateWindow ((LPSTR)"PGM6",
                               (LPSTR)"Popup Windows!",
                               WS_POPUPWINDOW | WS_CAPTION |
                                      WS_MINIMIZEBOX | WS_MAXIMIZEBOX |
                                      WS_THICKFRAME,
                               PopupX, PopupY, PopupW, PopupH,
                               NULL,
                               NULL,
                               hInst,
                               (LPSTR)NULL);
          }
        hMenu = GetSystemMenu (hWnd, FALSE);
        ChangeMenu (hMenu, 0, NULL, 999, MF_APPEND | MF_SEPARATOR);
        ChangeMenu (hMenu, 0,
             (WindowStyle == WS_POPUP) ?
                                    (LPSTR)"Overlapped" : (LPSTR)"Popup",
             1000, MF_APPEND | MF_STRING);
        ShowWindow (hWnd, SHOW_OPENWINDOW);
        break;

      default:
        return DefWindowProc (hWnd, msg, wParam, lParam);
      }
    break;

  case WM_SIZE:
  case WM_MOVE:
    if (WindowStyle == WS_POPUP)
      {
      GetWindowRect (hWnd, (LPRECT)&rect);
      switch (msg)
        {
        case WM_SIZE:
          PopupW = rect.right - rect.left;
          PopupH = rect.bottom - rect.top;
          break;

        case WM_MOVE:
          PopupX = rect.left;
          PopupY = rect.top;
          break;
        }
      }
    break;

  case WM_DESTROY:
    PostQuitMessage (0);
    break;

  default:
    return DefWindowProc (hWnd, msg, wParam, lParam);
    break;
  }
return (0L);
```

```
  }

int PASCAL WinMain (hInstance, hPrevInstance, lpszCmdLine, cmdShow)
  HANDLE        hInstance;
  HANDLE        hPrevInstance;
  LPSTR         lpszCmdLine;
  int           cmdShow;
  {
  MSG           msg;
  HWND          hWnd;
  PWNDCLASS     pMainClass;

  if (hPrevInstance)
    return FALSE;

  pMainClass = (PWNDCLASS)LocalAlloc (LPTR, sizeof(WNDCLASS));

  pMainClass->hCursor       = LoadCursor (NULL, IDC_ARROW);
  pMainClass->hIcon         = LoadIcon (NULL, IDI_APPLICATION);
  pMainClass->lpszMenuName  = (LPSTR)NULL;
  pMainClass->lpszClassName = (LPSTR)"PGM6";
  pMainClass->hbrBackground = (HBRUSH)GetStockObject (WHITE_BRUSH);
  pMainClass->hInstance     = hInstance;
  pMainClass->style         = CS_HREDRAW | CS_VREDRAW;
  pMainClass->lpfnWndProc   = MainWndProc;

  if (!RegisterClass ((LPWNDCLASS)pMainClass))
    return FALSE;

  LocalFree ((HANDLE)pMainClass);

  hWnd = CreateWindow ((LPSTR)"PGM6",
                       (LPSTR)"Popup Windows!",
                       WS_POPUPWINDOW | WS_CAPTION |
                                 WS_MINIMIZEBOX | WS_MAXIMIZEBOX |
                                 WS_THICKFRAME,
                       PopupX, PopupY, PopupW, PopupH,
                       NULL,
                       NULL,
                       hInst = hInstance,
                       (LPSTR)NULL);

  hMenu = GetSystemMenu (hWnd, FALSE);
  ChangeMenu (hMenu, 0, NULL, 999, MF_APPEND | MF_SEPARATOR);
  ChangeMenu (hMenu, 0, (LPSTR)"Overlapped", 1000, MF_APPEND | MF_STRING);

  lpDefaultWndProc = MakeProcInstance ((FARPROC)DefaultWndProc, hInst);

  ShowWindow (hWnd, cmdShow);
  UpdateWindow (hWnd);

  while (GetMessage ((LPMSG)&msg, NULL, 0, 0))
    {
    TranslateMessage ((LPMSG)&msg);
    DispatchMessage ((LPMSG)&msg);
    }

  FreeProcInstance (lpDefaultWndProc);

  return (int)msg.wParam;
  }
/*-----------------------------------------------------------------------*/
/* End of file:  PGM6.C                                                  */
/*************************************************************************/
```

To create PGM6's window, we'll change several fields in the **CreateWindow** function call in **WinMain:**

```
hWnd = CreateWindow ((LPSTR)"PGM6",
(LPSTR)"Popup Windows!",
WS_POPUPWINDOW | WS_CAPTION | WS_MINIMIZEBOX
                                        | WS_MAXIMIZEBOX,
PopupX,
PopupY,
PopupW,
PopupH,
NULL,
NULL,
hInst = hInstance,
(LPSTR)NULL);
```

Instead of **WS_OVERLAPPEDWINDOW**, we use **WS_POPUPWINDOW | WS_CAPTION | WS_MINIMIZEBOX | WS_MAXIMIZEBOX**. This gives us a popup window that has a title bar and minimize and maximize boxes. The next two arguments, **PopupX** and **PopupY**, specify the location (in screen coordinates) of the popup window's upper left corner. **PopupW** and **PopupH** describe the size of the window.

Note that in the second **ChangeMenu** call we set the **wIDChangeItem** field to **1000**. In **MainWndProc_WM SYSCOMMAND** we switch on case **1000:**

```
ChangeMenu (hMenu, 0, (LPSTR)"Overlapped", 1000,
                                MF_APPEND | MF_STRING);
```

9.3.1 Switching between Overlapped and Popup Windows

Selecting "Overlapped" or "Popup" from the system menu gets us to **MainWndProc**. To switch from a popup window to overlapped or vice versa, we want to:

1. Point to a dummy routine.
2. Destroy the window.
3. Create a new window.

4 Change the system menu.
5 Call a function to show the window.

First, we need to point to a dummy routine because we don't really want to quit when we destroy our window. Also, we don't want to confuse Windows about where this code belongs. So, we simply point Windows at a new routine to destroy the window:

```
SetWindowLong (hWnd, GWL_WNDPROC,
                              (LONG)lpDefaultWndProc);
```

SetWindowLong is used to change an attribute of the given window **hWnd**. In this case, we want to change the window function that is called to process the window associated with **hWnd** (this procedure is currently **MainWndProc**). **GWL_WNDPROC** is the flag to change the window function. **lpDefaultWndProc** is the pointer to our new window function that will handle closing and destroying the current window.

DefaultWndProc is a procedure that simply passes messages on to the default window function, **DefWndProc:**

```
long FAR PASCAL DefaultWndProc (hWnd, msg,
                                    wParam, lParam)
HWND    hWnd;
int     msg;
WORD    wParam;
LONG    lParam;
{
return (DefWindowProc (hWnd, msg, wParam, lParam));
}
```

Next, we want to destroy our current window:

```
DestroyWindow (hWnd);
```

The window associated with **hWnd** will be destroyed, but a "quit" message will not be posted because the default action of **DefWndProc** does not call **PostQuitMessage**. This keeps PGM6 running.

Next, we want to create a new window. If the previous window was an overlapped window, we want to create a popup window. If it was a popup window, we want to create an overlapped window. Then we change the system menu.

```
if (WindowStyle == WS_POPUP)
  {
  WindowStyle = WS_OVERLAPPED
  hWnd = CreateWindow ((LPSTR) "PGM6",
                       (LPSTR)"Overlapped Windows!",
                       WS_OVERLAPPEDWINDOW,
                       GetSystemMetrics (SM_CXSCREEN) / 4,
                       GetSystemMetrics (SM_CYSCREEN) / 4,
                       GetSystemMetrics (SM_CXSCREEN) / 2,
                       GetSystemMetrics (SM_CYSCREEN) / 2,
                       NULL, NULL, hInst, (LPSTR) NULL);
  }
  else
  {
  WindowStyle = WS_POPUP
  hWnd = CreateWindow ((LPSTR) "PGM6",
                       (LPSTR)"Popup Windows!",
                       WS_POPUPWINDOW | WS_CAPTION |
                          WS_MINIMIZEBOX | WS_MAXIMIZEBOX |
                          WS_THICKFRAME,
                       PopupX, PopupY, PopupW, PopupH,
                       NULL,
                       NULL,
                       hInst,
                       (LPSTR)NULL);
  }
hMenu = GetSystemMenu (hWnd, FALSE);
ChangeMenu (hMenu, 0, NULL, 999, MP_APPEND | MF_SEPARATOR);
ChangeMenu (hMenu, 0,
       (WindowStyle == WS_POPUP ?
                       (LPSTR)"Overlapped" : (LPSTR)"Popup",
        1000, MF_APPEND | MF_STRING;
```

And finally, we place the call to show our new window:

```
ShowWindow (hWnd, SHOW_OPENWINDOW);
```

In all previous sample programs, we have used **ShowWindow (hWnd, cmdShow)**, where **cmdShow** was passed to us by Windows. This time, we substitute **SHOW_OPENWINDOW** for **cmdShow**—this tells Windows to show our window. Windows allows you to use

cmdShow only once—thereafter you must use the flags such as **SHOW_OPENWINDOW**, as defined in WINDOWS.H.

9.3.2 Handling Changes in the Window's Size or Position

The **WM_SIZE** and **WM_MOVE** messages are sent when a window is resized or moved, respectively. If the popup window is altered, we want to remember its last position so that it will be displayed in the correct place the next time it is made into a popup window:

```
GetWindowRect (hWnd, (LPRECT)&rect);
```

Windows will fill the rectangle data structure pointed to by **&rect** with information regarding the screen coordinates of PGM6's window. We can use that to extract the size and location. We'll save this information until the next time **CreateWindow** is called, when it will be used to properly size and locate the popup window.

9.4 THE MODULE DEFINITION FILE: PGM6.DEF

```
;*************************************************************:
; Filename:     PGM6.DEF                                      :
;                                                             :
; Description:  Link definition file                          :
;-------------------------------------------------------------:
NAME     PGM6

DESCRIPTION 'Sample program 6'

STUB     '..\WINSTUB.EXE'

CODE     MOVEABLE
DATA     MOVEABLE MULTIPLE

HEAPSIZE  1024
STACKSIZE 4096

EXPORTS
    MainWndProc          @1
    DefaultWndProc       @2

;-------------------------------------------------------------:
; End of file:  PGM6.DEF                                      :
;*************************************************************:
```

9.5 THE MAKE FILE: PGM6.

```
#*********************************************************************#
# Filename:      PGM6.                                                #
#                                                                     #
# Description:  PGM6.EXE "MAKE" description file                      #
#---------------------------------------------------------------------#

pgm6.obj: pgm6.c
    cl -d -c -AS -Gsw -Os -Zpe pgm6.c

pgm6.exe: pgm6.obj pgm6.def
    link4 pgm6, pgm6/align:16,, slibw, pgm6.def

#---------------------------------------------------------------------#
# End of file:  PGM6.                                                 #
#*********************************************************************#
```

. . . .

In this chapter, you've learned to create and manage popup windows. In Chapter 10, you'll see how scroll bars, which are tiny child windows, are added to an application's main window.

10

ADDING SCROLL BARS AND CHILD WINDOWS

- Introduction To PGM7
- The C Language File: PGM7.C
- The Module Definition File: PGM7.DEF
- The Make File: PGM7.

To allow mouse users to scroll the information displayed in windows, you can add scroll bars, which are special types of child windows, to your application's main window. This chapter examines a sample program, PGM7, that adds scroll bars to a window. As usual, Windows will handle the operation of the scroll bars; all we need to worry about is the processing of various messages that Windows will send when events occur.

Basically, there are two methods of "ordering" a scroll bar. The first applies to windows, and is done by specifying that the window is to have a horizontal and/or vertical bar. The second method applies to dialog boxes, and is done by explicitly specifying a scroll bar as a control in the .RC file. In this chapter, we'll focus on the first method: creating windows with both horizontal and vertical scroll bars.

10.1 INTRODUCTION TO PGM7

PGM7 requires only three files:

PGM7.C	The source code file
PGM7.DEF	The module definition file
PGM7.	Input instructions to the MAKE utility

We have omitted the .RC and .H files. The program does not need a .RC file because it requires no resources; the .H file is not needed because the program has no .RC file.

Figure 10.1 illustrates what this program does: it displays nine horizontal and nine vertical scroll bars. Beside or under each bar is a numerical value representing the bar's current value. The user can drag the mouse cursor to move the scroll box (sometimes called a "thumb" or "elevator") in any of the bars.

Figure 10.1

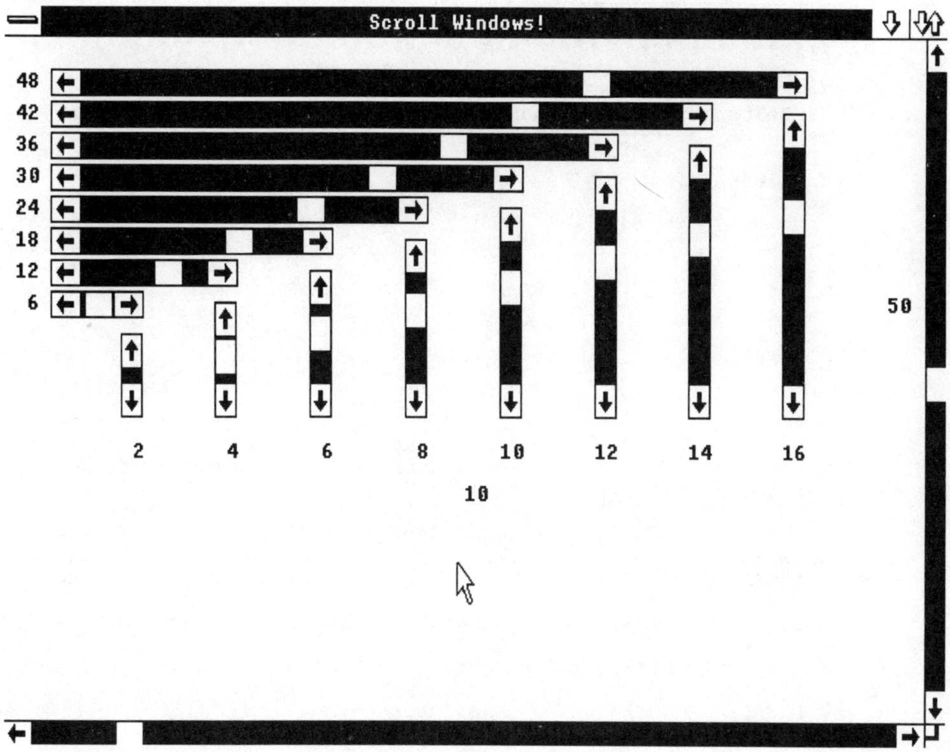

A window may not have more than one horizontal and one vertical bar. Hence, the bars on the extreme right and bottom belong to our program's main window. To display the other scroll bars, we create 16 child windows. Each child window is one vertical or horizontal scroll bar.

When the user clicks in a child window, the parent window is notified. This means each scroll bar doesn't really need a window function; the parent's window function can manage the whole show. (Actually, each scroll bar has a window function of its own, but Windows manages these functions.)

10.2 THE C LANGUAGE FILE: PGM7.C

```
/***************************************************************************/
/* Filename:     PGM7.C                                                    */
/*                                                                         */
/* Description:  PGM7.EXE source code                                      */
/*-------------------------------------------------------------------------*/

#include "windows.h"
struct {
  HWND               hSbar;          /* handle to scroll bar         */
  int                value;          /* current value of scroll bar  */
  int                X;              /* X coord for sbar value       */
  int                Y;              /* Y coord for sbar value       */
  int                high;           /* High end of range            */
  int                nBar;           /* SB_VERT, SB_HORZ, or SB_CTL  */
  } sBar[18];                        /* [00] = Main window horiz bar */
                                     /* [01] = Main window vert  bar */
                                     /* [02]-[09] = Child  horiz bar */
                                     /* [10]-[17] = Child  vert  bar */
  int                fontHeight;     /* height of font               */
  int                fontWidth;      /* avg width of font            */
  int                i;              /* working integer              */
  char               szNum[17];      /* working storage for strings  */
  DWORD              textColor;      /* RGB color of text            */
  DWORD              bkColor;        /* RGB color of background      */
  HANDLE             hInst;          /* handle to instance           */

  long FAR PASCAL    MainWndProc (HWND, unsigned, WORD, LONG);

int PASCAL WinMain (hInstance, hPrevInstance, lpszCmdLine, cmdShow)
  HANDLE             hInstance;
  HANDLE             hPrevInstance;
  LPSTR              lpszCmdLine;
  int                cmdShow;
  {
  MSG                msg;
  HWND               hWnd;
  HDC                hDC;
  PTEXTMETRIC        pTextMetric;
  PWNDCLASS          pClass;

  if (hPrevInstance)
    return FALSE;

  pClass = (PWNDCLASS)LocalAlloc (LPTR, sizeof(WNDCLASS));
  pClass->hCursor       = LoadCursor (NULL, IDC_ARROW);
  pClass->hIcon         = LoadIcon (NULL, IDI_APPLICATION);
  pClass->lpszMenuName  = (LPSTR)NULL;
  pClass->lpszClassName = (LPSTR)"Pgm7";
  pClass->hbrBackground =
              CreateSolidBrush (bkColor = GetSysColor(COLOR_WINDOW));
  pClass->hInstance     = hInstance;
  pClass->style         = CS_HREDRAW | CS_VREDRAW;
  pClass->lpfnWndProc   = MainWndProc;

  if (!RegisterClass((LPWNDCLASS)pClass))
    return FALSE;
  LocalFree ((HANDLE)pClass);

  hInst = hInstance;
  hWnd = CreateWindow ((LPSTR)"PGM7", (LPSTR)"Scroll Windows!",
```

```
    WS_OVERLAPPEDWINDOW | WS_VSCROLL | WS_HSCROLL,
    GetSystemMetrics (SM_CXSCREEN) / 4, GetSystemMetrics (SM_CYSCREEN) / 4,
    GetSystemMetrics (SM_CXSCREEN) / 2, GetSystemMetrics (SM_CYSCREEN) / 2,
    (HWND)NULL, (HMENU)NULL, (HANDLE)hInst, (LPSTR)NULL);
hDC = GetDC (hWnd);
pTextMetric = (PTEXTMETRIC)LocalAlloc (LPTR, sizeof(TEXTMETRIC));
GetTextMetrics (hDC, (PTEXTMETRIC)pTextMetric);
ReleaseDC (hWnd, hDC);
textColor = GetSysColor(COLOR_WINDOWTEXT);
fontHeight = (int) pTextMetric->tmHeight;
fontWidth = (int) pTextMetric->tmAveCharWidth;
LocalFree ((HANDLE)pTextMetric);

sBar[0].X = 39*fontWidth;
sBar[0].Y = 21*fontHeight;
sBar[0].value = 0;
SetScrollRange (sBar[0].hSbar = hWnd,
                sBar[0].nBar = SB_HORZ,
                0,
                sBar[0].high=99,
                FALSE);
SetScrollPos (sBar[0].hSbar, SB_HORZ, sBar[0].value = 10, TRUE);

sBar[1].X = 75*fontWidth;
sBar[1].Y = 12*fontHeight;
sBar[1].value = 0;
SetScrollRange (sBar[1].hSbar = hWnd, sBar[1].nBar = SB_VERT,
                                      0, sBar[1].high=99, FALSE);
SetScrollPos (sBar[1].hSbar, SB_VERT, sBar[1].value = 50, TRUE);

for (i=0; i<=7; i++)
  {
  sBar[i+2].hSbar = CreateWindow (
          (LPSTR) "ScrollBar",
          (LPSTR) "",
          WS_CHILD | WS_VISIBLE | SBS_HORZ | SBS_TOPALIGN,
          fontWidth*4,
          (i+1)*fontHeight*3/2,
          fontWidth*(8-i)*8,
          fontHeight,
          hWnd,
          1,
          hInst,
          (LPSTR)NULL);
  sBar[i+2].X = fontWidth;
  sBar[i+2].Y = (i+1)*fontHeight*3/2;
  SetScrollRange (sBar[i+2].hSbar, sBar[i+2].nBar = SB_CTL,
                             0, sBar[i+2].high = (8-i)*8, FALSE);
  SetScrollPos (sBar[i+2].hSbar, SB_CTL, sBar[i+2].value = (8-i)*6, TRUE);
  ShowWindow (sBar[i+2].hSbar, SHOW_OPENWINDOW);
  sBar[i+10].hSbar = CreateWindow (
          (LPSTR) "ScrollBar",
          (LPSTR) "",
          WS_CHILD | WS_VISIBLE | SBS_VERT | SBS_LEFTALIGN,
          66*fontWidth-8*fontWidth*i,          /* 4x + 8x(8-i) - 2x    */
          (fontHeight*3*i+fontHeight*7)/2,     /* 3x(i+1)/2 + 2x       */
          fontWidth*2,
          (29*fontHeight-3*i*fontHeight)/2,    /* 18x - (3x(i+1)/2+2x) */
          hWnd,
          1,
          hInst,
          (LPSTR)NULL);
  sBar[i+10].X = 66*fontWidth-8*fontWidth*i;  /* 4x + 8x(8-i) - 2x    */
  sBar[i+10].Y = 19*fontHeight;
```

```
      SetScrollRange (sBar[i+10].hSbar, sBar[i+10].nBar = SB_CTL,
                              0, sBar[i+10].high = (8-i)*8, FALSE);
      SetScrollPos (sBar[i+10].hSbar, SB_CTL,
                              sBar[i+10].value = (8-i)*2, TRUE);
      ShowWindow (sBar[i+10].hSbar, SHOW_OPENWINDOW);
      }

    ShowWindow (hWnd, cmdShow);
    UpdateWindow (hWnd);

    while (GetMessage ((LPMSG)&msg, NULL, 0, 0))
      {
      TranslateMessage((LPMSG)&msg);
      DispatchMessage((LPMSG)&msg);
      }
    return (int)msg.wParam;
    }

  printNum (hDC, value, x, y)
    HDC   hDC;
    int   value,  x,  y;
    {
    itoa (value, szNum, 10);
    if (value < 10)
      {
      szNum[1] = szNum[0];
      szNum[0] = ' ';
      }
    TextOut (hDC, x, y, (LPSTR)szNum, 2);
    }

  scrollFunc (hWnd, i, wParam, lParam)
    HWND  hWnd;
    int   i;
    WORD  wParam;
    LONG  lParam;
    {
    HDC   hDC;
    switch (wParam)
      {
      case SB_LINEUP:
        sBar[i].value--;
        break;
      case SB_PAGEUP:
        sBar[i].value /= 2;
        break;
      case SB_LINEDOWN:
        sBar[i].value++;
        break;
      case SB_PAGEDOWN:
        sBar[i].value += ((sBar[i].high-sBar[i].value)/2);
        break;
      case SB_THUMBPOSITION:
        sBar[i].value = LOWORD(lParam);
        break;
      case SB_TOP:
        sBar[i].value = 0;
        break;
      case SB_BOTTOM:
        sBar[i].value = 99;
        break;
      }
    sBar[i].value = max (0, min(sBar[i].high, sBar[i].value));
    SetScrollPos (sBar[i].hSbar, sBar[i].nBar, sBar[i].value, TRUE);
    hDC = GetDC (hWnd);
```

```
  SetBkColor (hDC, bkColor);
  SetTextColor (hDC, textColor);
  printNum (hDC, sBar[i].value, sBar[i].X, sBar[i].Y);
  ReleaseDC (hWnd, hDC);
  }

long FAR PASCAL MainWndProc (hWnd, msg, wParam, lParam)
  HWND                  hWnd;
  unsigned              msg;
  WORD                  wParam;
  LONG                  lParam;
  {
  switch (msg)
    {
    case WM_HSCROLL:
    case WM_VSCROLL:
      for (i=2; i<18; i++)
        {
        if (sBar[i].hSbar == HIWORD (lParam))
          {
          scrollFunc (hWnd, i, wParam, lParam);
          break;
          }
        }
      if (i==18)                          /* didn't find a match? */
        scrollFunc (hWnd, ((msg == WM_HSCROLL) ? 0 : 1), wParam, lParam);
      break;

    case WM_PAINT:
      {
      PAINTSTRUCT       ps;

      BeginPaint (hWnd, (LPPAINTSTRUCT)&ps);
      SetTextColor (ps.hdc, textColor);
      SetBkColor (ps.hdc, bkColor);
      for (i=0; i<18; i++)
        printNum (ps.hdc, sBar[i].value, sBar[i].X, sBar[i].Y);
      EndPaint (hWnd, (LPPAINTSTRUCT)&ps);
      break;
     }

    case WM_DESTROY:
      PostQuitMessage (0);
      break;

    default:
      return DefWindowProc (hWnd, msg, wParam, lParam);
      break;
    }
  return (0L);
  }

/*--------------------------------------------------------------------*/
/* End of file:  PGM7.C                                               */
/**********************************************************************/
```

WinMain starts off a little differently from our previous programs. There is no **MainInit** procedure; instead, we've incorporated that procedure into **WinMain** for simplicity. Note the first line:

```
if (hPrevInstance)
return FALSE;
```

Recall that **hPrevInstance** has the handle of a previous instance of this program. What we are saying here is, "If this is another instance, exit now." This code prevents multiple occurrences.

The next few lines build our class structure, register, and create our window. Following that, we grab a DC (display context). You've seen this code in several previous chapters.

10.2.1 Allocating Space for Fonts

Next, we allocate space for the data structure **TEXTMETRIC**:

```
pTextMetric = (PTEXTMETRIC) LocalAlloc (LPTR,
        sizeof(TEXTMETRIC));
```

TEXTMETRIC is defined in WINDOWS.H. It contains fields that define the basic metrics of a physical font. To ask Windows to fill in the fields, we use:

```
GetTextMetrics (hDC, (PTEXTMETRIC)pTextMetric);
```

The storage pointed to by **pTextMetric** is loaded with information about the current font. We are interested in two fields within this structure: **tmHeight** and **tmAveCharWidth**, the font height and average character width:

```
fontHeight = (int) pTextMetric->tmHeight;
fontWidth = (int) pTextMetric->tmAveCharWidth;
```

Finally, we de-allocate the local storage:

```
LocalFree ((HANDLE)pTextMetric);
```

10.2.2 Setting Scroll Bar Positions and Ranges

We have defined a global data structure at the top of our program:

```
struct {
HWND,     hSbar;         /* handle to scroll bar          */
int       value;         /* current value of scroll bar   */
int       X;             /* X coord for sbar value        */
int       Y;             /* Y coord for sbar value        */
int       high;          /* High end of range             */
int       nBar;          /* SB_VERT, SB_HORZ, or SB_CTL   */
} sBar[18];              /* [00] = Main window horiz bar  */
                         /* [01] = Main window vert  bar  */
                         /* [02]-[09] = Child  horiz bar  */
                         /* [10]-[17] = Child  vert  bar  */
```

We'll control all scroll bars through this structure. The first field, **hSbar**, contains the handle of the window that particular scroll bar is in. Every scroll bar will have a value that is dependent on the position of the scroll box; we'll keep that value in **value**. For every scroll bar, we want to display a numerical value: **X** and **Y** will contain the coordinates for placing the number. Every scroll bar has a range within which it varies. All of our scroll bars start at zero and go to **high**.

A scroll bar can have one of the following attributes: **SB_VERT, SB_HORZ,** or **SB_CTL**, depending on whether it is the window's vertical scroll bar, the window's horizontal scroll bar, or a child scroll bar (vertical or horizontal). We have one vertical scroll bar, one horizontal scroll bar, and 16 child scroll bars.

The next statements set the X and Y coordinates for displaying **value**. Following that is the statement:

```
SetScrollRange (sBar[0].hSbar = hWnd,
                sBar[0].nBar = SB_HORZ,
                0,
                sBar[0].high=99,
                FALSE);
```

This call to Windows does exactly what its name implies: it sets the range of a scroll bar. We are setting our overlapped window's **hWnd** horizontal (**SB_HORZ**) scroll bar to range from zero (**0**) to **99**. We do not want Windows to redraw the scroll bar yet (FALSE), because we still want to set an initial position:

```
SetScrollPos (sBar[0].hSbar,
              SB_HORZ,
              sBar[0].value = 10,
              TRUE);
```

This call sets the scroll box of the horizontal scroll bar belonging to window **sBar[0].hSbar** to the value of **10**. TRUE means that we want Windows to redraw the scroll bar.

Next, we'll create 16 child windows, each the size of a scroll bar. To do this, we use a loop that repeats eight times. The only lines that require discussion in the **CreateWindow** call are:

```
WS_CHILD | WS_VISIBLE | SBS_HORZ | SBS_TOPALIGN,
-or-
WS_CHILD | WS_VISIBLE | SBS_VERT | SBS_LEFTALIGN,
```

This tells Windows that we want a child window that is visible, and that we want a scroll bar (horizontal or vertical) that is top-aligned or left-aligned. The four lines following the flags specify the position and size. In this program, we use the height and width of the current font to control consistency.

```
SetScrollRange (sBar[i+2].hSbar,
                sBar[i+2].nBar = SB_CTL,
                0,
                sBar[i+2].high = (8-i)*8,
                FALSE);
SetScrollPos (sBar[i+2].hSbar,
              SB_CTL,
              sBar[i+2].value = (8-i)*6,
              TRUE);
```

Note that the calls to **SetScrollRange** and **SetScrollPos** are nearly identical, with the exception of **SB_CTL**. This flag indicates that this scroll bar is not in this window, but rather in a child window.

The rest of **WinMain** is business as usual.

10.2.3 Processing Scroll Bar Messages

Before looking at the scroll bar processing logic, let's look briefly at **WM_PAINT** in **MainWndProc**. As usual, we place a call to **BeginPaint** to get things going. Next, we want to set the foreground and background colors. Windows will use these values when drawing our text (the numbers).

```
SetTextColor (ps.hdc, textColor);
SetBkColor (ps.hdc, bkColor);
```

SetTextColor specifies the RGB color to use in drawing characters when **TextOut** is called. **SetBkColor** specifies the RGB color to use as the background. The default (issued with the DC when **GetDC** is called) is black text on white background.

We now introduce two new "WM_" messages:

```
case, WM_HSCROLL:
case WM_VSCROLL:
```

These messages are sent by the window function of a scroll bar whenever activity occurs in the scroll bar. **wParam** contains a code telling why Windows has made this call. For example, if the top (or right) arrow in the scroll bar was clicked on, Windows will send **wParam** equal to **SB_LINEUP**. See Figure 10.2 for a summary of these messages, which can be found in WINDOWS.H.

Figure 10.2

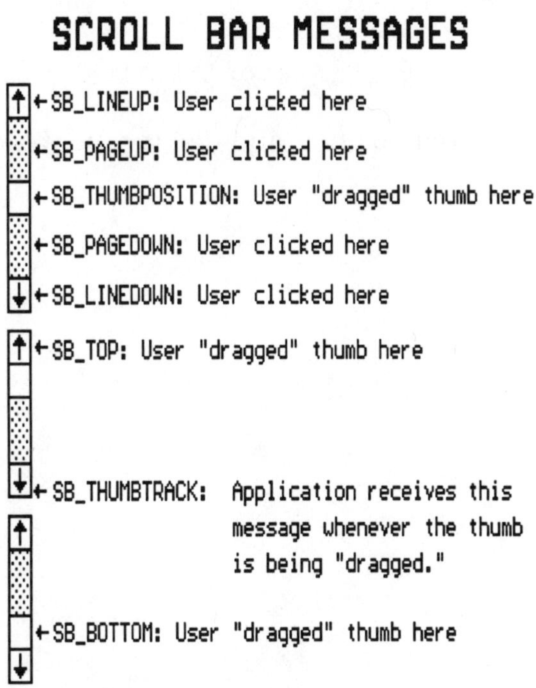

Because we are processing three types of scroll bars (**SB_HORZ, SB_VERT,** and **SB_CTL**) with the same piece of code, we loop through the 16 **SB_CTL** fields and check:

```
if (sBar[i].hSbar == HIWORD (lParam))
```

HIWORD (lParam) contains the child window handle of the scroll bar in which the event occurred. Remember, a parent window receives the scroll bar messages of its children, so **MainWndProc** receives not only **WM_VSCROLL** and **WM_HSCROLL** for its own two scroll bars, but for all 16 children as well. So, we key on the "offending" window handle. If it is equal to one of the children, we call our internal procedure **scrollFunc**. If we cannot find a match, we must assume the message comes from the main window. A simple test of **msg** tells us which scroll bar (horizontal or vertical) we are to act on (remember that (0) is the index in our array for horizontal and (1) corresponds to vertical).

Finally, let's take a quick look at **scrollFunc**. As discussed previously, Windows will tell us exactly what happened in the scroll bar via **wParam**. So we **switch** on it:

```
switch (wParam)
```

Just to be sure that none of our calculations overran the scroll bar limits, we use the following:

```
sBar[i].value = max (0, min(sBar[i].high, sBar[i].value
```

Last, we set the new scroll position and display the value.

10.3 THE MODULE DEFINITION FILE: PGM7.DEF

```
;*****************************************************************:
; Filename:     PGM7.DEF                                         :
;                                                                :
; Description:  Link definition file                             :
;----------------------------------------------------------------:

NAME    PGM7

DESCRIPTION 'Sample program 7'

STUB    '..\WINSTUB.EXE'

CODE    MOVEABLE
DATA    MOVEABLE MULTIPLE

HEAPSIZE  128
STACKSIZE 4096

EXPORTS
    MainWndProc         @1

;----------------------------------------------------------------:
; End of file:  PGM7.DEF                                         :
;*****************************************************************:
```

10.4 THE MAKE FILE: PGM7.

```
#*********************************************************************#
# Filename:     PGM7.                                                 #
#                                                                     #
# Description:  PGM7.EXE "MAKE" description file                      #
#---------------------------------------------------------------------#

pgm7.obj: pgm7.c
    cl -d -c -AS -Gsw -Os -Zpe pgm7.c

pgm7.exe: pgm7.obj pgm7.def
    link4 pgm7,/align:16,,slibw,pgm7.def

#---------------------------------------------------------------------#
# End of file:  PGM7.                                                 #
#*********************************************************************#
```

. . . .

In this chapter, you've learned to add child windows and scroll bars to your application's main window. In Chapter 11, you'll learn how Windows manages memory.

11

INTRODUCTION TO MEMORY MANAGEMENT

- Overview of Memory Management
- The Windows Memory Model
- Memory Allocation
- Memory Re-Allocation
- Locking Storage
- Freeing and Discarding Memory
- Compacting Memory
- Miscellaneous Memory Functions
- Using of C Runtime Memory Functions with Windows
- Testing An Application in Moveable Memory Environment: Using Shaker and Heapwalker
- Running PGM8 to Use Memory Management Calls

Any operating environment that simultaneously supports more than one user or application must provide a mechanism for dividing central memory among the concurrent processes. In this chapter, you'll see how Windows manages memory. At the end of the chapter are listings for a sample program, PGM8, that lets you directly use the memory management calls.

11.1 OVERVIEW OF MEMORY MANAGEMENT

Many multiprogramming systems divide memory into blocks, with each process being assigned to a different block. These partitions may be predefined in size and position (*fixed blocks*), or they may be allocated dynamically according to the requirements of the tasks being executed (*variable blocks*).

Generally speaking, using variable blocks results in more efficient use of memory than using fixed blocks, although copying tasks from one location in memory to another may require a substantial amount of time. When you use variable blocks, you don't have to select block sizes in advance. However, the memory manager must keep track of which areas of memory are allocated and which are free. The memory manager usually does this by maintaining a linked list of free memory areas. This list is scanned when a new block is allocated, and the block is placed either in the first free area that it will fit in (*first-fit allocation*), or in the smallest free area that it will fit in (*best-fit allocation*). When a block is released, its assigned memory is returned to the free list and combined with any adjacent free areas.

Using variable blocks sometimes causes *memory fragmentation*, a problem which occurs when the available free memory is split into several separate blocks, with each block being too small to be of use. One possible solution is *relocation*. To fill an allocation request that is greater than any individual fragment, the remaining free blocks are moved toward one end of memory, thereby gathering all the available memory together into one contiguous block. If this does not fulfill the allocation request, another technique may be applied: *discarding*. Certain memory blocks may be marked as "discardable," meaning the memory manager may, if necessary, reuse the space.

Figure 11.1 illustrates a typical Windows memory management problem: how to allocate a block that is greater in size than any one free block. A request for 30KB of memory is put to the memory manager.

40KB of memory is free within the system: however, it is fragmented into three areas of 10KB, 10KB, and 20KB.

Figure 11.2 illustrates how Windows solves the problem through relocation. Allocated blocks are moved to the lower end of storage, and the free areas are collected at the high end. This yields a block of 40KB from which an allocation of 30KB can be made.

Figure 11.1

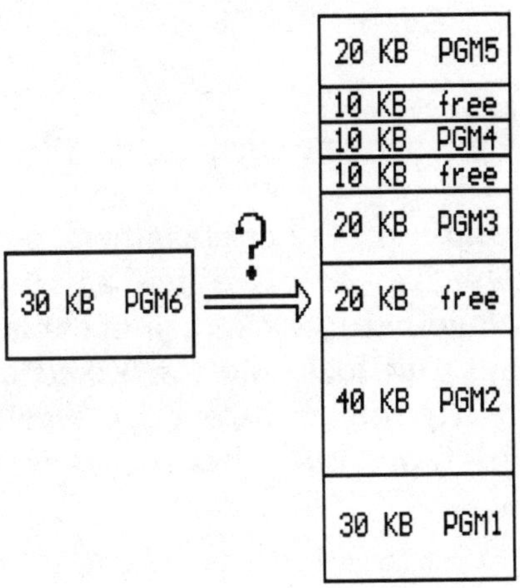

Figure 11.2

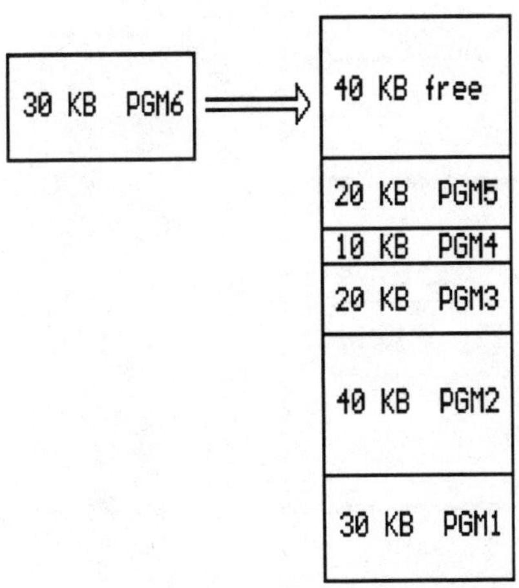

11.2 THE WINDOWS MEMORY MODEL

A Windows application has two types of storage available for general use: global and local. *Global memory* is all of system memory that is not allocated to any particular task. Global means BIG, usually greater than 64K in size. Global addresses are 32-bit pointers. *Local memory* is allocated from within an application's heap, is 64K or less, and is allocated in the module's link definition file statement:

```
HEAPSIZE bytes
```

where **bytes** is an integer that specifies the heap size. A local pointer is a 16-bit offset.

Both global and local storage may be classified as *fixed* or *moveable*. Moveable storage may also be classified as *discardable*. Figure 11.3 illustrates relative placement of fixed, moveable, and discardable allocations within global and local blocks. Fixed allocations are placed lower in memory in an attempt to thwart the development of "beachheads" or "roadblocks," which prevent other blocks from moving around.

Figure 11.3

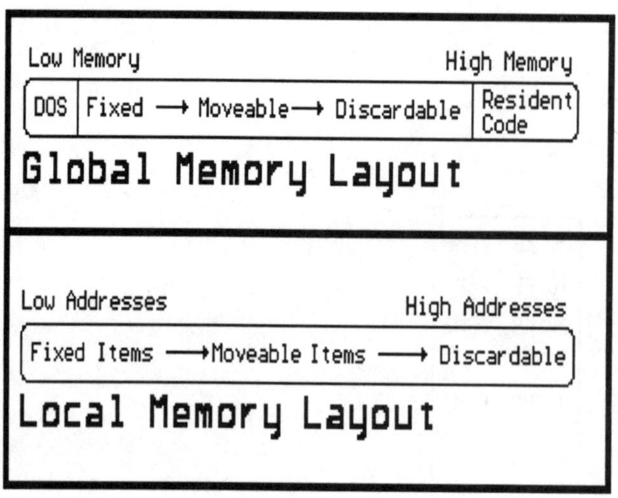

Figure 11.4 illustrates the integration of global and local allocations to form local objects. It should be noted that even though a local object may be fixed, the entire local segment may be a moveable global object. The local fixed object will remain fixed within the local segment, but could still be moved with the rest of the local segment.

Figure 11.4

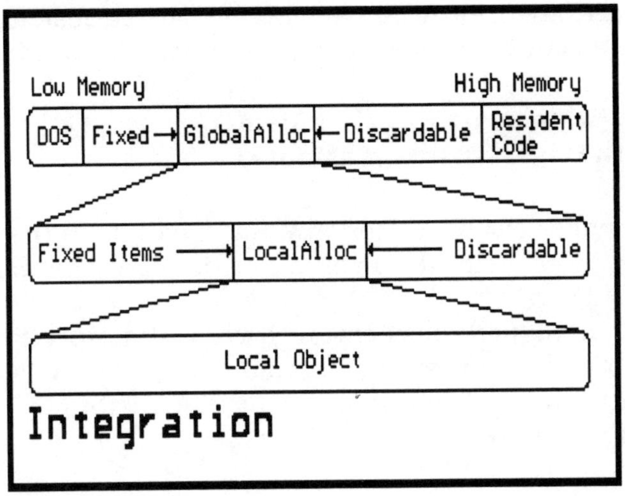

When a moveable memory block is marked as discardable, Windows may use this block to fulfill a memory allocation request from some other application. Windows keeps track of discardable storage in a "least recently used" chain.

Code segments are, by default, discardable. This means they may be reread from disk. Note that discarding and swapping are not the same: discarding does not involve a physical write to disk.

When Windows receives a storage allocation request, it scans memory on a "first-fit" basis in an attempt to immediately satisfy the allocation. Windows performs this scan from low to high memory addresses or from high to low memory addresses depending on whether a fixed or moveable block is required. If the allocation request cannot be met, Windows moves blocks until the request is met or until no more blocks can be moved. If the allocation still has not been achieved, Windows discards blocks until there are no more blocks to discard or the allocation has been met. If the allocation cannot be made, Windows returns an error.

11.3 MEMORY ALLOCATION

All global memory related functions begin with "Global," and most local memory functions begin with "Local." A formal request for storage allocation is made via one of these two functions:

GlobalAlloc (wFlags, dwBytes) : hMem
LocalAlloc (wFlags, wBytes) : hMem

If Windows makes the allocation, **hMem**, a handle to the memory, returns non-zero. If the allocation could not be made, **hMem** returns NULL.

wFlags is an unsigned short integer (word) that specifies exactly what type of allocation is desired. Its value can take on any of the following attributes, or any combination of these attributes, providing the combination makes sense:

FIXED	memory is fixed
MOVEABLE	memory is moveable
ZEROINIT	memory is initialized to zero
DISCARDABLE	memory is discardable
NOCOMPACT	compaction and discarding to satisfy the allocation will not be performed

When Windows makes an allocation, it also allocates an additional 16 bytes to the front of the memory block. These 16 bytes are called the *arena header*, which stores the segment's attributes and parameters.

Local fixed handles may be directly used as pointers. For example:

```
char *LocMemPtr;
if (LocMemPtr = (char *) LocalAlloc (wBytes, LMEM_FIXED))
  *LocMemPtr = 'Q';
```

If **LocalAlloc** returns a handle (not NULL, thus TRUE), the constant '*Q*' is assigned to the location specified by the handle. Note that this works *only* for local FIXED handles.

11.4 MEMORY RE-ALLOCATION

You can modify a memory block's size using one of the re-allocation calls. Also, if a block has been discarded, you can attempt to recover that storage. The re-allocation functions are:

```
GlobalReAlloc (hMem, dwBytes, wFlags) : hNewMem
LocalReAlloc (hMem, wBytes, wFlags) : hNewMem
```

These calls work much like the allocation functions. The only significant difference is that you also pass **hMem**, the memory handle of the block you want to have re-allocated.

For example, suppose you had used **GlobalAlloc** to allocate some number of FIXED storage blocks, and you now want to increase that storage to **dwBytes**, change it to MOVEABLE, and initialize the new bytes to zero. You'd use:

```
hMem = GlobalReAlloc (hMem, dwBytes,
                      GMEM_MOVEABLE | GMEM_ZEROINIT);
```

11.5 LOCKING STORAGE

To use storage allocated by the Windows memory manager, an application must "lock" it down. The act of locking yields a physical address where the memory block resides, and temporarily fixes the storage, thus protecting it from movement and discarding. The locking functions are:

```
GlobalLock (hMem) : lpAddress
LocalLock (hMem) : pAddress
```

GlobalLock generates a 32-bit physical address. **LocalLock** generates a 16-bit physical offset.

Before returning control to Windows, an application should unlock memory:

```
GlobalUnlock (hMem) : bResult
LocalUnLock (hMem) : bResult
```

bResult returns the Boolean value TRUE or FALSE indicating success or failure.

Here's an example of locking a global handle:

```
HANDLE hGlobal;
char   *GlobalPtr;
hGlobal = GlobalAlloc (...)
GlobalPtr = GlobalLock (hGlobal);
*GlobalPtr = ...
GlobalUnlock (hGlobal);
```

Windows keeps track of memory locking by using a field within the arena header called *lock count*. Calling one of the locking functions causes the *lock count* to be incremented. Calling one of the unlocking functions causes the *lock count* to be decremented.

By default, an application's data segment is created with a lock count of (1). This can be overridden in the module definition file with the statement:

```
DATA MOVEABLE
```

If an application has a moveable data segment and you want to fix it in memory, you can use these two functions:

```
LockData (Dummy)
UnlockData (Dummy)
```

Dummy is not used and can be set to zero.

The following situations can invalidate 32-bit pointers, so you'll need to either lock down the data segment with **LockData** or reestablish the outstanding pointer:

1 When an application calls the **GetMessage** or **PeekMessage** functions, the data segment's lock count is decremented, thereby allowing the segment to move about while other applications are running. Returning from these functions increments the lock count.

2 The **LocalAlloc** function can decrement an application's data segment lock count to zero and expand the local heap.

If an application makes a request for local storage greater than what is immediately available, Windows will attempt to compact the local heap. If you don't want to have the heap compacted, you'll use the following functions:

```
LocalFreeze (Dummy)
LocalMelt (Dummy)
```

Again, **Dummy** is not used and can be set to zero.

Local moveable objects may be addressed as follows:

```
char                *LocMemPtr;
HANDLE              hLocMem;
hLocMem = LocalAlloc (wBytes, LMEM_MOVEABLE)
LocMemPtr = LocalLock (hLocMem);
*LocMemPtr = 'Q';
LocalUnlock (hLocMem);
```

11.6 FREEING AND DISCARDING MEMORY

Windows is a *cooperative* environment: if an application doesn't need storage, it should free the handle to that storage or allow the handle to be discarded. To "free" a handle is to relinquish the handle and its associated storage. To "discard" a handle means to relinquish the memory allocated to a handle, but the handle itself remains valid.

The freeing functions are:

```
GlobalFree (hMem) : hOldMem
LocalFree (hMem) : hOldMem
```

hMem is the handle issued by the allocation or re-allocation function. **hOldMem** is NULL if the function is successful, otherwise it is equal to **hMem**.

Applications are required to free any global memory allocated to them. Applications should also free local memory when appropriate, although Windows will automatically free this storage when the application terminates.

As discussed previously, DISCARDABLE blocks will automatically be discarded during the allocation process. If an application wants to discard a block, it may use one of the discarding functions:

```
GlobalDiscard (hMem) : hOldMem
LocalDiscard (hMem) : hOldMem
```

Just like the freeing functions, **hMem** is a memory handle and **hOld-Mem** returns NULL if successful; otherwise it is equal to **hMem**. The discarding function marks the block as DISCARDABLE, but may not actually discard it. The next time the block is locked determines whether or not it is still valid.

11.7 COMPACTING MEMORY

Compacting can be performed if a request for storage allocation cannot be met using the "first-fit" technique. The compaction functions tell how much memory is available and cause Windows to compact if necessary.

The compaction functions are:

```
GlobalCompact (dwMinFree) : dwLargest
LocalCompact (wMinFree) : wLargest
```

MinFree is the argument in the question, "Is **MinFree** bytes available?" Windows returns the answer, "**Largest** is the largest number of bytes available." If **MinFree** is NULL, Windows will return **Largest**, but will not actually compact memory; thus **Largest** may not truly be the largest block that could be generated by moving and discarding.

11.8 MISCELLANEOUS MEMORY FUNCTIONS

Windows has two "size" functions that return the current size of a specified memory block:

```
GlobalSize (hMem) : dwBytes
LocalSize (hMem) : wBytes
```

Windows also has two "flag" functions that return status information about a specified memory block:

```
GlobalFlags (hMem) : wFlags
LocalFlags (hMem) : wFlags
```

wFlags is a word whose low byte contains the current lock count, and whose high byte contains flags indicating SWAPPED, DISCARDED, and DISCARDABLE.

11.9 USING OF C RUNTIME MEMORY FUNCTIONS WITH WINDOWS

The C runtime functions **calloc, malloc, realloc,** and **free** will work in all memory models. They are associated with the "Local. . ." functions as follows:

```
#define calloc (n,size)       LocalAlloc (LMEM_ZEROINIT,
                                                n*size);
#define malloc (size)         LocalAlloc (0, size);
#define free (p)              LocalFree (p);
#define realloc(p, size)      LocalReAlloc (p, size,
                                         LMEM_ZEROINIT);
```

11.10 TESTING AN APPLICATION IN MOVEABLE MEMORY ENVIRONMENT: USING SHAKER AND HEAPWALKER

Microsoft provides two test programs with the Development Kit: SHAKER and HEAPWALKER. SHAKER is designed to test an application in the moveable memory environment, and HEAPWALKER permits viewing the global heap.

You should routinely use SHAKER and HEAPWALKER as part of your development process. If the application continues to function with these two programs jogging the system memory, you can be fairly confident that your program will survive in the field.

11.11 RUNNING PGM8 TO USE MEMORY MANAGEMENT CALLS

```
/*******************************************************************/
/* Filename:     PGM8.H                                            */
/*                                                                 */
/* Description:  Header file                                       */
/*-----------------------------------------------------------------*/

#define IDITEM01        1001
#define IDITEM02        1002
#define IDITEM03        1003
#define IDITEM04        1004
#define IDITEM05        1005
#define IDITEM06        1006
#define IDITEM07        1007
#define IDITEM08        1008
#define IDITEM09        1009
#define IDITEM10        1010
#define IDITEM11        1011
#define IDITEM12        1012
#define IDITEM13        1013
#define IDITEM14        1014
#define IDITEM15        1015
#define IDITEM16        1016

#define IDALLOCATE      1021
#define IDLOCK          1022
#define IDUNLOCK        1023
#define IDFLAGS         1024
#define IDFREE          1025
#define IDDISCARD       1026
#define IDSIZE          1027
#define IDLOCALFREEZE   1028
#define IDLOCALMELT     1029
#define IDLOCKDATA      1030
#define IDUNLOCKDATA    1031
#define IDGLOBALCOMPACT 1032
#define IDLOCALCOMPACT  1033
#define MEMDLGBOX       1034
#define IDRBGLOBAL      1035
#define IDRBLOCAL       1036
#define IDRBFIXED       1037
#define IDRBMOVEABLE    1038
#define IDRBDISCARDABLE 1039
#define IDRBNODISCARD   1040
#define IDRBNOCOMPACT   1041
#define IDETSIZE        1042

/*-----------------------------------------------------------------*/
/* End of file:  PGM8.H                                            */
/*******************************************************************/
```

```
/********************************************************************/
/* Filename:     PGM8.RC                                            */
/*                                                                  */
/* Description:  Resource description file                          */
/*------------------------------------------------------------------*/

#include "style.h"
#include "pgm8.h"

MainMenu MENU
BEGIN
  POPUP "Item"
  BEGIN
    MENUITEM    " 1",                       IDITEM01
    MENUITEM    " 5",                       IDITEM05
    MENUITEM    " 9",                       IDITEM09
    MENUITEM    "13",                       IDITEM13
    MENUITEM    " 2",                       IDITEM02, MENUBARBREAK
    MENUITEM    " 6",                       IDITEM06
    MENUITEM    "10",                       IDITEM10
    MENUITEM    "14",                       IDITEM14
    MENUITEM    " 3",                       IDITEM03, MENUBARBREAK
    MENUITEM    " 7",                       IDITEM07
    MENUITEM    "11",                       IDITEM11
    MENUITEM    "15",                       IDITEM15
    MENUITEM    " 4",                       IDITEM04, MENUBARBREAK
    MENUITEM    " 8",                       IDITEM08
    MENUITEM    "12",                       IDITEM12
    MENUITEM    "16",                       IDITEM16
  END
  POPUP "&Options"
  BEGIN
    MENUITEM    " ",                        IDALLOCATE
    MENUITEM    SEPARATOR
    MENUITEM    "&Lock",                    IDLOCK
    MENUITEM    "&UnLock",                  IDUNLOCK
    MENUITEM    "&Flags",                   IDFLAGS,        MENUBARBREAK
    MENUITEM    "Fr&ee",                    IDFREE
    MENUITEM    "&Discard",                 IDDISCARD
    MENUITEM    "&Size",                    IDSIZE
    MENUITEM    "LocalFree&ze",             IDLOCALFREEZE,  MENUBARBREAK
    MENUITEM    "Local&Melt",               IDLOCALMELT
    MENUITEM    "Loc&kData",                IDLOCKDATA
    MENUITEM    "UnlockDa&ta",              IDUNLOCKDATA

  END
  POPUP "&Compact"
  BEGIN
    MENUITEM    "&Global",                  IDGLOBALCOMPACT
    MENUITEM    "&Local",                   IDLOCALCOMPACT
  END
END

MEMDLGBOX DIALOG   10, 50, 192, 56
STYLE WS_BORDER | WS_CAPTION | WS_DLGFRAME | WS_POPUP
BEGIN
 GROUPBOX    "Colour",      -1,            2,  2, 60, 36
 RADIOBUTTON "Global",      IDRBGLOBAL,    4, 12, 56, 12,WS_TABSTOP
 RADIOBUTTON "Local",       IDRBLOCAL,     4, 24, 56, 12,WS_TABSTOP
```

```
 GROUPBOX     "Flavor",      -1,               66,  2, 60, 36
 RADIOBUTTON "Fixed",        IDRBFIXED,        68, 12, 56, 12,WS_TABSTOP
 RADIOBUTTON "Moveable",     IDRBMOVEABLE,     68, 24, 56, 12,WS_TABSTOP
 RADIOBUTTON "Discardable", IDRBDISCARDABLE,132,  2, 56, 12,WS_TABSTOP
 RADIOBUTTON "NoDiscard",    IDRBNODISCARD,   132, 14, 56, 12,WS_TABSTOP
 RADIOBUTTON "NoCompact",    IDRBNOCOMPACT,   132, 26, 56, 12,WS_TABSTOP
 LTEXT        "Size:",       -1,                2, 44, 20,  8
 EDITTEXT                    IDETSIZE,         34, 42, 28, 12
 PUSHBUTTON  "Ok",           IDOK              66, 42, 60, 12
 PUSHBUTTON  "Cancel",       IDCANCEL,        130, 42, 60, 12
END

/*------------------------------------------------------------------*/
/* End of file:  PGM8.RC                                            */
/********************************************************************/
```

```
/********************************************************************/
/* Filename:      PGM8.C                                            */
/*                                                                  */
/* Description:  Program source                                     */
/*------------------------------------------------------------------*/

#include "windows.h"
#include "pgm8.h"

typedef BOOL FAR * LPBOOL;

  HANDLE                 hInst;
  FARPROC                lpAllocProc;
  int                    i,               index;
  char                   szString[80],    szNumber[17],    szStr[4];
  HMENU                  hMenu;
  HANDLE                 hOldMem;
  unsigned int           flags;

struct {
  HANDLE                 hMem;            /* handle to memory block  */
  unsigned int           flags;           /* allocation flags        */
  BOOL                   colour;          /* T: Global  F: Local     */
  unsigned int           size;            /* block size              */
  } memory[16];

  unsigned int           item             = 0;     /* current item */
  BOOL                   bValOK;
  BOOL                   bLocalFreeze     = FALSE;
  BOOL                   bLockData        = FALSE;

/*------------------------------------------------------------------*/

long FAR PASCAL MainWndProc (hWnd, msg, wParam, lParam)
  HWND           hWnd;
  unsigned       msg;
  WORD           wParam;
  LONG           lParam;
  {
  PAINTSTRUCT    ps;
  int            lineNum;
```

```
  switch (msg)  {
    case WM_CREATE:
      hMenu = GetMenu (hWnd);
      EnableMenuItem (hMenu, IDLOCALMELT, MF_GRAYED);
      EnableMenuItem (hMenu, IDUNLOCKDATA, MF_GRAYED);
      break;

    case WM_DESTROY:
      for (i=0; i<16; i++)               /* Free any allocations */
        if (memory[i].hMem)
          if (memory[i].colour)
            GlobalFree (memory[i].hMem);
          else
            LocalFree (memory[i].hMem);
      PostQuitMessage (0);
      break;

    case WM_PAINT:
      BeginPaint (hWnd, (LPPAINTSTRUCT)&ps);
      for (i=0, lineNum = 2; i<16; i++) {
        if (memory[i].hMem) {
          itoa (i+1, szNumber, 10);
          index = StrCopy (szString, 0, szNumber, 2, TRUE);
          index = StrCopy (szString, index, "  ", 2, FALSE);
          itoa (memory[i].hMem, szNumber, 16);
          index = StrCopy (szString, index, szNumber, 4, TRUE);
          index = StrCopy(szString, index, (memory[i].colour)
                        ? ("  GLOBAL  ") : ("  LOCAL   "), 10, FALSE);
          TextOut (ps.hdc, 8, lineNum += 12, (LPSTR)szString, index);
          }
        }
      EndPaint (hWnd, (LPPAINTSTRUCT)&ps);
      break;

    case WM_INITMENU:
      hMenu = GetMenu (hWnd);
      CheckMenuItem (hMenu, item + IDITEM01, MF_CHECKED);
      if (memory[item].hMem)
        ChangeMenu (hMenu, IDALLOCATE, (LPSTR)"&ReAllocate",
                IDALLOCATE, MF_CHANGE | MF_BYCOMMAND);
      else                                   /* here if item free */
        ChangeMenu (hMenu, IDALLOCATE, (LPSTR)"&Allocate",
                IDALLOCATE, MF_CHANGE | MF_BYCOMMAND);
      break;

    case WM_COMMAND:
      MainWndWMCommand (hWnd, msg, wParam, lParam);
      break;
    default:
      return DefWindowProc (hWnd, msg, wParam, lParam);
      break;
    }
  return (0L);
  }

MainWndWMCommand (hWnd, msg, wParam, lParam)
  HWND          hWnd;
  unsigned      msg;
```

```
WORD          wParam;
LONG          lParam;
{
if ((wParam >= IDITEM01)
 && (wParam <= IDITEM16)) {
  hMenu = GetMenu (hWnd);
  CheckMenuItem (hMenu, item + IDITEM01, MF_UNCHECKED);
  CheckMenuItem (hMenu, wParam, MF_CHECKED);
  item = wParam - IDITEM01;
  itoa (item+1, szStr, 10);
  SetWindowText (hWnd, (LPSTR)szStr);
  }
else {
  switch (wParam) {
    case IDALLOCATE:
      if (DialogBox(hInst, MAKEINTRESOURCE(MEMDLGBOX),
                                        hWnd, lpAllocProc))
        InvalidateRect (hWnd, (LPRECT)NULL, TRUE);
      break;


    case IDFREE:
      if (memory[item].hMem) {
        if (memory[item].colour)
          hOldMem = GlobalFree (memory[item].hMem);
        else
          hOldMem = LocalFree (memory[item].hMem);
        if (hOldMem)
          MessageBox (hWnd, (LPSTR)"Free function failed",
                           (LPSTR)NULL, MB_OK | MB_ICONHAND);
        else
          memory[item].hMem = 0;
          InvalidateRect (hWnd, (LPRECT)NULL, TRUE);
        }
      break;

    case IDDISCARD:
      if (memory[item].hMem) {
        hOldMem = FALSE;
        if (memory[item].colour) {
          if (HIBYTE(GlobalFlags(memory[item].hMem))
                                    & GMEM_DISCARDABLE)
            hOldMem = GlobalDiscard (memory[item].hMem);
          }
        else {
          if (HIBYTE(LocalFlags(memory[item].hMem))
                                    & LMEM_DISCARDABLE)
            hOldMem = LocalDiscard (memory[item].hMem);
          }
        if (hOldMem)
          MessageBox (hWnd, (LPSTR)"Discard function failed",
                           (LPSTR)NULL, MB_OK | MB_ICONHAND);
        else
          InvalidateRect (hWnd, (LPRECT)NULL, TRUE);
        }
      break;
```

```
case IDFLAGS:
  if (memory[item].hMem) {
    index = StrCopy(szString, 0, "Lock Count: ", 12, FALSE);
    if (memory[item].colour) {
      flags = GlobalFlags(memory[item].hMem);
      itoa (flags & GMEM_LOCKCOUNT, szNumber, 10);
      index = StrCopy (szString, index, szNumber, 4, TRUE);
      if (flags & GMEM_SWAPPED)
        index = StrCopy (szString, index, "  SWAPPED",
                                              9, FALSE);
      if (flags & GMEM_DISCARDED)
        index = StrCopy (szString, index, "  DISCARDED",
                                              11, FALSE);
      if (flags & GMEM_DISCARDABLE)
        index = StrCopy (szString, index, "  DISCARDABLE",
                                              13, FALSE);
      }
    else {
      flags = LocalFlags(memory[item].hMem);
      itoa (flags & LMEM_LOCKCOUNT, szNumber, 10);
      index = StrCopy (szString, index, szNumber, 4, TRUE);
      if (flags & LMEM_DISCARDED)
        index = StrCopy (szString, index, "  DISCARDED",
                                              11, FALSE);
      if (flags & LMEM_DISCARDABLE)
        index = StrCopy (szString, index, "  DISCARDABLE",
                                              13, FALSE);
      }
    MessageBox(hWnd, (LPSTR)szString, (LPSTR)"Flags",MB_OK);
    }
  break;

case IDSIZE:
  if (memory[item].hMem) {
    if (memory[item].colour)
      ltoa (GlobalSize(memory[item].hMem), szNumber, 10);
    else
      itoa (LocalSize(memory[item].hMem), szNumber, 10);
    index = StrCopy (szString, 0, szNumber, 4, TRUE);
    StrCopy (szString, index, " BYTES", 6, FALSE);
    MessageBox (hWnd, (LPSTR)szString, (LPSTR)"Size",MB_OK);
    }
  break;

case IDGLOBALCOMPACT:
  GlobalCompact ((long)-1);
  break;

case IDLOCALCOMPACT:
  LocalCompact (-1);
  break;

case IDLOCALFREEZE:
case IDLOCALMELT:
  bLocalFreeze ? LocalMelt (0) : LocalFreeze (0);
  bLocalFreeze = !bLocalFreeze;
  hMenu = GetMenu (hWnd);
```

```
        EnableMenuItem (hMenu, IDLOCALFREEZE,
                     bLocalFreeze ? MF_GRAYED : MF_ENABLED);
        EnableMenuItem (hMenu, IDLOCALMELT,
                     bLocalFreeze ? MF_ENABLED : MF_GRAYED);
        break;

      case IDLOCKDATA:
      case IDUNLOCKDATA:
        bLockData ? LockData (0) : UnlockData (0);
        bLockData = !bLockData;
        hMenu = GetMenu (hWnd);
        EnableMenuItem (hMenu, IDLOCKDATA,
                     bLockData ? MF_GRAYED : MF_ENABLED);
        EnableMenuItem (hMenu, IDUNLOCKDATA,
                     bLockData ? MF_ENABLED : MF_GRAYED);
        break;

      case IDLOCK:
        if (memory[item].hMem) {
          LPSTR Addr = 0;
          if (memory[item].colour)
            Addr = GlobalLock (memory[item].hMem);
          else
            Addr = (LPSTR)LocalLock (memory[item].hMem);
          if (Addr) {
            index = StrCopy(szString, 0, "Address: ", 9, FALSE);
            if (memory[item].colour) {
              ltoa (Addr, szNumber, 16);
              StrCopy (szString, index, szNumber, 8, TRUE);
              }
            else {
              itoa (LOWORD(Addr), szNumber, 16);
              StrCopy (szString, index, szNumber, 4, TRUE);
              }
            MessageBox (hWnd, (LPSTR)szString,
                                       (LPSTR)"Lock", MB_OK);
            }
          else
            MessageBox (hWnd, (LPSTR)"Function Failed",
                                       (LPSTR)"Lock", MB_OK);
          }
        break;

      case IDUNLOCK:
        if (memory[item].hMem)
          MessageBox (hWnd,
                     ((memory[item].colour
                      ? GlobalUnlock (memory[item].hMem)
                      : LocalUnlock (memory[item].hMem))
                     ? (LPSTR)"Block still locked"
                     : (LPSTR)"Block now unlocked"),
                     (LPSTR)"Unlock",
                     MB_OK);
        break;
      }
    }
}
```

```
/*-------------------------------------------------------------*/

BOOL FAR PASCAL AllocProc (hWnd, msg, wParam, lParam)
  HWND          hWnd;
  unsigned      msg;
  WORD          wParam;
  LONG          lParam;
  {
  switch (msg) {
    case WM_INITDIALOG:
      if (memory[item].hMem) {
        SetWindowText (hWnd, (LPSTR)"ReAllocate");
        SetDlgItemInt (hWnd, IDETSIZE, memory[item].size, FALSE);
        if (memory[item].colour) {
          CheckRadioButton (hWnd, IDRBGLOBAL, IDRBLOCAL, IDRBGLOBAL);
          CheckRadioButton (hWnd, IDRBFIXED, IDRBMOVEABLE,
                 (memory[item].flags & GMEM_MOVEABLE) ?
                                IDRBMOVEABLE : IDRBFIXED);
          CheckDlgButton (hWnd, IDRBDISCARDABLE,
               (memory[item].flags & GMEM_DISCARDABLE) ? 1 : 0);
          CheckDlgButton (hWnd, IDRBNODISCARD,
             (memory[item].flags & GMEM_NODISCARD) ? 1 : 0);
          CheckDlgButton (hWnd, IDRBNOCOMPACT,
             (memory[item].flags & GMEM_NOCOMPACT) ? 1 : 0);
          }
        else {
          CheckRadioButton (hWnd, IDRBGLOBAL, IDRBLOCAL, IDRBLOCAL);
          CheckRadioButton (hWnd, IDRBFIXED, IDRBMOVEABLE,
                 (memory[item].flags & LMEM_MOVEABLE) ?
                                IDRBMOVEABLE : IDRBFIXED);
          CheckDlgButton (hWnd, IDRBDISCARDABLE,
               (memory[item].flags & LMEM_DISCARDABLE) ? 1 : 0);
          CheckDlgButton (hWnd, IDRBNODISCARD,
             (memory[item].flags & LMEM_NODISCARD) ? 1 : 0);
          CheckDlgButton (hWnd, IDRBNOCOMPACT,
             (memory[item].flags & LMEM_NOCOMPACT) ? 1 : 0);
          }
        }
      else {
        EnableWindow (GetDlgItem (hWnd, IDOK), FALSE);
        SetWindowText (hWnd, (LPSTR)"Allocate");
        SetDlgItemText (hWnd, IDETSIZE,  (LPSTR)"");
        for (i=IDRBGLOBAL; i<=IDRBNOCOMPACT; i++)
          CheckDlgButton (hWnd, i, FALSE);
        }
      return TRUE;

    case WM_COMMAND:
      switch (wParam) {
        case IDRBGLOBAL:
        case IDRBLOCAL:
          if (!memory[item].hMem)
            CheckRadioButton (hWnd, IDRBGLOBAL, IDRBLOCAL, wParam);
          IsAllocOK (hWnd);
          break;

        case IDRBFIXED:
        case IDRBMOVEABLE:
```

```
    CheckRadioButton (hWnd, IDRBFIXED, IDRBMOVEABLE, wParam);
    if (wParam == IDRBFIXED)
      CheckDlgButton (hWnd, IDRBDISCARDABLE, FALSE);
    IsAllocOK (hWnd);
    break;


  case  IDRBDISCARDABLE:
    if (IsDlgButtonChecked (hWnd, IDRBDISCARDABLE))
      CheckDlgButton (hWnd, IDRBDISCARDABLE, FALSE);
    else
      if (IsDlgButtonChecked (hWnd, IDRBMOVEABLE))
        CheckDlgButton (hWnd, IDRBDISCARDABLE, TRUE);
    break;

  case  IDRBNOCOMPACT:
    CheckDlgButton (hWnd, IDRBNOCOMPACT,
                !IsDlgButtonChecked (hWnd, IDRBNOCOMPACT));
    break;

  case  IDRBNODISCARD:
    CheckDlgButton (hWnd, IDRBNODISCARD,
                !IsDlgButtonChecked (hWnd, IDRBNODISCARD));
    break;

  case IDETSIZE:
    if (HIWORD(lParam) == EN_CHANGE)
      IsAllocOK (hWnd);
    break;

  case IDOK:
    memory[item].flags = 0;
    memory[item].size =
        GetDlgItemInt (hWnd, IDETSIZE, (LPBOOL)&bValOK, FALSE);
    if (IsDlgButtonChecked (hWnd, IDRBGLOBAL)) {  /* global */
      memory[item].colour = TRUE;
      if (IsDlgButtonChecked (hWnd, IDRBMOVEABLE))
        memory[item].flags |= GMEM_MOVEABLE;
      if (IsDlgButtonChecked (hWnd, IDRBDISCARDABLE))
        memory[item].flags |= GMEM_DISCARDABLE;
      if (IsDlgButtonChecked (hWnd, IDRBNODISCARD))
        memory[item].flags |= GMEM_NODISCARD;
      if (IsDlgButtonChecked (hWnd, IDRBNOCOMPACT))
        memory[item].flags |= GMEM_NOCOMPACT;
      }
    else {                                            /* local */
      memory[item].colour = FALSE;
      if (IsDlgButtonChecked (hWnd, IDRBMOVEABLE))
        memory[item].flags |= LMEM_MOVEABLE;
      if (IsDlgButtonChecked (hWnd, IDRBDISCARDABLE))
        memory[item].flags |= LMEM_DISCARDABLE;
      if (IsDlgButtonChecked (hWnd, IDRBNODISCARD))
        memory[item].flags |= LMEM_NODISCARD;
      if (IsDlgButtonChecked (hWnd, IDRBNOCOMPACT))
        memory[item].flags |= LMEM_NOCOMPACT;
      }
    EndDialog(hWnd, memory[item].hMem =
          (memory[item].hMem
```

```
                ? (IsDlgButtonChecked (hWnd, IDRBGLOBAL)
                 ? GlobalReAlloc (memory[item].hMem, (unsigned long)
                        memory[item].size, memory[item].flags)
                 : LocalReAlloc (memory[item].hMem,
                        memory[item].size, memory[item].flags))
                : (IsDlgButtonChecked (hWnd, IDRBGLOBAL)
                 ? GlobalAlloc (memory[item].flags,
                        (unsigned long) memory[item].size)
                 : LocalAlloc (memory[item].flags,
                                    memory[item].size))));
          break;

        case IDCANCEL:
          EndDialog(hWnd, FALSE);
          break;
        }                                     /* end of switch        */
      break;                                  /* end of WM_COMMAND    */

    default:
      return FALSE;
    }
  return TRUE;
  }

BOOL IsAllocOK (hWnd)
  HWND  hWnd;
  {
  GetDlgItemInt (hWnd, IDETSIZE,  (LPBOOL)&bValOK, FALSE);
  if (!bValOK)
    EnableWindow (GetDlgItem (hWnd, IDOK), FALSE);
  else
    if ((IsDlgButtonChecked (hWnd, IDRBGLOBAL)
      || IsDlgButtonChecked (hWnd, IDRBLOCAL))
     && (IsDlgButtonChecked (hWnd, IDRBFIXED)
      || IsDlgButtonChecked (hWnd, IDRBMOVEABLE)))
      {
      EnableWindow (GetDlgItem (hWnd, IDOK), TRUE);
      return TRUE;
      }
  return FALSE;
  }

int StrCopy (new, newIndex, old, width, padleft)
  char  new[],  old[];
  int   width,  newIndex;
  BOOL  padleft;
  {
  int   n,      oldStrLen;

  for (oldStrLen=0; old[oldStrLen]; oldStrLen++);
  if (padleft) {
    if (width != oldStrLen)
    for (n = width - oldStrLen; n; n--, newIndex++)
      new[newIndex] = ' ';
  }
for (n=0; new[newIndex]=old[n]; n++, newIndex++);
return newIndex;
}
```

```
/*-----------------------------------------------------------------*/

int PASCAL WinMain (hInstance, hPrevInstance, lpszCmdLine, cmdShow)
  HANDLE                hInstance;
  HANDLE                hPrevInstance;
  LPSTR                 lpszCmdLine;
  int                   cmdShow;
  {
  MSG                   msg;
  HWND                  hWnd;

  if (!hPrevInstance)
    {
    if (!MainInit (hInstance))
      return FALSE;
    }

  hWnd = CreateWindow ((LPSTR)"PGM8", (LPSTR)"1", WS_OVERLAPPEDWINDOW,
        GetSystemMetrics (SM_CXSCREEN) / 4, GetSystemMetrics (SM_CYSCREEN) /
 4,
        GetSystemMetrics (SM_CXSCREEN) / 2, GetSystemMetrics (SM_CYSCREEN) /
 2,
        (HWND)NULL, (HMENU)NULL, (HANDLE)hInstance,  (LPSTR)NULL);

  hInst       = hInstance;
  lpAllocProc = MakeProcInstance ((FARPROC)AllocProc, hInstance);

  ShowWindow (hWnd, cmdShow);
  UpdateWindow (hWnd);

  while (GetMessage((LPMSG)&msg, NULL, 0, 0))
    {
    TranslateMessage ((LPMSG)&msg);
    DispatchMessage ((LPMSG)&msg);
    }

  FreeProcInstance (lpAllocProc);

  return (int)msg.wParam;
  }

BOOL MainInit (hInstance)
  HANDLE        hInstance;
  {
  PWNDCLASS pMainClass = (PWNDCLASS)LocalAlloc(LPTR,sizeof(WNDCLASS));
  pMainClass->hCursor         = LoadCursor (NULL, IDC_ARROW);
  pMainClass->hIcon           = LoadIcon (NULL, IDI_APPLICATION);
  pMainClass->lpszMenuName    = (LPSTR)"MainMenu";
  pMainClass->lpszClassName   = (LPSTR)"PGM8";
  pMainClass->hbrBackground   = (HBRUSH)GetStockObject (WHITE_BRUSH);
  pMainClass->hInstance       = hInstance;
  pMainClass->style           = CS_HREDRAW | CS_VREDRAW;
  pMainClass->lpfnWndProc     = MainWndProc;
  if (!RegisterClass((LPWNDCLASS)pMainClass))
    return FALSE;
  LocalFree ((HANDLE)pMainClass);
  return TRUE;
  }

/*-----------------------------------------------------------------*/
/* End of file:  PGM8.C                                            */
/*******************************************************************/
```

```
;***************************************************************:
; Filename:     PGM8.DEF                                        :
;                                                               :
; Description:  Link definition file                            :
;---------------------------------------------------------------:

NAME    PGM8

STUB    '..\WINSTUB.EXE'

CODE    MOVEABLE
DATA    MOVEABLE MULTIPLE

HEAPSIZE  4096
STACKSIZE 4096

EXPORTS
    MainWndProc @1
    AllocProc   @2

;---------------------------------------------------------------:
; End of file:  PGM8.DEF                                        :
;***************************************************************:
```

```
#***************************************************************#
# Filename:     PGM8.                                           #
#                                                               #
# Description:  "MAKE" description file                         #
#---------------------------------------------------------------#

pgm8.obj: pgm8.c pgm8.h
    cl -d -c -AS -Gsw -Os -Zpe pgm8.c

pgm8.res: pgm8.rc pgm8.h
    rc -r pgm8.rc

pgm8.exe: pgm8.obj pgm8.res pgm8.def
    link4 pgm8,/align:16,/map,slibw,pgm8.def
    rc pgm8.res

#---------------------------------------------------------------#
# End of file:  PGM8                                            #
#***************************************************************#
```

PGM8 lets you directly use the Windows memory management function calls and immediately see their effect. Because the interface is intuitive, we won't go into a detailed discussion of the program's operation.

To gain a greater appreciation of this program, you should concurrently run HEAPWALKER. As an example of the effect of running PGM8 and HEAPWALKER, Figure 11.5 illustrates a global memory allocation. The allocation is reflected in the HEAPWALKER window. Remember that the arena header takes 16 bytes; the physical address is one paragraph later. Figure 11.6 illustrates the effect of freeing the memory.

Figure 11.5

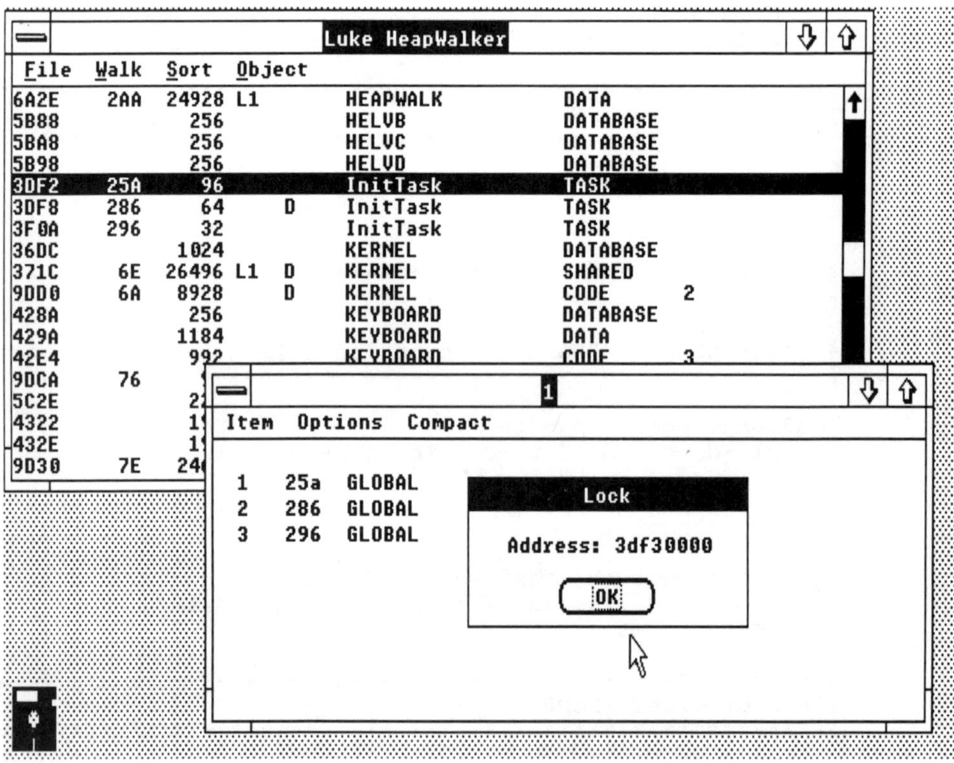

Figure 11.6

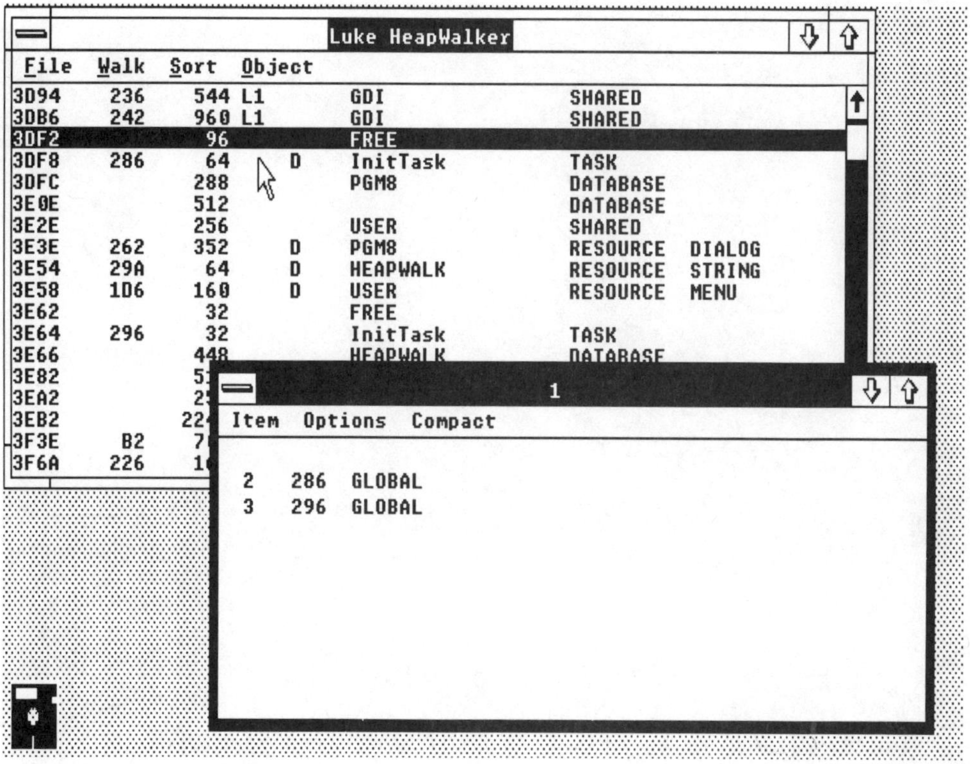

. . . .

In this chapter, you've learned about how Windows manages memory. In Chapter 12, you'll see how to transfer data between your application and the Windows clipboard.

12

USING THE CLIPBOARD

- Introduction to PGM9
- The Header File: PGM9.H
- The Resource Script File: PGM9.RC
- The C Language Source File: PGM9.C
- The Module Definition File: PGM9.DEF
- The Make File: PGM9.

One of the key features of the Windows environment is that users can move data between applications. Windows provides a unique and powerful medium, called the clipboard, for data interchange between concurrent tasks. In this chapter, we'll examine a sample program, PGM9, that moves data to and from the Windows clipboard.

12.1 INTRODUCTION TO PGM9

The simple program presented in this chapter, PGM9, is designed to move data to and from the clipboard. The clipboard is an area in global storage and is administered by Windows.

PGM9 requires five files:

PGM9.H	C header file
PGM9.RC	Resource script file
PGM9.C	C language source file
PGM9.DEF	Module definition file
PGM9.	Input instructions to the MAKE utility

Figure 12.1 illustrates what you'll see upon executing PGM9 and selecting the "Select" menu option. Note that the options "Cut" and "Copy" are grayed. This is because our program is holding no data; it's "empty." Note also that "Paste" is gray, because the clipboard is also empty.

Figure 12.1

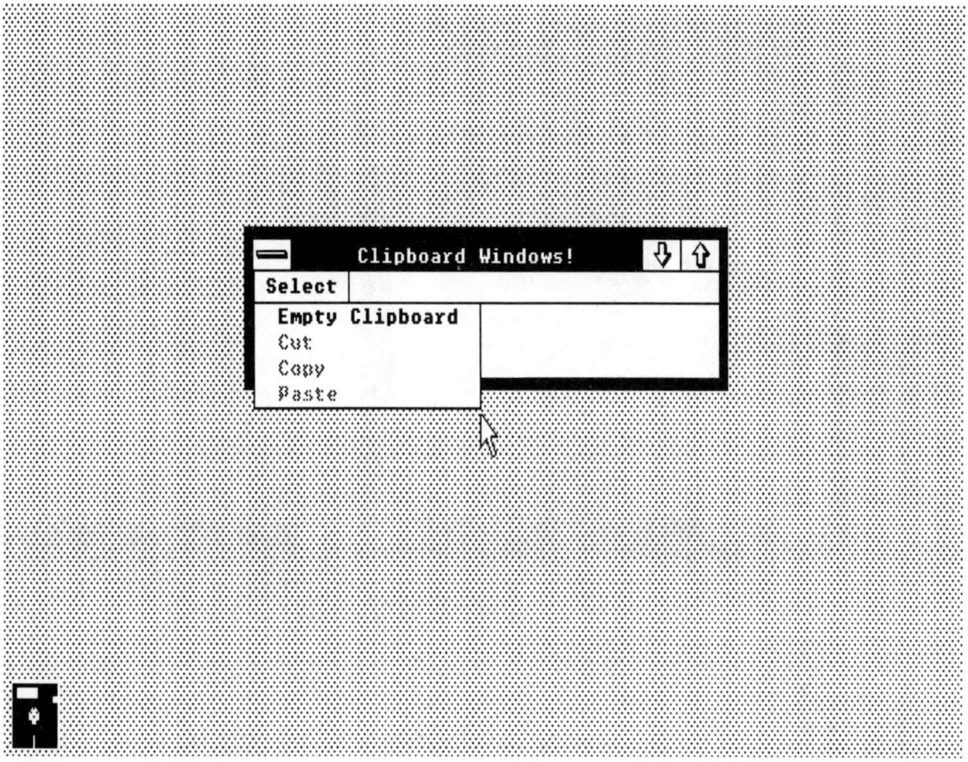

Windows is shipped with a program called CLIPBOARD. This program is simply a viewer: it allows the user to peek at the clipboard's contents. It *cannot* alter the clipboard contents in any way. Remember, the clipboard itself is internal to Windows; it is *not* the program CLIPBOARD.

Figure 12.2

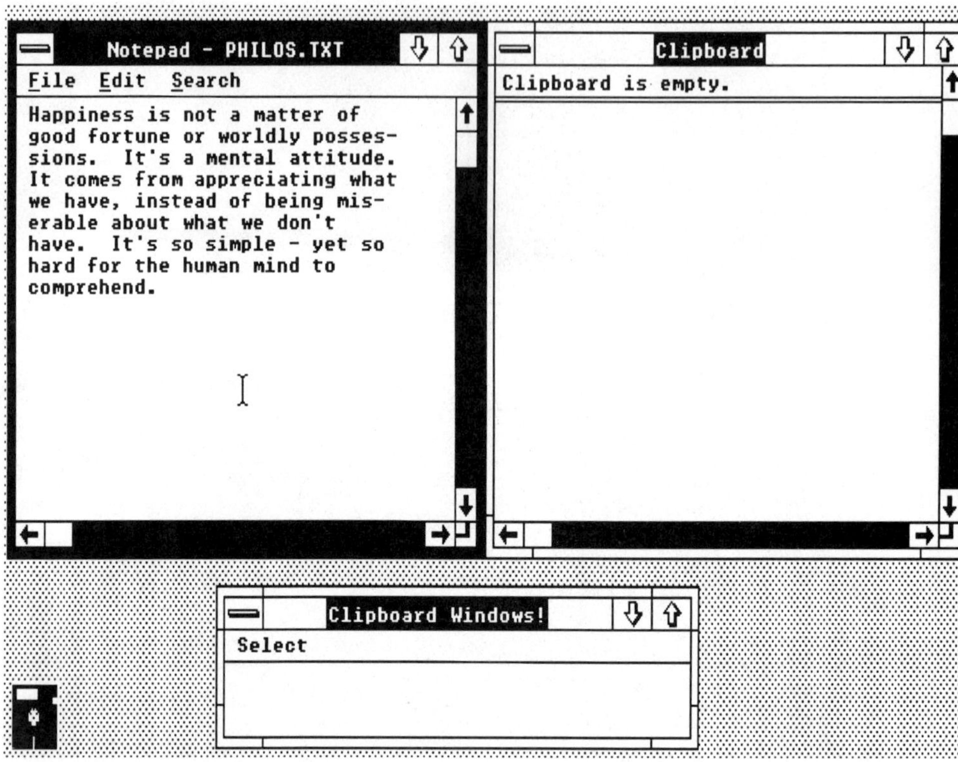

Now we'll examine what PGM9 does. Figure 12.2 shows three windows: **Notepad, Clipboard,** and **Clipboard Windows!** Within the **Notepad** window you'll find a paragraph which can be transferred to the clipboard. To do so, place the I-beam cursor at the beginning of the text, press and hold the left mouse button, drag the I-beam to the text's end, and release the button. Figure 12.3 illustrates what the window should look like at this point.

Figure 12.3

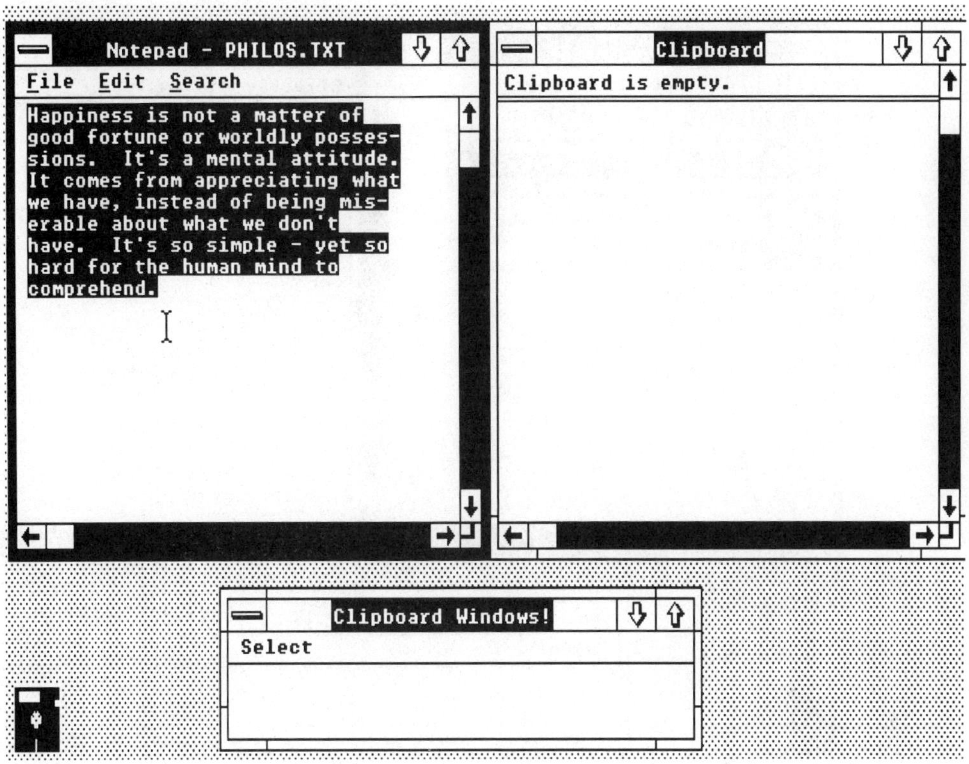

To transfer the highlighted data to the clipboard, select the "Edit Cut" command in the **Notepad** window (see Figure 12.4). This causes the text to be cut, or moved, from **Notepad** into the clipboard. The **Clipboard** window then displays the text (see Figure 12.5).

Figure 12.4

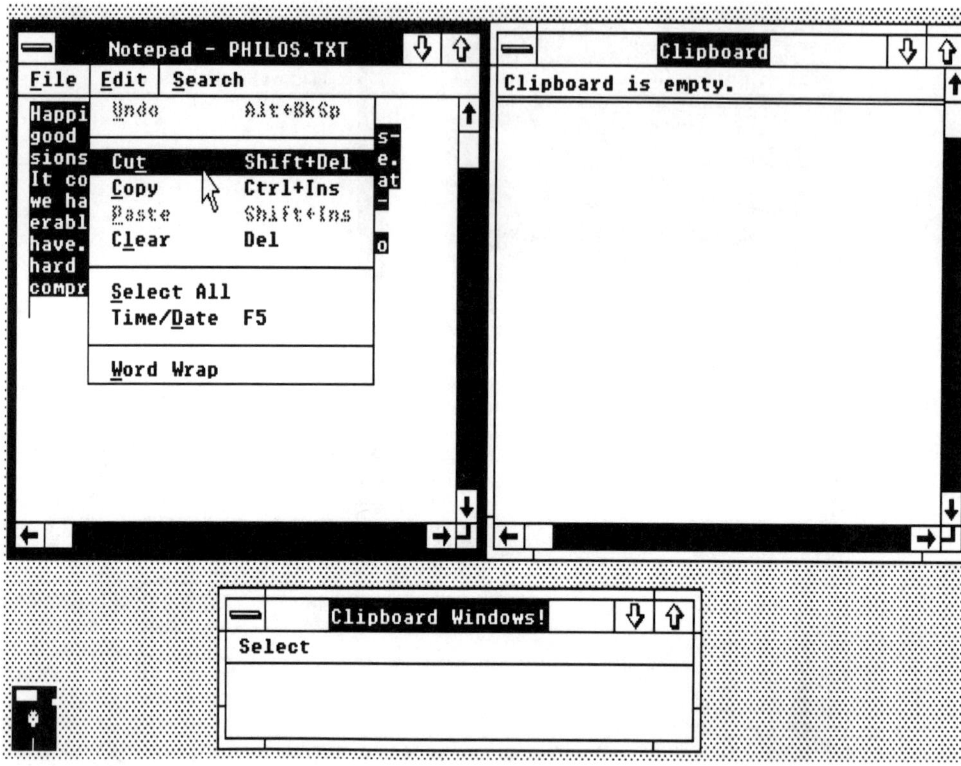
Notepad - PHILOS.TXT
File
Edit
Search
Undo Alt+BkSp
Cut Shift+Del
Copy Ctrl+Ins
Paste Shift+Ins
Clear Del
Select All
Time/Date F5
Word Wrap
Clipboard
Clipboard is empty.
Clipboard Windows!
Select

Figure 12.5

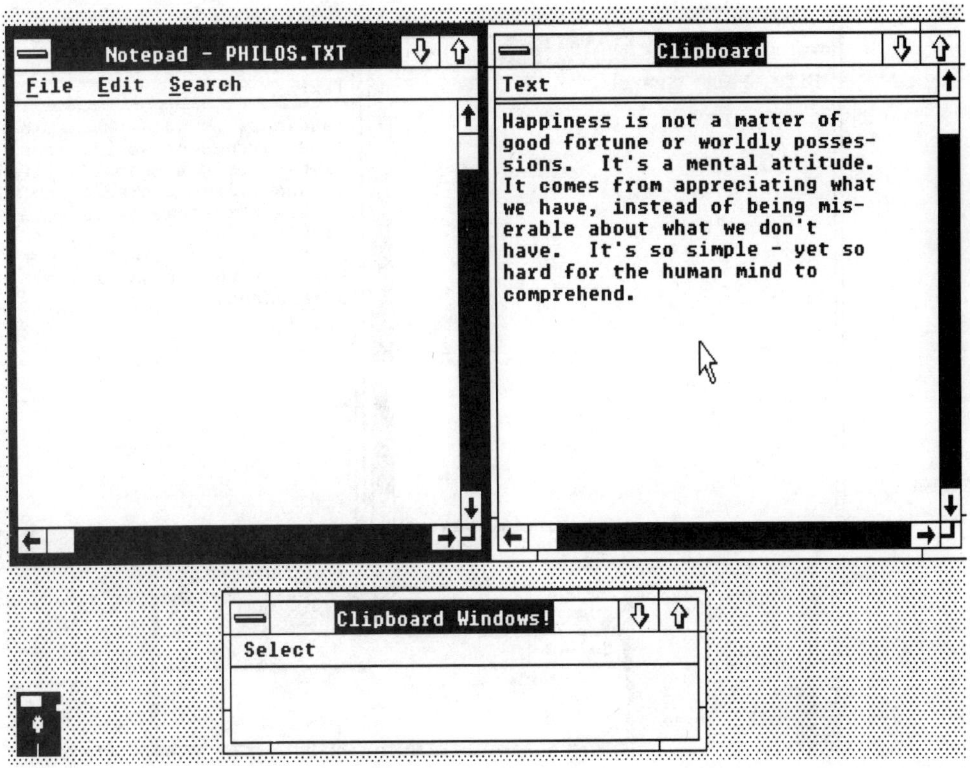

Next, to copy the data on the clipboard into our **Clipboard Windows!** program, highlight "Select Paste" in the **Clipboard Windows!** window (Figure 12.6). Note that "Paste" is now an option, because there is data within the clipboard. Upon selecting "Paste," you will not see anything displayed within the **Clipboard Windows!** window. The code is not needed to illustrate the point we want to make in this chapter.

Figure 12.6

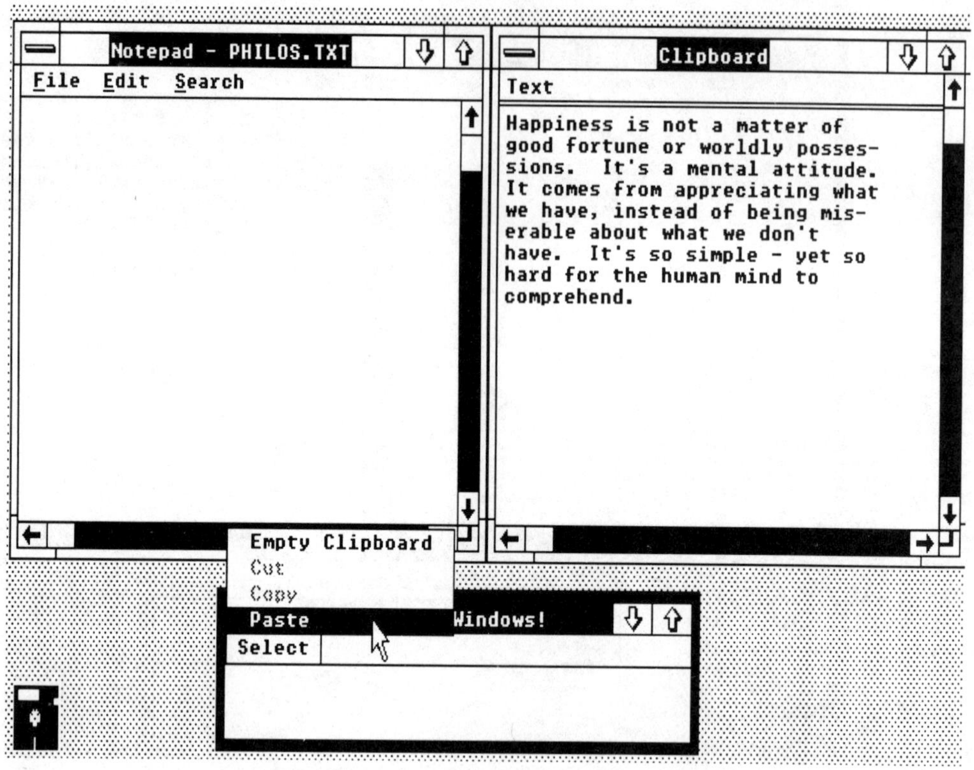

If you click on "Select" in the **Clipboard Windows!** window, you'll see that the options "Cut" and "Copy" are now enabled (Figure 12.7), because our window now contains data. "Select Empty Clipboard" will empty the clipboard, as illustrated in Figure 12.8.

Figure 12.7

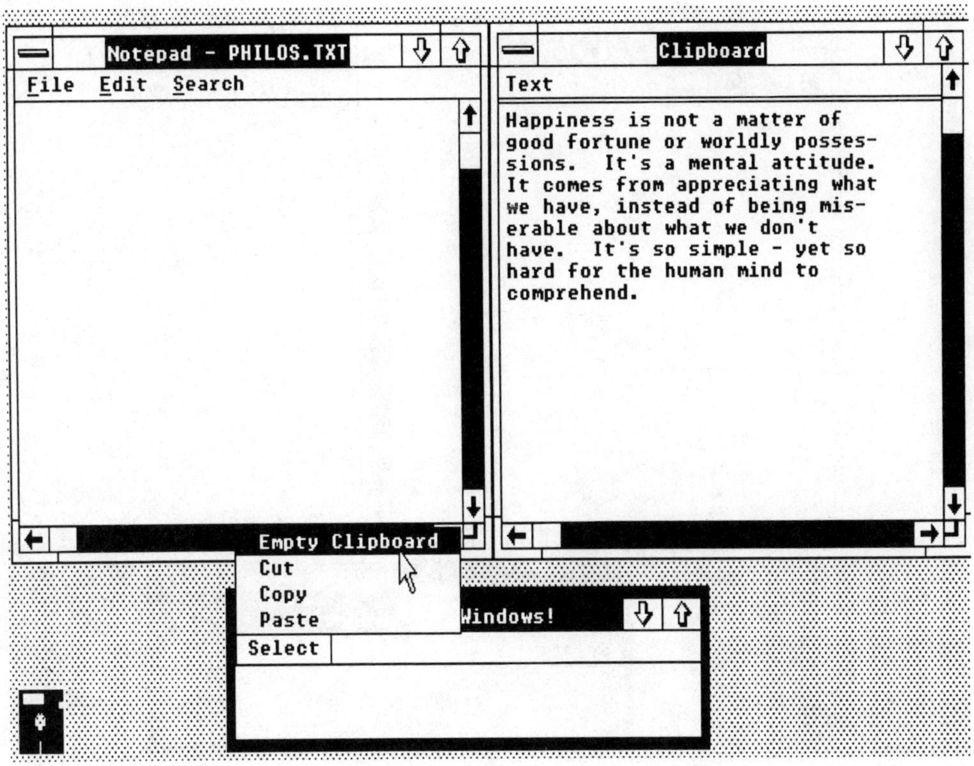
Notepad - PHILOS.TXT
File Edit Search
Clipboard
Text
Happiness is not a matter of
good fortune or worldly posses-
sions. It's a mental attitude.
It comes from appreciating what
we have, instead of being mis-
erable about what we don't
have. It's so simple - yet so
hard for the human mind to
comprehend.
Empty Clipboard
Cut
Copy
Paste
Windows!
Select

Figure 12.8

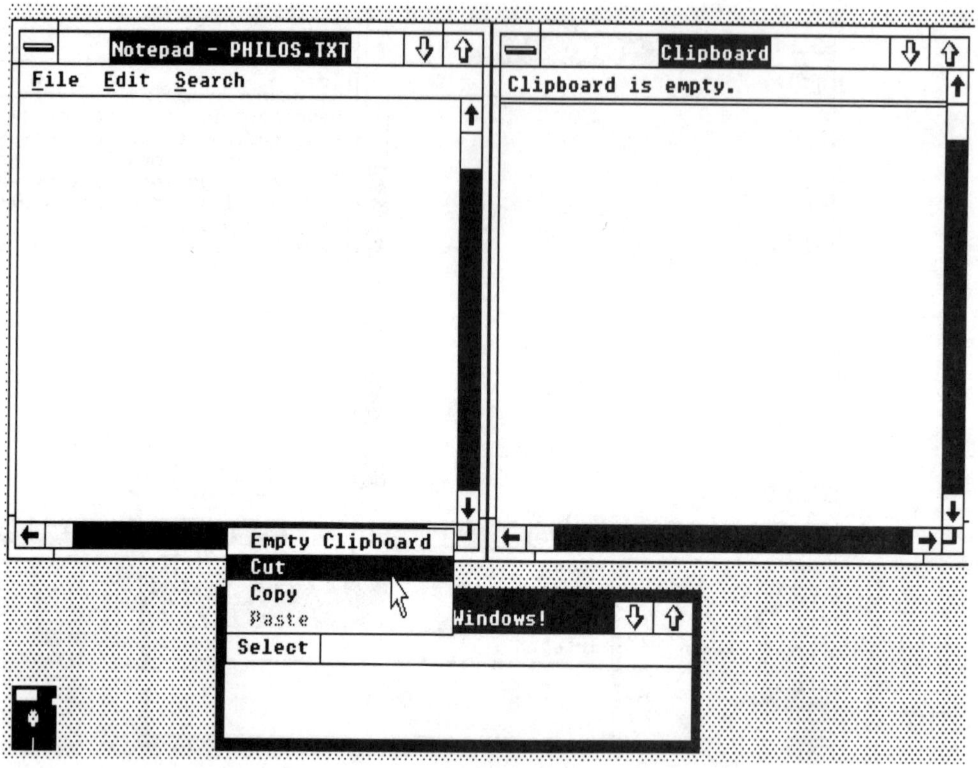

Let's turn around and move the data back into **Notepad**. "Select Cut" will move the data from our program's buffer into the clipboard. From **Notepad,** "Edit Paste" (Figure 12.9) will copy the data back into the **Notepad** program (Figure 12.10).

Figure 12.9

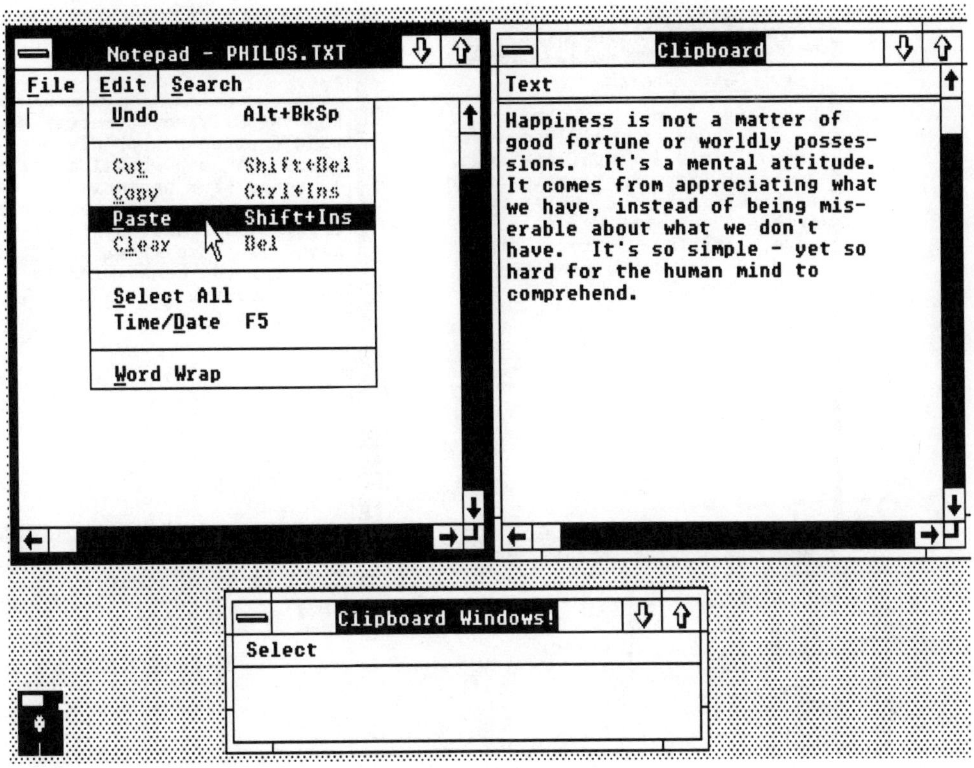
Notepad - PHILOS.TXT
File
Edit
Search
Undo Alt+BkSp
Cut Shift+Del
Copy Ctrl+Ins
Paste Shift+Ins
Clear Del
Select All
Time/Date F5
Word Wrap
Clipboard
Text
Happiness is not a matter of good fortune or worldly possessions. It's a mental attitude. It comes from appreciating what we have, instead of being miserable about what we don't have. It's so simple - yet so hard for the human mind to comprehend.
Clipboard Windows!
Select

Figure 12.10

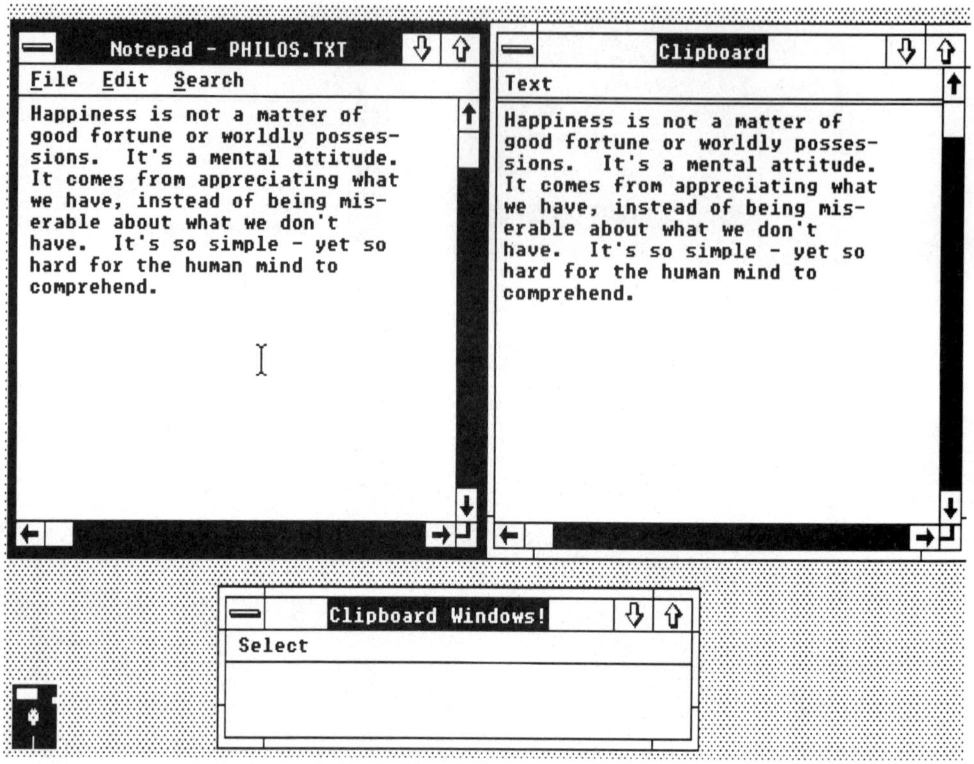

Now for the truly amazing part: let's see just how simple our program really is!

12.2 THE HEADER FILE: PGM9.H

```
/***************************************************************************/
/* Filename:     PGM9.H                                                    */
/*                                                                         */
/* Description:  PGM9.C  header file                                       */
/*-------------------------------------------------------------------------*/

#define MENU_EMPTY       1010
#define MENU_CUT         1020
#define MENU_COPY        1030
#define MENU_PASTE       1040

/*-------------------------------------------------------------------------*/
/* End of file:  PGM9.H                                                    */
/***************************************************************************/
```

12.3 THE RESOURCE SCRIPT FILE: PGM9.RC

```
/***************************************************************************/
/* Filename:     PGM9.RC                                                   */
/*                                                                         */
/* Description:  PGM9.EXE resources                                        */
/*-------------------------------------------------------------------------*/

#include "pgm9.h"

MainMenu MENU
BEGIN
    POPUP "Select"
    BEGIN
        MENUITEM        "Empty Clipboard",              MENU_EMPTY
        MENUITEM        "Cut",                          MENU_CUT
        MENUITEM        "Copy",                         MENU_COPY
        MENUITEM        "Paste",                        MENU_PASTE
    END
END

/*-------------------------------------------------------------------------*/
/* End of file:  PGM9.RC                                                   */
/***************************************************************************/
```

12.4 THE C LANGUAGE SOURCE FILE: PGM9.C

```
/***************************************************************************/
/* Filename:     PGM9.C                                                    */
/*                                                                         */
/* Description:  PGM9.EXE source code                                      */
/*-------------------------------------------------------------------------*/

#include "windows.h"
#include "pgm9.h"

  long FAR PASCAL       MainWndProc (HWND, unsigned, WORD, LONG);

  HANDLE                hInst;
  PWNDCLASS             pMainClass;
  HANDLE                hData = NULL;
  HANDLE                hTempData;

int PASCAL WinMain (hInstance, hPrevInstance, lpszCmdLine, cmdShow)
  HANDLE                hInstance;
  HANDLE                hPrevInstance;
  LPSTR                 lpszCmdLine;
  int                   cmdShow;
  {
  MSG                   msg;
  HWND                  hWnd;
  HMENU                 hMenu;

  if (hPrevInstance)
    return FALSE;
```

```
  pMainClass = (PWNDCLASS)LocalAlloc (LPTR, sizeof(WNDCLASS));
  pMainClass->hCursor        = LoadCursor (NULL, IDC_ARROW);
  pMainClass->hIcon          = LoadIcon (NULL, IDI_APPLICATION);
  pMainClass->lpszMenuName   = (LPSTR)"MainMenu";
  pMainClass->lpszClassName  = (LPSTR)"PGM9";
  pMainClass->hbrBackground  = (HBRUSH)GetStockObject (WHITE_BRUSH);
  pMainClass->hInstance      = hInstance;
  pMainClass->style          = CS_HREDRAW | CS_VREDRAW;
  pMainClass->lpfnWndProc    = MainWndProc;

  if (!RegisterClass((LPWNDCLASS)pMainClass))
    return FALSE;

  LocalFree ((HANDLE)pMainClass);

  hWnd = CreateWindow  ((LPSTR)"PGM9", (LPSTR)"Clipboard Windows!",
      WS_OVERLAPPEDWINDOW,
      GetSystemMetrics (SM_CXSCREEN) / 4, GetSystemMetrics (SM_CYSCREEN) / 4,
      GetSystemMetrics (SM_CXSCREEN) / 2, GetSystemMetrics (SM_CYSCREEN) / 2,
      (HWND)NULL, (HMENU)NULL, (HANDLE)hInstance, (LPSTR)NULL);

  hInst = hInstance;            /* Save instance handle for Dialog box  */

  ShowWindow (hWnd, cmdShow);
  UpdateWindow (hWnd);

  while (GetMessage ((LPMSG)&msg, NULL, 0, 0))
    {
    TranslateMessage((LPMSG)&msg);
    DispatchMessage((LPMSG)&msg);
    }
  return (int)msg.wParam;
  }

long FAR PASCAL MainWndProc (hWnd, msg, wParam, lParam)
  HWND                  hWnd;
  unsigned              msg;
  WORD                  wParam;
  LONG                  lParam;
  {
  switch (msg)
    {
    case WM_DESTROY:
      PostQuitMessage (0);
      break;

    case WM_INITMENU:
      {
      HMENU     hMenu = GetMenu (hWnd);
      int       pasteMenuFlag = MF_GRAYED;
      int       wFormat = 0;

      if (OpenClipboard (hWnd))
        {
        while (wFormat = EnumClipboardFormats (wFormat))
          {
          if (wFormat == CF_TEXT)
            {
            pasteMenuFlag = MF_ENABLED;
            break;
            }
          }
        CloseClipboard ();
        }
```

```
    EnableMenuItem (hMenu, MENU_PASTE, pasteMenuFlag);
    EnableMenuItem (hMenu, MENU_CUT,   hData ? MF_ENABLED : MF_GRAYED);
    EnableMenuItem (hMenu, MENU_COPY,  hData ? MF_ENABLED : MF_GRAYED);
    break;
    }

  case WM_COMMAND:
    switch (wParam)
      {
      HANDLE          hClipData;
      LPSTR           szSource,       szDest;

      case MENU_EMPTY:
        if (OpenClipboard (hWnd))
          {
          EmptyClipboard ();
          CloseClipboard ();
          }
        break;

      case MENU_COPY:
        if (!(hTempData = GlobalAlloc (GMEM_MOVEABLE,
                                        GlobalSize (hData))))

          break;
        szSource = GlobalLock (hData);
        szDest   = GlobalLock (hTempData);
        for (; *szDest++ = *szSource++;);
        GlobalUnlock (hData);
        GlobalUnlock (hTempData);
                                              /* fall thru */
      case MENU_CUT:
        if (OpenClipboard(hWnd))
          {
          SetClipboardData (CF_TEXT, hData);
          CloseClipboard ();
          hData = (wParam == MENU_COPY) ? hTempData : NULL;
          }
        break;

      case MENU_PASTE:
        if (hData)
          GlobalFree (hData);

        if (OpenClipboard(hWnd))
          {
          if ((hClipData = GetClipboardData(CF_TEXT))
            && (hData = GlobalAlloc (GMEM_MOVEABLE,
                                        GlobalSize (hClipData))))

            {
            szSource = GlobalLock (hClipData);
            szDest   = GlobalLock (hData);
            for (; *szDest++ = *szSource++;);
            GlobalUnlock (hClipData);
            GlobalUnlock (hData);
            }
          CloseClipboard ();
          }
        break;
      }
    break;
```

```
    default:
      return DefWindowProc (hWnd, msg, wParam, lParam);
      break;
    }
  return (0L);
  }

/*----------------------------------------------------------------------*/
/* End of file:  PGM9.C                                                 */
/************************************************************************/
```

The first page of code is pretty standard stuff that you'll recognize by now. As you've noticed, the menu items are "white" and "gray" (enabled or disabled) during various phases of execution. You know from earlier lessons that the menu items are controlled through the interception of the **WM_INITMENU** message. Let's look at that process.

12.4.1 Accessing the Clipboard

Because only one task can use the clipboard at a time, and every program needs access to it, we must open the clipboard, access it, then close it, every time we want to use it.

To begin, we grab a menu handle and initialize some flags. Next, we use:

```
if (OpenClipboard (hWnd))
```

To open the clipboard, we simply place a call to **OpenClipboard,** passing it the window handle. This function returns a Boolean value indicating success or failure. If all goes well, we make our next move:

```
while (wFormat = EnumClipboardFormats (wFormat))
```

This routine uses **EnumClipboardFormats** to rifle through the available data formats. The formats can be enumerated by calling this function in this fashion. Returned is a non-zero number indicating the next format. Possible clipboard formats are:

Format	*Contents*
CF_TEXT	Null-terminated text
CF_BITMAP	A bitmap

CF_METAFILEPICT	A metafile picture structure
CF_SYLK	Data in SYLK format
CF_DIF	Data in DIF format

In this program, we want text, or **CF_TEXT**, format. If this format is found, we know that text data exists on the clipboard and is available for pasting, hence we set the flag to enable the menu item and break out:

```
if (wFormat == CF_TEXT)
  {
  pasteMenuFlag = MF_ENABLED;
  break;
  }
```

We must now close the clipboard:

```
CloseClipboard ();
```

To complete **WM_INITMENU**, we place the **EnableMenuItem** calls:

```
EnableMenuItem (hMenu, MENU_PASTE, pasteMenuFlag);
EnableMenuItem (hMenu, MENU_CUT, hData ? MF_ENABLED :
                                                MF_GRAYED);
EnableMenuItem (hMenu, MENU_COPY, hData ? MF_ENABLED :
                                                MF_GRAYED);
```

hData is a global variable that contains either a NULL or a global memory handle. We'll use this variable soon. For now just remember that if **hData** is not NULL, then we have a buffer with something in it that may be placed on the clipboard. Translation: if **hData** is NULL, gray the menu item, else enable it.

12.4.2 Controlling the Clipboard from Menus

You know the scenario used here: the user selects a menu item, and Windows calls **MainWndProc WM_COMMAND** with **wParam** containing the selected menu item. We switch on it:

```
switch (wParam)
```

The first case is "Empty Clipboard." Empty or not, here we come . . .

```
case MENU_EMPTY:
if (OpenClipboard (hWnd))
  {
  EmptyClipboard ();
  CloseClipboard ();
  }
break;
```

Pretty simple, right? We open the clipboard, empty it, and close it. For something a little more challenging, let's move on to "Paste."

"Paste" means to copy data from the clipboard to our buffer. But what if we already have data in our buffer? We'll use:

```
case MENU_PASTE:
if (hData)
GlobalFree (hData);
```

hData is a handle to a global memory block. We'll keep it NULL when we're not using it. Therefore, if it's not NULL, we want to go ahead and free the storage.

After opening the clipboard, we want to get the memory handle to the data currently in the clipboard and allocate another global block of the exact same size:

```
if ((hClipData = GetClipboardData(CF_TEXT))
&& (hData = GlobalAlloc (GMEM_MOVEABLE, GlobalSize
                                        (hClipData))))
```

GetClipboardData returns a handle to the data retrieved from the clipboard. **CF_TEXT** specifies the data format: text. After securing a block of identical size, we want to copy the data from the clipboard into our private storage:

```
szSource = GlobalLock (hClipData);
szDest   = GlobalLock (hData);
for (; *szDest++ = *szSource++;);
GlobalUnlock (hClipData);
GlobalUnlock (hData);
```

And we don't want to forget to close the clipboard:

```
CloseClipboard ();
```

Now, let's reverse the process and move data from our buffer to the clipboard. We have two choices: "Cut" or "Copy." "Cut" means "move," and "Copy" means just what it says.

12.4.3 Moving Data to the Clipboard

When we put something into the clipboard, we are really "giving" it to Windows; we can no longer use the memory handle because Windows invalidates it. This means that we are not responsible for freeing this memory.

To copy into the clipboard, we must first make a copy of our data for ourselves since we'll be giving our original to Windows.

```
case MENU_COPY:
if (!(hTempData = GlobalAlloc
                 (GMEM_MOVEABLE, GlobalSize(hData))))
  break;
szSource = GlobalLock (hData);
szDest   = GlobalLock (hTempData);
for (; *szDest++ = *szSource++;);
GlobalUnlock (hData);
GlobalUnlock (hTempData);           /* fall thru */
```

The copy logic falls right into "Cut":

```
case MENU_CUT:
if (OpenClipboard(hWnd))
  {
  SetClipboardData (CF_TEXT, hData);
  CloseClipboard ();
  hData = (wParam == MENU_COPY) ? hTempData : NULL;
  }
break;
```

SetClipboardData accepts the text (**CF_TEXT**) data belonging to the memory handle **hData. hData** is no longer valid to us. After closing, we set **hData** to either **hTempData** (the handle of the copy of the data) or NULL (if this was a "Cut" operation). Note that up in **WM_INITMENU** we enabled or grayed the "Cut" and "Copy" menu options depending on whether **hData** was NULL or not.

12.5 THE MODULE DEFINITION FILE: PGM9.DEF

```
;**************************************************************:
; Filename:     PGM9.DEF                                       :
;                                                              :
; Description:  Link definition file                           :
;--------------------------------------------------------------:
NAME    PGM9

DESCRIPTION 'Sample program 9'

STUB    '..\WINSTUB.EXE'

CODE    MOVEABLE
DATA    MOVEABLE MULTIPLE

HEAPSIZE  128
STACKSIZE 4096

EXPORTS
    MainWndProc         @1

;--------------------------------------------------------------:
; End of file:  PGM9.DEF                                       :
;**************************************************************:
```

12.6 THE MAKE FILE: PGM9.

```
#**********************************************************************#
# Filename:     PGM9.                                                  #
#                                                                      #
# Description:  PGM9.EXE "MAKE" description file                       #
#----------------------------------------------------------------------#

PGM9.OBJ: PGM9.C PGM9.H
    cl -d -c -AS -Gsw -Os -Zpe PGM9.C

PGM9.RES: PGM9.RC PGM9.H
    rc -r PGM9.RC

PGM9.EXE: PGM9.OBJ PGM9.RES PGM9.DEF
    LINK4 PGM9,/ALIGN:16,/MAP,SLIBW,PGM9.DEF
    RC PGM9.RES

#----------------------------------------------------------------------#
# End of file:  PGM9.                                                  #
#**********************************************************************#
```

. . . .

In this chapter, you've learned to manipulate the Windows clipboard. In Chapter 13, you'll learn to use atoms to save memory space for strings.

13

USING ATOMS

- Introduction To Atoms
- Introduction to PGM10: An Atom Manager
- The Header File: PGM10.H
- The Resource Script File: PGM10.RC
- The C Language Source File: PGM10.C
- The Module Definition File: PGM10.DEF
- The Make File: PGM10.

Some applications use many character strings, which implies that they must maintain large arrays to store their character data. If this data is constant, it might prove more efficient to allow Windows to manage the data storage and retrieval process by using atoms. *Atoms* are integers that uniquely identify null-terminated ASCII strings. This chapter examines a sample program that manages atoms.

13.1 INTRODUCTION TO ATOMS

When you add a string to Windows' atom table, Windows returns to you an atom, a unique identifier to that string. Then, instead of passing entire strings from routine to routine, you need only pass the atom.

Memory for atoms is allocated out of the application's data segment; therefore, the absolute limit of memory size is the size of the caller's DS. The limit to the number of characters in an atom is 255. If an application declares many atoms but uses only a few, the only penalty is the memory used.

13.2 INTRODUCTION TO PGM10: AN ATOM MANAGER

Our sample program, **PGM10**, will exercise most of the atom functions. PGM10 requires five files:

PGM10.H	C header file
PGM10.RC	Resource script file
PGM10.C	C language source file
PGM10.DEF	Module definition file
PGM10.	Input instructions to the MAKE utility

Upon execution of PGM10, you'll see a display that looks like Figure 13.1. If you select the only menu item, "Atom . . ," you'll see a dialog box, shown in Figure 13.2. Because our atom table is currently empty, only one operation, "Add," is available for selection and is initially selected.

Figure 13.1

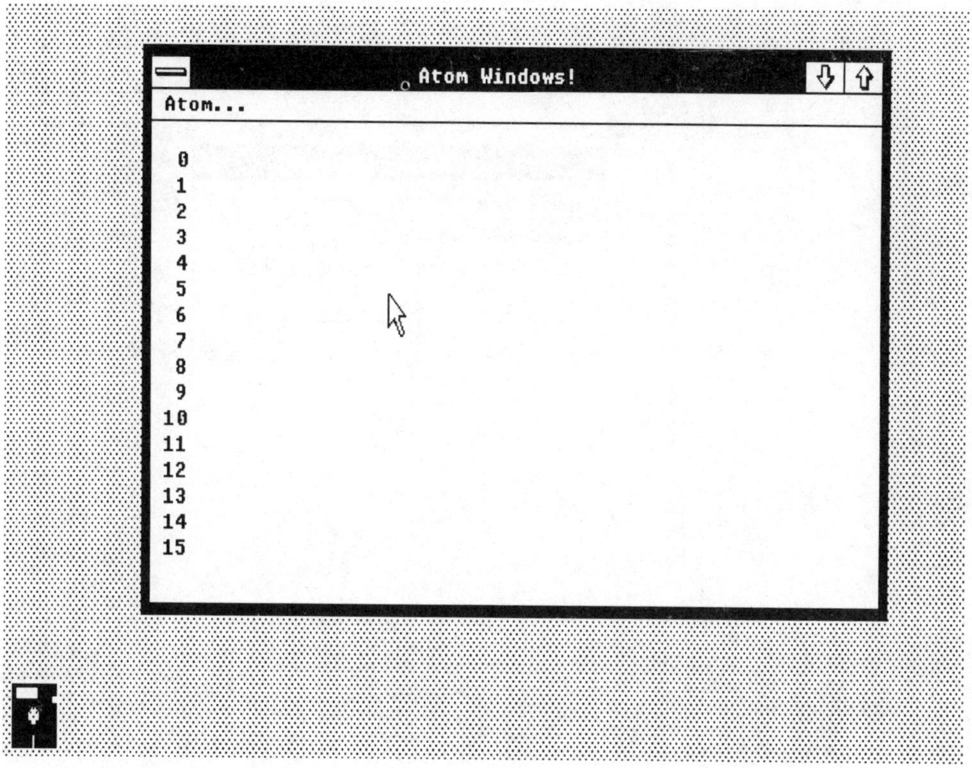

Figure 13.2

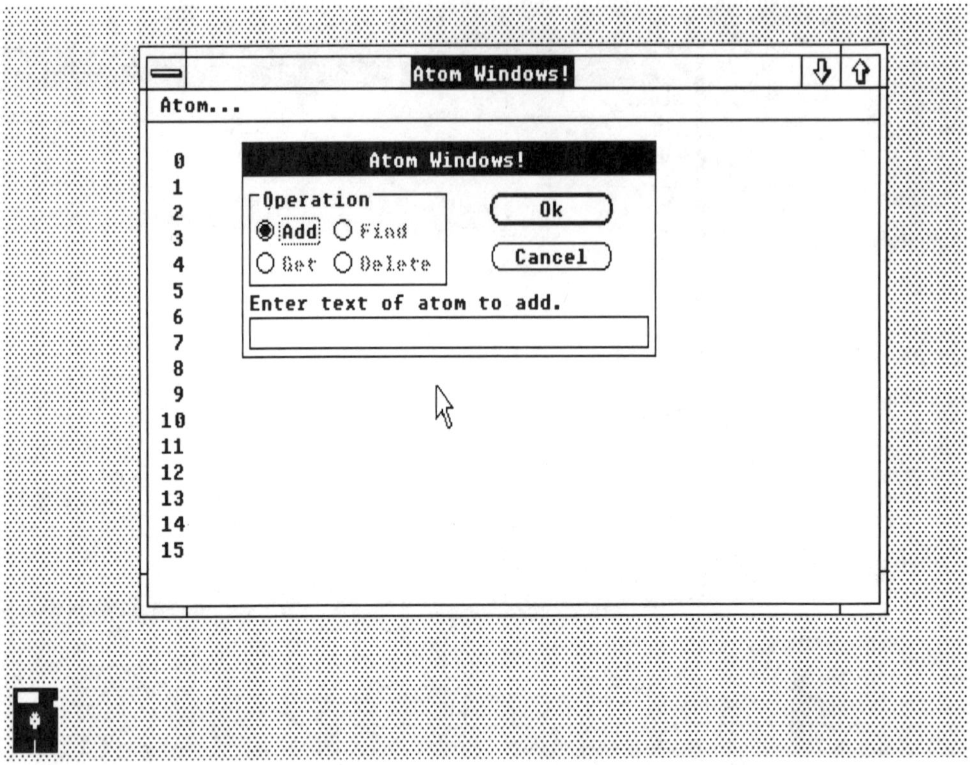

If you enter some text, such as

<-- This is the "Atom Number"

and press the "Ok" button, you'll see the text displayed in the main window. Immediately to the left of the text is a hexadecimal number between the range of 0xC000 and 0xFFFF. This is called the *atom number*, and was given to us by Windows. (This number may vary from the number shown in the figure.)

If you select "Atom. . ." again, all four options will be available (as shown in Figure 13.3). If you repeat the "Add" process several more times, you'll end up with several atoms in your table.

Figure 13.3

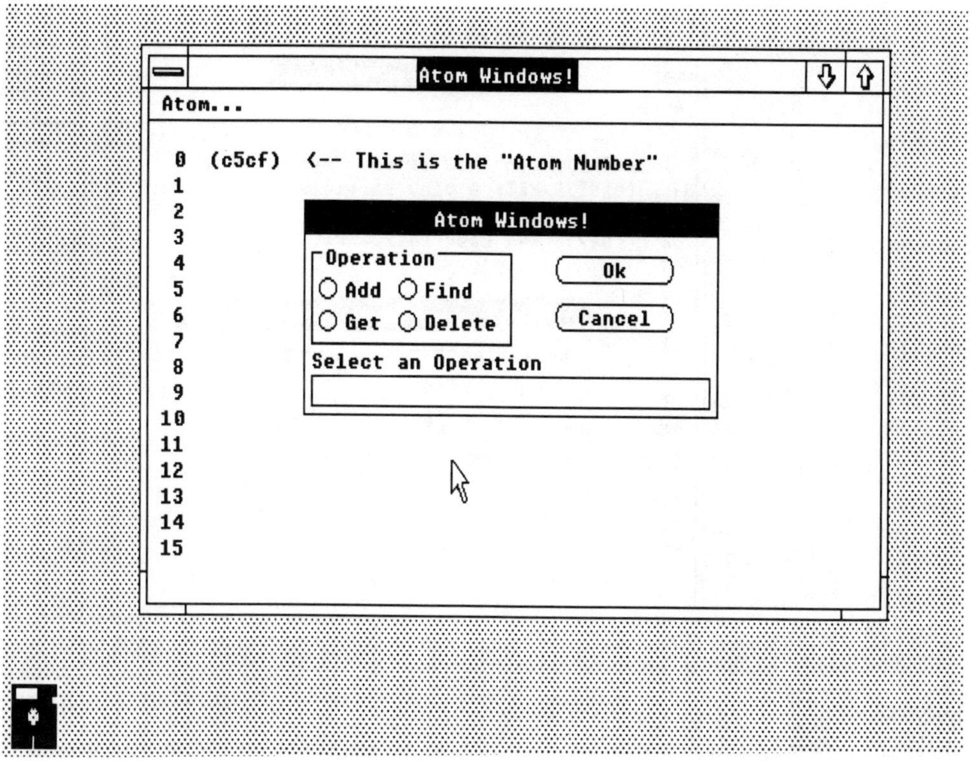

We know the contents of our atom table because the table is displayed on the screen. But let's pretend that we know only the atom number. To see what the text of the atom is, we use the "get" function (see Figure 13.4). For simplicity, we won't enter the actual hexadecimal number, but rather the *index number*. (The index number is simply the number down the left side of the screen—0, 1, 2, etc.) Our program will fetch the actual number from a table. As illustrated, entering a number causes Windows to return the actual text of the atom (see Figure 13.5).

Figure 13.4

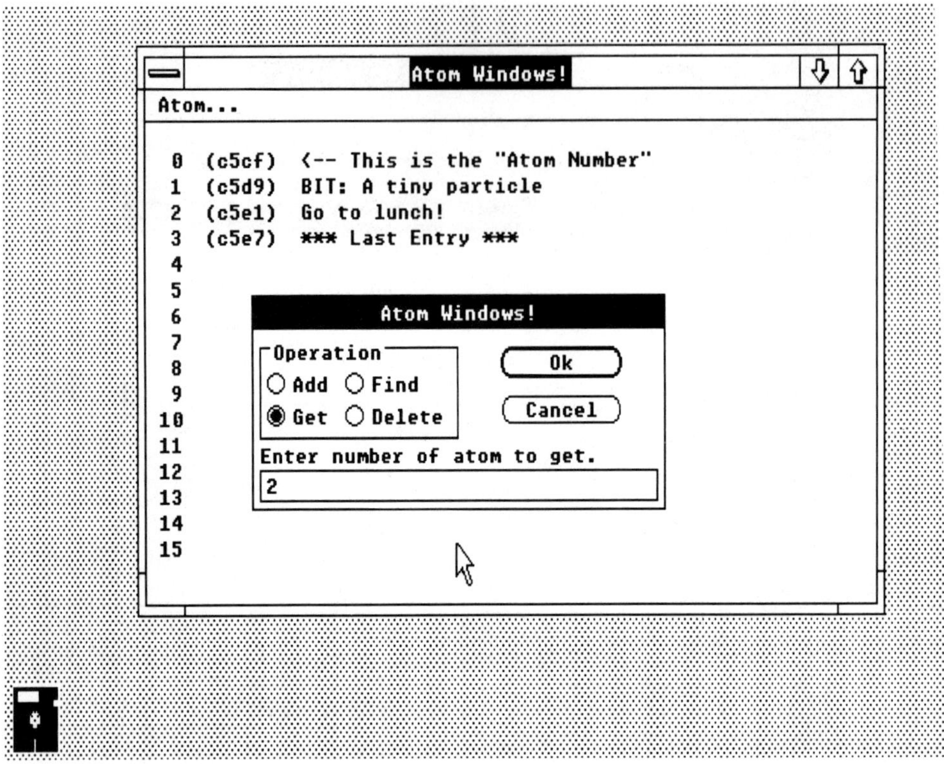
Atom Windows!
Atom...
0 (c5cf) <-- This is the "Atom Number"
1 (c5d9) BIT: A tiny particle
2 (c5e1) Go to lunch!
3 (c5e7) *** Last Entry ***
4
5
6
7
8
9
10
11
12
13
14
15
Atom Windows!
Operation
Add
Find
Get
Delete
Ok
Cancel
Enter number of atom to get.
2

Figure 13.5

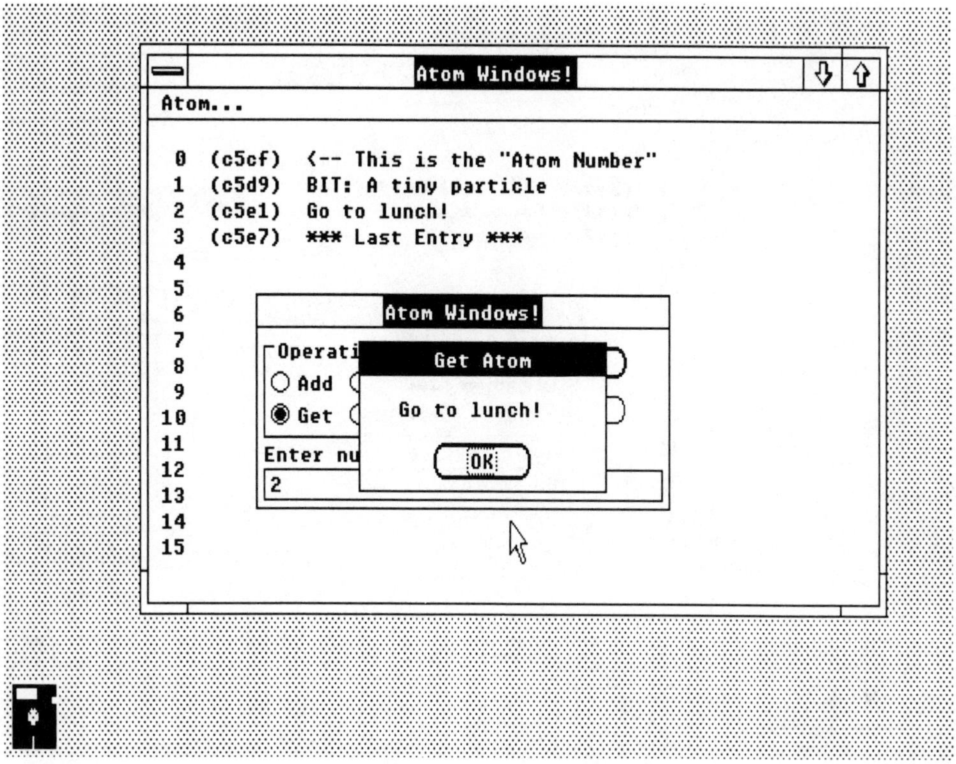

The reverse of this process is to give Windows some text and to have Windows return to you an atom number, as illustrated in Figure 13.6.

Figure 13.6

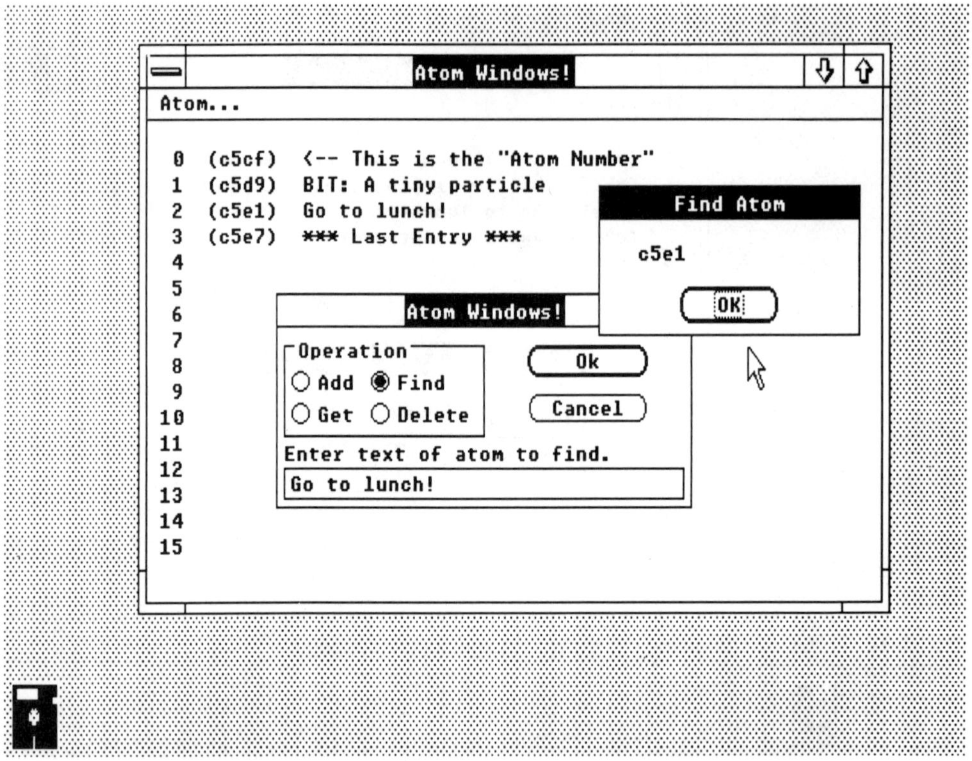

To delete our atoms, we'll supply an index, just as with the "get" operation. In Figure 13.7, we selected atom number (1). Pressing the "Ok" button causes the atom to be deleted, as illustrated in Figure 13.8.

Figure 13.7

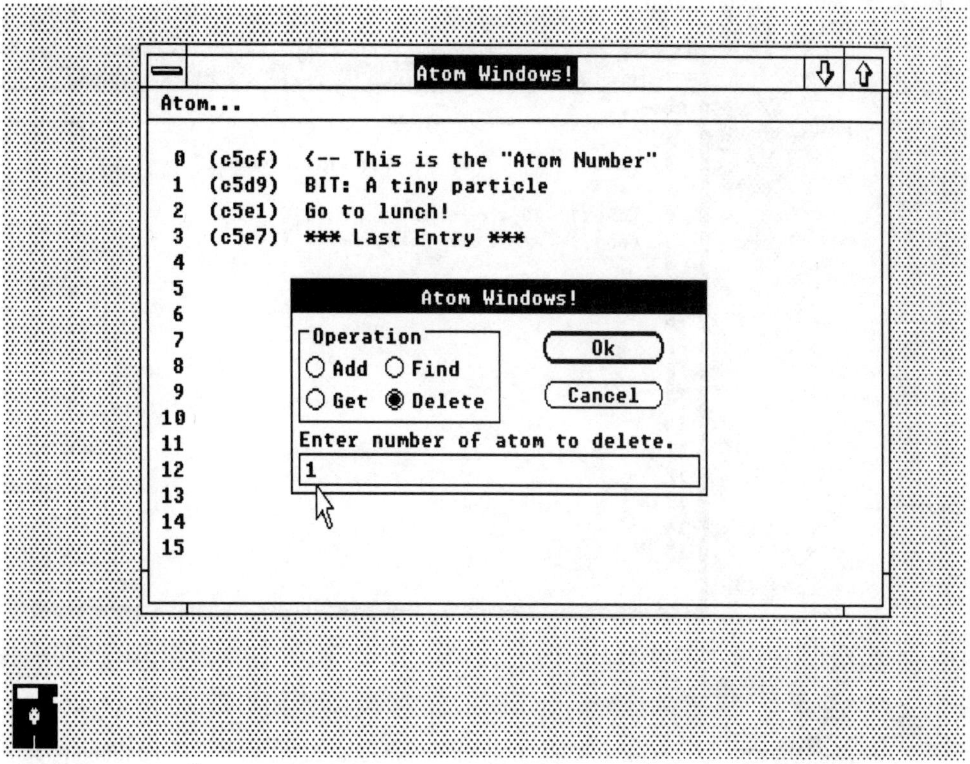
Atom Windows!
Atom...
0 (c5cf) <-- This is the "Atom Number"
1 (c5d9) BIT: A tiny particle
2 (c5e1) Go to lunch!
3 (c5e7) *** Last Entry ***
4
5
6
7
8
9
10
11
12
13
14
15
Atom Windows!
Operation
Add
Find
Get
Delete
Ok
Cancel
Enter number of atom to delete.
1

Figure 13.8

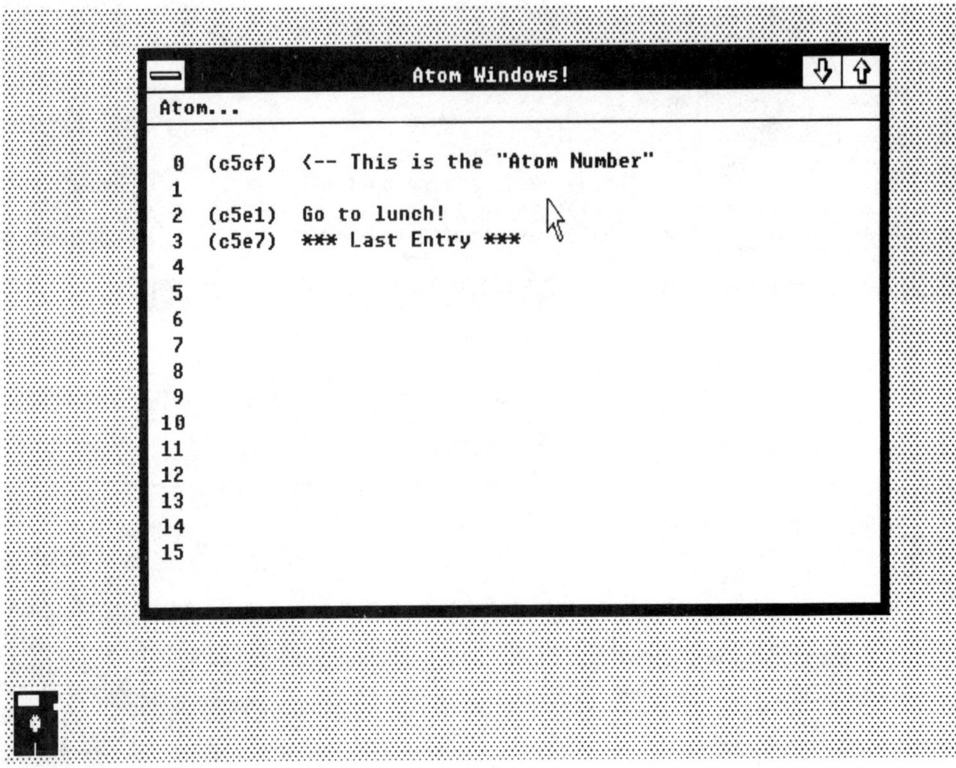

13.3 THE HEADER FILE: PGM10.H

```
/************************************************************************/
/* Filename:     PGM10.H                                                */
/*                                                                      */
/* Description:  Header file                                            */
/*----------------------------------------------------------------------*/

#define IDMATOM          1000
#define ATOMDLG          1001
#define IDRBADD          1002     /* Of the 4 radiobuttons,        */
#define IDRBGET          1003     /* IDRBADD must be the first,    */
#define IDRBFIND         1004     /* and IDRBDELETE must be last.  */
#define IDRBDELETE       1005     /* Reason: CheckRadioButton(..)  */
#define IDSHELP          1006
#define IDEDIT           1007

/*----------------------------------------------------------------------*/
/* End of file:  PGM10.H                                                */
/************************************************************************/
```

13.4 THE RESOURCE SCRIPT FILE: PGM10.RC

```
/*****************************************************************/
/* Filename:     PGM10.RC                                        */
/*                                                               */
/* Description:  Resource description file                       */
/*---------------------------------------------------------------*/

#include "style.h"
#include "pgm10.h"

MainMenu MENU
BEGIN
  MENUITEM      "&Atom...",     IDMATOM
END

ATOMDLG DIALOG   30, 20, 136, 66
STYLE WS_BORDER | WS_CAPTION | WS_DLGFRAME | WS_POPUP
CAPTION "Atom Windows!"
BEGIN
  GROUPBOX      "Operation",    -1,              2,  2,  66, 38
  RADIOBUTTON   "&Add",         IDRBADD,         4, 14,  24, 12
  RADIOBUTTON   "&Get",         IDRBGET,         4, 26,  24, 12
  RADIOBUTTON   "&Find",        IDRBFIND,       30, 14,  28, 12
  RADIOBUTTON   "&Delete",      IDRBDELETE,     30, 26,  36, 12
  LTEXT         "Select an Operation", IDSHELP,  2, 42, 132,  8
  EDITTEXT                      IDEDIT,          2, 52, 132, 12
  PUSHBUTTON    "&Ok",          IDOK,           82,  6,  40, 12
  PUSHBUTTON    "&Cancel",      IDCANCEL,       82, 24,  40, 12
END

/*---------------------------------------------------------------*/
/* End of file:  PGM10.RC                                        */
/*****************************************************************/
```

13.5 THE C LANGUAGE SOURCE FILE: PGM10.C

```
/*****************************************************************/
/* Filename:     PGM10.C                                         */
/*                                                               */
/* Description:  Program source                                  */
/*---------------------------------------------------------------*/

#include "windows.h"
#include "pgm10.h"
typedef BOOL FAR * LPBOOL;
#define NATOMS  16

  unsigned int          atomTable[NATOMS];
  HANDLE                hInst;
  int                   i,      j;
  FARPROC               lpAtomProc;

/*===============================================================*/
```

```
long FAR PASCAL MainWndProc (hWnd, msg, wParam, lParam)
  HWND          hWnd;
  unsigned      msg;
  WORD          wParam;
  LONG          lParam;
  {
  PAINTSTRUCT   ps;
  int           lineNum;

  switch (msg)  {
    case WM_CREATE:
      for (i=0; i<NATOMS; i++)
        atomTable[i] = 0;
      break;

    case WM_PAINT:
      BeginPaint (hWnd, (LPPAINTSTRUCT)&ps);
      for (i=0; i<NATOMS; i++)
        {
        int     index,          len;
        char    szStr80[80],    szStr17[17],    szStr33[33];

        itoa (i, szStr17, 10);
        index = StrCopy (szStr80, 0, szStr17, 2, TRUE);
        if (atomTable[i])
          {
          index = StrCopy (szStr80, index, "  (", 3, FALSE);
          itoa (atomTable[i], szStr17, 16);
          index = StrCopy (szStr80, index, szStr17, 4, TRUE);
          index = StrCopy (szStr80, index, ")  ", 3, FALSE);
          len = GetAtomName (atomTable[i], (LPSTR)szStr33, 33);
          index = StrCopy (szStr80, index, szStr33, len, TRUE);
          }
        TextOut (ps.hdc, 8, (i+1)*12, (LPSTR)szStr80, index);
        }
      EndPaint (hWnd, (LPPAINTSTRUCT)&ps);
      break;

    case WM_DESTROY:
      PostQuitMessage (0);
      break;

    case WM_COMMAND:
      if (DialogBox (hInst, MAKEINTRESOURCE(ATOMDLG), hWnd, lpAtomProc))
        InvalidateRect (hWnd, (LPRECT)NULL, TRUE);
      break;

    default:
      return DefWindowProc (hWnd, msg, wParam, lParam);
      break;
    }
  return (0L);
  }

/*=================================================================*/

char *HelpText (wParam)
  int wParam;
  {
  switch (wParam)
    {
    case IDRBADD:        return "Enter text of atom to add.";
    case IDRBGET:        return "Enter number of atom to get.";
```

```
    case IDRBFIND:      return "Enter text of atom to find.";
    case IDRBDELETE:    return "Enter number of atom to delete.";
    }
  }

int StrCopy (new, newIndex, old, width, padleft)
  char  new[],  old[];
  int   width,  newIndex;
  BOOL  padleft;
  {
  int   n,      oldStrLen;

  for (oldStrLen=0; old[oldStrLen]; oldStrLen++);
  if (padleft) {
    if (width != oldStrLen)
      for (n = width - oldStrLen; n; n--, newIndex++)
        new[newIndex] = ' ';
    }
  for (n=0; new[newIndex]=old[n]; n++, newIndex++);
  return newIndex;
  }

getRBName (hWnd, first, last)
  HWND  hWnd;
  int   first, last;
  {
  for (; first <= last; first++)
    if (IsDlgButtonChecked (hWnd, first))
      return (first);

  }

/*==============================================================*/

BOOL FAR PASCAL AtomProc (hWnd, msg, wParam, lParam)
  HWND          hWnd;
  unsigned      msg;
  WORD          wParam;
  LONG          lParam;
  {
  switch (msg)
    {
    case WM_INITDIALOG:
      for (i=j=0; i<NATOMS; i++)
        if (atomTable[i])
          j++;
      if (!j)
        {
        EnableWindow (GetDlgItem (hWnd, IDRBGET),    FALSE);
        EnableWindow (GetDlgItem (hWnd, IDRBFIND),   FALSE);
        EnableWindow (GetDlgItem (hWnd, IDRBDELETE), FALSE);
        SetDlgItemText (hWnd, IDSHELP, (LPSTR)HelpText(IDRBADD));
        CheckRadioButton(hWnd, IDRBADD, IDRBDELETE, IDRBADD);
        }
      else
        if (j == NATOMS)
          EnableWindow (GetDlgItem (hWnd, IDRBADD),  FALSE);
      break;

    case WM_COMMAND:
      switch (wParam)
        {
        case IDRBADD:
        case IDRBGET:
        case IDRBFIND:
```

```
case IDRBDELETE:
  CheckRadioButton(hWnd, IDRBADD, IDRBDELETE, wParam);
  SetDlgItemText (hWnd, IDSHELP, (LPSTR)HelpText(wParam));
  break;

case IDOK:
  switch (getRBName(hWnd, IDRBADD, IDRBDELETE))
    {
    char szBuff[33];
    BOOL bValOK;
    int  num;

    case IDRBADD:
      if (GetDlgItemText (hWnd, IDEDIT, (LPSTR)szBuff, 33))
        {
        num = AddAtom ((LPSTR)szBuff);
        if (num)
          {
          for (i=0; i<NATOMS; i++)
            if (atomTable[i] == num)
                {
                EndDialog(hWnd, FALSE);
                return;
                }
           for (i=0; i<NATOMS; i++)
             if (!atomTable[i])
                {
                atomTable[i] = num;
                break;
                }
           }
         EndDialog(hWnd, TRUE);
         }
       break;

     case IDRBFIND:
       if (GetDlgItemText (hWnd, IDEDIT, (LPSTR)szBuff, 33))
         {
         itoa (FindAtom ((LPSTR)szBuff), szBuff, 16);
         MessageBox(hWnd,(LPSTR)szBuff, (LPSTR)"Find Atom", MB_OK);
         EndDialog(hWnd, TRUE);
         }
       break;

     case IDRBGET:
       num = GetDlgItemInt (hWnd, IDEDIT, (LPBOOL)&bValOK, FALSE);
       if (!bValOK)
         break;
       if ((num >= 0)
        && (num < NATOMS)
        && (atomTable[num]))
         {
         GetAtomName (atomTable[num], (LPSTR)szBuff, 33);
         MessageBox(hWnd, (LPSTR)szBuff, (LPSTR)"Get Atom", MB_OK);
         }
       EndDialog(hWnd, TRUE);
       break;

     case IDRBDELETE:
       num = GetDlgItemInt (hWnd, IDEDIT, (LPBOOL)&bValOK, FALSE);
       if (!bValOK)
         break;
       if ((num >= 0)
```

```
              && (num < NATOMS)
              && (atomTable[num]))
               atomTable[num] = DeleteAtom (atomTable[num]);
             EndDialog(hWnd, TRUE);
             break;
           }
         break;

       case IDCANCEL:
         EndDialog(hWnd, FALSE);
         break;
       }

     break;

   default:
     return FALSE;
   }
 return TRUE;
 }

/*==================================================================*/

int PASCAL WinMain (hInstance, hPrevInstance, lpszCmdLine, cmdShow)
  HANDLE                    hInstance;
  HANDLE                    hPrevInstance;
  LPSTR                     lpszCmdLine;
  int                       cmdShow;
  {
  MSG                       msg;
  HWND                      hWnd;
  PWNDCLASS                 pMainClass;

  if (hPrevInstance)
    return FALSE;

  pMainClass = (PWNDCLASS)LocalAlloc(LPTR,sizeof(WNDCLASS));
  pMainClass->hCursor         = LoadCursor (NULL, IDC_ARROW);
  pMainClass->hIcon           = LoadIcon (NULL, IDI_APPLICATION);
  pMainClass->lpszMenuName    = (LPSTR)"MainMenu";
  pMainClass->lpszClassName   = (LPSTR)"PGM10";
  pMainClass->hbrBackground   = (HBRUSH)GetStockObject (WHITE_BRUSH);
  pMainClass->hInstance       = hInstance;
  pMainClass->style           = CS_HREDRAW | CS_VREDRAW;
  pMainClass->lpfnWndProc     = MainWndProc;
  if (!RegisterClass((LPWNDCLASS)pMainClass))
    return FALSE;

  LocalFree ((HANDLE)pMainClass);

  hWnd = CreateWindow ((LPSTR)"PGM10", (LPSTR)"Atom Windows!",
    WS_OVERLAPPEDWINDOW,
    GetSystemMetrics (SM_CXSCREEN) / 4, GetSystemMetrics (SM_CYSCREEN) / 4,
    GetSystemMetrics (SM_CXSCREEN) / 2, GetSystemMetrics (SM_CYSCREEN) / 2,
    (HWND)NULL, (HMENU)NULL, (HANDLE)hInstance, (LPSTR)NULL);
  hInst = hInstance;
  lpAtomProc = MakeProcInstance ((FARPROC)AtomProc, hInstance);

  ShowWindow (hWnd, cmdShow);
  UpdateWindow (hWnd);

  while (GetMessage((LPMSG)&msg, NULL, 0, 0)) {
    TranslateMessage ((LPMSG)&msg);
    DispatchMessage ((LPMSG)&msg);
    }
```

```
FreeProcInstance (lpAtomProc);
  return (int)msg.wParam;
  }

/*------------------------------------------------------------*/
/* End of file:  PGM10.C                                       */
/*************************************************************/
```

13.5.1 The Atom Management Functions

We'll assume that by now you can make your own way through the **WinMain** and **MainWndProc** procedures. There's only one new function presented in the painting procedure: **GetAtomName.** After we examine the dialog box processing procedure, you should see how the paint procedure retrieves and displays the text of atoms. We'll discuss **GetAtomName** in depth with the rest of the atom calls later in this chapter.

The procedure we'll focus on first is **AtomProc,** which is called when the user selects "Atom. . ." from the menu bar.

13.5.2 Processing Dialog Box Messages

Before displaying our dialog box, we'll check a few things. If there are no atoms in the atom table, we want to disable three of the radio buttons (seen in Figure 13.2). Also, if our array of 16 elements is full, we want to disable the "Add" option. We have used all of these functions in previous programs, so we won't dwell on them here.

As usual, **WM_COMMAND** will be called whenever the user does something in the dialog box. We are only interested in knowing when a radio or push button is "pressed".

It should be noted that if we don't have atoms in the atom table, then the **WM_INITDIALOG** code will disable three of the radio buttons. This implies that we'll never receive a message from any of these buttons unless there is at least one atom defined.

When the user presses a radio button, all we want to do is to select it and de-select the others. We have done this before, in Chapter 6, so let's move on.

The condition we are really interested in is the "Ok" push button, **IDOK**. It is here that we'll do whatever work is requested. We begin by doing a little fancy footwork with the switch:

```
switch (getRBName (hWnd, IDRBADD, IDRBDELETE)) {
```

The function **getRBName,** defined before **AtomProc,** returns the identifier of the currently selected radio button. We switch it on because we want to use the function that is selected (add, get, find, or delete).

The first function we process is "add," or **IDRBADD**. After getting the text from the edit field, we'll add it to the atom table:

```
num = AddAtom ((LPSTR)szBuff);
```

AddAtom adds the text found in **szBuff** to the atom table. Returned is the actual atom. If the function fails, then NULL is returned.

If the string is identical to one that is already in the atom table, Windows won't really add this one, but rather will return the atom of the previous entry. What we do is to look through our atom table and see if a match is found. If so, we just exit. If not, we look for the first empty entry and store our newly created atom.

The next case is "find," or **IDRBFIND**. "Find" means to pass Windows some text, which causes Windows to return the atom number of that text if the text is in the atom table. If we successfully retrieve some text from the edit field, then we'll use:

```
itoa (FindAtom ((LPSTR)szBuff), szBuff, 16);
```

FindAtom returns the actual atom for the text passed in **szBuff**. We take that number and pass it to the standard C function **itoa,** which converts integers into ASCII text and places the text in the buffer **szBuff**. We then display a message box with the atom number.

IDRBGET is used to get the text associated with an atom. Given a valid index (0 to 15), we'll ask Windows to put the text into our buffer:

```
GetAtomName (atomTable[num], (LPSTR)szBuff, 33);
```

atomtable[num] is the atom that we had stored in **IDRBADD**. Windows will place the text, which cannot exceed 33 characters, in the specified buffer (33 is the limit we specified, not a Windows limitation). Note that **GetAtomName** is also used in the paint procedure to display the text in the main window.

Finally, we'll delete atoms. After getting an integer value within the range of zero to 15, we make a call to the delete function:

```
atomTable[num] = DeleteAtom (atomTable[num]);
```

If the function is successful, a NULL will be returned. Otherwise, the atom is returned and re-assigned to **atomTable.**

13.6 THE MODULE DEFINITION FILE: PGM10.DEF

```
;*****************************************************************:
; Filename:      PGM10.DEF                                        :
;                                                                 :
; Description:  Link definition file                              :
;-----------------------------------------------------------------:

NAME     PGM10

STUB     '..\WINSTUB.EXE'

CODE     MOVEABLE
DATA     MOVEABLE MULTIPLE

HEAPSIZE  4096
STACKSIZE 4096

EXPORTS
    MainWndProc           @1
    AtomProc              @2

;-----------------------------------------------------------------:
; End of file:  PGM10.DEF                                         :
;*****************************************************************:
```

13.7 THE MAKE FILE: PGM10.

```
#*************************************************************#
# Filename:     PGM10.                                        #
#                                                             #
# Description:  "MAKE" description file                       #
#-------------------------------------------------------------#

pgm10.obj: pgm10.c pgm10.h
    cl -d -c -AS -Gsw -Os -Zpe pgm10.c

pgm10.res: pgm10.rc pgm10.h
    rc -r pgm10.rc

pgm10.exe: pgm10.obj pgm10.res pgm10.def
    link4 pgm10,/align:16,/map,slibw,pgm10.def
    rc pgm10.res

#-------------------------------------------------------------#
# End of file:  PGM10                                         #
#*************************************************************#
```

. . . .

In this chapter, you've learned about using atoms to manage strings. In Chapter 14, you'll learn to use timers to prompt the user for action.

14

SETTING TIMERS AND FLASHING FOR ATTENTION

- Introduction To Timers
- Introduction To PGM11: Timer Windows!
- The C Header File: PGM11.H
- The Resource Script File: PGM11.RC
- The C Language Source File: PGM11.C
- The Module Definition File: PGM11.DEF
- The Make File: PGM11.

Because Windows is a cooperative environment in which many applications can be running at the same time, your window may not always have the user's attention when you want it. To check how much time has elapsed after an event, you'll use a *timer*, a device that tells you when a certain time period is up. To signal the user that your application needs the input focus, you'll *flash* your window. This chapter will show you how to set and kill timers, and how to flash for attention.

14.1 INTRODUCTION TO TIMERS

Because timers operate independently of the program code, they are considered to be *asynchronous*. When we ask Windows to start a timer, we'll pass the duration of the time period and the address of a routine that is to receive control when the period expires.

The time duration is expressed in milliseconds and is an unsigned word argument. The greatest time period that can be used is 65,535 milliseconds or slightly more than 65 seconds.

14.2 INTRODUCTION TO PGM11: TIMER WINDOWS!

PGM11 requires five files:

PGM11.H	C language program header
PGM11.RC	Resource script file
PGM11.C	Code for PGM11
PGM11.DEF	Definition file (required by LINK4)
PGM11.	Input instructions to the MAKE utility

Figure 14.1 illustrates what you'll see upon executing PGM11. If you select the menu item "Timer," the program displays a popup menu with two items: "Begin" and "End." "End" is grayed until "Begin" is selected. At that time, "Begin" will become grayed.

Figure 14.1

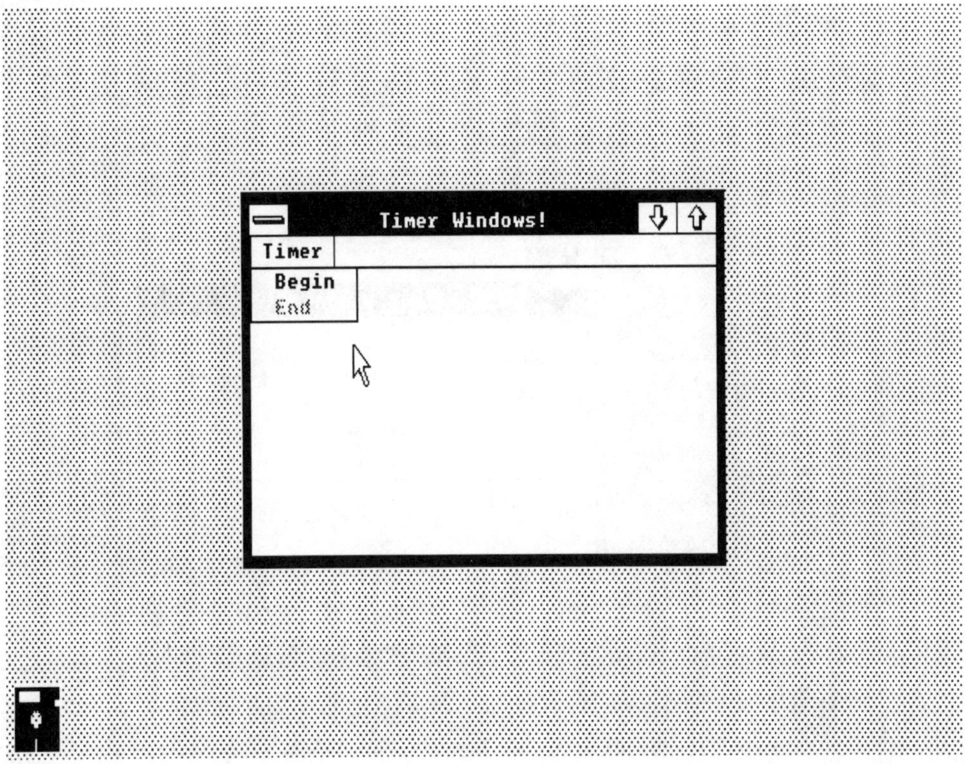

Selecting "Begin" starts a timer with a duration of 10,000 milliseconds, or 10 seconds. When the time expires, you should see a message box as illustrated in Figure 14.2. When the "Ok" pushbutton is pressed, the timer will begin the 10-second countdown again.

Figure 14.2

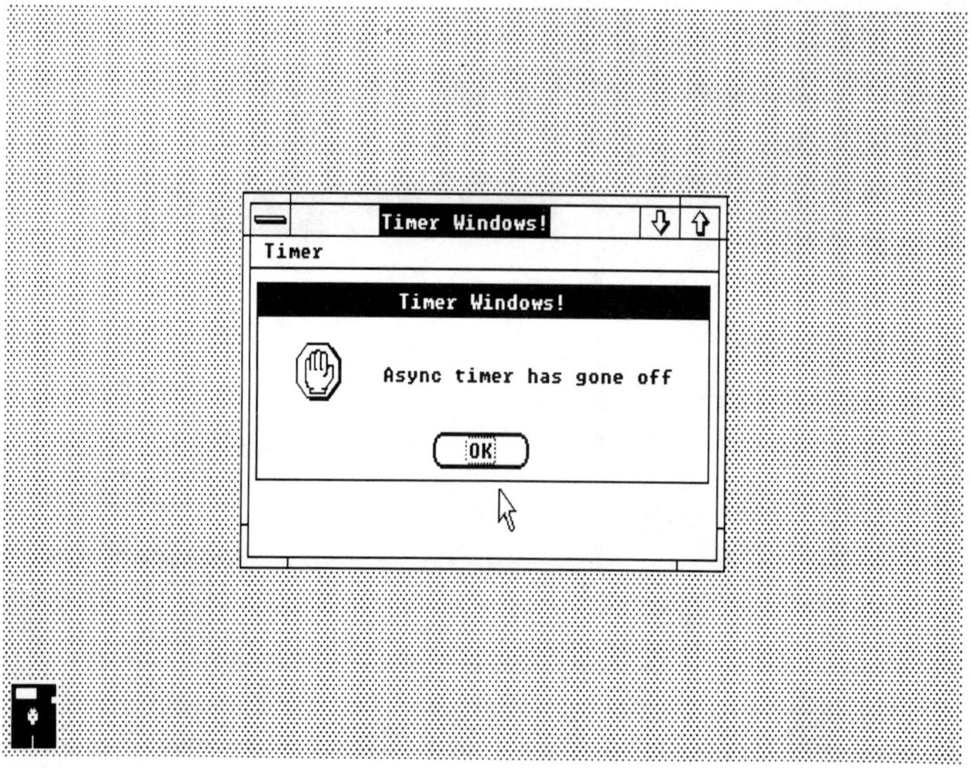

If PGM11's window does not have the input focus at the time the program needs to display the message box, the program will flash the title bar to signal the user that the window requires attention. Flashing involves repeatedly changing the window's title bar from the "inactive" state to the "active" state and back again.

If our application's window is in iconic form at the time it needs to display the message box, we cannot flash the title bar, so we'll change the background color of the icon to flash the icon. Flashing may sound complicated, but you'll see that it requires only one call to Windows.

PGM11 also displays a dialog box, shown in Figure 14.3, that gives the user a chance to return to the application after selecting "Quit" from the system menu or double-clicking the system menu icon. This gives the user a chance to reconsider and an opportunity to save any unsaved work.

Figure 14.3

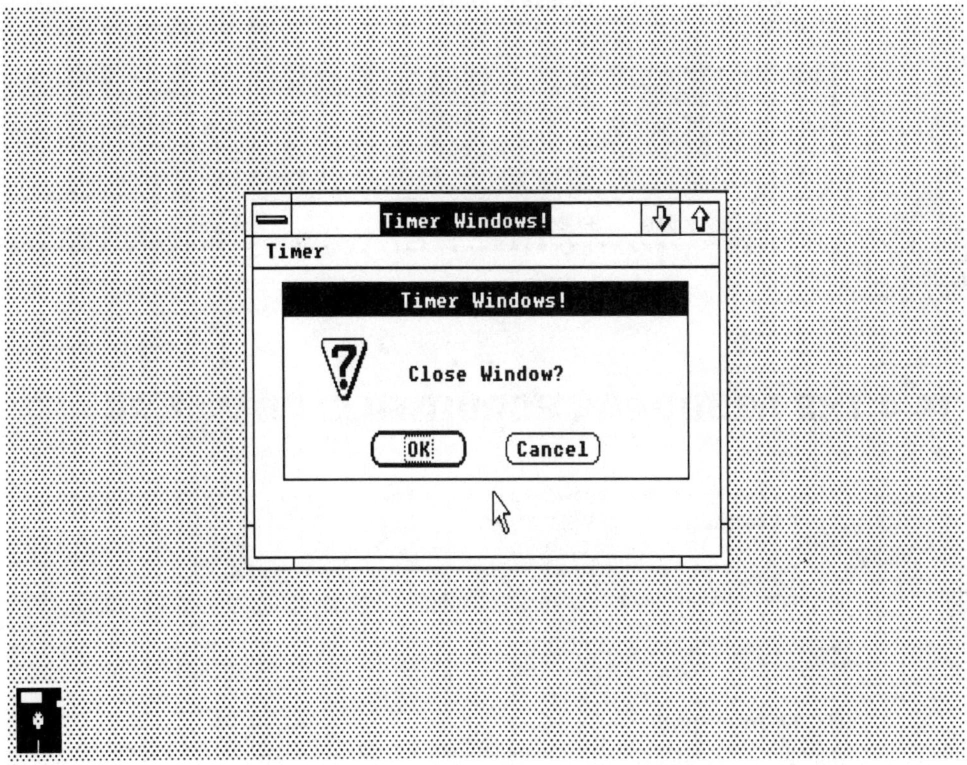

14.3 THE C HEADER FILE: PGM11.H

```
/*****************************************************************/
/* Filename:     PGM11.H                                         */
/*                                                               */
/* Description:  Header file                                     */
/*---------------------------------------------------------------*/

#define IDMBEGIN        1000
#define IDMEND          1001
#define IDTASYNC        1002
#define IDTFLASH        1003

/*---------------------------------------------------------------*/
/* End of file:  PGM11.H                                         */
/*****************************************************************/
```

14.4 THE RESOURCE SCRIPT FILE: PGM11.RC

```
/*****************************************************************/
/* Filename:     PGM11.RC                                        */
/*                                                               */
/* Description:  Resource description file                       */
/*---------------------------------------------------------------*/

#include "style.h"
#include "pgm11.h"

MainMenu MENU
BEGIN
  POPUP         "&Timer"
  BEGIN
    MENUITEM    "&Begin",       IDMBEGIN
    MENUITEM    "&End",         IDMEND,         GRAYED
  END
END

/*---------------------------------------------------------------*/
/* End of file:  PGM11.RC                                        */
/*****************************************************************/
```

14.5 THE C LANGUAGE SOURCE FILE: PMG11.C

```
/*****************************************************************/
/* Filename:     PGM11.C                                         */
/*                                                               */
/* Description:  Program source                                 */
/*---------------------------------------------------------------*/

#include "windows.h"
#include "pgm11.h"

  HANDLE                   hInst;
  FARPROC                  lpprocTimerFunction;
  BOOL                     bAsync = FALSE;
  BOOL                     bFlash = FALSE;

/*===============================================================*/

AsyncMessage (hWnd)
  HWND  hWnd;
  {
  bFlash = FALSE;
  KillTimer (hWnd, IDTASYNC);
  KillTimer (hWnd, IDTFLASH);
  FlashWindow(hWnd, FALSE);
  MessageBox (hWnd,
              (LPSTR)"Async timer has gone off",
              (LPSTR)"Timer Windows!",
              MB_OK | MB_ICONHAND);
  if (bAsync)
      SetTimer (hWnd, IDTASYNC, 10000, lpprocTimerFunction);
  }

/*===============================================================*/

FAR PASCAL TimerFunction (hWnd, msg, nIDEvent, dwTime)
  HWND            hWnd;
  unsigned        msg;
  WORD            nIDEvent;
  DWORD           dwTime;
  {
  switch (nIDEvent)
    {
    case IDTASYNC:
      KillTimer (hWnd, IDTASYNC);
      if (GetFocus() == hWnd)
        AsyncMessage (hWnd);
      else
        {
        bFlash = TRUE;
        SetTimer (hWnd, IDTFLASH, 1000, lpprocTimerFunction);
        FlashWindow (hWnd, TRUE);
        }
      return (FALSE);

    case IDTFLASH:
      FlashWindow (hWnd, TRUE);
```

```
    }
  }

/*===================================================================*/

long FAR PASCAL MainWndProc (hWnd, msg, wParam, lParam)
  HWND          hWnd;
  unsigned      msg;
  WORD          wParam;
  LONG          lParam;
  {
  HMENU         hMenu;

  switch (msg)  {
    case WM_COMMAND:
      hMenu = GetMenu (hWnd);
      switch (wParam)
        {
        case IDMBEGIN:
          EnableMenuItem (hMenu, IDMBEGIN, MF_GRAYED);
          EnableMenuItem (hMenu, IDMEND,   MF_ENABLED);
          bAsync = TRUE;
          bFlash = FALSE;
          SetTimer (hWnd, IDTASYNC, 10000, lpprocTimerFunction);
          break;

        case IDMEND:
          EnableMenuItem (hMenu, IDMBEGIN, MF_ENABLED);
          EnableMenuItem (hMenu, IDMEND,   MF_GRAYED);
          KillTimer (hWnd, IDTASYNC);
          KillTimer (hWnd, IDTFLASH);
          bAsync = FALSE;
          bFlash = FALSE;
          break;
        }
      break;

      case WM_ACTIVATE:
        if (wParam && !HIWORD(lParam))
          SetFocus (hWnd);
        break;

      case WM_SETFOCUS:
        if (bFlash)
          AsyncMessage (hWnd);
        break;

    case WM_CLOSE:
      if (MessageBox (hWnd,
                     (LPSTR)"Close Window?",
                     (LPSTR)"Timer Windows!",
                     MB_OKCANCEL | MB_ICONQUESTION)
       == IDOK)
        DestroyWindow(hWnd);
      break;
```

```
    case WM_DESTROY:
      PostQuitMessage (0);
      break;

    default:
      return DefWindowProc (hWnd, msg, wParam, lParam);
      break;
    }
  return (0L);
  }

/*===================================================================*/

int PASCAL WinMain (hInstance, hPrevInstance, lpszCmdLine, cmdShow)
  HANDLE                hInstance;
  HANDLE                hPrevInstance;
  LPSTR                 lpszCmdLine;
  int                   cmdShow;
  {
  MSG                   msg;
  HWND                  hWnd;
  PWNDCLASS             pMainClass;

  if (hPrevInstance)
    return FALSE;

  pMainClass = (PWNDCLASS)LocalAlloc(LPTR,sizeof(WNDCLASS));
  pMainClass->hCursor         = LoadCursor (NULL, IDC_ARROW);
  pMainClass->hIcon           = LoadIcon (NULL, IDI_APPLICATION);
  pMainClass->lpszMenuName    = (LPSTR)"MainMenu";
  pMainClass->lpszClassName   = (LPSTR)"PGM11";
  pMainClass->hbrBackground   = (HBRUSH)GetStockObject (WHITE_BRUSH);
  pMainClass->hInstance       = hInstance;
  pMainClass->style           = CS_HREDRAW | CS_VREDRAW;
  pMainClass->lpfnWndProc     = MainWndProc;
  if (!RegisterClass((LPWNDCLASS)pMainClass))
    return FALSE;

  LocalFree ((HANDLE)pMainClass);
  hWnd = CreateWindow ((LPSTR)"PGM11", (LPSTR)"Timer Windows!",
      WS_OVERLAPPEDWINDOW, GetSystemMetrics (SM_CXSCREEN)/4,
      GetSystemMetrics (SM_CYSCREEN)/4, GetSystemMetrics (SM_CXSCREEN)/2,
      GetSystemMetrics (SM_CYSCREEN)/2, (HWND)NULL, (HMENU)NULL,
      (HANDLE)hInstance, (LPSTR)NULL);
  hInst = hInstance;
  lpprocTimerFunction = MakeProcInstance ((FARPROC)TimerFunction, hInst);
  ShowWindow (hWnd, cmdShow);
  UpdateWindow (hWnd);

  while (GetMessage((LPMSG)&msg, NULL, 0, 0)) {
    TranslateMessage ((LPMSG)&msg);
    DispatchMessage ((LPMSG)&msg);
    }
```

```
  FreeProcInstance (lpprocTimerFunction);

  return (int)msg.wParam;
  }
/*---------------------------------------------------------------*/
/* End of file:  PGM11.C                                         */
/*****************************************************************/
```

14.5.1 Starting a Timer

You'll recognize most of the code by now: the user selects a menu item, we get the **WM_COMMAND** message, and **wParam** contains the identifier.

If the user selects "Begin," we need to change the colors of the menu items and start a timer. We also set two Boolean variables:

```
bAsync = TRUE;
bFlash = FALSE;
```

These variables remind us of the type of timer we're using. Right now we're using what we'll call the "async" timer, the timer that will control the time interval before putting up the message box. You'll soon see how to use a timer to control flashing. For now, we simply remind ourself that the "flash" timer is "off."

Next, we'll start the async timer:

```
SetTimer (hWnd, IDTASYNC, 10000, lpprocTimerAsync);
```

IDTASYNC is the timer event identifier that PGM11 and Windows will use to reference this timing action. **10000** is the time period in milliseconds. **lpprocTimerAsync** is a long pointer to the timer event function, which will gain control after the ten-second period expires. (You'll learn more about **lpprocTimerAsync** in the next section.)

When the user selects "Begin" from the menu, the "End" menu item becomes available. If the user selects "End," we need to enable "Begin" and disable "End," kill any timers running, and set flags to remind ourselves that no timers are active:

```
KillTimer (hWnd, IDTASYNC);
```

This reverses the process we started earlier with **SetTimer** by killing the timer event associated with the **IDTASYNC** identifier.

14.5.2 Checking the Input Focus

We'll receive the **WM_ACTIVATE** message whenever our window becomes active or inactive. **wParam** holds the key identifying the event that has occurred. If **wParam** is zero, the window has become inactive. If **wParam** is non-zero, the window is becoming active and the non-zero number will have one of the two values:

Value	*Meaning*
(1)	The window became active via the keyboard or via a function call such as **SetWindowActive**.
(2)	The window became active via a mouse click.

lParam contains more information about our window's state. If the high order word is zero, the window is not iconic; if the high order word is non-zero, the window is iconic. The contents of the low order word depend on **wParam**. If **wParam** is zero (the window is becoming inactive), the low order word is the handle of the window that is becoming active. If **wParam** is non-zero (the window is becoming active), the low order word is the handle of the window becoming inactive (the low order word may be NULL if no window is becoming active).

If our window is not iconic and is becoming active, we'll set the input focus to our window:

```
case WM_ACTIVATE:
   if (wparam && !HIWORD(lParam))
     SetFocus (hWnd);
   break;
```

SetFocus simply points the focus to the window with the handle **hWnd** (our application's window).

We'll discuss the **WM_SETFOCUS** and **WM_CLOSE** messages after studying the **TimerFunction** procedure.

14.5.3 Controlling Flashing

We started the asynchronous timer above in **MainWndProc WM_COMMAND case IDMBEGIN**. When the interval expires, control is transferred to **TimerFunction** (when we called **SetTimer** earlier, we specified that **TimerFunction** would gain control when a timer event occurred). Like most functions that are defined by the application but called by Windows, **TimerFunction** must be declared FAR PASCAL. Just like other functions, **TimerFunction** passes a window handle, a message, a word parameter and a double-word parameter:

```
FAR PASCAL TimerFunction (hWnd, msg, nIDEvent, dwTime)
HWND            hWnd;
unsigned        msg;
WORD            nIDEvent;
DWORD    dwTime;
{
```

Instead of **wParam** and **lParam,** we have **nIDEvent** and **dwTime. nIDEvent** is the identification number of the timer event that caused invocation of this procedure. This implies that more than one timer can use this procedure. **dwTime** is the current system time. Because we're using two timers and pointing both to this routine, we'll immediately branch:

```
    switch (nIDEvent)
    {
```

nIDEvent can take one of two values: **IDTASYNC** or **IDTFLASH,** depending on how we used the **SetTimer** function. We'll see momentarily how it gets **IDTFLASH**. For now, let's look at what happens when the asynchronous timer goes off:

```
    case IDTASYNC:
    KillTimer (hWnd, IDTASYNC);
    if (GetFocus() == hWnd)
            AsyncMessage (hWnd);
```

We begin by killing the timer, because it may take a while before the user gets around to acknowledging our signal and we don't want the timer going off again. Next, we want to find out which window has the input focus. If our window has it, we want to call the **AsyncMessage** function, which, among other things, displays the message box. If we don't have the input focus, we want to begin the flashing operation.

To begin flashing, we set a timer in motion, but this time we use the ID **IDTFLASH** and set the interval at **1000** milliseconds, or one second. Next, we call **FlashWindow:**

```
bFlash = TRUE;
SetTimer (hWnd, IDTFLASH, 1000, lpprocTimerFunction);
FlashWindow (hWnd, TRUE);
```

FlashWindow has two arguments: **hWnd** and a Boolean value. TRUE means flash, or invert the window from whatever it was. FALSE means set the window to its correct state (active or inactive).

So, we killed the async timer and started the flash timer. Guess where control goes when the flash timer goes off?

```
    case IDTFLASH:
    FlashWindow (hWnd, TRUE);
```

Right! This flashes the title bar or icon background to get the user's attention.

14.5.4 Killing Timers

AsyncMessage is called when the async timer goes off and our window has the input focus. Let's take a look at it:

```
bFlash = FALSE;
KillTimer (hWnd, IDTASYNC);
KillTimer (hWnd, IDTFLASH);
FlashWindow(hWnd, FALSE);
MessageBox (hWnd,
                  (LPSTR)"Async timer has gone off",
                  (LPSTR)"Timer Windows!",
                  MB_OK | MB_ICONHAND);
if (bAsync)
  SetTimer (hWnd, IDTASYNC, 10000, lpprocTimerFunction);
```

First, we remind ourselves that we are not flashing. Then, we kill both timers. Next, we return the title bar to the correct state (using the FALSE argument). After displaying the message box, we reset the timer for another 10-second interval.

14.5.5 Processing the WM_SETFOCUS and WM_CLOSE Messages

Now, let's revisit **MainWndProc** and wrap things up. There are two more cases that we purposely neglected to study earlier: **WM_SETFOCUS** and **WM_CLOSE.**

MainWndProc will get the **WM_SETFOCUS** message after our window gets the input focus. We trap this message because the flash timer may have been trying to get the user's attention. Once we get the focus, we want to display the message box and kill the timers. A call to **AsyncMessage** takes care of all of this:

```
case WM_SETFOCUS:

if (bFlash)
AsyncMessage (hWnd);
break;
```

If the flash timer is running, a call to **AsyncMessage** will kill it, display the message, and restart the async timer.

PGM11 gives the user the option of returning to the application after selecting "Close" from the system menu. Before our window is closed, we receive the following message from Windows:

```
case WM_CLOSE:
```

To check the intentions of the user, we display a message box:

```
if (MessageBox (hWnd,
                        (LPSTR)"Close Window?",
                        (LPSTR)"Timer Windows!",
                        MB_OKCANCEL | MB_ICONQUESTION)
== IDOK)
DestroyWindow(hWnd);
```

If the user responds with "Ok," **MessageBox** will return TRUE, in which case we place a call to **DestroyWindow**. Otherwise, **MessageBox** returns FALSE, we don't place the call, and the program resumes operation.

14.6 THE MODULE DEFINITION FILE: PGM11.DEF

```
;*****************************************************************:
; Filename:     PGM11.DEF                                         :
;                                                                 :
; Description:  Link definition file                              :
;-----------------------------------------------------------------:

NAME    PGM11

STUB    '..\WINSTUB.EXE'

CODE    MOVEABLE
DATA    MOVEABLE MULTIPLE

HEAPSIZE  4096
STACKSIZE 4096

EXPORTS
    MainWndProc         @1
    TimerFunction       @2

;-----------------------------------------------------------------:
; End of file:  PGM11.DEF                                         :
;*****************************************************************:
```

14.7 THE MAKE FILE: PGM11.

```
#*****************************************************************#
# Filename:     PGM11.                                            #
#                                                                 #
# Description:  "MAKE" description file                           #
#-----------------------------------------------------------------#

pgm11.obj: pgm11.c pgm11.h
    cl -d -c -AS -Gsw -Os -Zpe pgm11.c

pgm11.res: pgm11.rc pgm11.h
    rc -r pgm11.rc

pgm11.exe: pgm11.obj pgm11.res pgm11.def
    link4 pgm11,/align:16,/map,slibw,pgm11.def
    rc pgm11.res

#-----------------------------------------------------------------#
# End of file:  PGM11                                             #
#*****************************************************************#
```

. . . .

In this chapter, you've learned to set timers and flash the application window. In Chapter 15, you'll learn how to read from and write to a disk file.

15

READING AND WRITING DISK FILES

- Introduction To PGM12
- The Header File: PGM12.H
- The Resource Script File: PGM12.RC
- The C Language Source File: PGM12.C
- The Module Definition File: PGM12.DEF
- The Make File: PGM12.

Since we're assuming that you are a seasoned C language programmer, we also assume that you are at least somewhat familiar with the following C language function calls: **open, close, read,** and **write.** If you are proficient in using these and other disk I/O calls, you'll find it easy to learn how to use them from Windows.

Use C function calls from Windows? Yes, indeed! Basically, you only need to learn one new call: **OpenFile,** which replaces the C **open** function. There are a few more distinctions, but you'll find that file I/O isn't much different in the Windows world. In this chapter, we'll study a program that writes a file to disk, and then reads that file back.

15.1 INTRODUCTION TO PGM12

To create PGM12, we modified PGM9 ("Clipboard Windows!", examined in Chapter 12) to write the data in the clipboard to a disk file or read a file into the clipboard. PGM12 requires five files:

PGM12.H	C language program header
PGM12.RC	Resource script file
PGM12.C	Code for PGM12
PGM12.DEF	Definition file (required by LINK4)
PGM12.	Input instructions to the MAKE utility

Figure 15.1 shows PGM12's window and its "Select" menu. There's nothing in the clipboard to write to a disk file, so the menu items "Empty" and "Write file from" are grayed.

Figure 15.1

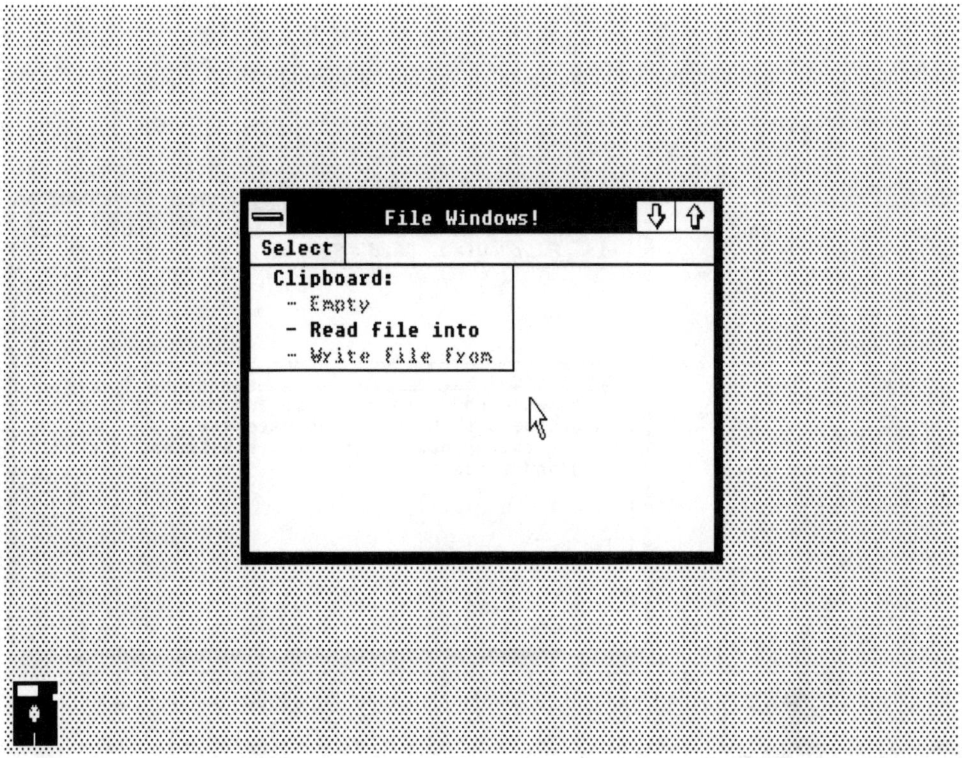

We'll use the Windows **Cardfile** program to put some data into the clipboard. Figure 15.2 shows the **Cardfile** window and a card containing a few sentences. To transfer this text to the clipboard, we first select the text by moving the I-beam cursor to the left of the letter "S," pressing the left mouse button, and dragging the cursor beyond the exclamation point (!) to highlight the text.

Figure 15.2

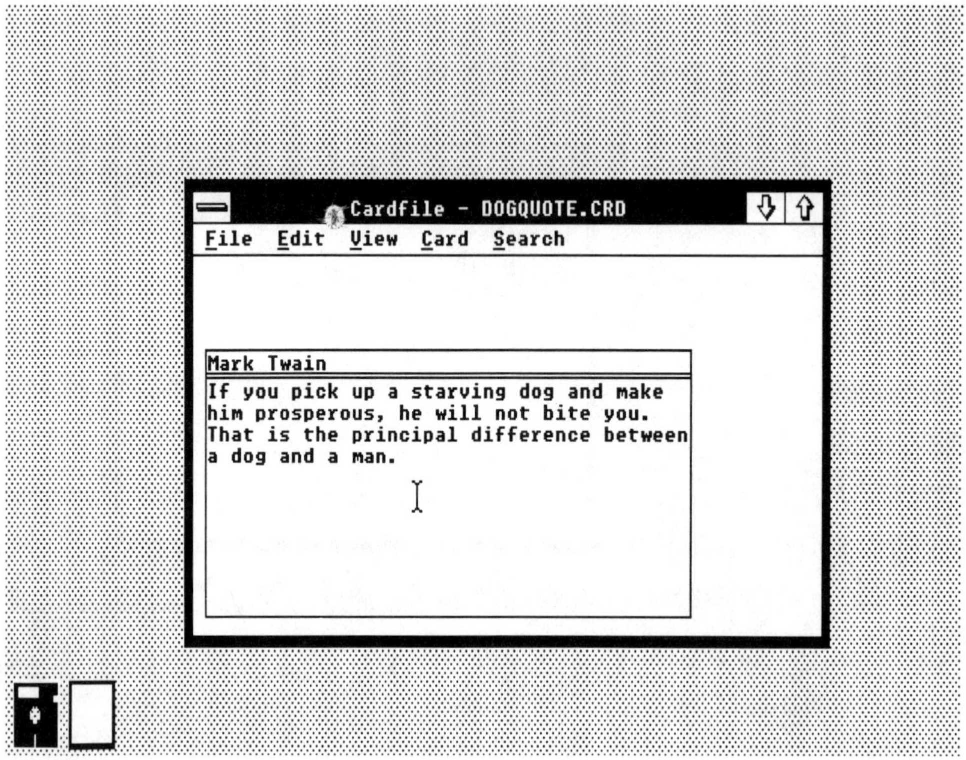

Then we use **Cardfile's** "Edit Cut" menu item, as shown in Figure 15.3, to cut the text from the card and place it on the clipboard. Figure 15.4 shows the data in the **Clipboard** window.

Figure 15.3

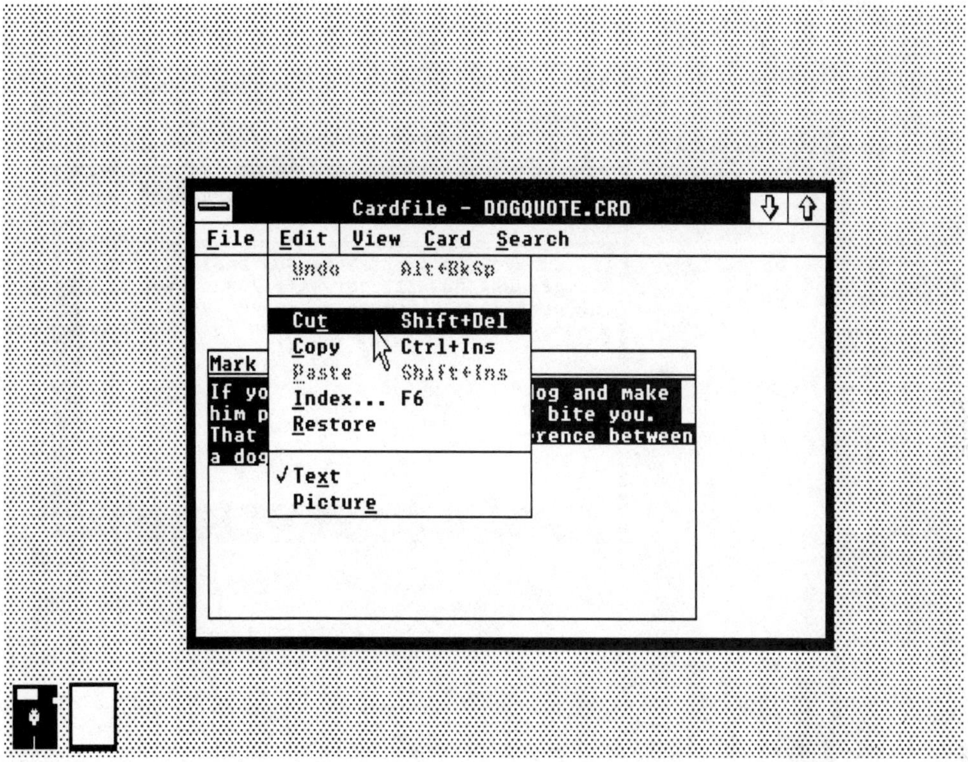
Cardfile - DOGQUOTE.CRD
File
Edit
View
Card
Search
Undo Alt+BkSp
Cut Shift+Del
Copy Ctrl+Ins
Paste Shift+Ins
Index... F6
Restore
Text
Picture
Mark
If yo
him p
That
a dog
log and make
bite you.
rence between

Figure 15.4

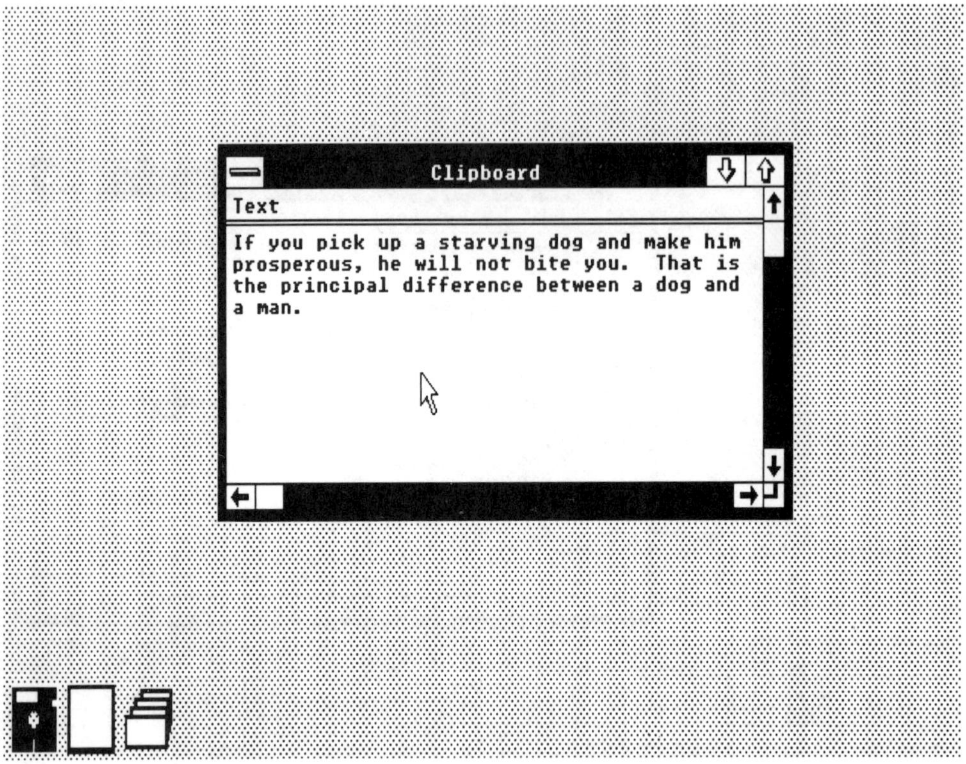
Clipboard
Text
If you pick up a starving dog and make him
prosperous, he will not bite you. That is
the principal difference between a dog and
a man.

In our program's window, shown in Figure 15.5, the menu items "Empty" and "Write file from" are available, because the clipboard now contains data. To write this data to a disk file, we select "Write file from."

Figure 15.5

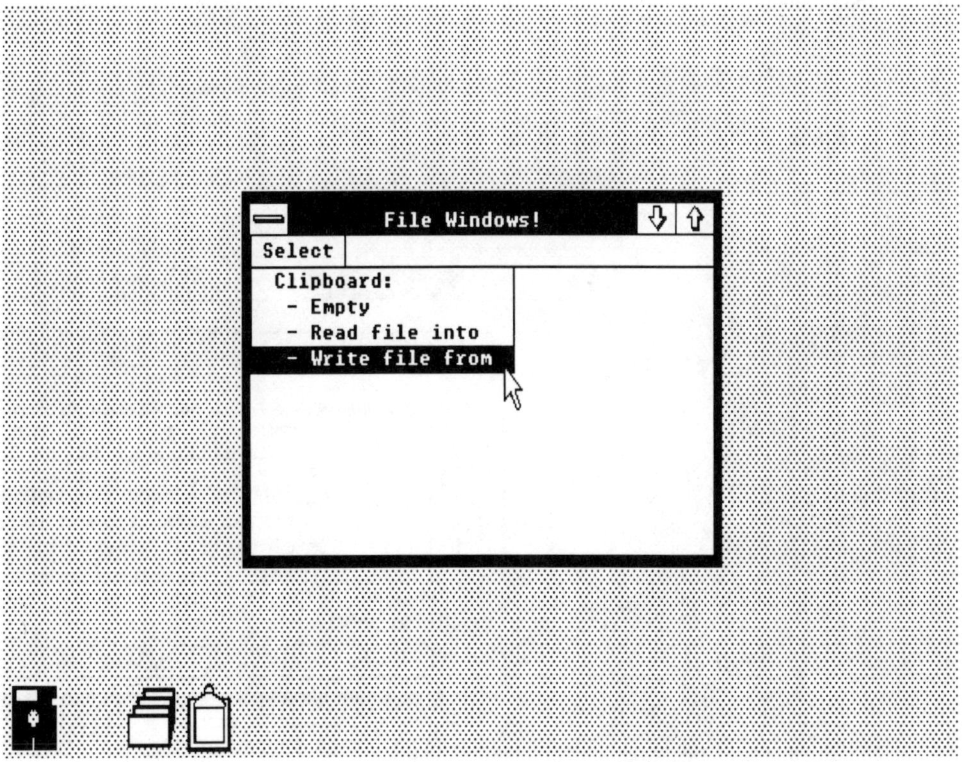

PGM12 displays a dialog box that prompts for a filename (Figure 15.6). If there were files in the list, we could select one to overwrite, but for now we enter a name, "QUOTE.CLP." When we press the ENTER key or select "Ok," the data is copied from the clipboard into the disk file. The new file's name is added to the MS-DOS Executive window, as shown in Figure 15.7.

Figure 15.6

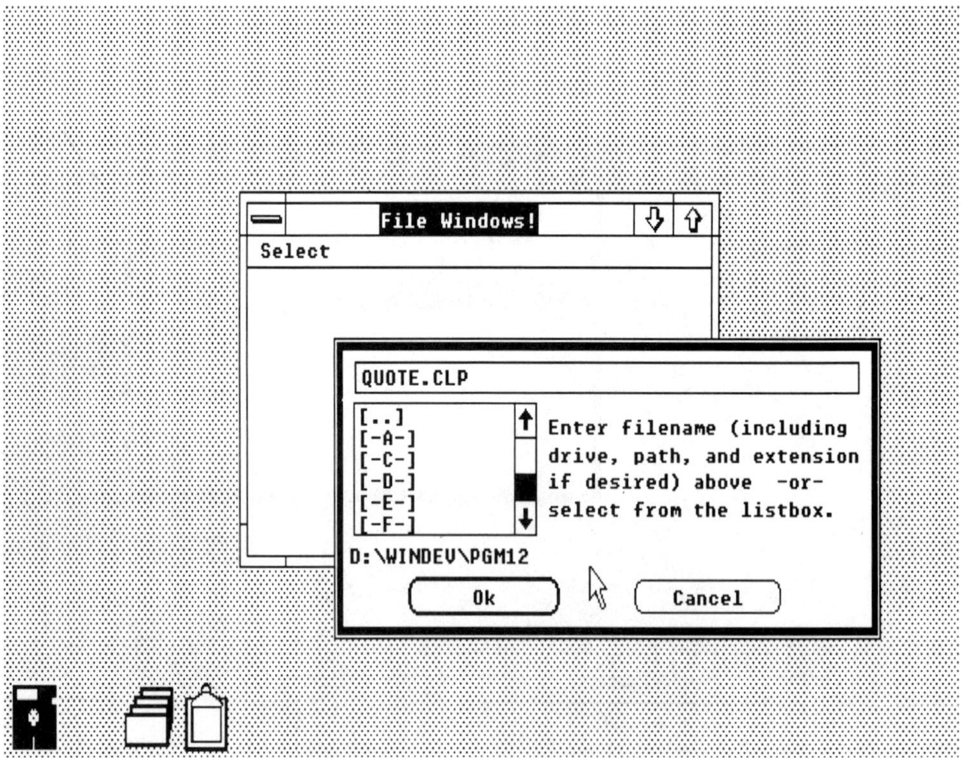

Figure 15.7

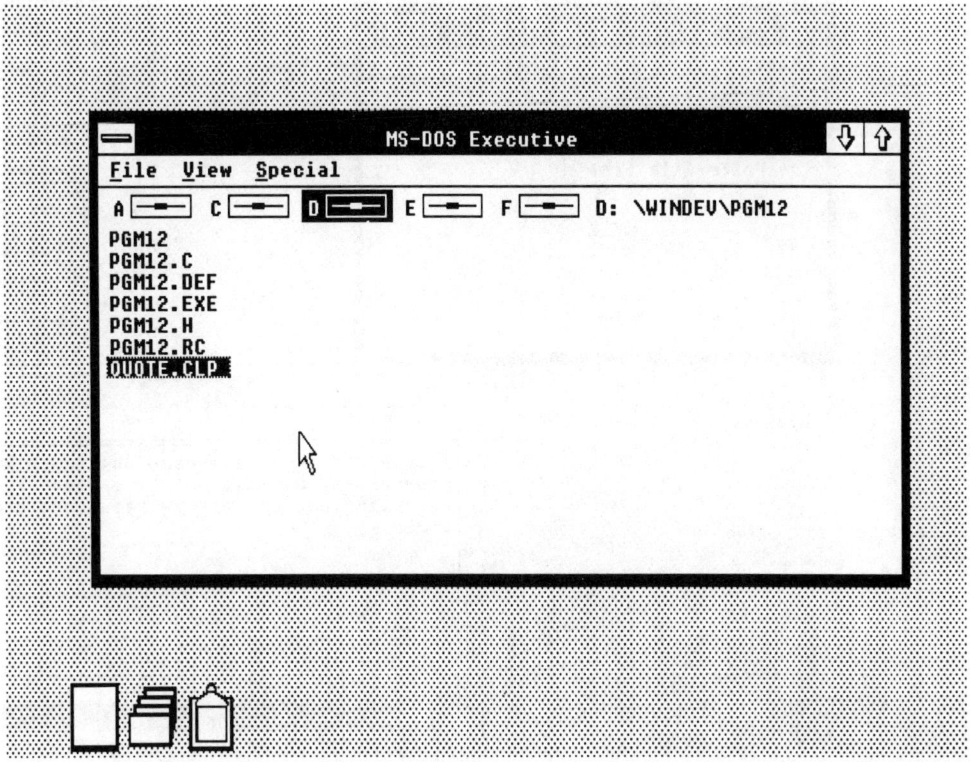

To empty the clipboard, we pick "Empty" (Figure 15.8) from our application's menu. Earlier we "cut" the data from the cardfile and put it into the clipboard, and now we have emptied the clipboard, so that data is gone forever.

Figure 15.8

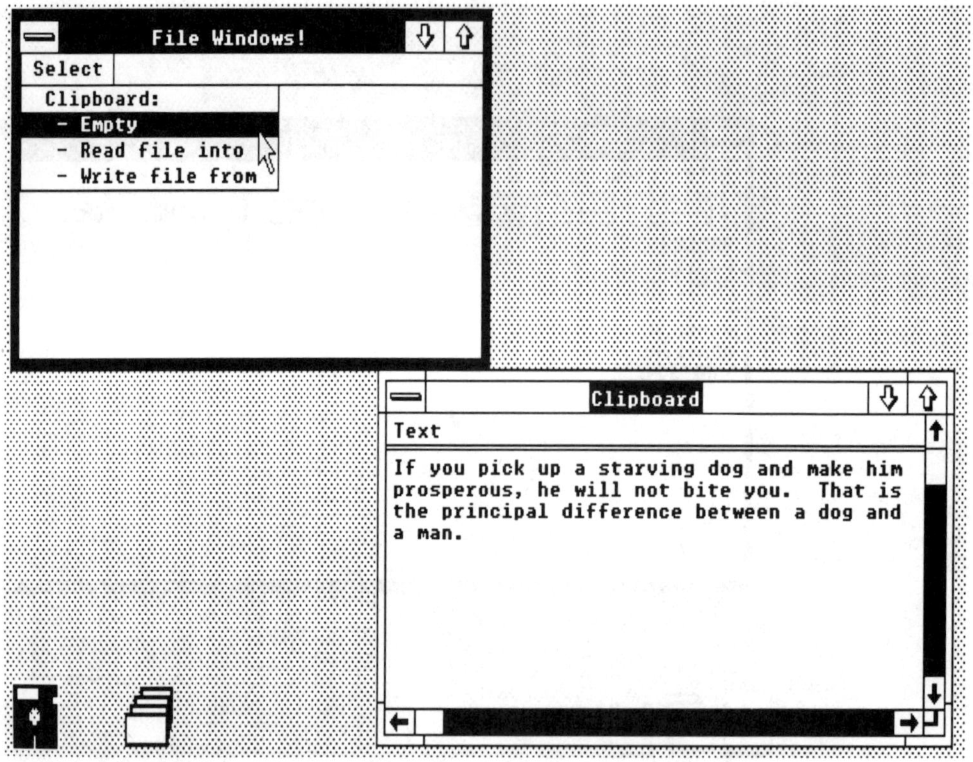
File Windows!
Select
Clipboard:
- Empty
- Read file into
- Write file from
Clipboard
Text
If you pick up a starving dog and make him prosperous, he will not bite you. That is the principal difference between a dog and a man.

Figure 15.9

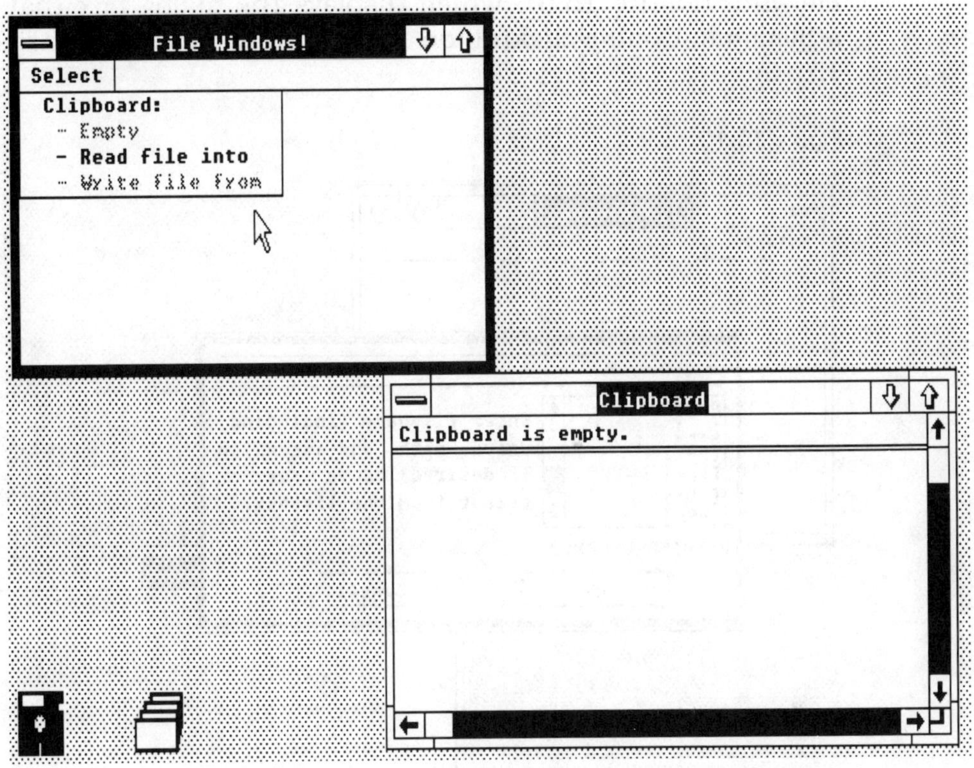
File Windows!
Select
Clipboard:
- Empty
- Read file into
- Write file from
Clipboard
Clipboard is empty.

Now, to read our file back into the clipboard, choose "Select Read file into" (Figure 15.9), which displays the dialog box that requests a filename. Double-clicking on "QUOTE.CLP" will do the trick (Figure 15.10).

Figure 15.10

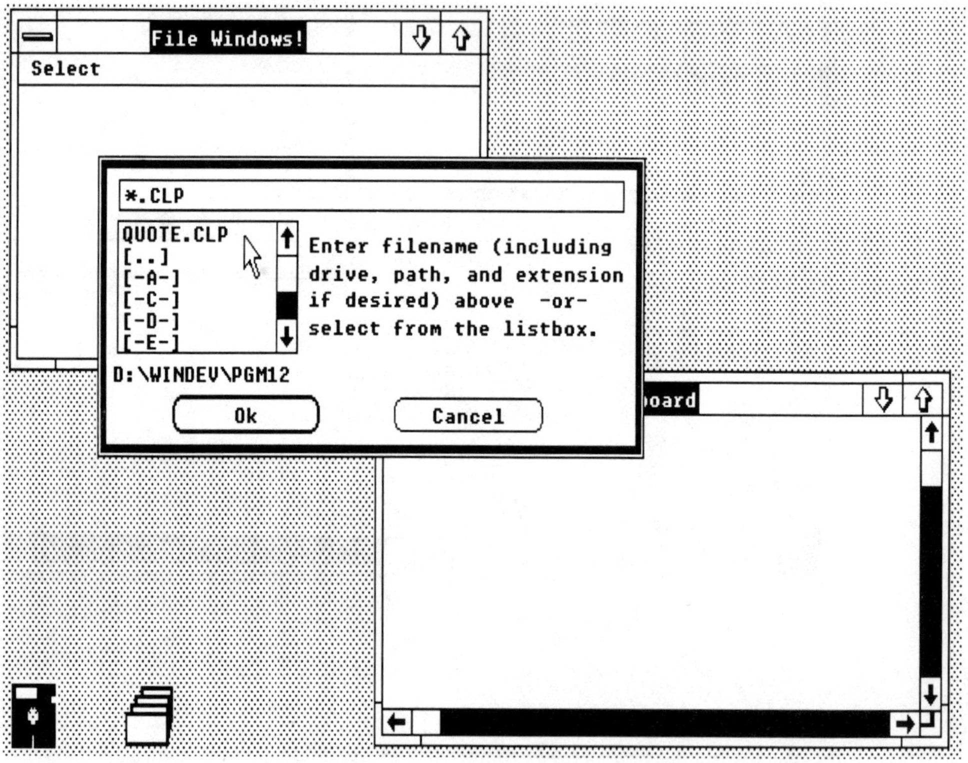

"Empty" and "Write file from" are enabled, indicating that the clipboard contains data. The **Clipboard** window confirms that the file transfer worked (Figure 15.11). It is now a small matter to return to the **Cardfile** window and paste the data back onto a card (Figures 15.12 and 15.13).

Figure 15.11

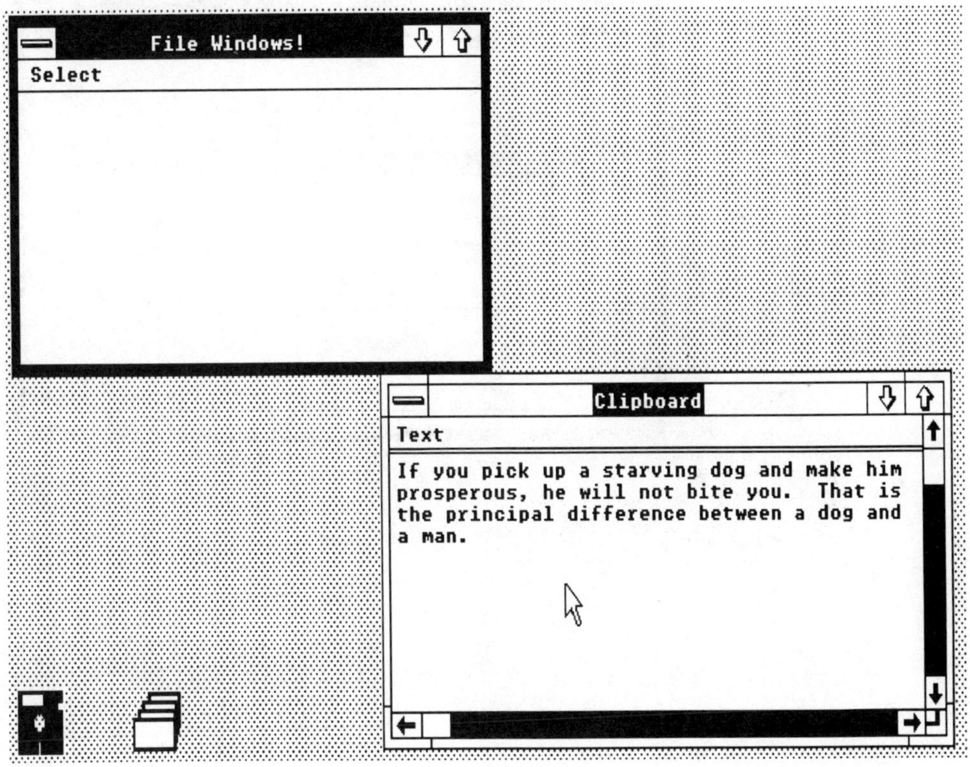

Figure 15.12

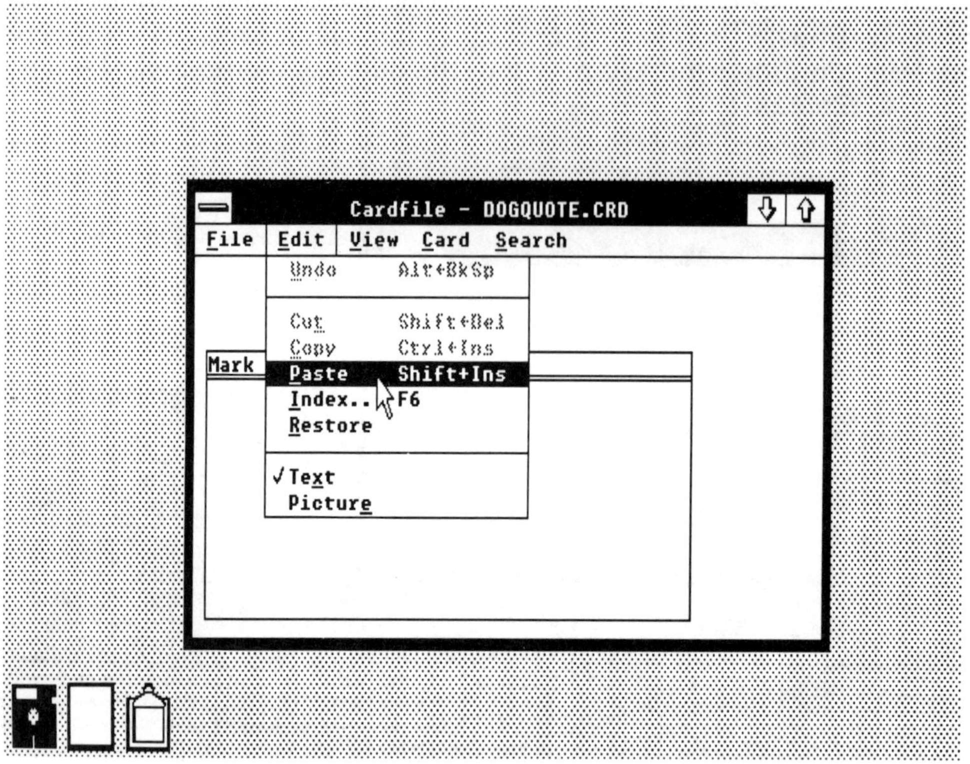
Cardfile - DOGQUOTE.CRD
File
Edit
View
Card
Search
Undo Alt+BkSp
Cut Shift+Del
Copy Ctrl+Ins
Paste Shift+Ins
Index... F6
Restore
Text
Picture
Mark

Figure 15.13

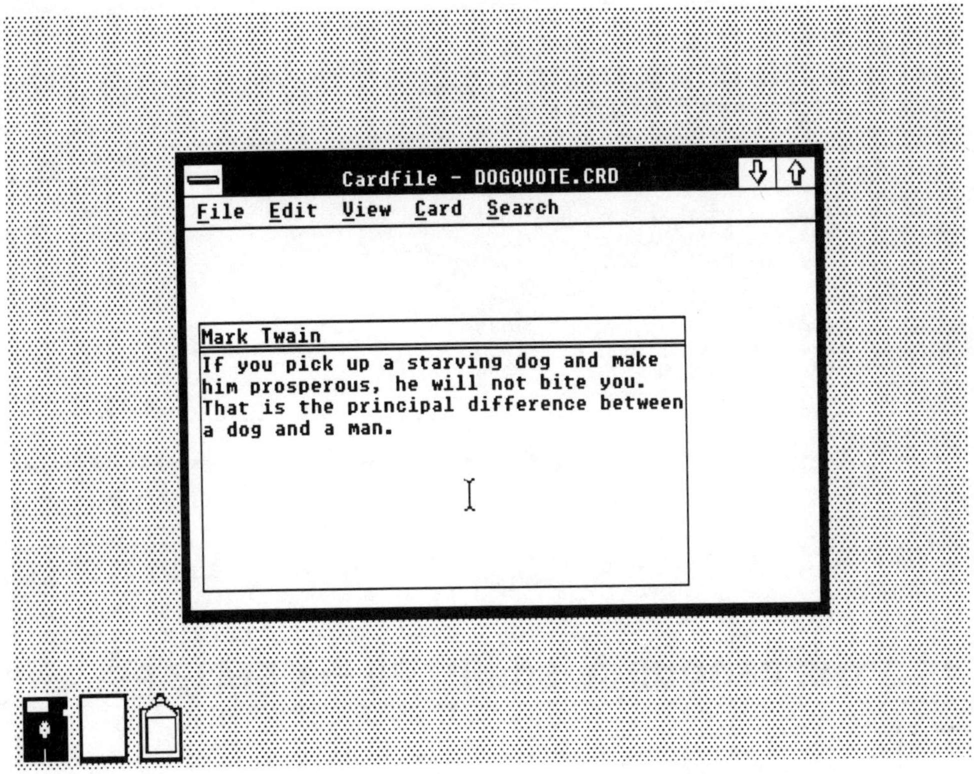
Cardfile - DOGQUOTE.CRD
File Edit View Card Search
Mark Twain
If you pick up a starving dog and make
him prosperous, he will not bite you.
That is the principal difference between
a dog and a man.

15.2 THE HEADER FILE: PGM12.H

```
/****************************************************************************/
/* Filename:     PGM12.H                                                    */
/*                                                                          */
/* Description:  PGM12.C  header file                                       */
/*--------------------------------------------------------------------------*/

#define MENU_EMPTY      1000
#define MENU_READ       1010
#define MENU_WRITE      1020

#define FILENAME        1030
#define IDCEDIT         1040
#define IDCLISTBOX      1050
#define IDPATH          1060

/*--------------------------------------------------------------------------*/
/* End of file:  PGM12.H                                                    */
/****************************************************************************/
```

15.3 THE RESOURCE SCRIPT FILE: PGM12.RC

```
/****************************************************************************/
/* Filename:     PGM12.RC                                                   */
/*                                                                          */
/* Description:  PGM12.EXE resources                                        */
/*--------------------------------------------------------------------------*/

#include "windows.h"
#include "pgm12.h"

MainMenu MENU
BEGIN
    POPUP "&Select"
    BEGIN
        MENUITEM        "Clipboard:",            -1,             INACTIVE
        MENUITEM        " - &Empty",             MENU_EMPTY
        MENUITEM        " - &Read file into",    MENU_READ
        MENUITEM        " - &Write file from",   MENU_WRITE
    END
END
```

```
#define EDITSTYLE       WS_TABSTOP | WS_GROUP | ES_AUTOHSCROLL
#define LISTBOXSTYLE    LBS_STANDARD | WS_TABSTOP | WS_GROUP

FILENAME DIALOG 30, 30, 176, 102
STYLE WS_POPUP | WS_DLGFRAME
BEGIN
    EDITTEXT                         IDCEDIT,     4,  4, 168, 12, EDITSTYLE
    LISTBOX                          IDCLISTBOX,  4, 20,  60, 48, LISTBOXSTYLE
    LTEXT          "",               IDPATH,      2, 72, 168,  8
    DEFPUSHBUTTON  "Ok",             IDOK,       22, 84,  50, 14, WS_GROUP
    PUSHBUTTON     "Cancel"          IDCANCEL,   96, 84,  50, 14, WS_GROUP
    LTEXT "Enter filename (including ", -1, 68, 24, 104,  8
    LTEXT "drive, path, and extension", -1, 68, 34, 104,  8
    LTEXT "if desired) above  -or-   ", -1, 68, 44, 104,  8
    LTEXT "select from the listbox.  ", -1, 68, 54, 104,  8
END

/*-----------------------------------------------------------------------*/
/* End of file:  PGM12.RC                                                */
/*************************************************************************/
```

15.4 THE C LANGUAGE SOURCE FILE: PGM12.C

```
/*************************************************************************/
/* Filename:     PGM12.C                                                 */
/*                                                                       */
/* Description:  PGM12.EXE source code                                   */
/*-----------------------------------------------------------------------*/

#include "windows.h"
#include "pgm12.h"

  WORD                   FileStyle;
  HANDLE                 hFile;
  HANDLE                 hInst;
  int                    i;
  int                    j;
  unsigned long          lCount;
  unsigned long          lJ;
  FARPROC                lpOpenFileProc;
  char                   *pLocal;
  OFSTRUCT               ReOpenBuff;
  char                   *szSearchFilespec      = "*.CLP";
  char                   *szTitle               = "File Windows!";
  char                   *szFileHeader          = "Clipboard";
  char                   *szInFileHeaderBuff    = "         ";
  int                    wFormat;

/*---------------------------------------------------------------*/

int far PASCAL OpenFileProc (hWnd, msg, wParam, lParam)
  HWND          hWnd;
  unsigned      msg;
  WORD          wParam;
  LONG          lParam;
  {
  char          szFileName[64];
```

```
switch (msg)
  {
  case WM_INITDIALOG:
    SetDlgItemText (hWnd, IDCEDIT, (LPSTR)szSearchFilespec);
    DlgDirList (hWnd, (LPSTR)szSearchFilespec,
                                 IDCLISTBOX, IDPATH, 0x4010);
    break;

  case WM_COMMAND:
    switch (wParam)
      {
      case IDOK:
        GetDlgItemText (hWnd, IDCEDIT, (LPSTR)szFileName, 64);
        if (DlgDirList (hWnd, (LPSTR)szFileName,
                                 IDCLISTBOX, IDPATH, 0x4010))
          {
          SetDlgItemText (hWnd, IDCEDIT, (LPSTR)szFileName);
          break;
          }
        EndDialog (hWnd, OpenFile ((LPSTR)szFileName,

                                         (LPOFSTRUCT)&ReOpenBuff,
                                         FileStyle));
        break;

      case IDCANCEL:
          EndDialog(hWnd, 0);
          break;
      case IDCLISTBOX:
        switch (HIWORD(lParam))
          {
          case 1:
            if (DlgDirSelect (hWnd, (LPSTR)szFileName, IDCLISTBOX))
              {
              for (i=0; szFileName[i]; i++);
              for (j=0; szFileName[i++] = szSearchFilespec[j++];);
              }
            SetDlgItemText (hWnd, IDCEDIT, (LPSTR)szFileName);
            break;

          case 2:
            if (DlgDirList (hWnd, (LPSTR) szFileName,
                                         IDCLISTBOX, IDPATH, 0x4010))
              {
              SetDlgItemText (hWnd, IDCEDIT, (LPSTR)szFileName);
              break;
              }
            EndDialog (hWnd, OpenFile ((LPSTR)szFileName,
                                         (LPOFSTRUCT)&ReOpenBuff,
                                         FileStyle));
            break;
          }
        break;

      case IDCEDIT:
        if (HIWORD(lParam) == EN_CHANGE)
          EnableWindow (GetDlgItem (hWnd, IDOK),
                     SendMessage (GetDlgItem (hWnd, IDCEDIT),
                                  WM_GETTEXTLENGTH, 0, 0L));
        break;

      default:
        return(FALSE);
      }
    break;
```

```
    default:
      return FALSE;
    }
  return TRUE;
  }
/*----------------------------------------------------------------*/

long FAR PASCAL MainWndProc (hWnd, msg, wParam, lParam)
  HWND                  hWnd;
  unsigned              msg;
  WORD                  wParam;
  LONG                  lParam;
  {
  switch (msg)
    {
    case WM_DESTROY:
      PostQuitMessage (0);
      break;

    case WM_INITMENU:
      {
      HMENU     hMenu = GetMenu (hWnd);
      int       MenuFlag = MF_GRAYED;

      if (OpenClipboard (hWnd))
        {
        if (CountClipboardFormats() == CF_TEXT)
          MenuFlag = MF_ENABLED;
        CloseClipboard ();
        }
      EnableMenuItem (hMenu, MENU_EMPTY, MenuFlag);
      EnableMenuItem (hMenu, MENU_WRITE, MenuFlag);
      break;
      }

    case WM_COMMAND:
      switch (wParam)
        {
        HANDLE          hClipData;
        LPSTR           szSource,       szDest;
        int             count;

        case MENU_EMPTY:
          if (OpenClipboard (hWnd))
            {
            EmptyClipboard ();
            CloseClipboard ();
            }
          break;

        case MENU_WRITE:
          if (!OpenClipboard (hWnd))
            {
            MessageBox (hWnd, (LPSTR)"Problem opening clipboard.",
                        (LPSTR)szTitle, MB_OK | MB_ICONEXCLAMATION);
            break;
            }
```

```
         FileStyle = OF_WRITE | OF_CREATE | OF_PROMPT;
         hFile = DialogBox (hInst, MAKEINTRESOURCE(FILENAME),
                                               hWnd, lpOpenFileProc);
         switch (hFile)
           {

           case -1:
             MessageBox (hWnd, (LPSTR)"Problem opening file.",
                         (LPSTR)szTitle, MB_OK | MB_ICONEXCLAMATION);
           case 0:
             CloseClipboard ();
             break;

           default:
             write (hFile, szFileHeader, 9);
             wFormat = EnumClipboardFormats (0);
             if (!wFormat)
               {
               close (hFile);
               CloseClipboard ();
               break;
               }
             write (hFile, &wFormat, 2);
             pLocal = (char *)LocalAlloc (LPTR, 1024);
             if (hClipData = GetClipboardData (wFormat))
               {
               long    lCount, lJ;

               lCount = lJ = GlobalSize (hClipData);
               write (hFile, &lCount, 4);
               szSource = GlobalLock (hClipData);

               while (lJ != 0)
                 {
                 j = 1024;
                 if (lJ < 1024)
                   j = lJ;
                 for (i=0; i<j; i++)
                   pLocal[i] = *szSource++;
                 write (hFile, pLocal, j);
                 lJ -= j;
                 }
               GlobalUnlock (hClipData);
               }
             LocalFree ((HANDLE)pLocal);
             close (hFile);
             CloseClipboard ();
             break;
           }
         break;

       case MENU_READ:
         if (!OpenClipboard (hWnd))
           {
           MessageBox (hWnd, (LPSTR)"Problem opening clipboard.",
                       (LPSTR)szTitle, MB_OK | MB_ICONEXCLAMATION);
           break;
           }
         FileStyle = OF_READ;
         hFile = DialogBox (hInst, MAKEINTRESOURCE(FILENAME),
                                               hWnd, lpOpenFileProc);
         switch (hFile)
           {
```

```
        case -1:
          MessageBox (hWnd, (LPSTR)"Problem opening file.",
                     (LPSTR)szTitle, MB_OK | MB_ICONEXCLAMATION);
        case 0:
          CloseClipboard ();
          break;

        default:
          count = read (hFile, szInFileHeaderBuff, 9);
          for (i=j=0; szFileHeader[i]; i++)
            if (szFileHeader[i] != szInFileHeaderBuff[i])
              {
              j = 1;         /* set error flag   */
              break;         /* break out of FOR */
              }
          if ((count != 9)
           || (j == 1))
            {
            MessageBox (hWnd, (LPSTR)"File is not CLIPBOARD data.",
                       (LPSTR)szTitle, MB_OK | MB_ICONEXCLAMATION);
            break;
            }
          read (hFile, &wFormat, 2);
          read (hFile, &lCount,  4);

          pLocal = (char *)LocalAlloc (LPTR, 1024);

          if (hClipData = GlobalAlloc (GMEM_MOVEABLE, lCount))
            {
            lJ = lCount;
            szDest = GlobalLock (hClipData);

            while (lJ != 0)
              {
              j = 1024;
              if (lJ < 1024)
                j = lJ;
              read (hFile, pLocal, j);
              for (i=0; i<j; i++)
                *szDest++ =  pLocal[i];
              lJ -= j;
              }
            GlobalUnlock (hClipData);
            SetClipboardData (wFormat, hClipData);
            }
          LocalFree ((HANDLE)pLocal);
          close (hFile);
          CloseClipboard ();
          break;
        }
      break;
    }
  break;
default:
  return DefWindowProc (hWnd, msg, wParam, lParam);
  break;
}
return (0L);
}
```

```
/*-----------------------------------------------------------------*/

int PASCAL WinMain (hInstance, hPrevInstance, lpszCmdLine, cmdShow)
  HANDLE              hInstance;
  HANDLE              hPrevInstance;
  LPSTR               lpszCmdLine;
  int                 cmdShow;
  {
  MSG                 msg;
  HWND                hWnd;
  PWNDCLASS           pMainClass;

  if (hPrevInstance)
    return FALSE;

  pMainClass = (PWNDCLASS)LocalAlloc (LPTR, sizeof(WNDCLASS));
  pMainClass->hCursor         = LoadCursor (NULL, IDC_ARROW);
  pMainClass->hIcon           = LoadIcon (NULL, IDI_APPLICATION);
  pMainClass->lpszMenuName    = (LPSTR)"MainMenu";
  pMainClass->lpszClassName   = (LPSTR)"PGM12";
  pMainClass->hbrBackground   = (HBRUSH)GetStockObject (WHITE_BRUSH);
  pMainClass->hInstance       = hInstance;
  pMainClass->style           = CS_HREDRAW | CS_VREDRAW;
  pMainClass->lpfnWndProc     = MainWndProc;

  if (!RegisterClass((LPWNDCLASS)pMainClass))
    return FALSE;
  LocalFree ((HANDLE)pMainClass);

  hWnd = CreateWindow  ((LPSTR)"PGM12", (LPSTR)szTitle,
      WS_OVERLAPPEDWINDOW, GetSystemMetrics (SM_CXSCREEN)/4,
      GetSystemMetrics (SM_CYSCREEN)/4, GetSystemMetrics (SM_CXSCREEN)/2,
      GetSystemMetrics (SM_CYSCREEN)/2, (HWND)NULL, (HMENU)NULL,
      hInst = hInstance, (LPSTR)NULL);

  lpOpenFileProc = MakeProcInstance (OpenFileProc, hInst);
  ShowWindow (hWnd, cmdShow);
  UpdateWindow (hWnd);

  while (GetMessage ((LPMSG)&msg, NULL, 0, 0))
    {
    TranslateMessage((LPMSG)&msg);
    DispatchMessage((LPMSG)&msg);
    }

  FreeProcInstance (lpOpenFileProc);
  return (int)msg.wParam;
  }

/*-------------------------------------------------------------------------*/
/* End of file:  PGM12.C                                                   */
/***************************************************************************/
```

As usual, **MainWndProc** contains the bulk of the code. case **WM_INITMENU** is similar to PGM9: if the clipboard has some text data on it, enable the menu items **MENU_EMPTY** and **MENU_WRITE.**

In an attempt to keep this example small, PGM12 deals only with the **CF_TEXT** mode of the clipboard. This program could be easily expanded to handle the other clipboard modes as well.

MENU_EMPTY is straightforward: open the clipboard, empty it and close it. Both **MENU_WRITE** and **MENU_READ** begin the same way: open the clipboard. If that fails, put up a message box and break out. Next, we set a variable **FileStyle**, which we'll examine in just a moment. We then open the dialog box:

```
hFile = DialogBox (hInst, MAKEINTRESOURCE
     (FILENAME), hWnd, lpOpenFileProc);
```

You'll soon see that this function will return a handle to a file.

15.4.1 Setting Up the Dialog Box

As usual, we want to do some preprocessing before our dialog box is displayed. We want to (1) place the default search file specification in the edit control, and (2) list the current directory using the search file specification.

```
case WM_INITDIALOG:
SetDlgItemText (hWnd, IDCEDIT, (LPSTR)szSearchFilespec);
DlgDirList (hWnd, (LPSTR)szSearchFilespec,
                                    IDCLISTBOX, IDPATH, 0x4010);
break;
```

You've seen both these functions before. Let's briefly review **DlgDirList:** this function fills the list box control, specified by **IDCLISTBOX,** with all filenames that match the search specification **szSearchFilespec**. **IDPATH** specifies a control where **DirDlgList** can place the current path. The hexadecimal number **0x4010** specifies that we also want drives and subdirectories listed. (See PGM3.C in Chapter 6 if you want to review the details of this function.)

15.4.2 Selecting and Opening a File

We are interested in four events that can happen in our dialog box:

1. The user presses the "Ok" button.
2. The user presses the "Cancel" button.
3. The user types in the edit control field.
4. The user clicks or double-clicks on an item in the listbox.

The easiest event to handle is pressing the "Cancel" button. We simply say:

```
EndDialog (hWnd, 0);
```

The return value, **0**, means that the user pressed the "Cancel" button. Actually, the **DialogBox** call we made earlier expects a file handle to be returned. But DOS reserves the handles 0 through 4 for standard input, standard output, standard error, standard aux, and standard printer. Therefore, since we know that DOS will never return a handle with the value 0, we can special case, or redefine, it to be our own "internal" code.

The next easiest event to handle is typing in the edit control. In this case, we only want to enable or disable the "Ok" button. If the field is blank, we want "Ok" disabled.

```
case IDCEDIT:
if (HIWORD(lParam) == EN_CHANGE)
EnableWindow (GetDlgItem (hWnd, IDOK),
              SendMessage (GetDlgItem (hWnd,IDCEDIT),
                           WM_GETTEXTLENGTH, 0, 0L));
break;
```

If the text in the edit control was changed, we want to enable or disable the control that has the handle **GetDlgItem (hWnd, IDOK),** depending on the result of **SendMessage (. . .)**. You've seen all of these functions in previous chapters. **GetDlgItem (. . .)** returns a handle to a control that we use as input to **EnableWindow. SendMessage** with the command **WM_GETTEXTLENGTH** returns the length of the text in the control specified by the handle returned by **GetDlgItem (hWnd, IDCEDIT)**. If the length is zero (FALSE), then the "Ok" will be disabled; otherwise, it will be enabled.

Let's look at what happens when the "Ok" button is pressed:

```
case IDOK:
GetDlgItemText (hWnd, IDCEDIT, (LPSTR)szFileName, 64);
if (DlgDirList (hWnd, (LPSTR)szFileName,
IDCLISTBOX, IDPATH, 0x4010))
{
SetDlgItemText (hWnd, IDCEDIT, (LPSTR)szFileName);
break;
}
```

We begin by fetching the text in the edit control and placing it in **szFileName**. Then, we use **DlgDirList** to list matching entries. If **szFileName** does not contain a valid search string, **DlgDirList** returns FALSE.

For example, if **szFileName** contains the string "*.XYZ," then **DlgDirList** will return TRUE because "*.XYZ" is a valid search string. (Even if no files match that particular specification, **DlgDirList** will still return TRUE.) If **szFileName** had contained "ANYFILE.XYZ," **DlgDirList** would return FALSE because "ANYFILE.XYZ" is not a valid search string.

If **DlgDirList** returns TRUE, it will also parse the string, removing any drive and path information, leaving only the search file string. We want to put that string back into the edit field, then break back into the dialog box to allow further input.

If **DlgDirList** returns FALSE, we want to take down the dialog box and open the file that was specified. We return the handle of the open file to **MainWndProc.**

To open a file, we make a call to **OpenFile:**

```
EndDialog (hWnd, OpenFile ((LPSTR)szFileName,
                 (LPOFSTRUCT) &ReOpenBuff, FileStyle));
break;
```

Arguments to this function are a filename, a data structure called **OFSTRUCT**, and an open style. The filename is, of course, **szFileName** **&ReOpenBuff** is a pointer to a data structure of type **OFSTRUCT**. (This structure can be found in WINDOWS.H). It will be filled in by the **OpenFile** call, and contains information about the medium (fixed disk or floppy), an error code if the open fails, and the complete path name.

FileStyle is a word that describes how to open the file. Back in **MainWndProc,** before we placed the call to **DialogBox(...)**, we set **FileStyle** to a specific mode. If we were processing case **MENU_WRITE**, we used:

```
FileStyle = OF_WRITE | OF_CREATE;
```

OF_WRITE opens the file for writing only. We combine this with **OF_CREATE,** which creates the file if it does not exist. If we were processing case **MENU_READ**, we used:

```
FileStyle = OF_READ;
```

OF_READ means open the file for reading only.

If **OpenFile** is successful, it will return a file handle. Otherwise, it will return (1).

We have one other case to look at: the list box message **case IDCLISTBOX.** We have presented this case before in PGM3 in Chapter 6, so we'll be brief. The high word of **lParam** contains **1** or **2: 1** for a single click and **2** for a double-click.

If we're responding to a single click, we want to get the selection from the list box. **DlgDirSelect** returns TRUE if a directory name was selected, and then we want to append the default search file specification. Finally, we want to set the edit field to the selection.

If we're responding to a double-click, we know that the single click has already been processed. So we need only do the same thing as the "Ok" logic: try to list the directory. If successful, we set the edit field text. Otherwise, we take down the dialog box and open the file. When we've successfully taken down the dialog box, we need to act on the file handle returned by the **OpenFile** function. Three cases can occur:

1. The user selected "Cancel," to which we assigned the "handle" zero (0).

2. The **open** call failed (1).

3. The **open** call was successful.

On entry to case **MENU_READ** or **MENU_WRITE,** we opened the clipboard. Now we've opened a file. Next we'll transfer information from the clipboard to that file.

15.4.3 Writing to a File

The first thing we want to write is a "signature" into our file, marking it as a file written by this program. To do this, we'll write the nine characters in the field **szFileHeader,** "Clipboard," using the standard library function **write**:

```
write (hFile, szFileHeader, 9);
```

Next, we get the current clipboard format (a word value) and write it out:

```
write (hFile, &wFormat, 2);
```

We're ready to begin writing the clipboard data. Because the clipboard is in global memory and the **write** function works out of the data segment, we'll need to transfer the bytes into our data segment before writing. To accomplish this task, we allocate a piece of the heap for a buffer, transfer data into it, write, then release the storage.

Finally, we close up shop by closing our file and the clipboard:

```
close (hFile);
CloseClipboard ();
```

close (hFile) is the standard C call.

15.4.4 Reading from a File

Read is just the reverse of **write.** We read in the signature characters to verify that the file is clipboard data, using the standard library call, **read:**

```
count = read (hFile, szInFileHeaderBuff, 9);
```

Next, we read in the format and count:

```
read (hFile, &wFormat, 2);
read (hFile, &lCount, 4);
```

Now, we go into our memory allocation routine, then read the file into memory and transfer it to global memory. Finally, we close the file and clipboard.

15.5 THE MODULE DEFINITION FILE: PGM12.DEF

```
;*****************************************************************:
; Filename:     PGM12.DEF                                         :
;                                                                 :
; Description:  Link definition file                              :
;-----------------------------------------------------------------:
NAME    PGM12

DESCRIPTION 'Sample program 12'

STUB    '..\WINSTUB.EXE'

CODE    MOVEABLE
DATA    MOVEABLE MULTIPLE

HEAPSIZE  1536
STACKSIZE 4096

EXPORTS
    MainWndProc         @1
    OpenFileProc        @2

;-----------------------------------------------------------------:
; End of file:  PGM12.DEF                                         :
;*****************************************************************:
```

15.6 THE MAKE FILE: PGM12.

```
#***********************************************************************#
# Filename:     PGM12.                                                  #
#                                                                       #
# Description:  PGM12.EXE "MAKE" description file                       #
#-----------------------------------------------------------------------#

PGM12.OBJ: PGM12.C PGM12.H
    cl -d -c -AS -Gsw -Os -Zpe PGM12.c

PGM12.RES: PGM12.RC PGM12.H
    rc -r PGM12.RC

PGM12.EXE: PGM12.OBJ PGM12.RES PGM12.DEF
    LINK4 PGM12,/ALIGN:16,/MAP,SLIBW,PGM12.DEF
    RC PGM12.RES

#-----------------------------------------------------------------------#
# End of file:  PGM12.                                                  #
#***********************************************************************#
```

. . . .

In this chapter, you've learned to read to and write from disk files. In Chapter 16, you'll learn how your application can directly address the printer.

16

USING THE PRINTER

- Introduction To Printing From Windows
- Introduction To PGM13: Print Windows!
- The C Language Source File: PGM13.C
- The Module Definition File: PGM13.DEF
- The Make File: PGM13.

In most situations, a Windows application never communicates to any program or device except through Windows. For example, when addressing the display, the flow of execution travels from the application through the Graphics Display Interface to a device driver that talks to the video hardware.

An exception to this translation scheme will occur when printing, because there might be occasions when you'll want your application to "talk" directly to the device driver. For example, you might want to eject the current page. In this chapter, you'll learn how to make your application talk to the printer.

16.1 INTRODUCTION TO PRINTING FROM WINDOWS

Because several tasks may be trying to address the printer at the same time, Windows controls who "has" the printer through *spooling*. Instead of going directly to the printer, data is spooled to a disk file. Once the application has completed sending data to the spooler, it will begin moving it to the printer, provided that the printer is not printing another job.

Figure 16.1 illustrates the data flow of a typical Windows application printing operation. The application can talk to GDI using a function (**LineTo, Polygon,** etc.), or it can talk directly to the device driver using "escape" functions. The device driver then talks to the spooler which, in turn, talks to the printer.

Figure 16.1

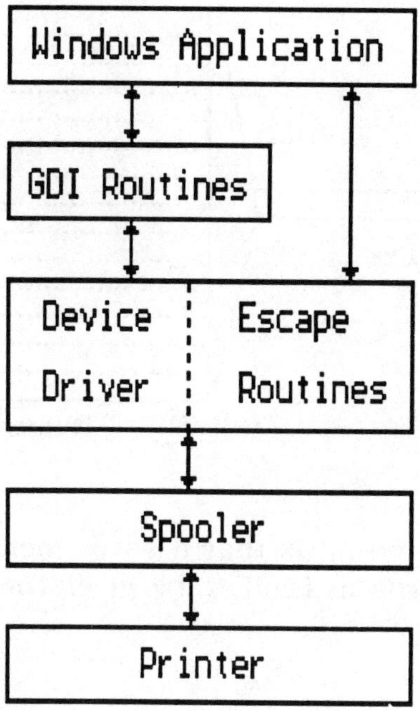

Windows presents a unique problem when it comes to printing, because all the images seen on the display are graphics, not text. You can't transfer the images from the screen as character data. Instead, you must work at the pixel, or bit, level. Also, you can't simply transfer a bitmap from the screen to the printer; you must use an intermediate staging area, a memory display context.

Figure 16.2 illustrates the technique known as "banding." We divide the display and printer page into a number of segments. Band by band, we perform a **StretchBlt** operation, moving bits from the display into the memory staging area. **StretchBlt** resizes bits (expands or compresses them) as necessary to fit into the target area. Once they are secured in memory, the bits are moved out to the printer using the **BitBlt** transfer function. You'll recall from previous chapters that **BitBlt** transfers a bitmap from one place to another.

Figure 16.2

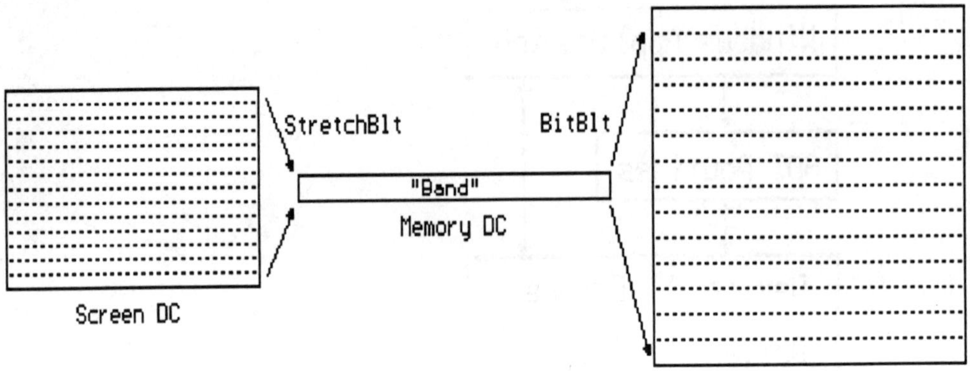

The primary advantage of banding is that it saves memory. You can make the band as wide or narrow as is allowable given the system's resources (available memory).

16.2 INTRODUCTION TO PGM13: PRINT WINDOWS!

The sample program that we'll examine in this chapter transfers the display image to the printing device. To operate this program, you must have a printer installed with Windows. Within WIN.INI, the Windows initialization file, you should have a statement similar to:

```
[windows]
...
device=EPSON,Epson FX-80,LPT1:
...
```

If your WIN.INI doesn't contain a print device statement, you should run the Windows application CONTROL.EXE to install your printing device.

PGM13 requires only three files:

PGM13.C	Program code
PGM13.DEF	Module definition file
PGM13.	Input instructions to the MAKE utility

PGM13 does not use any resources, so we have dispensed with the .H and .RC files.

Figure 16.3 illustrates what you'll see when you run PGM13. The program displays a popup window with a title bar and a very small client area. Clicking on the system menu icon will reveal the menu shown in Figure 16.4. Selecting the "PrtSc" menu item invokes the screen printing logic. Then the "Print Screen" window will be hidden, the spooler will be started and the screen image will be transferred to the spooler for printing.

Figure 16.3

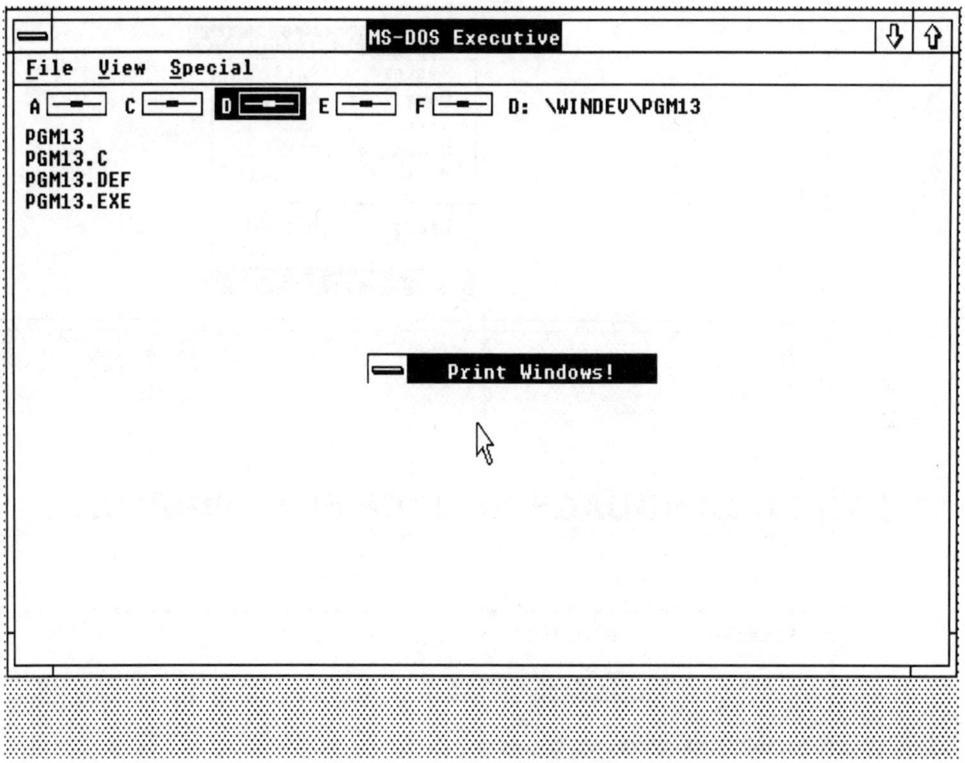

Figure 16.4

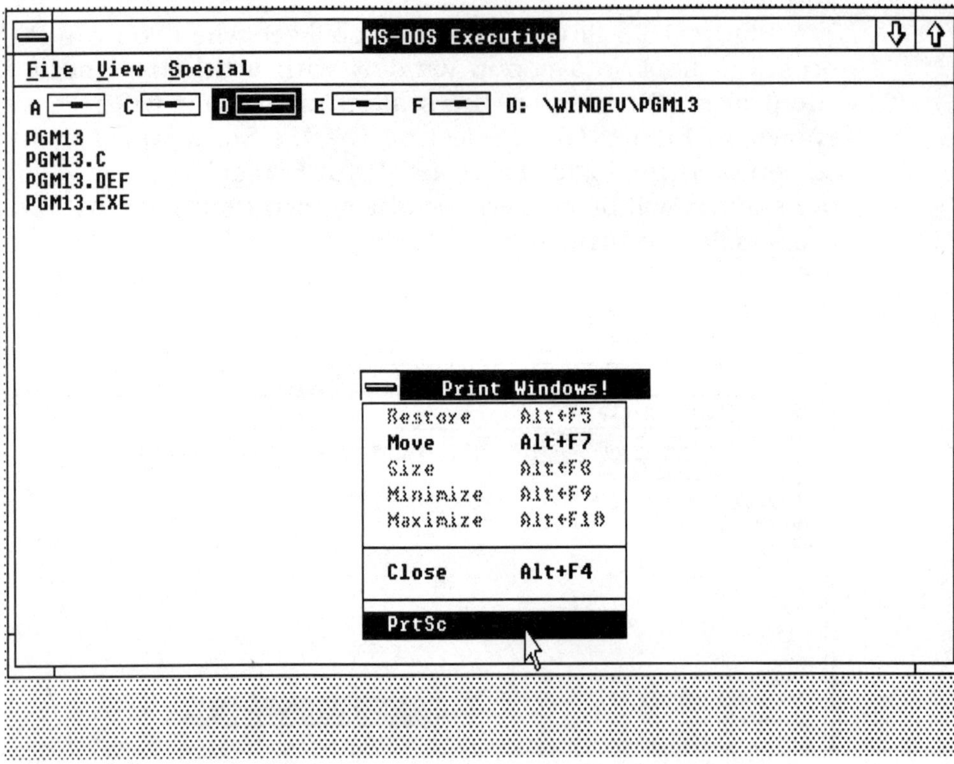

16.3 THE C LANGUAGE SOURCE FILE: PGM13.C

```
/*****************************************************************/
/* Filename:     PGM13.C                                         */
/*                                                               */
/* Description:  Program source                                  */
/*---------------------------------------------------------------*/

#include "windows.h"

#define BANDS 25         /* The screen is divided into BANDS bands       */

  FARPROC       lpEnumProc;
  HWND          hWndSave;
  FARPROC       lpAbortFunc;

/*-------------------------------------------------------------------------*/
```

```
BOOL FAR PASCAL EnumProc (hWnd, lpData)
  HWND          hWnd;
  LPSTR         lpData;
  {
  EnumChildWindows (hWnd, lpEnumProc, 0L);
  if (IsWindowVisible (hWnd))
    UpdateWindow (hWnd);
  return TRUE;
  }

/*---------------------------------------------------------------------*/

Message (hWnd, pStr)
  HWND  hWnd;
  PSTR  pStr;
  {
  MessageBox (hWnd,
             (LPSTR)pStr,
             (LPSTR)" Print Screen ",
             MB_OK | MB_ICONHAND);
  }

/*---------------------------------------------------------------------*/

int FAR PASCAL AbortFunc (hPR, code)
  HDC           hPR;
  int           code;
  {
  switch (code)
    {
    case SP_ERROR:
      Message (hWndSave, "General error writing to spooler.");
      break;

    case SP_APPABORT:
      Message (hWndSave, "Application aborts printer.");
      break;

    case SP_USERABORT:
      Message (hWndSave, "User aborts printer.");
      break;

    case SP_OUTOFDISK:
      Message (hWndSave, "No disk space for spool file.");
      break;

    case SP_OUTOFMEMORY:
      Message (hWndSave, "No memory for spool file.");
      break;
    }
  return TRUE;
  }

/*---------------------------------------------------------------------*/

long FAR PASCAL MainWndProc (hWnd, msg, wParam, lParam)
  HWND          hWnd;
  unsigned      msg;
  WORD          wParam;
  LONG          lParam;
  {
```

```
unsigned int  bands;
HDC           hScreenDC;
HBITMAP       hMemBitmap;
HDC           hMemDC;
HDC           hPrinterDC;
char          *pch;
char          *pchDriver;
char          *pchPort;
unsigned int  PrinterBandDeltaY;
unsigned int  PrinterBandHeight;
unsigned int  PrinterHorzRes;
unsigned int  PrinterHorzSize;
unsigned int  PrinterHorzSz;
unsigned int  PrinterVertRes;
unsigned int  PrinterVertSize;
unsigned int  PrinterVertSz;
char          ReturnedString[40];
HBITMAP       hSaveBitmap;
unsigned int  ScreenBandDeltaY;
unsigned int  ScreenBandHeight;
unsigned int  ScreenHorzRes;
unsigned int  ScreenHorzSize;
unsigned int  ScreenVertRes;
unsigned int  ScreenVertSize;

switch (msg)
  {
  case WM_SYSCOMMAND:
    switch (wParam)
      {
      case 1000:
        if (!(hScreenDC = CreateDC ((LPSTR)"DISPLAY",
                                     (LPSTR) 0,
                                     (LPSTR) 0,
                                     (LPSTR) 0)))
          {
          Message (hWnd, "Cannot access display driver.");
          PostQuitMessage (0);
          break;
          }

        if (!(hMemDC = CreateCompatibleDC(hScreenDC)))
          {
          DeleteDC (hScreenDC);
          Message (hWnd, "Cannot create memory DC.");
          PostQuitMessage (0);
          break;
          }

        GetProfileString ((LPSTR)"Windows",
                          (LPSTR)"Device",
                          (LPSTR)"",
                          (LPSTR)ReturnedString,
                          40);

        for (pch = ReturnedString; *pch && (*pch != ','); ++pch);
        if (*pch)
          *pch++ = 0;
        while (*pch && (*pch <= ' '))
          pch++;
        pchDriver = pch;
```

```
while (*pch && (*pch != ',') && (*pch > ' '))
  pch++;
if (*pch)
  *pch++ = 0;
while (*pch && ((*pch <= ' ') || (*pch == ',')))
  pch++;
pchPort = pch;
while (*pch && (*pch > ' '))
  pch++;
*pch = 0;

if (!(hPrinterDC = CreateDC ((LPSTR)pchDriver,
                   (LPSTR)ReturnedString,
                   (LPSTR)pchPort,
                   (LPSTR)0)))
  {
  DeleteDC (hMemDC);
  DeleteDC (hScreenDC);
  Message (hWnd, "Cannot access printer driver.");
  PostQuitMessage (0);
  break;
  }
ScreenHorzSize  = GetDeviceCaps (hScreenDC, HORZSIZE);
ScreenVertSize  = GetDeviceCaps (hScreenDC, VERTSIZE);
ScreenHorzRes   = GetDeviceCaps (hScreenDC, HORZRES);
ScreenVertRes   = GetDeviceCaps (hScreenDC, VERTRES);
PrinterHorzSz   =
PrinterHorzSize = GetDeviceCaps (hPrinterDC, HORZSIZE);
PrinterVertSz   =
PrinterVertSize = GetDeviceCaps (hPrinterDC, VERTSIZE);
PrinterHorzRes  = GetDeviceCaps (hPrinterDC, HORZRES);
PrinterVertRes  = GetDeviceCaps (hPrinterDC, VERTRES);

if ((100 * PrinterHorzSize / ScreenHorzSize) >
    (100 * PrinterVertSize / ScreenVertSize))
  {
  PrinterHorzSize = ScreenHorzSize *
                         PrinterVertSize / ScreenVertSize;
  PrinterHorzRes = (unsigned long)PrinterHorzSize *
                         PrinterHorzRes / PrinterHorzSz;
  }
else
  {
  PrinterVertSize = ScreenVertSize *
                         PrinterHorzSize / ScreenHorzSize;
  PrinterVertRes = (unsigned long)PrinterVertSize *
                         PrinterVertRes / PrinterVertSz;
  }

PrinterBandHeight = PrinterVertRes / BANDS;
ScreenBandHeight  = ScreenVertRes / BANDS;

if (!(hMemBitmap = CreateBitmap (PrinterHorzRes,
                         PrinterBandHeight,
                         1,
                         1,
                         (LPSTR)NULL)))
  {
  DeleteDC (hPrinterDC);
  DeleteDC (hMemDC);
  DeleteDC (hScreenDC);
  Message (hWnd, "Out of memory.");
  PostQuitMessage (0);
  break;
  }
```

```
ShowWindow (hWnd, HIDE_WINDOW);
EnumWindows (lpEnumProc, 0L);
hSaveBitmap = SelectObject (hMemDC, hMemBitmap);
Escape(hPrinterDC, SETABORTPROC, 0, (LPSTR)lpAbortFunc, (LPSTR)0);
Escape(hPrinterDC, STARTDOC,     6, (LPSTR)"Screen",     (LPSTR)0);

for (ScreenBandDeltaY = PrinterBandDeltaY = 0,
          bands = BANDS;
     bands--;
     ScreenBandDeltaY += ScreenBandHeight,
          PrinterBandDeltaY += PrinterBandHeight)
  {
  StretchBlt (hMemDC,
                0,
                0,
                PrinterHorzRes,
                PrinterBandHeight,
                hScreenDC,
                0,
                ScreenBandDeltaY,
                ScreenHorzRes,
                ScreenBandHeight,
                SRCCOPY);
  BitBlt (hPrinterDC,
            0,
            PrinterBandDeltaY,
            PrinterHorzRes,
            PrinterBandHeight,
            hMemDC,
            0,
            0,
            SRCCOPY);
  }
if (bands = (ScreenVertRes % BANDS))
  {
  StretchBlt (hMemDC,
                0,
                0,
                PrinterHorzRes,
                PrinterBandHeight,
                hScreenDC,
                0,
                ScreenBandDeltaY,
                ScreenHorzRes,
                bands,
                SRCCOPY);
  BitBlt (hPrinterDC,
            0,
            PrinterBandDeltaY,
            PrinterHorzRes,
            PrinterVertRes - (PrinterBandHeight * BANDS),
            hMemDC,
            0,
            0,
            SRCCOPY);
  }
Escape (hPrinterDC, NEWFRAME, 0, (LPSTR)0, (LPSTR)0);
Escape (hPrinterDC, ENDDOC,   0, (LPSTR)0, (LPSTR)0);
```

```
      hMemBitmap = SelectObject (hMemDC, hSaveBitmap);
      DeleteObject (hMemBitmap);
      DeleteDC (hPrinterDC);
      DeleteDC (hMemDC);
      DeleteDC (hScreenDC);
      Message (hWnd, "Screen sent to spooler...");
      PostQuitMessage (0);
      break;

    default:
      return DefWindowProc (hWnd, msg, wParam, lParam);
      break;

    case WM_DESTROY:
      PostQuitMessage (0);
      break;

    default:
      return ((LONG)DefWindowProc (hWnd, msg, wParam, lParam));
      break;
    }

  return 0L;
  }

/*-------------------------------------------------------------------*/

int PASCAL WinMain (hInstance, hPrev, lpszCmdLine, cmdShow)
  HANDLE        hInstance;
  HANDLE        hPrev;
  LPSTR         lpszCmdLine;
  int           cmdShow;
  {
  HDC           hIC;
  HMENU         hMenu;
  MSG           msg;
  PWNDCLASS     pMainClass;
  PTEXTMETRIC   pTM;
  int           PopupHeight;
  int           PopupWidth;

  if (hPrev)
    return FALSE;

  pMainClass = (PWNDCLASS) LocalAlloc (LPTR, sizeof(WNDCLASS));
  pMainClass->style         = CS_VREDRAW | CS_HREDRAW;
  pMainClass->cbClsExtra    = 0;
  pMainClass->cbWndExtra    = 0;
  pMainClass->hInstance     = hInstance;
  pMainClass->hIcon         = LoadIcon (NULL, IDI_APPLICATION);
  pMainClass->hCursor       = LoadCursor (NULL, IDC_ARROW);
  pMainClass->hbrBackground = (HBRUSH) GetStockObject (WHITE_BRUSH);
  pMainClass->lpfnWndProc   = MainWndProc;
  pMainClass->lpszMenuName  = (LPSTR) NULL;
  pMainClass->lpszClassName = (LPSTR) "PGM13";
  if (!RegisterClass((LPWNDCLASS)pMainClass))
    return FALSE;
  LocalFree ((HANDLE)pMainClass);
```

```
 if (hIC = CreateIC ((LPSTR)"DISPLAY", (LPSTR)0, (LPSTR)0, (LPSTR)0))
   {
   pTM = (PTEXTMETRIC) LocalAlloc (LPTR, sizeof(TEXTMETRIC));
   GetTextMetrics (hIC, (LPTEXTMETRIC)pTM);
   PopupWidth = pTM->tmMaxCharWidth * 24;
   PopupHeight = pTM->tmHeight+4; /* *3/2; */
   LocalFree ((HANDLE)pTM);
   hWndSave = CreateWindow ((LPSTR)"PGM13",
                     (LPSTR)" Print Windows! ",
                     WS_POPUP | WS_VISIBLE | WS_CAPTION | WS_SYSMENU,
                     (GetDeviceCaps (hIC, HORZRES) - PopupWidth) / 2,
                     (GetDeviceCaps (hIC, VERTRES) - PopupHeight) / 2,
                     PopupWidth,
                     PopupHeight,
                     (HWND)0,
                     (HMENU)0,
                     (HANDLE)hInstance,
                     (LPSTR)NULL);
   DeleteObject (hIC);

   if (hWndSave)
     {
     ShowWindow (hWndSave, cmdShow);
     UpdateWindow (hWndSave);

     lpEnumProc = MakeProcInstance (EnumProc, hInstance);
     lpAbortFunc = MakeProcInstance (AbortFunc, hInstance);

     hMenu = GetSystemMenu (hWndSave, FALSE);
     ChangeMenu (hMenu, 0, NULL, 999, MF_APPEND | MF_SEPARATOR);
     ChangeMenu (hMenu, 0, (LPSTR)"PrtSc", 1000, MF_APPEND | MF_STRING);

     while (GetMessage((LPMSG)&msg, NULL, 0, 0 ))
       {
       TranslateMessage ((LPMSG)&msg);
       DispatchMessage ((LPMSG)&msg);
       }
     FreeProcInstance (lpEnumProc);
     FreeProcInstance (lpAbortFunc);
     }
   }
 return (int)msg.wParam;
 }

/*-----------------------------------------------------------------*/
/* End of file:  PGM13.C                                           */
/*****************************************************************/
```

16.3.1 Creating an Information Context

The only statement within **WinMain** that needs discussion is:

```
hIC = CreateIC ((LPSTR)"DISPLAY", (LPSTR)0, (LPSTR)0,
                                                (LPSTR)0)
```

An *IC*, or *information context*, is very similar to a DC (display context), except that no resources are allocated. ICs are used to get device information, as you'll see when we use the functions **GetText Metrics** and **GetDeviceCaps.**

16.3.2 Creating a Screen Display Context

The only case we want to trap–other than the usual **WM_DESTROY** —is **WM_SYSCOMMAND.** Recall that Windows sends **WM_SYSCOMMAND** whenever an item is selected from the system menu. Of course, we want to know when the user selects "PrtSc," or case **1000:**.

We assigned case **1000** to our program back in **WinMain** using the **ChangeMenu** function. You already know how to use **ChangeMenu,** so let's move on . . .

Windows uses device drivers for all physical input/output. Each of these drivers has a specific name. The name of the display driver is "DISPLAY". We'll begin by creating a display context for the system display, which will allow us to access the entire display:

```
if (!(hScreenDC = CreateDC ((LPSTR)"DISPLAY",
                                        (LPSTR) 0,
                                        (LPSTR) 0,
                                        (LPSTR) 0)))
{
Message (hWnd, "Cannot access display driver.");
PostQuitMessage (0);
break;
}
```

The only piece of information we need supply is the driver name: DISPLAY. If this function is not successful, we want to post a message box describing the failure and close the window.

16.3.3 Creating a Memory Context

After we have successfully created the screen DC, we want to create a compatible memory DC:

```
if (!(hMemDC = CreateCompatibleDC (hScreenDC)))
{
DeleteDC (hScreenDC);
Message (hWnd, "Cannot create memory DC.");
PostQuitMessage (0);
break;
}
```

If a non-zero number is returned, Windows successfully created a DC that is compatible with the display DC, and **hMemDC** corresponds to the "memory DC" shown in Figure 16.2. If zero is returned, we want to delete the display DC, post a message box with an error message, and terminate (abend).

16.3.4 Getting Information about the Printer

Next, we need to know about the printer. For that information, we turn to the WIN.INI file. Microsoft supplies us with a dandy little function for getting at this file:

```
GetProfileString ((LPSTR)"Windows",
                          (LPSTR)"Device",
                          (LPSTR)"",
                          (LPSTR)ReturnedString,
                          40);
```

GetProfileString searches WIN.INI for the "application name," which is:

```
[windows]
```

Once it finds the application name, it looks for a keyword, which is, in our case:

```
Device=
```

If **GetProfileString** finds these two strings, it copies the text following the keyword into the string **ReturnedString**. If it does not find a match, it copies whatever we supply as a default. We have supplied the NULL string. **40** is the maximum length to transfer. For example, if an Epson FX-80 printer is connected to LPT1:, we should get the string:

```
EPSON,Epson FX-80,LPT1:
```

Following the **GetProfileString** statement are a few lines of code that parse the above string looking for the three fields.

16.3.5 Creating a Printer Display Context

Once the string has been parsed and secured, we need to create a DC for the printer. This is similar to the usual procedure for creating a display context, except that we use a few more parameters to specify the unit we are addressing:

```
if (!(hPrinterDC = CreateDC ((LPSTR)pchDriver,
                              (LPSTR)ReturnedString,
                              (LPSTR)pchPort,
                              (LPSTR)0)))
{
DeleteDC (hMemDC);
DeleteDC (hScreenDC);
Message (hWnd, "Cannot access printer driver.");
PostQuitMessage (0);
break;
}
```

If we can't create the printer DC, we want to delete the other two display contexts that we created, post a message, and terminate.

16.3.6 Creating a Memory Bitmap

We now have our three DCs: screen, memory (sometimes called a "shadow" display context) and printer. Next, we want to find out more about the screen and the printer. Specifically, we need to know the horizontal and vertical sizes and resolutions for both the display and the printer. To get this information, we repeatedly call **GetDeviceCaps,** specifying the proper DC and index. For example, to get the printer's vertical resolution, we use:

```
PrinterVertRes   = GetDeviceCaps (hPrinterDC, VERTRES);
```

The next few lines of code determine which is the constraining factor: the display or the printer. In most cases, the display will constrain. For example, if the display is wider than it is high and a printed page is higher than it is wide, and we are using portrait mode on the printer, then we want to fill the page as w-i-d-e as possible, and set the height proportionally.

Next, we want to divide the display and printer into an *integer* number of bands. In PGM13 we're using **BANDS** bands where **BANDS** equals 25. There is no particular reason that we chose 25; a wise programmer would compute a value based on available resources and the given configuration.

Now we create our actual memory bitmap:

```
if (!(hMemBitmap = CreateBitmap (PrinterHorzRes,
                                 PrinterBandHeight,
                                 1,
                                 1,
                                 (LPSTR)NULL)))
{
DeleteDC (hPrinterDC);
DeleteDC (hMemDC);
DeleteDC (hScreenDC);
Message (hWnd, "Out of memory.");
PostQuitMessage (0);
break;
}
```

Our bitmap is **PrinterHorzRes** by **PrinterBandHeight** and is monochrome (one bit per pixel and one plane). We assign the bitmap handle to the variable **hMemBitmap.** If this fails, we want to delete the three DCs, post a message, and terminate. It's all downhill from here . . .

16.3.7 Updating the Display

Next, we hide the popup window (so it won't be printed):

```
ShowWindow (hWnd, HIDE_WINDOW);
```

HIDE_WINDOW does just that: it instructs Windows to hide (remove) this window from the display. Unfortunately, **HIDE_WINDOW** leaves a hole where the popup window was. (Remember that Windows *does not* remember what the screen looks like; you are responsible for refreshments.) To remedy this little problem, we use:

```
EnumWindows (lpEnumProc, OL);
```

This function enumerates all the windows seen on the display by passing the window handle to the function specified by **lpEnumProc.** We assigned **EnumProc** during the **WinMain** initialization process. The windows are enumerated in the following order:

1 Tiled windows
2 Iconic windows
3 Popup windows
4 Hidden popups

The second parameter is a long argument to pass to **EnumProc**. In this program, we won't pass anything.

Next, let's examine the **EnumProc.** To close the hole left by the removal of our popup window, we need to enumerate all the windows. One by one, we'll enumerate all child windows, and if a window is visible, we'll update (paint) it:

```
BOOL FAR PASCAL EnumProc (hWnd, lpData)
HWND            hWnd;
LPSTR                     lpData;
{
EnumChildWindows (hWnd, lpEnumProc, OL);
if (IsWindowVisible (hWnd))
UpdateWindow (hWnd);
return TRUE;
}
```

Remember that we invoked this function by the call:

```
EnumWindows (lpEnumProc, OL);
```

This function repeatedly calls **EnumProc** passing **hWnd,** the handle of a window on the screen. For each window, we first enumerate its children (and their children and their children, etc.), using the function **EnumChildWindows.** This does essentially the same thing as **EnumWindows** except that it affects child windows. Note that we pass the address of **EnumProc. EnumProc** will be called recursively until all children (and grandchildren, etc.) have been enumerated.

Following the enumeration, we check each window to see if it is visible. If it is, we place a call to update it. Eventually, all windows will get the command to update (paint) themselves.

16.3.8 Moving Information to the Printer Driver

Let's review where we stand:

1 We created three display contexts.

   a) Display

   b) Memory (compatible to display)

   c) Printer

2 We computed the constraining device.

3 We computed band heights.

4 We created a monochrome memory bitmap.

5 We hid our popup window and filled the "hole" left behind.

Next, we need to connect the memory DC with the memory bitmap:

```
hSaveBitmap = SelectObject (hMemDC, hMemBitmap);
```

You'll recall that **SelectObject** returns the handle of the previously selected object. We'll save that handle so we can restore the selection prior to termination. Now we'll get to the heart of this program: talking to the printer device driver.

We can get at the printer driver directly via a special **Escape** function. The general form of **Escape** is:

```
Escape (hDC, function, count, lpInData, lpOutData) : result
```

where **hDC** is a display context, **function** is the escape function name, **count** is the count of bytes in the input buffer **lpInData,** and the output buffer is **lpOutData**. **Escape** returns **result.**

The first **Escape** function we use is **SETABORTPROC:**

```
Escape (hPrinterDC, SETABORTPROC, 0,
                    (LPSTR)lpAbortFunc, (LPSTR)0);
```

SETABORTPROC gives the driver a place to go when an error occurs. Just like **EnumProc,** we filled the variable **lpAbortFunc** with the address of **AbortFunc** during the initialization of **WinMain.** Let's take a moment to look at **AbortFunc.**

16.3.9 Handling Printer Errors

If something traumatic happens in the printer driver, such as an out-of-disk-space or out-of-memory error, the driver needs a place to go to get instructions on what to do next and how to let the user know that this condition has occurred. **AbortFunc** is just that place.

As usual, we declare **AbortFunc** a FAR PASCAL procedure. It contains two arguments: **hPR**, the handle to the printer display context, and **code,** the reason the function was called:

```
int FAR PASCAL AbortFunc (hPR, code)
HDC     hPR;
int     code;
{
switch (code)  {
```

We'll handle all cases by posting a message box. The cases are:

Case	*Explanation*
SP_ERROR	General error in writing to spooler.
SP_APPABORT	Application aborts printer.
SP_USERABORT	User aborts printer.
SP_OUTOFDISK	No disk space for spool file.
SP_OUTOFMEMORY	No memory for spool file.

16.3.10 Controlling Printing

After setting the **AbortProc,** we begin our printing job:

```
Escape (hPrinterDC, STARTDOC, 6, (LPSTR)"Screen", (LPSTR)0);
```

STARTDOC informs the driver that we are starting a new job, and that all the following pages are part of this job. This insures that other jobs do not intermix pages with ours.

6 is the count of characters passed in the next argument: **(LPSTR)"Screen."** This is the name of the document, and is displayed in the spooler window. The last argument is not used and is set to zero.

Next comes the real work. We'll *transfer* and *stretch* all bands from the display to memory, and then from memory to the printer:

```
StretchBlt (hMemDC, 0, 0, PrinterHorzRes, PrinterBandHeight,
            hScreenDC, 0, ScreenBandDeltaY, ScreenHorzRes,
                   ScreenBandHeight, SRCCOPY);
```

StretchBlt transfers a bitmap from the display to the memory DC. The target coordinates in memory are (**0,0**) for a width of **PrinterHorzRes** and a height of **PrinterBandHeight** (the size of our bitmap). The source is the screen (**0, ScreenBandDeltaY**) with a width of **ScreenHorzRes** and a height of **ScreenBandHeight.** The operation is **SRCCOPY,** which overwrites the destination.

StretchBlt stretches or compresses the bits as needed to fit the target bitmap. This may cause pixels to be deleted or added: if this is undesirable, you should adjust the size of your target bitmap. Of course this implies that the entire page width or height will not be used.

After moving into the staging area with **StretchBlt,** we need to move the bits onward to the printer with the **BitBlt** function:

```
BitBlt (hPrinterDC, 0, PrinterBandDeltaY, PrinterHorzRes,
                                        PrinterBandHeight,

        hMemDC, 0, 0, SRCCOPY);
```

After all bits have been run through the band, we begin the actual printing operation:

```
Escape (hPrinterDC, NEWFRAME, 0, (LPSTR)0, (LPSTR)0);
```

NEWFRAME tells the printer driver that we're finished writing to this page and the printer may print it. Finally, we send:

```
Escape (hPrinterDC, ENDDOC, 0, (LPSTR)0, (LPSTR)0);
```

ENDDOC tells the driver that we are done talking to it, and it may release the job to the spooler for printing.

Before exiting, we must clean up by re-selecting the previous bitmap, deleting our DCs, and posting a message telling the user that this program is terminating.

```
hMemBitmap = SelectObject (hMemDC, hSaveBitmap);
DeleteObject (hMemBitmap);
DeleteDC (hPrinterDC);
DeleteDC (hMemDC);
DeleteDC (hScreenDC);
Message (hWnd, "Screen sent to spooler...");
PostQuitMessage (0);
break;
```

16.4 THE MODULE DEFINITION FILE: PGM13.DEF

```
;*************************************************************:
; Filename:     PGM13.DEF                                      :
;                                                              :
; Description:  Link definition file                           :
;-------------------------------------------------------------:

NAME    PGM13

STUB    '..\WINSTUB.EXE'

CODE    MOVEABLE
DATA    MOVEABLE

HEAPSIZE  4096
STACKSIZE 4096

EXPORTS
    MainWndProc         @1
    EnumProc            @2
    AbortFunc           @3

;-------------------------------------------------------------:
; End of file:  PGM13.DEF                                      :
;*************************************************************:
```

16.5 THE MAKE FILE: PGM13.

```
#*****************************************************************#
# Filename:     PGM13.                                            #
#                                                                 #
# Description:  "MAKE" description file                           #
#-----------------------------------------------------------------#

pgm13.obj: pgm13.c
    cl -c -Asnw -Gsw -Oas -Zped pgm13.c

pgm13.exe: pgm13.obj pgm13.def
    link4 pgm13,pgm13,,slibw, pgm13.def;

#-----------------------------------------------------------------#
# End of file:  PGM13                                             #
#*****************************************************************#
```

. . . .

In this chapter, you've learned to make your application talk directly to the printer.

GLOSSARY

ACCELERATOR: A "short-cut" key or key combination that lets a user perform the action of a menu item instead of selecting the item by highlighting it. An accelerator is commonly a function key or an ALT key or CONTROL key combination.

ANISOTROPIC MAPPING MODE: A mapping mode in which the programmer determines the coordinate system.

ATOM: A short integer equated to a string, used to save memory space when moving strings between routines.

BANDING: A printing technique whereby an image to be printed is divided into bands (slices) and each band is sent separately to the printer. This technique allows printing of complex images without creating the entire image in memory, thereby substantially reducing memory requirements.

BITBLT: An operation that transfers a bitmap from one place to another.

BITMAP: A memory image of a portion of a display device (a CRT, printer, or other output device). A Windows bitmap is a data structure containing a pointer to the memory image and information about the display device. Memory requirements for bitmaps depend on the capabilities and pixel resolution of the display device. While bitmaps are device dependent, Windows provides GDI transfer routines for manipulating them in a device-independent manner.

BRUSH: A pattern used to fill objects.

BUTTON: A small rectangle or circle in a dialog box or message box, which the user can turn on or off by placing a mouse pointer on it and clicking the mouse button.

CHILD WINDOW: A window that is defined and maintained within the client area of another window. Typically, child windows are used to divide the client area into several functional areas.

CLASS: A data structure that defines the attributes of a window. These attributes are defined in the data structure PWNDCLASS. Every window must belong to a window class.

CLIENT AREA: The work area of a window. The client area is the exclusive property of that window: an application may do whatever it wants within its client area.

CLIPBOARD: A global data area through which Windows applications can exchange data.

CLIPPING REGION: The area of the client area in which GDI routines can write, draw, or paint. When objects are drawn on the screen, only the portion of the object within the clipping region is copied.

CONTROLS: Child windows whose behavior is predefined by Windows; Microsoft has already written their window functions. Primarily used in dialog boxes.

DEFAULT WINDOW FUNCTION: A function provided by Windows, **DefWindowProc,** that will process any messages not processed by other window functions. An application must specifically call **DefWindowProc** when it doesn't want to process a message itself.

DEFINITION FILE: A file required by the linker, used during the compilation and linking process. A definition file includes information about the application's name, the size of the stack and heap, and the import and export list, as well as other data about the application.

DIALOG BOX: A child window that contains controls, designed to get input from the user.

DISPLAY CONTEXT (DC): A data structure that contains information about the size and location of a window. DCs are used by many GDI functions.

DYNAMIC DATA EXCHANGE (DDE): The passage of data between Windows applications, achieved by using specific message types, protocols for processing messages, and data types.

DYNAMIC LINKING: The process of loading library routines at run time. Through dynamic linking, several Windows applications can use one copy of a library routine and thus reduce the amount of memory required.

EVENT: Any occurrence that Windows defines as being of interest to an application, such as mouse movements, keyboard actions, mouse clicks, and so forth.

EXPORT LIST: A list of routines within an application or library that can be called by another application or library. The export list is contained within the application's definition file.

EXTENT: The number of units in the X and Y direction from the *origin* required to set the second point for a window's rectangle.

FONT: An assortment of type of one size and style.

GLOBAL MEMORY: Memory in Windows' memory area that is dynamically allocated to applications.

GRAPHICS DEVICE INTERFACE (GDI): The Windows library that contains routines that produce and display device-independent graphics. GDI routines control clipping and mapping, and provide graphics tools such as pens, brushes, and fonts.

GROUP BOX: A frame, sometimes including a title, that "groups" together several controls within a dialog box.

GROUPED CONTROLS: Controls positioned within a group box in a dialog box.

HANDLE: A unique, fixed integer that identifies a window, display context, instance, pen, brush, menu, or other object, required as an input argument by most Windows routines. The data types for Windows handles are defined in WINDOWS.H.

ICON: A small pictorial device, usually representing an application or a process.

ICON AREA: The portion of the screen in which Windows puts icons representing applications that are executing but are not displayed in windows.

IMPORT LIST: A list of routines within another library that will be called by this application or library. The import list is contained within the application's definition file.

INPUT FOCUS: A device that tells Windows which window is to receive keyboard input. Only one window can have the input focus at any given time.

INSTANCE: An instance is an occurrence of an application within the Windows environment. An application may have multiple instances. All instances share the same code segment and have their own data segment.

ISOTROPIC MAPPING MODE: A mapping mode in which logical coordinates are converted into screen coordinates in a way that preserves the aspect ratio (the shape) of a drawing, but allows the drawing to change size.

LOGICAL COORDINATE SYSTEM: A virtual coordinate system that extends from plus 32K to minus 32K in the X and Y directions. Logical coordinates are used as input arguments for GDI routines, which then translate them to the appropriate screen coordinates.

MAPPING MODE: Mapping modes allow setting window and viewport extents into common pre-defined configurations. This effectively changes the scale component of the transformation equations.

MENU: A list of menu items from which the user can choose. Sometimes called a "popup" or "drop-down" menu.

MESSAGE: A data structure that contains a message identifier and message parameters.

MESSAGE BOX: A popup window displayed by the MessageBox routine, which can contain a brief message, an icon, a title bar, and push buttons.

NONPREEMPTIVE MULTITASKING: The form of multitasking implemented in Windows. In this environment, a nonpreemptive scheduler manages multiple cooperating tasks. Each task periodically yields control back to the scheduler, thus forming a multitasking system.

ORIGIN: The upper left corner of a window's rectangle.

OVERLAPPED WINDOW: A window normally used as the main window for an application.

PAINT: To fill in or update a window.

PAINT PROCEDURE: A procedure that handles paint messages for a window function.

PARENT WINDOW: A window containing child or popup windows.

PEN: A solid-color object used to draw lines.

PHYSICAL COORDINATE SYSTEM: A coordinate system determined by a physical device.

POPUP WINDOW: A popup window is a window that can be painted and maintained anywhere on the screen. Popups lie on top of the other windows making their complete contents visible at all times.

QUEUES: Windows maintains several queues: the hardware queue (keyboard, timer, and mouse events), and application queues (events from hardware queue, Windows, itself, and other applications). All queues are 30 events deep.

RASTER OPERATION (ROP) CODES: ROP codes define how the source bitmap, the currently selected brush, and the destination bitmap are combined with the Boolean operators OR, XOR, AND, and NOT. ROP codes are used by the **PatBlt, BitBlt,** and **StretchBlt** functions.

RESOURCE: Data or objects kept in resource script (.RC) files separate from the source code. Resources can include icons, cursors, menus, strings, and dialog boxes.

TASK: Any program that executes as an independent unit. Each instance of an application is a task.

TITLE BAR: The bar at the top of a window that usually contains the application's name. Mouse users can move a window by pointing to the title bar, pressing a mouse button, and dragging the window.

VIEWPORT: A rectangular part of the screen coordinate system, used with the logical window to map logical coordinates to physical coordinates in isotropic or anisotropic mapping modes.

WINDOW CLASS: A group of windows having the same attributes. All messages for a window class are processed by the same window procedure, so all windows in a class behave similarly. Every window must belong to a window class.

WINDOW FUNCTION: The function responsible for processing an application's messages.

INDEX

Introduction to Windows Programming Diskette Offer

All the programs from this book are available on diskette for the IBM PC. Also available are numerous other supplemental example programs designed to aid programmers in learning how to write Windows applications. You can order these diskettes directly from the author.

Shipping information Please print

Name ______________________________

Company ______________________________

Street ______________________________

City ____________________ ST __________ ZIP __________

Country (if outside U.S.A.) ______________________________

Please send me:

- Diskette accompaniment(s) containing all the programs from this book in source code format .... $9.95 each
- Diskette supplement(s) containing numerous example programs in source form and designed to accompany this book .... $14.95 each
- Both diskettes described above .... $19.95 pair

Price includes postage & handling and applicable sales tax.
Outside U.S.A. add $5.00 per item for additional P & H.
Price and availability subject to change without notice.

Payment method: Cash, check or money order only in US Dollars.

Mail to: Guy Quedens
190 Vahalla Drive
Southern Pines, NC 28387

Here's how to receive your free catalog and save money on your next book order from Scott, Foresman and Company.

Simply mail in the response card below to receive your free copy of our latest catalog featuring computer and business books. After you've looked through the catalog and you're ready to place your order, attach the coupon below to receive $1.00 off the catalog price of Scott, Foresman and Company Professional Books Group computer and business books.

- YES, please send me my *free* catalog of your latest computer and business books! I am especially interested in

- IBM
- MACINTOSH
- AMIGA
- COMMODORE
- Programming
- Business Applications
- Networking/Telecommunications
- Other ______

Name (please print) ______

Company ______

Address ______

City ______ State ______ Zip ______

Mail response card to:

Scott, Foresman and Company
Professional Books Group
1900 East Lake Avenue
Glenview, IL 60025

PUBLISHER'S COUPON NO EXPIRATION

DATE

SAVE $1.00

Limit one per order. Good only on Scott, Foresman and Company Professional Books Group publications. Consumer pays any sales tax. Coupon may not be assigned, transferred, or reproduced. Coupon will be redeemed by Scott, Foresman and Company Professional Books Group, 1900 East Lake Avenue, Glenview, IL 60025.

Customer's Signature ______